"Greaves' intimate experience with, and in-dept[...]
political and institutional forces that faced Canada's activists over the last
half-century shines through in this collection. The fearless, persistent,
and creative actions of the feminist leaders who contributed to this
book, had a profound influence on the women's movement and changed
Canada's entire health system. These women challenged established
norms and demanded unprecedented approaches and inventive
alternatives that altered the values, policies, and practices that shape the
health of women and girls to this day."

—MARILYN EMERY
President and Chief Executive Officer, Women's College Hospital

"This is a very compelling and pan-Canadian gathering of stories and
analyses about the past 50 years of the women's health movement. It
chronicles the determination, courage, and creativity of many different
groups of women trying to make the world safer and more responsive
to their varied needs. It is also an excellent lens through which to
remember how far we have come and to understand how much farther
there is to go."

—CHAVIVA HOSEK
OC PhD LLD

"...a must-read for all women, especially those working for change in
the arena of women's health in Canada. I was very touched by the book.
It is a stark reminder of how much work, dedication, commitment, and
plain old slogging it has taken to keep Canadian women's bodies free of
unwanted interference. It is still far from clear sailing, and we are seeing
south of the border just how easily the clock can be turned back. A big
cheer for the courageous women and men who have fought so hard to
protect our right to health on our own terms."

—PENNY BALLEM
MD FRCP FCAHS

A FEMINIST HISTORY SOCIETY BOOK

Personal

— and —

Political

*Stories from the Women's
Health Movement 1960–2010*

edited by Lorraine Greaves

Second Story Press

Library and Archives Canada Cataloguing in Publication

Personal and political : stories from the women's health movement
1960-2010 / Lorraine Greaves, editor.

Issued in print and electronic formats.
ISBN 978-1-77260-079-7 (softcover).–ISBN 978-1-77260-080-3 (HTML)

1. Women's rights–Canada–History–20th century. 2. Second-wave
feminism–Canada. 3. Women–Health and hygiene–Canada–History–
20th century. 4. Women–Canada–Social conditions–20th century.
I. Greaves, Lorraine, editor

HQ1453.P473 2018   305.420971   C2018-904063-7
                           C2018-904064-5

"A Feminist History Society Book."
Issued in print and electronic formats.
ISBN 978-1-77260-079-7 (softcover).-
ISBN 978-1-77260-080-3 (ebook)

Cover art © 2018 Jamie Lawson
Editor: Andrea Knight
Book design: Ellie Sipila
Original series design by Zab Design & Typography

Printed and bound in Canada

*Second Story Press gratefully acknowledges the support of the
Ontario Arts Council and the Canada Council for the Arts for our
publishing program. We acknowledge the financial support of the
Government of Canada through the Canada Book Fund.*

ONTARIO ARTS COUNCIL
CONSEIL DES ARTS DE L'ONTARIO

Canada Council   Conseil des Arts
for the Arts   du Canada

Funded by the Government of Canada
Financé par le gouvernement du Canada   Canada

Published by
Second Story Press
20 Maud Street, Suite 401
Toronto, ON M5V 2M5
www.secondstorypress.ca

CONTENTS

FOREWORD

I want to thank all of the brave women who contributed to this book. Their stories are essential to our understanding of the women's health movement in Canada. Since the beginning of this project in 2016, I have been constantly inspired by, and amazed at, the depth and detail of these stories. Many of the women who have contributed had to dig deep into their memories or their archives or consult long-ago friends. Some had to dig into painful memories, both personal and political, and I thank all of them. I am grateful that you all agreed to do this hard work. But these stories are only the tip of an iceberg and reflect only a small selection of the legions of other women who braved the system in order to make change in communities across Canada. These untold stories are still out there, and I encourage you to share them.

I had my own journey in creating this book. I spoke to many women, who put me in touch with many other women, and on it went. I had thought I knew about the women's health movement in Canada, having been part of it, but I was surprised, amused, educated, angered, shocked, and re-energized as I uncovered these stories. In particular, I want to thank Liz Whynot, a long-time Vancouver feminist physician who linked me to many of the West Coast storytellers. From the other coast, I want to thank Wendy Williams, a radical nurse whose memories of Newfoundland politics are stellar. And in between, of course, the consistent and persistent Feminist History Society collective members: Beth Atcheson, Constance Backhouse, Diana Majury, and Beth Symes, who, with me, continue on our quest to record the activities of the second wave women's movement in Canada.

Finally, a big thanks to Andrea Knight, who superbly edited this volume and proved to be a kindred spirit from the women's health movement; Jan Trainor for her historical research; Glenda Morris for her administrative support, and Margie Wolfe, the stalwart feminist publisher who believes in the vision of the Feminist History Society. Onward!

Lorraine Greaves
2018

INTRODUCTION

Lorraine Greaves

There is perhaps nothing more central to women's liberation than women's health, personally and collectively. This book details some of the many innovative, courageous, and creative actions that emerged in Canada during the "second wave" of the women's movement between 1960 and 2010, actions that not only (re) claimed our bodies, but went on to create and claim spaces that were separate and apart from the medically dominated health care system. Feminists working in the Canadian women's health movement challenged many elements of that medically dominated system and of our culture, including the care we were being offered and the way we saw our bodies and ourselves.

We filled in service gaps with new approaches to care and treatment, and challenged established knowledge and perspectives about what was health and what was illness. It is fair to say that the robust, aggressive, and multi-faceted women's health movement that emerged during this period ultimately changed the entire health system. Arguably, it was also the pivot and foundation for the broader women's movement in Canada. It is, and continues to be, a force for change, activism, research, and insight. It created both the demand for new approaches and our own inspired alternatives; it developed within us the strategic abilities to shift big systems on behalf of women. This book offers a glimpse of how those changes came to be, and into the actions of many women who were part of this ground-up, contentious, and difficult re-building of women's health, including women's reproductive autonomy, health care practices, policies, and research.

Women in Canada in the 1960s and 1970s were fed up. The women's liberation movement that seeded itself in the 1960s set the stage for women's bodily empowerment along with a range of demands for political empowerment. Yet we still lived in a country where contraception and abortion were illegal, only supplied by brave renegades who risked a tremendous amount to do so. Similarly, women who needed contraception or abortion were forced to take huge risks, sometimes life threatening, with their bodies, their lives, and their reputations.

This only began to change in 1969, first with the introduction of new federal laws in Canada that relaxed restrictions on birth control and sexual practices, and then followed by more activist efforts by feminists on a range of reproductive freedoms such as access to abortion, women-controlled childbirth, and the (re) introduction of midwifery. At the same time, the women's health movement in the USA was maturing. In particular, a popular self-help reference book called *Our Bodies, Ourselves* published by the Boston Women's Health Collective marked a sea change in how women thought about themselves, their bodies, and their rights. That book is still available almost fifty years later, speaking to an ongoing hunger for information about our bodies.

Centuries of sexism and patriarchal control of medicine had rendered women's wisdom, women's health professions, and women's bodies marginal, stigmatized, or invisible. But during this period, it slowly became obvious that when it came to disease or treatment, women were not just "small men". As the contributors in this book show, the "new" women's health movement produced a pervasive reawakening generated by a self-help approach, collective efforts, and a "never say die" determination. Every woman has a body, and those bodies were being reclaimed, sometimes one by one.

Along the way, claiming power over childbirth, pelvic exams, contraception, abortion, and our views of our own bodies and, indeed, ourselves, turned out to be a gateway to health and political power. A rejection of the patriarchal, medical model preceded a do-it-ourselves approach to figuring out how to look after ourselves, our own bodies, our own bodily processes, and our own health. The personal was *never* more political.

This book details some of that vibrant Canadian activism. It is full of energy, failure, success, despair, creativity, strategy, risk, and doggedness. It goes without saying that in 2018, these stories are still highly relevant to the well-being of girls and women in Canada, and to our continued advocacy and engagement with feminism. It verges on the obvious, but without our health, we are nothing: we are not activists, we are not able to participate in life as full political players or full family members, and we are not able to be change-makers. The contributors describe the incredible awakening that birthed the women's health movement during second-wave feminism in Canada. The causes, ideas, initiatives, and failures described here give deep meaning to the right to health and powered our collective right to govern our health.

The contributors to this collection detail only some of those activities and highlight only some of the many initiatives of the second-wave women's health movement in Canada. Many players and groups were involved in cities and towns across the country. They nagged and cajoled to create better systems of care for women, and often created those alternatives themselves. They reframed issues and badgered those with power to challenge the mainstream understanding of women's health, its antecedents, and its future. The movement and the women who have been part of it have had a huge impact on women's health care, prevention, treatment, policy, and research. They have, without a doubt, had a huge impact on how we see ourselves and how we are seen, treated, and studied.

The first section describes some of the activities that are emblematic of the women's health movement in Canada. However, its beginnings were, for the most part, white, middle class, heterosexist, and often lesbophobic. It took a safe approach to women's health, even among those writing in the feminist media. It relied on activist feminist medical practitioners to make the transition to woman-centred care. It focused at first, on heterosexual women's issues of contraception, abortion, and birthing. It was less radical and inclusive in its agenda than we would, from a 2018 point of view, likely wish. Nevertheless, the do-it-yourself element was the most critical and radical phase and set the stage for the more evolved questions and topics to follow. It worked on raising consciousness among a broad swath of women, tapping into the anger we probably all felt about how we were being treated. We were awakened to the need to control our own health, to question our practitioners, to critique information about drugs and treatments, to question the underlying research, and to analyze health from a political point of view.

It questioned why we were collectively beholden to others for decisions about our bodies, especially when it came to birthing, pregnancy, or abortion. Who was in charge of our bodies? Who was telling us what we could do with them, and what they should look like? It certainly did not seem to be us.

The second section of the book details those fights. Just who defined when or if we could get an abortion? Who defined what our contraceptive options were? Who defined who could look up whose vaginas, or claim a "delivery" or assist in birthing? Who decided who needed a Pap smear, and how, when, where, and by whom they could get it? In those heady days of the women's health movement, we looked up each other's vaginas, caught each other's babies, and arranged each other's illegal abortions. We also discussed who defined what was an acceptable body for a woman, and who got to describe it. Those days were full. They represent the women's health movement pushing off from the dock, leaving the stability of an often unquestioned, patronizing and patriarchal medical system behind, and floating out to chart a new direction entirely navigated by us. But what were we to do to create better responses?

The third section details some of the incredibly radical activism in creating the services to replace patriarchal options and to offer better alternatives for women and girls. The battles! The tediousness of creating new options! The time involved! The commitment! The volunteer hours! The audacity! The scheming! The political acumen! But how empowering it was, and is, to take control of defining, changing, and creating services that actually respect and serve all women as opposed to swallowing hard and submitting ourselves to unquestioned, tired approaches, with (in those days, usually male) doctors literally hovering over us. This section reflects on some daring, creative, and courageous initiatives, and their relevance, success, failure, permanence, or not, and most of all, the lessons. Some of these efforts led to reform in the system and were no longer needed. Some of these efforts petered out as women found other alternatives to health and health care that were more responsive and becoming mainstreamed. Some of these efforts required energies that were unsustainable. Some of those fights are still not won and continue to affect our health and well-being. Some of the institutions and services built in this period have been retracted, defunded, chipped away at, or eroded. And others survive. It is clear that maintaining our collective health requires ongoing attention and considerable vigilance. It also soon became clear that root solutions were needed to reform women's health care.

The fourth section details some of those efforts. How could we challenge and replace a medical model of health with an approach that resonated with respect for women? Who defined what constituted a diagnosis? Who defined what was an appropriate treatment? Was there any accountability and safety for women patients in the health care system? Was the preponderance and type of drugs dispensed to women appropriate? More fundamentally, was mainstream medicine able to treat the effects of patriarchy: sexual abuse, incest, domestic violence, addiction, and smoking? Or was it just responding with over-prescriptions, misguided psychotherapeutic analysis, one-size-fits-all treatments, and more layers of obfuscation? Was it just perpetuating the same? It takes ongoing ingenuity to respond to medical models of health care, but some of the earliest feminist arguments for a social model of health, woman-centred care, linking violence and trauma to health, and incorporating women's experiences into health care are now mainstream. At its core, the women's health movement aimed to unpeel these questions and create new ways of learning about ourselves. The work involved was extensive. Unlearning old ways, questioning authority, and raising consciousness were the bulwarks of creating new knowledge among women about our health, preparing ourselves to go out and make change.

Finally, the systems underpinning our health and our experiences with the health system were to get our attention. How were we to limit the effects of the patriarchy on our health going forward? We soon realized that the very research on which treatment, drug development, policy, and practice was based was sexist, partial, and exclusionary. We were not included in the research questions and designs, so how could we possibly be treated accurately and safely? The norm for research was gender-blind, which meant males were the subjects, even among rats and mice, let alone humans. The health workers in charge were men and the helpers were women. How was nurses' knowledge going to be mined, and how could nurses' activism be nurtured?

How could the predominant view of vulnerable women be shifted to generate respect, not blame? Women who were experiencing addiction or poverty, violence or disempowerment were often dismissed, shamed, or repeatedly violated. How could women become central to understanding disease, treatment, research, policy solutions, and health information? These were such big questions, requiring a seismic shift of the entire health and social system in Canada. But no questions were too big for the women's health movement. All of these questions were taken on, chipped away at, and indeed, continue to create fundamental changes in Canada in how we see women's health. These challenges persist, but the issues raised by feminists about stigma, patient and consumer rights, health literacy, inclusion, and gendered research approaches are now top of mind in Canadian policy and programme design, even if not in practice.

This book details and reveals the amazing amount of energy expended to make these changes, and the incredible persistence of women's health activists in Canada during the "second wave" feminist movement. Between 1960 and 2010 feminists in Canada tackled numerous contentious and difficult issues from abortion access to inclusive research to addressing psychoactive drug over-prescribing to sustaining women's hospitals. While the movement emerged in the context of a newly awakened feminist movement in the 1960s and 1970s, the demands were based on years, if not decades and centuries, of foment about bodily autonomy and reproductive choice. Centuries of silent and pervasive sexism in the form of paternalistic medical personnel and a range of oppressive laws and norms was eventually confronted by a tsunami of challenge, resistance, demand, and critique. That anger at those centuries-old systems and legions of oppressive practices became the fuel for activism. It carries us still in our quest for better health.

have you considered, using a DIAPHRAGM ?

a safer, effective method of birth control
a menstrual cup   # woman-controlled
a way of becoming more in touch with your body

the diaphragm fitters collective provides :

• appointments during the day, evenings, weekends
• fittings done in our homes and at the Health Collective
• a relaxed atmosphere for women that includes diaphragm rap, cervical self-exam, and free fitting
• the opportunity for women to learn to fit diaphragms
• re-checks   • Kids' play area available

For further information call 736-6696 or drop in at the Vancouver Women's Health Collective, 1501 W. Broadway corner of Granville

hours: Mondays 1:30-7:30
Tuesdays, Thursdays 1:30-5:30 and Fridays
Saturdays 12-4

From *Healthsharing*, 1982.

SECTION ONE:
TRYING TO MAKE CHANGE

The early years of the second-wave women's health movement in Canada were bristling with indignation-fuelled activity. Consciousness-raising gave way to anger and anger fuelled change-making efforts across Canada. This section opens with a reflection piece first published by the Canadian Women's Health Network in 1996, when an impending joint USA-Canada health meeting produced a number of papers and initiatives. It captures the scene at the time, and the key events of the prior twenty-five years. But this was not a very inclusive movement. Trainor illustrates the homophobia of the early years of the women's health movement by tracing the invisibility of lesbian health in the feminist media of the era. Atcheson et al. discuss a two-year effort in the late 1970s to establish a women's hospital in Toronto that would provide well-woman care as well as abortions. The effort failed, but the authors' account highlights the politics and legalities of making changes to health care delivery and the formidable obstacles of sexism, condescension, and dismissal in the medical, legal, and political spheres of the day.

In the same era, Cohen and Backhouse wrote about the deficiencies of women's health care, and Backhouse provides a retrospective commentary on their position, reflecting on the article's capacity to still astonish her and asking how much has changed. Meanwhile in Vancouver, the famous Vancouver Women's Health Collective was fully operational, influenced by west coast USA politics and activists, but quickly developing its own style. Buhler, Whynot, Frost, and Conn reminisce about the collective and its legacy. The collective was a prime example of women taking direct action on their health, all the way down to fitting each other's diaphragms in private homes. This section illustrates how women made their own health care, sometimes learning on the job, but avoiding inadequate male-dominated systems.

As some of these authors suggest, these early efforts were often forged in the name of a unitary concept of "women," blind to the nuances of multiple impacts on women's health such as race, class, sexual orientation, and education. Nowhere was this more evident than in Indigenous (then referred to as Aboriginal) women's health, where racism and sexism and colonialism collided to perpetuate poor health. Bourassa et al. document these pressures and how they affected Indigenous women to an even greater extent than they did Indigenous men. Finally, Williams documents the many efforts in Newfoundland and Labrador to organize a powerful women's health lobby and to generate a radical shift in women's health policy, research, and provision of services.

These efforts to make change were born of anger, fear, indignation, and despair. A sense of "not taking any more" paternalistic, medicalized treatment from a male-dominated system, governed by patriarchal and colonial legal systems and medical hierarchies washed across Canada from coast to coast. Women in every city and town and beyond decided, in some way, to take health matters into their own hands. The women's health movement was in full swing.

THE WOMEN'S HEALTH MOVEMENT IN CANADA: LOOKING BACK AND MOVING FORWARD

*Madeline Boscoe, Gwynne Basen, Ghislaine Alleyne,
Barbara Bourrier-Lacroix, and Susan White of the
Canadian Women's Health Network*

Reprinted from Canadian Women's Studies/les cahiers de la femme,
Volume 24, Number 1 (Fall 2004), 7–13.

You would be hard-pressed to find anyone who works in, or thinks about health in Canada today who did not agree, at least publicly, on the importance of social and economic conditions such as education, housing, environment, and gender on a person's health status. This broadened approach to health reflects a profound change in thinking and can be credited, in part, to the work of the women's health movement. This social movement was the first to bring together women's own experiences with health services and their own opinions about their health concerns with new visions, new information, and new methods of research and outcome evaluations.

The publication of this edition of *Canadian Woman Studies* devoted to women's health and well-being provides us at the Canadian Women's Health Network (CWHN) with an opportunity to share our reflections on the past, our comments on the present, and our speculations on the future of women's health in Canada.

IN THE BEGINNING
The 1960s, 1970s, and 1980s saw a rebirth of the women's movement and, directly associated with it, the women's health movement in Canada and around the world. Women came together to share experiences and knowledge. We looked at our cervixes, fit diaphragms, helped get each other off mood-altering drugs, and "caught" babies. We shared stories about our interactions with the medical system. We started asking questions. We understood that

knowledge was power and sought information. Through debate and sharing, we developed new approaches. We realized that we could understand medical information if it was presented in an accessible form. We came to recognize the impact of issues such as violence and racism on our health. We realized that those who formulated the research questions controlled the answers. We understood that women's health is a political, social, and economic matter. We were, as Sue Sherwin wrote, "Patient No More" and would be, to quote Sharon Batt (1994), "No Longer Patient."

Women gathered in discussion groups, educational forums, and consciousness-raising sessions. We created new avenues to develop our concerns and our ideas that broke down isolation and allowed for individual and group action. No one was just a "patient" or a doctor or a nurse or a therapist or an academic. Health was something that mattered to all women.

The women's health movement made links and formed partnerships with other groups who shared our issues:

- consumer groups and self-help movements dealing with issues such as cancer, mental health, and addictions;
- anti-racism groups and those working on equity and access issues including First Nations and rural communities;
- those providing alternative and traditional healing;
- environmental and anti-nuclear groups;
- disability rights activists;
- medical reform groups, including those interested in health promotion and community development; and
- the legal community, who helped us push companies and providers to be more responsive and responsible.

In part, the strength and endurance of the women's health movement has been a result of this network.

SHAPING OUR ISSUES

Over the years, the women's health movement has focused on three main issues: the health care delivery system, the development and analysis of the social determinants of health, and a commitment to increase the participation of women in all aspects of health care.

The movement's critique of a health care system dominated by white male health professionals began with exposing how lack of information prevented women from making informed decisions; how the power dynamics between health professionals (doctors [usually male] and nurses [female]) and between physicians and patients made it hard to question professional expertise or refuse treatment; how sexism, racism, paternalism, and other power oppressions within the system led to our priorities not being addressed; how the growing pervasiveness of drugs and other technologies distorted the treatment and prevention programmes women really needed (Cohen and Sinding; Beck; Status of Women Canada; Batt 2002).

Women also learned that some institutions had interests in conflict with ours. For example, the commercial push to market a drug and increase profits could supersede the obligation to make safe and effective medicines available and to do follow-up on a drug's safety.

The emphasis was on a woman-centred vision of health and wellness. We knew that improving the health status of women meant paying attention to education, economic and social policies, housing, and the environment. Gender was put up front and centre as a critical determinant of health. The analyses recognized and respected the diverse needs and realities of women's lives and the impact of these on their health status.

Women worked for the increased presence of women throughout the health care system. We looked at the research used to rationalize the existing approaches to our health concerns. We saw that women's issues and voices were absent in both asking the questions and seeking the answers and that none of it was "neutral." We saw that women were often excluded from clinical trials for new drugs and couldn't know if the medicine we were given was safe for us.

We fought for greater participation of women in all levels of the health care system including policy-making. We pressed for, and finally got, Women's Health Bureaus or departments in provincial governments, women's health committees in research and professional groups such as the Medical Research Council, a Women's Health Bureau inside Health Canada, women's health research centres in Ontario, and the establishment of the Centres of Excellence in Women's Health.

CREATING WOMAN-CENTRED PROGRAMMES AND SERVICES

Not satisfied with just offering critiques, women's health advocates also developed programmes that reflected our vision of woman-centred care (Barnett, White, and Horne). When we found existing services unresponsive or unyielding to our issues, we founded new creative ones where all women would have opportunities to learn and freely discuss their concerns. We developed more equitable, non-hierarchical ways for health service providers to work with each other—and to work with women.

These activities fuelled a new approach to women's health and health services, one that required much more than pink walls or even "nicer" female doctors. We called for providers to listen to women's voices, putting women, not care providers, centre stage in the health care system. This approach, which we called a *woman-centred model*, had several themes or principles. These included:

- user control of health care delivery systems;
- establishing innovative services;
- creating resource centres;
- emphasizing self-help and peer support;
- obtaining appropriate and effective health promotion and education;
- deprofessionalizing medical knowledge and health service jobs;
- developing programmes examining health issues in their social context;
- demanding equity in hiring practices;
- understanding that women are experts in their own needs and issues;
- providing continuity of care and care providers; and
- having access to female practitioners.

From these principles came activities, programmes, and services. One of the earliest was *Side Effects*, a play and popular education campaign about women and pharmaceuticals that made a remarkable cross-country tour in the early 1980s (Tudiver and Hall). Other examples included the formation of home birth and midwifery coalitions, the launching of the still-published *A Friend Indeed* newsletter on women and menopause, woman-centred tobacco programmes, the Montreal Health Press, environmental action groups, women and AIDS activities, endometriosis and breast cancer action groups, the disability rights organization DAWN, feminist counselling programmes, women's shelters, traditional healing study groups, *HealthSharing* magazine, sexual assault support and action groups, anti-racism work, and community-based women's services such as Le Regroupement des centres de santé des femmes du Quebec, Winnipeg's Women's Health Clinic, or the Immigrant Women's Health Centre in Toronto to name a few.

These organizations, programmes, and services were characterized by innovation and social action. Their work recognized that women's health and well-being are deeply affected by poverty and class and by experiences of abuses and racism. Women who sought services in woman-centred programmes experienced group-learning methods, peer support, or new types of care providers, such as nurse practitioners. Women experienced alternative delivery models, which increased their knowledge and sense of autonomy and competence. The programmes provided examples of outreach to those women whom conventional medical service providers considered "hard-to-reach."

The development and evolution of these programmes and services is the "happy" part of the story. Sadder, if not tragic, is that, despite women's best efforts, most of these programmes and services, no matter their effectiveness, remained marginalized within the mainstream health delivery sector and/or have had their funding severely if not completely cut. Those that survive are the exception to the rule, and even these have never received the funding that would make them universally accessible.

BUILDING THE CANADIAN WOMEN'S HEALTH NETWORK

In the 1970s and 80s, groups of women across the country began talking about creating a formal women's health network to create a national presence and strengthen ties among women working in women's health. They saw a need for a network of networks that would encourage dialogue and discussion about strategies and policies and empower women to make informed choices about health (Tudiver).

Networking is a challenging task in Canada with its vast geographic distances and its linguistic, cultural, and regional diversities. But women across the country rose to the task. It was a time of severe cutbacks in government spending on health and social services and far-reaching attacks on Medicare and medical care as a right in Canada. The cutbacks were targeted to the poor and the poorest of the poor—women on welfare, persons with disabilities requiring home care services, shelters, and other services for abused women and children. Women's health activists knew how severely these cuts would affect women's health.

In 1993, after a decade of consultation and discussion with women across the country, the Canadian Women's Health Network was created. Eleven years later, the Canadian Women's Health Network continues to build and strengthen the women's health movement in Canada through information sharing, education, and advocacy with the goal of changing inequitable health policies and practices for women and girls.

Many of the visions expressed when the CWHN was born have become realities. The CWHN has established a national presence for women's health issues and is on the "consultation" list of the federal government and national organizations when health issues are being discussed. Our bilingual information centre now has over 2,500 organizations listed in its database and over 5,000 resources on women's health; and we are a major source for media seeking information on women's health. Our website and *Network* magazine are popular sources of knowledge. Our electronic newsletter and e-mail discussion lists are busy and well subscribed. CWHN has links with a variety of research and policy networks.

MOVING FORWARD

Women's health concerns have become very popular and "acknowledged" in the mainstream. This has proved to be both a blessing and a curse. Women's health advocates have achieved a certain level of recognition, but are always in danger of being co-opted or used by those who control the health system. The language of the women's movement has been taken on by governments and media, but too often without a deep commitment to giving women a real voice in health care policy and planning.

We in the CWHN know that there is still much to be accomplished. Today we can identify five broad challenges ahead for women's health in Canada.

1. Health reform and health service restructuring

The erosion of our publicly funded, not-for-profit health insurance system and the accelerating growth of a two-tiered health system is a significant women's health issue. Though women and men are both affected by government cutbacks and rising health care expenditures, they do not have the same financial resources to cope with them and the impacts are different. Women, on average, earn less than men, are less likely to have supplementary health insurance coverage through their paid employment, and are more likely to live in poverty (Donner, Busch, and Fontaine). As a result, women face a greater burden when health care costs are privatized.

And it is women who bear the burden when health care services are off-loaded from the institution to the home. Women provide 80 per cent of both paid and unpaid health care (Armstrong et al.; National Coordinating Group on Health Care Reform and Women). This inequitable situation results in increased stress, poverty, and social exclusion for these female caregivers.

Despite a 2002 Royal Commission on Health Care that clearly demonstrated the support for and superiority of the Canadian Medicare system (Romanow), action is missing. The commission report itself was also lacking in almost any mention of women's health issues and concerns (National Coordinating Group on Health Care Reform and Women, 2003). The movements toward national home care and pharmacare programmes seem to be fading. Primary care discussions make little if any mention of community health centres. Midwifery and feminist counselling services remain small and under-funded. Through the establishment of the Canadian Institutes for Health Research (CIHR) there has been an increase in support for academic research in gender health. But there is little funding for innovation or demonstration projects such as support for women's second stage housing, women centred smoking cessation or addiction treatment, or mothering support.

The federal government, as well as some provinces, has a commitment to undertake gender sensitive policy and programme development, with, at the very least, uneven results. Provincial governments may have identified women as a priority population, produced a women's health plan or set up Women's Health departments but without much effort on care. The hopes and requests for woman-centred models of care remain.

There have been and continue to be huge cuts to the groups and ad hoc organizations that have provided much of the infrastructure for the women's health movement. Women's centres, community health centres, national and regional organizations such as DES Action, *HealthSharing*, the Vancouver Women's

Health Collective, and innovative demonstration projects have all had their funding dramatically reduced or withdrawn altogether. Burn-out is common as staff members grow exhausted from unrealistic workloads to which are added the need to write seemingly endless funding proposals and reports (Scott, 2003). The loss of these groups and programmes is a "double-whammy": women lose services and programmes providing practical examples of woman-centred approaches, and also lose their work in promoting a health determinants approach in all service and policy areas.

2. The continuing medicalization of women's health

The biomedical-corporate model continues to dominate our health care system. Institutions, professional groups, and corporations in the medical field have significant built-in inertia, if not conflicts of interest, with the reforms envisioned by the women's health movement and the Beijing *Platform for Action* (United Nations), and indeed, Canadian government policy statements such as "Health For All" (Epp). For most, it is business as usual.

Despite years of mobilization and analysis, women's bodies and women's health issues continue to be over-medicalized, with women seen as incompetent and *all* our health issues in need of medical intervention. Among the latest examples are the widespread prescribing of hormone replacement for all menopausal women and the increasing use of epidural anaesthesia for birthing women (O'Grady; *Giving Birth in Canada*).

This biomedical focus on the treatment of acute medical problems continues to colour the approach of health care providers as well as the media and politicians. In this reactive role, the health system continually allocates resources that result in questionable policy "choices" such as:

- Paying for breast cancer screening by mammography, but not for breast cancer support groups or smoking awareness and cessation programmes, or for research into possible environmental causes (O'Leary Cobb).

- Directing some $100 million in federal/provincial "economic development" funds to drug companies to produce hormonal drugs for older women, with little or no support allocated to health education, menopause research, or ensuring streets are safe enough to encourage women to prevent osteoporosis through exercise (Batt 2002).

- Investing large amounts of public and private funds into "new" reproductive technologies while midwifery continues to struggle for recognition and resources to support mothering and to address environmental contaminants that may lead to infertility are basically non-existent (Hawkins and Knox).

- Over-prescribing of benzodiazepines. Women are not only more likely to be prescribed benzodiazepines compared to men, but are also more likely to be prescribed benzodiazepines for longer periods of time (Currie 2003).

- Overprescribing selective serotonin uptake inhibitors (SSRIs) to treat depression and other mental health conditions while other effective interventions such as counselling or exercise remain unfunded and under-utilized — and systemic changes in workplaces and elsewhere that lead to stress and depression are ignored (Currie forthcoming).

It took two decades of lobbying by women's health advocates before legislation to regulate the new reproductive technologies was introduced and passed into law (*An Act Respecting Assisted Human Reproduction and Related Research*). The act is just one step towards an overall strategy to improve the reproductive and sexual health of Canadians, a commitment made by the government several years ago in yet one more "green" paper. This strategy must include increasing access to emergency contraception and ensuring reliable, accessible information on sex education for women and girls across their life spans.

3. Quality health information for women

For women to make informed choices, we must have access to accurate, timely, women-sensitive health information. But programmes that used to fund groups creating information tools no longer exist. And while the explosive growth of the Internet seems to have created access to an enormous amount of information, it is not necessarily the knowledge women need or can access. In addition, most health research continues to lack an analysis of the differences between men and women or between women (Health Canada).

Community-based health providers have responded to the demand for health information by creating material, but have been constrained by limited funding and time. By contrast, advertising by the pharmaceutical industry has continued to permeate our media, not only to promote new products to professionals with expensive sophisticated techniques, but to produce health "information" brochures and other material that really should come from impartial, trusted, non-commercial sources. These same companies push their products to women—often flouting laws that prohibit direct-to-consumer advertising (Mintzes and Baraldi, 2001).

4. Public policy—Is it going to be healthy or not?

While the federal government takes pride in its progressive health policy statements, we need actions, not words.

Those government policy frameworks that emphasize a broad range of health determinants and have goals to achieve population health (Federal/Provincial/Territorial Advisory Committee on Population Health) overlap with a woman-centred holistic approach. However, many of the government's actions appear to ignore these commitments. No action has ever been taken to build in health impact assessments that would evaluate new policies or programmes as possible causes of inequities in women's health.

The growing gap between the rich and the poor, both within Canada and internationally, points to a societal failure to protect citizens and increases ill health, not just for the impoverished, but for everyone. Poverty is increasingly becoming feminized. The dismantling of social programmes such as housing and income support are felt everywhere in Canada, but this has a particular impact on the lives and health of women and children. Poverty is hazardous to women's health.

5. Changes in the women's health movement

Women's health activists continue to struggle with whether or not to put our energies into modifying existing institutions or building new ones. Funding restraints make it more difficult for *all* the services envisioned by grassroots groups to be developed. When they are (under) funded they immediately develop long waiting lists, and meeting needs becomes difficult if not impossible.

We are grappling with a sisterhood made up of women who live at different levels of power and privilege. Our sisterhood's members have many different issues, priorities, and perspectives. How to prioritize issues and resource allocation is far from clear.

Midwifery is an example of this potential stress—in effect, a competition for services between rich and poor women. Midwifery, fought for by a broad coalition of consumers, midwives, and public health staff, has finally been implemented in most provinces and territories. How can equal access for all women be ensured? Will midwifery services, in short supply at the present, be "overused" by women who have resources, while women who would most profit from midwifery services (adolescents, women with multiple problems, rural and northern women who have to leave their communities to birth) have the least chance of getting access to them? It is clear that many women would seek to improve their birth experience if they had the opportunity. What happens to the women most in need, whose voices are often absent?

PROTECTING OUR VISION
The women's health movement has broadened and matured. Some of the coalitions created long ago remain, but even those that have come apart have continuing ties that have created an underlying network of individuals and groups who remain active and connected. And women need this network: The issues we have fought for remain as current and as real today as they were three decades ago. New problems have an all too familiar ring. The task is clearly not an easy one.

The changes that have been won have been the result of persistence and, at times, anger and pain. Not only has the health care system resisted us, but frequently women's wishes and concerns have been disregarded, no matter how clearly they were articulated, while at other times they have been co-opted. Gender parity in medical schools and the recognition of nurse practitioners is wonderful, but his is only a small step toward our vision. Having women in positions of power as physicians, health administrators, and politicians will continue to have some positive effect. But this is not the only mechanism that we can rely on. As we all know, women frequently experience "glass ceilings" and "sticky floors." We also know that one's values cannot be automatically assumed because of gender.

We need to move from "the personal is the political" to "the communal good is in everyone's interest." Individual health cannot exist without social justice. As individuals, we need to work on issues that are best for the community of women, even when these are not necessarily our personal priorities. Those of us working in the health service sector will need to join other groups to advocate for the systemic changes that will remove inequities such as poverty and racism that so strongly affect health. We need to ensure that whatever changes are made are not merely superficial or cosmetic changes laid over a biomedical service model, with no attention paid to the broader social determinants of health.

Women's health activists need not only to continue to lobby to reform and adapt existing institutions and professions, but we need to be sure this work doesn't lead to losing what has been achieved with the creation of alternative and new woman-centred services and service providers. We must stay on guard to protect woman-centred research. We also need to consider creating a long-term demonstration fund for community-based, consumer-controlled services, particularly for women. We are, after all, retooling an industry.

We need mechanisms throughout the system to ensure that this dynamic process continues. Grassroots groups and a diverse range of citizen voices must maintain a strong leadership role as we move forward. We know that in times of confusion and constraint, dissent and critiques can be hard to hear. We will need to continue to build new alliances and new coalitions.

The women's health movement has provided a dynamic environment for some of the most creative debates and positive visions for a better, healthier future. Given the opportunity, there is no reason why we can't take on the challenges ahead.

This paper is adapted and updated from a presentation by Madeline Boscoe, Executive Director for the Canadian Women's Health Network, to the delegates of the Canada-USA Women's Health Forum in 1996 and was edited by Ghislaine Alleyne, Gwynne Basen, Madeline Boscoe, Barbara Bourrier-LaCroiz, and Susan White and reviewed by the Executive Members of the CWHN's Board of Directors.

REFERENCES

An Act Respecting Assisted Human Reproduction and Related Research.
Ottawa: Ministry of Supply and Services Canada, 2004.

Armstrong, Pat, Carol Amaratunga, Jocelyne Bernier, Karen Grant, Ann
Pederson, and Kay Willson. *Exposing Privatization: Women and Health Care
Reform in Canada.* Aurora, ON: Garamond, 2001.

Barnett, Robin, Susan White, and Tammy Horne. *Voices From the Front
Lines: Models of Women-Centred Care in Manitoba and Saskatchewan.*
Winnipeg: Prairie Women's Health Centre of Excellence, 2002.

Batt, Sharon. *Patient No More: the Politics of Breast Cancer.* Charlottetown:
Gynergy, 1994.

Batt, Sharon. *Preventing Disease: Are Pills the Answer?* Toronto: Women and
Health Protection, 2002.

Beck, Christina S. *Partnership for Health: Building Relationships Between
Women and Health Caregivers.* Mawah, NJ: Lawrence Erlbaum Associates,
Inc., 1997.

Cohen, May and Chris Sinding. "Changing Concepts of Women's Health:
Advocating for Change." *Women's Health Forum: Canadian and American
Commissioned Papers.* Ottawa: Minister of Supply and Services Canada,
1996.

Currie, Janet. *Manufacturing Addiction: The Over-Prescription of Benzodiazepines and Sleeping Pills to Women in Canada.* Vancouver: British Columbia
Centre of Excellence for Women's Health, 2003.

Currie, Janet. *The Marketization of Depression: Prescribing of SSRI Antidepressants to Women.* Toronto: Women and Health Protection. Forthcoming.

Donner, Lissa, Angela Busch, and Nahanni Fontaine. *Women, Income and
Health in Manitoba: An Overview and Ideas for Action.* Winnipeg: Women's
Health Clinic, 2002.

Epp, Jake. *Achieving Health for All: A Framework for Health Promotion.*
Ottawa: Minister of Supply and Services Canada, 1986.

Federal/Provincial/Territorial Advisory Committee on Population Health.
Strategies for Population Health: Investing in the Health of Canadians.
Ottawa: Ministry of Supply and Services Canada, 1994.

Giving Birth in Canada: A Regional Profile. Ottawa: Canadian Institute for
Health Information, 2004.

Hawkins, Miranda and Sarah Knox. *The Midwifery Option: A Canadian
Guide to the Birth Experience.* Toronto: HarperCollins Canada Ltd., 2003.

Health Canada. Women's Health Bureau. *Exploring Concepts of Gender and
Health.* Ottawa: Minister of Supply and Services Canada, 2003.

Mintzes, Barbara and Rosanna Baraldi. *Direct-to-Consumer Prescription Drug Advertising: When Public Health Is no Longer a Priority.* Toronto: Women and Health Protection, 2001.

National Coordinating Group on Health Care Reform and Women. *Women and Health Care Reform.* Winnipeg: National Coordinating Group on Health Care Reform and Women, 2002.

National Coordinating Group on Health Care Reform. *Reading Romanow: The Implications of the Final Report of the Commission on the Future of Health Care in Canada for Women.* Winnipeg: National Coordinating Group on Health Care Reform, 2003.

O'Grady, Kathleen. "Reclaiming menopause: Another look at HRT and the medicalization of women's bodies." *Network* 5/6 (4/1) (2002): 3–4.

O'Leary Cobb, Janine. "Behind the screens: Mammograms." *A Friend Indeed* 10(4) (2003).

Romanow, Roy J. *Building on Values: The Future of Health Care in Canada.* Final Report of the Commission on the Future of Health Care in Canada. Saskatoon: Commission on the Future of Health Care in Canada, 2002.

Scott, Katherine. *Funding Matters: The Impact of Canada's New Funding Regime on Nonprofit and Voluntary Organizations.* Ottawa: Canadian Council on Social Development, 2003.

Sherwin, Susan. *No Longer Patient: Feminist Ethics and Health Care.* Philadelphia: Temple University Press, 1992.

Status of Women Canada. *What Women Prescribe: Report and Recommendations from the National Symposium "Women in Partnership: Working Towards Inclusive, Gender-Sensitive Health Policies."* Ottawa: Minister of Supply and Services Canada, 1995.

Tudiver, Sari. *The Strength of Links: Building the Canadian Women's Health Network.* Winnipeg: Women's Health Clinic, 1994.

Tudiver, Sari and Madelyn Hall. "Women and Health Services Delivery in Canada: A Canadian Perspective." *Women's Health Forum: Canadian and American Commissioned Papers.* Ottawa: Minister of Supply and Services Canada, 1996.

United Nations. Department of Public Information. *Platform for Action and the Beijing Declaration: Fourth World Conference on Women, Beijing, China, 4-15 September, 1995.* New York, 1996

DIGGING INTO THE FEMINIST MEDIA: LOOKING FOR LESBIAN HEALTH

Jan Trainor

> History, real solemn history, I cannot be interested in.... I read it a little as a duty but it tells me nothing that does not either vex or weary me. The quarrels of popes and kings, with wars and pestilences, in every page; the men all so good for nothing and hardly any women at all—it is very tiresome.[1]
>
> Jane Austen, *Northanger Abbey*

I set out to trace the history of lesbian health through the lens of the women's health movement during the "second wave" in Canada. It was, I found out, as confounding a task as that undertaken by Jane Austen. I wanted to know if and how *lesbian,* women, and health intersected in recent women's history. But it turned out that early feminist publications were tiresome too...if you were a lesbian. So, as it turns out, this is not necessarily about lesbians.

The victories in assuring women's dominion over their reproductive health were admittedly hard-won, yet it was 2017 before access to abortion was available in all Canadian provinces. As for lesbian women, their issues under the feminist flag or health file are hard to find. The feminist quest for sexual equality and reproductive dominion in Canada in the 1980s was almost exclusive to heterosexual women. Perhaps lesbians were best seen as feminist allies on matters related to women's health?

Some of the alternate voices heard by Canadian women who were fighting for women-specific health programming in the 1980s were in feminist publications. Some of the publications that Canadian women had access to included: *Broadside* (1979–1989), a monthly publication, which served Toronto and southern Ontario; *Pandora* (1985–1994), a quarterly publication, which served Halifax and the Maritimes; and Vancouver's *Kinesis* (1974–2001), a monthly publication, which was widely read by labour women. Ironically, although the editorial boards and collectives of these publications were largely lesbian, and lesbians were keen subscribers and contributors, the actual coverage of lesbian issues was very limited.

As Dr. Barbara M. Freeman notes in her essay, "Collective Visions" in her volume on feminist journalism, reportage, and publishing,[2] *Broadside* averaged between 4.5 and 15 per cent lesbian coverage, *Kinesis* averaged between 12 and 21 per cent lesbian coverage, and *Pandora* averaged from 8 to 10 per cent. *Healthsharing* (1979–1993) reached across Canada by doing thematic issues and encouraging regional voices to be heard on all matters that affected women's health but contained little on lesbians. Indeed, there is an element of compulsive heterosexuality in all the feminist publications despite their varied editorial boards. The gay press revealed the same bias. The *Body Politic* (1972–1987) was primarily a gay men's publication based in Toronto. But it also had a lesbian readership and the paper had lesbians on its editorial board and in their production offices. Nevertheless, studies show that only 12 per cent of *Body Politic* content was lesbian-focused. Again lesbians, although involved, were not an issue.

Broadside (www.broadsidefeminist.com) has digitized all its volumes, as has *Healthsharing* at www.cwhn.ca. The University of British Columbia put the *Kinesis* collection online at open.library. ubc.ca/collections/kinesis, and Western University in London, Ontario hosts the online version of *The Body Politic* at www.uwo. ca/pridelib/bodypolitic/bphome.htm. So it was easy for me to explore *Broadside,* a publication to which I subscribed and read regularly; I knew members of the editorial collective and many of the contributors. Dr. Freeman confirmed through her interviews with the collectives of all three feminist publications that there was a tension within the collectives between how much lesbian content to feature versus focusing on feminism for a broader readership. This tension reflected the schism between feminism and lesbianism…the lesbians, it was feared, tainted the feminist brand.

Broadside, for example, was very much against male heterosexual pornography and urged provincial and federal governments to stop the flow of pornography from other countries and to close down the venues that sold both print and video material in their communities. Ironically, this reliance on government to enforce the eradication of male heterosexual pornography resulted in a very aggressive government crackdown on print and media representations of male-to-male sex and female-to-female sex. This created tensions between straight and lesbian feminists and the broader gay and lesbian community who had to fight to read and see information on their culture and its representations. Notable too is that in these enforcement efforts books such as *Our Bodies, Ourselves,* and periodicals such as *off our backs* were banned as obscene by Canada Customs. But somehow, male heterosexual pornography continued to make its way by Canada Customs.

Broadside helpfully indexed their publication when they placed it online. For my purposes, in searching for information on lesbians and health, I used a quantitative approach. Using *Broadside's* index, health entries numbered one hundred; of those, thirty-six were about abortion, thirty-eight were about health, women's health, mental health, and addictions, while the remaining entries covered reproduction, sexuality, and disability. I note that any reference to lesbians is incidental in the health entries. *Broadside's* coverage of abortion over the years grew in sophistication in their analysis of the issue—the collective featured the work of legal and medical experts to explain the issue and promote access to safe and free abortion within free-standing women's health clinics. *Broadside* also started to include gender in their analysis, and they defined the power imbalance between the doctor (male) and the patient (female) under the patriarchal gaze of the state.

Violence against women was emerging as a women's health issue during this period. *Broadside* featured fifty-five articles on violence against women: eighteen were about the violence against women inherent in and deriving from male heterosexual pornography, eighteen articles were about the need for shelters and the need for meaningful laws to redefine domestic violence as woman assault and protect women from violence on the streets and in the home. Fourteen articles discussed sexual assault and the need for support and reform and enforcement of laws to deter and punish male sexual violence against women. Incest and child sexual abuse also got some coverage. These articles highlighted the prevailing problem: The patriarchal state paid little attention to the women and children who were victims, while male offenders, as the alleged breadwinners, were rarely prosecuted for assault and battery and infrequently jailed.

And still, lesbians are absent from the pages. Granted, we are but 10–12 per cent of the population, maybe even less. Granted, we have addictions, disabilities, and mental health issues, and yes, we have babies and probably abortions. Yet, back in the day, *Broadside, Kinesis,* and *Pandora* were just teasing with their lesbian content. Others were not satisfied and wrote specifically about lesbians. Mariana Valverde was a contributor to *Broadside* and the author of *Sex, Power, and Pleasure* (The Women's Press, 1985) in which she discussed heterosexual, bisexual, and lesbian sexual relations and practices. Her chapter on lesbians, "Lesbianism: A country that has no language," is a primer on how female love and sex have evolved culturally over the past one hundred years. She talks about lesbianism and compulsory heterosexuality, the state, lesbian culture and the women's movement—Valverde implored the women's movement to reach out to all sexual orientations.

Sharon Dale Stone edited *Lesbians in Canada* (Between the Lines, 1990), wherein Joanne Doucette wrote on disabled lesbians and Joan Blackwood wrote on lesbian sex. The lesbian as mother is introduced by Dian Day. Becki Ross, in researching her organizational study of the Lesbian Organization of Toronto (LOOT) in *The House that Jill Built* (University of Toronto Press, 1995), found that lesbians were still not mentioned in Canadian women's movement writings as late as 1995. Her work is a history of a lesbian community under development as it attempts to form an organization that would promote lesbian culture. In its short life (1976–77 to 1979–80), it alienated butches and femmes (too heterosexual), bisexuals (too undecided), straight feminists (too heterosexual), lipstick lesbians (too fashionable), and other gay and lesbian community groups. Coalition politics or collaborative politics were not LOOT's strength. And lesbian health was clearly not an issue.

It could be argued that the Canadian women's movement chose to purposefully exclude lesbians. This was reflected in their publications that despite having lesbian editors, show little evidence of lesbians as feminists, activists, contributors, and subscribers. Lesbian health, I can only assume, was so good that there was no need to mention any real or potential illnesses. Or, I suspect, it was a case of what Betty Friedan called in 1970, the "lavender menace"—feminists did not want to taint the heterosexual feminist brand. However you read it, the printed history of the women's health movement with respect to lesbian health is incomplete and indeed, tiresome.

THE IMPORTANCE OF BEING RELENTLESS: A TORONTO WOMEN'S HEALTH CLINIC

Beth Atcheson, Constance Backhouse, Diana Majury, and Beth Symes

On April 1, 1978, the four of us, along with Leah Cohen, Jane Grimwood, and Marilou McPhedran, applied under Ontario law to create a new public hospital, to be known as the Toronto Women's Health Clinic (TWHC). We designed the TWHC to meet the need for a stand-alone facility to provide the full spectrum of routine health care for women throughout their lives. We included abortion as one of the routine services that the clinic would provide.[3] We were ready to start. We had draft articles of incorporation and by-laws. We had identified the services, staff complement, physical space, and capital and operating expenses for the TWHC. We had detailed financial, staffing, and architectural plans; safety and referral plans within the Toronto health network; and evaluation plans ready for review.[4] But before we could go ahead, Ontario's Minister of Health had to approve our application to create the hospital under the *Public Hospitals Act*[5] and, in addition, to approve it as a hospital in which therapeutic abortions could be performed in accordance with section 251 of the *Criminal Code*.[6] We met with the minister, Dennis Timbrell, on April 21, 1978. Almost forty years later, on April 17, 2017, we four authors met to reflect on our TWHC project from political and personal perspectives. How did we get on that path, how did we navigate it, and what difference did it make?

Our group came together out of myriad personal connections. Constance Backhouse, Diana Majury, Marilou McPhedran, and Beth Symes (Beth S) had just graduated from law school. They all hailed from Winnipeg. Constance and Diana were best childhood friends but went to different law schools. Constance knew Marilou from Osgoode Hall Law, and Beth S knew her from articling.

Diana knew Beth S from Queen's Law. Diana, Marilou, and Beth S were finishing their articling year at different Toronto law firms. Constance was working at the Ontario Ministry of Labour, having finished her articles, where she had met Leah Cohen, a consultant in the private sector, at a business conference. During her articles, Beth S had met Jane Grimwood, a flight attendant and union activist with the Canadian Airline Flight Attendants' Association, who was a labour relations officer at the Ontario Labour Relations Board. Beth Atcheson (Beth A), from Fredericton, was going into in her final year at University of Toronto Law and roomed with Constance, having met years earlier through a national youth project. Constance, Diana, Marilou, and Beth S were contemplating the six-month Bar Admission Course in September 1977, anticipating that it would be boring and that they would have time on their hands. We each had some experience of feminism and activism and were excited by the possibilities for change; we wanted to do more of that work. Whether or not we had an awareness of our "privilege" as white, middle-class, non-disabled lawyers in training, a concept that would be applied and understood later, we were keen to put ourselves to work.

Over a drink at the Long Bar in the Sheraton Hotel on Queen Street West in May 1977, Constance and Beth S canvassed the possibilities. Reproductive rights, and in particular abortion, kept coming up as key issues. At that time, abortion was prohibited under the *Criminal Code of Canada* except in extremely limited circumstances. Amendments to the Code, enacted in 1969, had created an exception to the prohibition on abortion. It would not apply to a doctor performing an abortion or a female obtaining one if the abortion had been previously approved by the therapeutic abortion committee (TAC) of an accredited or approved hospital and was also carried out in an accredited or approved hospital. A TAC had to comprise three doctors, none of whom could at the same time be performing abortions. The TAC was required to certify, in writing, that the continuation of the pregnancy would or would be likely to endanger the life or "health" of the female. "Health" was not defined. There was no requirement that an accredited or approved hospital put a TAC in place. In *Morgentaler* v. *The Queen*, [1976] S.C.R. 616, the Supreme Court of Canada held that this law took away the "necessity defence" (*R. v. Bourne*, [1939] 3 All E. R. 615), so that the only way for doctors, and women seeking abortions, to avoid the risk of a criminal charge in providing or having an abortion (except in the case of an emergency) was through prior approval of the abortion by a TAC.

On the one hand, the TAC was a significant barrier. On the other, because of provincial jurisdiction over hospitals, the provinces had constitutionally clear scope to ameliorate the barrier. In 1978, abortion was firmly under the control of the medical profession and the hospital system.

Constance thought that we could perhaps collaborate on a brief. Beth S wanted us to be more proactive and suggested a "practical" project. We fanned out to speak with women's organizations and feminist activists to hear their ideas and views. Constance particularly remembers a luncheon at the Toronto Hilton with Laura Sabia, who was in her usual elegant hat. We met with a group of frontline workers in women's health services, and others who were working on a Morgentaler-style clinic as a way of both providing services and challenging the law in Ontario. Dr. Henry Morgentaler had been operating an abortion clinic in Montreal since 1969 that did not require approvals through a TAC, and was therefore subject to charges that it was violating section 251 of the *Criminal Code*. We were impressed by these frontline activists and decided that we wanted to work on an abortion clinic, but would come at it another way. We wanted to use the tools that existed "inside the box" of law (and, to some degree, politics) to create something new. We decided on a women's health clinic. The TWHC would do legal abortions and be an approved hospital with a TAC, but, just as importantly, the TWHC would be a well-women clinic with a holistic approach to women's health care, challenging the conventional medical model.

> Although women's health care needs have probably been constant over time, it is only recently that women have begun to analyze existing health care from the critical point of view... women are anxious to find means to become informed and active participants in their overall health maintenance. Topics of particular concern are female anatomy and physiology, nutrition, exercise, health habits, sexuality, venereal disease, reproduction, birth control, parenthood, childbearing and menopause. Routine health care is seen as an essential part of health care for women. If it is clear why women are now willing to take responsibility for their own health, it should be clear why routine health is now of such importance.[7]

We were taken with the simplicity and audacity of our plan: You need to be a hospital to perform legal abortions.... Okay, we will set up a hospital and we will make it a women's hospital.

Later in the project, we explored the possibility of combining forces with the other group working on a clinic, but we had two fundamental differences. First, the TWHC group decided that it could not embark on anything illegal. We were not prepared to risk prosecution. To a degree, we did take on risk—risk in our work and in our relationships—but those are different orders of risk. On being called to the bar, we would be swearing to uphold the law. We wanted to contribute as best we could within those bounds. Second, there were the politics. Whatever our personal politics were or became, at that time we would have been seen as mainstream. We did not have "radical," "left," grassroots," or "frontline" credentials. The other group nicknamed us the "Legal Beagles." It was not so far off. Would we have been in a better place if the two groups could have figured out how to combine our energies? It is an important question, not answered here. What is clear is that we understood the nature of prosecution risk and we respect those who are prepared to take it.

We were clear from the very beginning that we did not have any subject matter expertise, but we had confidence that we could learn what we needed to know. We had been "in training" in formal institutions for years and we wanted to "bust out" of the dominant values and constraints of these spaces, to do what we wanted to do, in the way we wanted to do it, to the full extent of our abilities. We had been in environments dominated by men and we had learned how to stand up for our points of view. We were trained in the use and integration of fact, law, and argument. The TWHC, amongst other things, was an exercise in advocacy. Following our training, our first step was research. Diana undertook a memorandum of the law, and we set out to learn the facts.

Our project was active for less than two years. But during that time, we developed our ideas through calling people we did not know, tapping their expertise and advice, and making decisions about how to integrate what we learned into the design of the TWHC. We learned in this process not to go alone to important meetings. Not only did it help to have more than one perspective on what was discussed, but we could also take different tacks at a meeting to bring out information or points of view, either pushing hard or playing nice. Going together helped us to plan tactics for our meetings, limit our nervousness going into meetings, and allowed us to mitigate attempts to intimidate us. We moved at speed, with intensity, and somehow met the requirements of our "day jobs." But by no means were we alone; there were hundreds of feminist activist projects at the time, all kinds of politics and all kinds of issues. We pushed, and were pushed, by other women and their work. We confronted what stood in our way. It was exhilarating.

Our choice of project made considerable sense in 1977–1978. During the (almost) ten years since limited access to legal abortion became available in 1969, the law had been continuously challenged, so some room to manoeuvre had been created.[8] The Canadian Association for the Repeal of the Abortion Law (CARAL, formed in 1974 and after 1980 called the Canadian Abortion Rights Action League) was the leading national voice for decriminalization of abortion through the repeal of section 251 of the *Criminal Code*. Dr. Henry Morgentaler, who performed abortions in a stand-alone, single-purpose clinic in Montreal, had been charged three times under section 251 and had been acquitted by a jury each time.

The Parti Québécois was elected in Québec on November 16, 1976, and weeks later, on December 11, the Québec justice minister announced that no further charges would be laid in respect of abortions performed by qualified medical personnel in clinics in Québec.[9] So, while the provinces had no authority over the *Criminal Code* provision itself, they controlled enforcement of the *Criminal Code*, a scope that the Province of Québec would use to circumvent the provision. At the time, there was no indication that Ontario would follow Québec's lead and refuse to lay charges if a clinic met certain requirements. Indeed, four years later, in the early 1980s, Ontario would lay charges against a Toronto abortion clinic. Those charges were challenged all the way to the Supreme Court of Canada, which would strike down section 251 in 1988.[10] We were working on the TWHC at the beginning of that key decade, testing what Ontario would do with respect to abortion within its constitutional jurisdiction.

In January 1977, the *Report of the Committee on the Operation of the Abortion Law* (Badgley Report) was released. The committee had been created in 1975 but was confined to fact-finding and its terms of reference forbade its making recommendations. Even the federal government and Otto Lang, minister of justice and attorney general from 1972 to 1975, who opposed abortion in principle, had had to recognize that there were gross inequities in the availability of abortion across Canada. The committee made clear findings on significant matters: the effects of hospitals being given the option of whether or not to have a therapeutic abortion committee; the varying processes used and the varying interpretations or definitions of "health" by TACs; and the significant percentage of successful applicants who faced extra billing for the procedure. It pointed out that for every five women who obtained an abortion in Canada, at least one left the country for that purpose.[11]

Abortion law aside, we were navigating the health care system ourselves and, as young women who came of age in the 1960s, found that it did not meet our expectations or needs. We were already encountering misogyny in public education, legal education, and the legal system; the misogyny was no less apparent or frustrating in the medical system. Many of our best teachers and allies in our work on the women's clinic had had their own trials in medical education and practice.

We decided that our project would not focus on reform or repeal of section 251 itself. Influenced by the Badgley Report and by our own paths as young lawyers-to-be, we opted to see what could be accomplished for women's health by treating abortion as an essential element on a spectrum of women's health needs. As we were focused only on legal abortion, the only option for our project was to become a hospital under section 251, with its own TAC.[12] Further, we did not want the TWHC to be directly affiliated with a conventional hospital and utilizing that hospital's TAC. This was in part about control, as we did not wish to import the politics of a larger, mainstream institution into the plans for, and future of, the TWHC. We also wanted the TWHC to be run as, and ultimately evaluated as, an alternative method for the delivery of routine health care to women.

As it turned out, the biggest challenge we faced did not arise from performing abortions in a clinic. It was clear that this could be done safely (it was being done safely in the Morgentaler clinic, and it was being done safely in many clinics in the US[13]). In fact, a key finding of the Badgley Report supported a clinic approach, as we explained in the brief that accompanied our application to be a public hospital:

> In the *Report of the Committee on the Operation of the Abortion Law*, (Ottawa, 1977), it was shown that the manner in which doctors and hospitals now process requests for abortion creates, on the average, an eight-week delay between a pregnant women's first visit to a doctor and eventual performance of an abortion. This delay itself creates

the risk of health complications. Furthermore, the *Report* says the complications occurred at a rate of 3.1 per 100 therapeutic abortions in 1974. It was suggested that the number and types of complications associated with therapeutic abortions might be reduced, *inter alia*, by the performance of all therapeutic abortions at an earlier stage of gestation and the concentration of the performance of the abortion procedure into specialized units with a full range of required equipment and staffed by experienced and specially trained nursing and medical personnel. Specialization in administration and procedure is therefore desirable in order to reduce the risk of complications and increase efficiency.

The challenges we faced were organizational and financial, and most significantly, political. In retrospect, one of the most interesting aspects of the TWHC was how much helpful advice we received from Ontario and City of Toronto public servants. We consulted about a dozen key officials in health care delivery and funding. Whatever they thought of our project, us, or abortion, we were treated professionally and given valuable advice. They were the ones who guided us through the regulatory route on how to create and fund the clinic. We were confident and optimistic that we could raise $135,00 for capital expenses (for renovations, equipment, and furnishings) privately, even though we had no experience in fundraising at that time. We now have a great deal indeed, some of it gained the hard way. The operating expenses were a different matter, as they could mostly be funded on a fee-for-service basis through the Ontario Health Insurance Plan (OHIP). In fact, the OHIP fees, particularly those generated from therapeutic abortions (surgery being recompensed at a higher rate than other services), would be enough to cover the staff and services essential to a well-woman clinic that could not be recovered under OHIP. Insured services could be used to subsidize uninsured services, allowing the TWHC to employ counsellors and nurses.

We knew that women had a wide range of health needs and interests. Our proposal made it clear that services were to be provided on a patient-centred basis:

> Essentially, the Toronto Women's Health Clinic will be a specialized clinic because it will be for

women; it will, however, have an expertise more comprehensive than most specialized clinics.... [I]t must be characterized by care that is both participatory and empathetic: it will be information- and discussion-intensive. General hospitals are certainly not structured to provide that type of care, but are disease and crisis oriented. Although public health clinics and doctors in private practice can and do provide that kind of care, their other responsibilities generally preclude the development of expertise that results from specialization.

Although we did not intend to appropriate the voices of "all women," we may have been seen as doing so because of the way in which we worked. We did not do very much, if any, research, outreach, or collaboration with specific women's communities in Toronto. In those pre-*Charter* days we were starting to appreciate the nature of discrimination other than our own, awkwardly expressed at that time as "double discrimination"—the reality that women often experienced discrimination not only because of sex or gender, but also because of other characteristics such as race, origin, religion, dis/ability, sexuality, or citizenship status. But we stayed within our own networks, or networks with which we were comfortable. We did not either "talk" or "walk" inclusion or what was later labelled as intersectionality in the way we did the project or in the TWHC proposal. Equally, there is no evidence that the government of Ontario had any concept of inclusion in evaluating the TWHC proposal.

We understood the political challenges of establishing the TWHC, although our approach to addressing them had some successes and strengths as well as weaknesses. We garnered significant support from Toronto city councillors (then called "aldermen") and from civil society organizations, including but also beyond women's groups, as we made a point of showing the breadth and depth of support for access to abortion. We have particularly strong and favourable memories of our meetings with Archbishop Ted Scott, then primate of the Anglican Church of Canada, and Dr. Robert B. McClure, a former moderator of The United Church of Canada, both of whom endorsed the TWHC. On the other hand we did not understand the Davis government and provincial politics very well, and so we did not spend enough time strategizing about Premier Davis and the Cabinet, nor did we operate on a cross-party basis and engage the opposition leaders and parties. There was a provincial election on June 9, 1977, that returned Premier Bill Davis's Progressive Conservatives as a minority government. Dr. Stuart Smith was the Liberal leader (and leader of the official opposition); the NDP leadership was in flux as Stephen Lewis resigned and Michael Cassidy stepped in as NDP leader. The Davis government had a history of resisting equality for women[14] and, although we did meet with one prominent Progressive Conservative, lawyer Eddie Goodman, who was supportive and contacted Dennis Timbrell to say so, we did not work the provincial political scene astutely or adequately.

While we had strong support from many prominent members of the medical community, we also met with considerable resistance on this front. The meeting that most stands out in our memory is with Dr. W. H. Allemang, Senior Staff, Obstetrics and Gynaecology at Toronto General Hospital. We were there because we wanted to establish a collaborative relationship with a hospital that would be close to the TWHC. The meeting turned out to be short, dominated by his views and our decision to say little, as we felt what would be the point when he saw us as stupid girls? He said women could not be obstetricians because they did not have the intellectual, moral, or physical fortitude to deliver babies and he was going to make sure that there was never a female obstetrician on staff. In his view, abortions were really dangerous. We understood him to say that the idea of doing them in a stand-alone clinic a block away was irresponsible, unsafe, and ludicrous. We underestimated the deeply entrenched misogynist views held by key players whose support we sought.

On March 15, 1978, *The Globe and Mail* published a Canadian Press item that read "Health Minister Dennis Timbrell said [in the Legislature] yesterday he does not support the establishment of private therapeutic abortion clinics in Ontario," indicating that "he has twice met" with groups advocating clinics. We were curious about this. We understood that he had met with the other Toronto group advocating for a clinic. Our meeting with the minister had been rescheduled several times and not yet held. Either there was a third group or the minister had also already decided the fate of the TWHC. In any event, our meeting was held on April 21, 1978. There was some dancing around whether a clinic might be approved if we could find a hospital that would agree to close beds, given that a clinic would divert patients away from hospitals.[15] But it became clear that this strategy was not really on the table. In response to a direct question, Minster Timbrell stated that even if we were successful in obtaining such an agreement, he would not recommend that cabinet approve our application. He said that due to his personal views, he could not "in good conscience" approve a free-standing clinic that would do abortions, even legal abortions. Our only option would be to affiliate with an existing hospital with a TAC.

We sat down to evaluate what we considered to be the "must haves" for the TWHC. We wanted to provide a full range of routine health care for women, health care in which women were full participants, not simply passive recipients of medical advice. We believed that first trimester abortion was part of the spectrum of service that could best be delivered in a clinic setting. As a practical matter, the only way to fund the operating costs of a full-service clinic was through OHIP. We would not, and could not, do a clinic without abortions. The minister's position meant that the only way to do abortions was in an existing public hospital. In the fall of 1978, we explored whether any hospital doors were open to the TWHC and quickly found that they were as uninterested in us as we had been in them. We concluded that our approach—"inside" the legal box and "outside" the traditional health care box—was not going to work. We have asked ourselves whether we felt all along that the minister would never take up the scope that section 251 gave to the provinces and to "hospitals" under provincial law, whether all along we knew in our hearts that we would be turned down, so that what we were really doing was testing and establishing beyond any doubt that section 251 could never work for women. But in truth, we did believe that there was a possibility of approval. In our process of planning and advocating for the clinic, we became more and more committed to it as a model for women's health care, and more and more hopeful that its clear benefits would quash the opposition. If the TWHC had been approved, however, our hard work would only have just begun, a reality that was not so clear to us at the time, but became obvious with experience. Had we achieved it, the TWHC would have changed the course of our lives.

We moved on to other women's projects. Constance and Leah published *The Secret Oppression: Sexual Harassment of Working Women* (MacMillan, 1978) and additional works. Diana joined with women who worked on the other clinic proposal to co-found *Healthsharing*, a women's health magazine. Beth S, Marilou, and Beth A worked on constitutional equality rights for women and the founding of the Women's Legal Education and Action Fund.

Feminists in Canada were relentless in the pursuit of change.

Each project required relentless work and advocacy. Win, lose, or draw in the shorter term, when we are relentless we ultimately prevail. The TWHC was part of a stream of unrelenting pressure to respond to women's demands for better health, reproduction, and abortion services. The clinic application for hospital status under section 251 of the *Criminal Code* pushed the Ontario government of the day and clearly established that it would be impossible to set up a legal abortion clinic under the existing law. The rigidity of the law and its application became a tool in tearing down the law itself. Politicians deal with us when they understand that we are not going away, that we are relentless, and that our demands go up when we are dismissed. This is how feminist activism operated—working in all kinds of ways, in all kinds of spaces, being new water wearing down the resistance of old and aging stone, that creates change, sometimes incremental and around the edges, sometimes in a deep and quick fracture.

WOMEN AND HEALTH:
THE GROWING CONTROVERSY

Leah Cohen and Constance Backhouse

Reprinted from Canadian Women's Studies/les cahiers de la femme, *Volume 1, Number 4 (1979).*

This article was prepared for publication in The Globe and Mail, *August 1978. Although it was accepted by a senior editor, his superiors decided that the subject matter was not timely and that women readers would be unable to comprehend the statistical data.*

In Ontario hospitals, student interns and residents routinely practise internal pelvic examinations on anaesthetized women patients. These patients, who are in hospital for gynecological operations, have not been informed of this practice, nor has the public at large.

The argument put forth by the medical community to justify this procedure is that it is necessary in order to train students. It is difficult to find unanaesthetized female patients who would willingly consent to have students practice pelvic examinations on them. Since the anaesthetized woman is unaware of what is occurring, the medical profession believes that there is nothing improper about the procedure.

This and other issues concerning the delivery of medical services to women are becoming points of controversy. At a time when health costs are soaring, grave concern has been expressed that the quality of health care provided to women may be questionable.

OVER-MEDICATION OF WOMEN

Why do doctors prescribe more mood-altering drugs for women than for men? A recent Canadian study on psychotropic drug use among women demonstrated that women exceed men in their consumption of psychotropic drugs in a consistent ratio of two to one. One explanation is that the doctor misinterprets his female patient's symptoms as imaginary because she speaks in cultural language that he does not understand.

A 1966 study on the way in which patients from two cultures describe their ailments suggests this possibility. While the study concerned the Irish and the Italian, medical researchers concluded it was also relevant to all males and females.

This study, published in the *American Sociological Review*, indicated that at the Eye, Ear, Nose and Throat Clinic of Massachusetts General Hospital, the Irish patients presented few symptoms and refused to admit pain to doctors. Italians with comparable ailments gave more symptoms, acknowledged their illnesses, and complained of pain. Doctors concluded that the Irish needed medical help more urgently than the Italians, even though the two groups had been matched for seriousness of illness.

The study suggests that the more stoical the patient, the more seriously the doctor tends to regard him or her. The more expansive the patient, the less seriously the physician takes him or her. In an update of the study, it was discovered that if no organic basis for the disease existed, doctors tended to describe an Italian as having emotional problems, but described an Irish patient in more neutral terms.

Dr. Linda Fidell, the author of a 1975 California drug-usage study, pointed out that in North American culture men generally act like the stoic Irish and women like the expansive Italians.

From childhood, Dr. Fidell observes, a female is encouraged to admit her pain and to ask for help freely. As a male (92 per cent of all doctors are male), the doctor is programmed to endure hardship rather than ask for help immediately. When confronted with a female who describes vague symptoms at length, the doctor, already assuming that women's ailments are often psychosomatic, may consider her problem an emotional one. So, Dr. Fidell concludes, the doctor prescribes a tranquilizer.

Drug advertisements also tend to foster such sexist assumptions, she maintains. A five-year study of leading medical journals concluded that medical advertising gives this message to physicians: Men have "real illness"; women have mental problems.

In numerous surveys of mental health practitioners who were asked to describe a healthy, mature, socially competent man, woman, and adult, the results have indicated that regardless of the sex of the practitioner, traits of a healthy adult were significantly less likely to be attributed to a woman than to a man. The studies indicated that many mental health practitioners believe a healthy woman differs from a healthy man by being "more submissive, less independent, less adventurous, less aggressive, more excitable in minor crises, less objective, disliking math and science." This analysis of a healthy woman, the surveys conclude, is not simply mere stereotyping, but rather suggestive of a powerful negative assessment of women.

Gena Corea, author of *The Hidden Malpractice: How American Medicine Treats Women as Patients and Professionals*, says there is the danger that doctors programmed to expect psychosomatic afflictions in all women may overlook a critical condition.

Dr. W. H. Allemang, senior gynecologist and obstetrician at Toronto General Hospital, believes that women are the recipients of mood-altering drugs more often than men due to their emotional make-up. "Women tend to react emotionally—it is part of the component of being a woman. Women are a little more feminine than men. Men are more rational."

Dr. Allemang has assessed that women are greater users of the health care system than men. They go to a general practitioner who is busy and has only approximately ten minutes to give to each patient. As a result, the reasons for anxiety are not discussed and the women are often given tranquilizers. However, he feels this is not a serious problem.

Dr. Harding LeRiche, a professor of epidemiology at the University of Toronto Faculty of Medicine believes that over-medication is one of the worst things that is happening at the present time. However, studies that he has done indicate that women have more psychiatric problems than men.

In Dr. LeRiche's view, women are generally "more timid, less aggressive, more sensitive, and more perceptive than men." He suggests that this is somewhat related to social conditioning. However, the net result is that women tend to go to doctors more easily than men and hence are the recipients of more medication. "Not only do they get treatment they need, but they probably also get treatment that is not needed."

Today in Canada 78 per cent of physicians prescribe more mood-altering drugs for women than for men. According to Jessica Hill, the Acting Director of Non-Medical Use of Drugs in Toronto, 70 per cent of all tranquilizers are prescribed by GPs. These GPs, she claims, are more likely to prescribe tranquilizers to women than to men presenting the same complaints.

Although these data surfaced as early as 1971, Ruth Cooperstock, a scientist at the Addiction Research Foundation in Toronto, maintains that there has been little response or change. "Doctors," she says, "have the role of confidant forced on them. Their education is geared to action. They generally won't say 'I don't know' or refer the patient to an agency outside the health care system.

"If a woman comes to a doctor describing anxiety and

emotional problems and asking for help, the doctor is not trained as a marriage counsellor or housing expert and finds it difficult to take the time to allow the patient to ventilate. But the doctor does know that drugs diminish anxiety for short periods of time and often thinks that prescribing a drug is the humane thing to do. Current medical education devotes little time to training doctors in pharmacology or the problems of addiction."

Dr. Eugene Vayda, in a February 1976 article in the *Canadian Medical Association Journal*, states: "Physicians need continuing training in clinical pharmacology...including teaching the properties of individual drugs and an understanding of the measures used to determine therapeutic effectiveness."

The problem is further exacerbated, Ruth Cooperstock observes, by the growing phenomenon of cross-addiction of alcohol and mood-altering drugs—the effect of which is synergistic—meaning that the same amount of alcohol and Valium, for example, has a more than doubling effect. In fact, Ontario statistics show 36 per cent of recovered women alcoholics were cross-addicted, usually with tranquilizers.

What happens, Ms. Cooperstock says, is that doctors are aware that the prognosis for alcoholism is poor, so they try to stay away from it. Doctors are given so little training in alcohol addiction that they do not know much about the process. Furthermore, there is a great stigma attached to the female alcoholic. "Women in our society are supposed to be the nurturing force and the bedrock of society," she says. "A drunk female is terribly threatening—there is no dinner, the house is dirty, and the children are neglected."

As a result, doctors do not generally ask their female patients about their rate of alcohol consumption. If they do, there is a generally-held misconception that if the doctor can reduce tension with mood-altering drugs, alcohol consumption will diminish. But Ms. Cooperstock's research indicates that the drugs can become addictive in themselves. The woman may be told to cut her drinking, to take Valium and if she fails to comply, is sent on to a psychiatrist.

Ms. Cooperstock believes that until we see a critical mass of women in the medical profession, very little will change. It is interesting to note, she adds, with women's new wave of feminism, female doctors are being rushed off their feet by female patients.

"More women have tried tranquilizers and are not pleased with the results," she concludes. "Younger women especially are seeking coping skills and life changes as opposed to solutions via a mood-altering drug."

UNNECESSARY SURGERY
Hysterectomies

Although discussion about the prevalence and perils of unnecessary surgery is a recent phenomenon, the historical background indicates that this was a problem of serious proportion for nineteenth-century women.

The commonly held nineteenth-century view was that women had no capacity for sexual feeling of any kind. If a woman did develop the illness of sexuality—called "nymphomania"—physicians cured her with a variety of techniques. Many doctors cauterized (burned) the clitoris, or removed it surgically.

Removal of both ovaries was another operation frequently performed in the nineteenth-century to cure female sexuality and non-conformity. American historian G. J. Barker-Benfield reports in his book, *The Horrors of the Half-Known Life: Male Attitudes Towards Women and Sexuality in Nineteenth-Century America*, that the medical indications for ovariotomy included "neurosis, insanity, troublesomeness, eating like a ploughman, masturbation, attempted suicide, erotic tendencies, persecution mania, and anything untoward in female behavior."

The modern controversy over unnecessary surgery rages about hysterectomy—the surgical removal of the uterus. The medical reasons for performing such a procedure are said to be uterine cancer, inexplicable menstrual bleeding, small non-malignant tumours, menstrual cramps, and vaginal laxness (a condition in which the vaginal walls lose their firmness, often as a result of childbearing).

Other doctors are not convinced and claim that for most of these symptoms, rest, relaxation, hormones, or scraping of the uterus (D&C) are all treatments that should be considered before major surgery. Despite this more cautious sector of opinion, hysterectomies have become the second most frequently performed operation on females in the USA. Further, the number of hysterectomies performed in the USA increased approximately 60 per cent between 1965 and 1973, far in excess of population growth.

Numerous American studies, including one by the University of Michigan Department of Obstetrics and Gynecology, have concluded that at least one-third of the hysterectomies performed are completely unwarranted, exposing women unnecessarily to the risks of anaesthesia reactions and post-operative complications such as pneumonia, blood clots, and infection.

The Canadian pattern of surgery is similar. Dr. Eugene Vayda, chairman of the Department of Health Administration, University of Toronto Faculty of Medicine, recently wrote in the *Canadian Journal of Surgery* that hysterectomy, which is done twice as frequently in Canada as in England and Wales, increased by 40 per cent between 1968 and 1972.

Vayda concluded: "It seems unlikely that these increases were due to changes in the prevalence of associated diseases." Instead he accounted for some of the increase by correlating it to such factors as the number of surgical personnel and bed to patient ratio. (The frequency of the procedure increased when more physicians and beds were available.)

The 40 per cent increase in Canadian hysterectomies evidenced between 1968 and 1972 seems to have levelled off, but except for a minor decrease, the rate has remained at the controversially high level. In 1971, there were 23,635 hysterectomies done in Ontario, compared to 23,197 in 1975. Across Canada the hysterectomy rate per 100,000 female population was 622 in 1971 and 572 in 1975.

When questioned about whether unnecessary hysterectomies were being done in Canada, Dr. W. H. LeRiche, professor of epidemiology, University of Toronto Faculty of Medicine, said, "A few years ago there were too many hysterectomies being done in Saskatchewan, but that has been stopped. As far as Ontario is concerned, when I studied it a few years ago, I found no unnecessary surgery in university centres."

"In smaller centres and medium-sized towns where there aren't any university medical schools, there may be some unnecessary hysterectomies." Despite the similarity of Canadian and American data, LeRiche said that "on the whole, it is not a problem in Canada as it is in the US Discipline on the medical profession is of a higher standard in Canada."

The Saskatchewan incident referred to is notorious among members of the medical profession. In Saskatchewan an increase in 75 per cent between 1964 and 1971 in the rate of hysterectomies was brought to the attention of the Saskatchewan College of Physicians and Surgeons.

The College appointed a special committee, which identified indications for hysterectomy and classified hysterectomies in 1970 and 1973 at selected hospitals as "justified" or "unjustified." Unjustified hysterectomy rates ranged from 1.7 to 58.6 per cent. Hospitals with low rates of unjustified hysterectomies were "commended" and those with high rates were sent five recommendations that included the statements that "unnecessary surgery should cease" and "Tissue Committees (which examine all tissues removed by physicians) should take a renewed interested in their responsibility." The committee reported a 50 per cent reduction in the rate of hysterectomy in the one Saskatchewan city with the highest "unjustified" hysterectomy rate, and an overall provincial reduction of 13 per cent, which they attributed, in part, to the review.

Dr. Eugene Vayda has recently suggested that perhaps the next step after criteria for "justified" and "unjustified" elective surgeries are agreed upon would be to allow hospital surgical utilization committees "to act prospectively to screen candidates for elective surgery and to pre-authorize elective operations." The most serious obstacle to this approach is that the medical profession cannot agree on the criteria indicating a hysterectomy.

One of the reasons why hysterectomy rates are so high is that physicians not only remove the uterus once they discover uterine cancer, but increasingly remove it to prevent any possibility of future cancer. Hysterectomy will, of course, prevent cancer. If you don't have a uterus, you can't get uterine cancer. Medical journalists bear witness to the current debate over whether gynecologists should remove the healthy reproductive organs of *all* women who reach a certain age to prevent development of cancer in the uterus and ovaries (*Audio Digest Obstetrics/Gynecology*, 1973).

As Dr. LeRiche says, "You can't have it both ways. While necessary hysterectomies may be alleged, cervical cancer is quite serious." However, according to Ralph Nader's Washington, DC's Health Research Group, the death rate for hysterectomy itself (1,000 out of every 1 million women annually) is, in fact, higher than the death rate for uterine/cervical cancer (100 out of every 1 million women each year).

In *Seizing Our Bodies: The Politics of Women's Health,* Claudia Dreifus reports that the American Planned Parenthood Foundation is taking issue with what they call "hacking preventively" at future possibly offending flesh. "Preventive lobotomies," says Planned Parenthood in an effort to point out the absurdity of the argument, "for young people at statistically high risk of developing violent psychoses at some future time have not been suggested by physicians writing in psychiatric journals."

Recently, some physicians have abandoned the question of which medical symptoms warrant surgical removal of the uterus, and have wholeheartedly endorsed this operation for the sole purpose of sterilization. Dr. W. H. Allemang, senior gynecologist and obstetrician at Toronto General Hospital, accounts for the "popularity" of hysterectomy because it is "a reasonable form of sterilization. The alternative of the sterilization procedure just leaves a useless uterus, except to get cancer. With a hysterectomy you prevent menstruation, which for a woman in her forties may be a bit out of control. It's that easy. It's an attractive package in this day and age both for the patient and the doctor."

When asked whether he felt too many hysterectomies were being done in Canada, Dr. Allemang said, "What is too much operating? No doubt there is an increasing trend in the area of hysterectomy, but these things become fetishes of the time. Which one is today's, which one will be next year's, I don't know. Surgery has in a sense become safer. Most physicians want to contribute the best they can. They develop theories that a certain procedure will solve the patient's problem. There is not very much risk associated with it."

In an environment where 92 per cent of all physicians are male, the type of reasoning that predominates was identified in a 1970 issue of *Medical World News*. This journal reported on a cancer conference where surgeons had agreed that they rarely hesitate to remove an ovary but think twice about removing a testicle. "The doctors readily admitted that such a sex-oriented viewpoint arises from the fact that most surgeons are male," the *News* reported. "Said one of them wryly, 'No ovary is good enough to leave in, and no testicle is bad enough to take out!'"

Breast surgery
The unresolved controversy over the various methods of treatment for breast cancer is more publicly visible than the issue of hysterectomy. A range of surgical procedures is used—from a radical mastectomy in which the breast, underlying lymph nodes, and the pectoral muscles are removed, through less drastic surgery such as the partial, modified, simple, or subcutaneous mastectomy.

The radical mastectomy was first devised by Williams Stewart Halsted in 1882, when, according to Gena Corea in *The Hidden Malpractice*, due to late diagnosis, tumours were much more massive by the time they were treated than they are now. His radical mastectomy quickly became the standard operation for breast cancer in the USA and Canada. Corea reports that even though there has been no proof that the Halsted radical is a superior treatment to more moderate procedures, no controlled study of the various procedures was undertaken until 1970.

At that point, the National Cancer Institute, on a test of 1,700 women, compared three treatments: the radical mastectomy, simple mastectomy, and simple mastectomy followed by radiation therapy. After two years, all three treatments had approximately the same 15 per cent recurrence rates of disease.

"It's a very sad business because there's no proof whatever surgery is done makes any difference—no proof that radical mastectomy does any more good than just taking out a lump. The evidence is that we don't really know what treatments are most effective," says Dr. LeRiche.

Dr. George Crile, Jr., author of *What Women Should Know About Breast Cancer*, takes a more extreme view. He reported in his book that many surgeons in North America and most of those in England now agree that there is no longer any place for the mutilating radical operation. "If the cancer is so advanced that it cannot be removed by an operation less than radical mastectomy, it has already spread through the system and is incurable by surgery."

Gena Corea reports that when American physicians detect a cancerous tumour in the breast, 90 per cent of them perform a Halsted radical mastectomy. British surgeons perform half as many radical mastectomies per 100,000 population as American surgeons. Dr. Crile noted in his book that Canadian surgeons appear to be abandoning radical mastectomy more rapidly than American surgeons. However, Dr. Eugene Vayda has reported that "The rates in Canada for the period from 1968–1972 for radical mastectomy have remained essentially the same."

After this period, the number of radical and extended radical mastectomies done in Ontario and Canada began to decline. In 1973, of the 3,574 mastectomies done in Ontario, there were 744 radical and extended radical; in 1976, of 4,523 mastectomies in Ontario, there were 595 radical and extended radical. The Canadian figures indicate that in 1971 there were twenty-eight radical mastectomies per 100,000 female population; in 1975, there were fifteen.

Many doctors in Canada criticize the findings of the National Cancer Institute, pointing out that the women tested must be followed for a number of years before any firm conclusions can be drawn. Author Dr. Crile, however, argues that for too long surgeons have assumed the entire burden of deciding how their patients with breast cancer should be treated.

He states, "Today there is no agreement on treatment, and the surgeon, therefore, has an obligation to inform the patient of the facts. Only when the patient is allowed to participate in the decision can she accept an operation on her breast with what can be known ethically as 'informed consent.'"

Cancer of the breast is by far the most common malignant tumour in women. Health and Welfare Canada reports that it is the third leading cause of death in all Canadian women. For women aged forty to forty-nine, it is the leading cause of death.

ESTROGEN REPLACEMENT THERAPY FOR MENOPAUSAL WOMEN

In her recently published book, *The Hidden Malpractice,* Gena Corea has reported that every woman reacts to the change of life differently. "But doctors tend to assume that all menopausal women will be psychologically and physically at risk. They are expected to have emotional breakdowns, lose their sexual appetites, experience hot flashes and sprout little moustaches. Their breasts and vaginas are supposed to shrivel up."

Dr. David Reuben asserted in his widely read book *Everything You Always Wanted to Know About Sex* that the menopausal woman was, "not really a man, but no longer a functional woman (living) in the world of intersex…. Having outlived their ovaries, menopausal women may have outlived their usefulness as human beings."

A 1966 book entitled, *Feminine Forever,* written by a respected American gynecologist, Dr. Robert A. Wilson, went one step further, referring to menopausal women as "living decay," "the death of womanhood," and "an individual who can't be entrusted with decision-making jobs."

According to Elaine Vayda, an assistant professor at York University's School of Social Work who developed a course in the Social Aspects of Health and Disease, "most women expect something horrific to take place at menopause, but in fact, the majority of women continue to produce sufficient amounts of the female hormone estrogen, to be well and functioning."

Professor Vayda says "the belief that menopause is a period of decay and an end usually coincides with a time when children leave home and husbands and wives experience life crises, which often result in separation, divorce, and a sense of failure."

All of this, she goes on to say, gets medicalized as menopause—a disease, and is then often treated with drugs, commonly known as Estrogen Replacement Therapy. Menopause is a normal, physical occurrence in most women, Professor Vayda concludes, but the whole social structure has made it into a far more significant event than it is.

The Consequences of treating menopausal women with ERT became apparent in 1975 when Dr. Donald F. Austin, the Chief of the California Tumor Registry, reported that from 1969 to 1973, the rate of invasive uterine cancer in California rose 80 per cent among white women fifty years and older. He linked the rise in cancer to the increased use of ERT. (The USA estrogen drug market had grown from $17M in 1962 to $69M in 1973.)

Concern was also recently expressed in the prestigious *New England Journal of Medicine* that published two studies that showed that post-menopausal women who take estrogen are five to fourteen times more likely to get cancer of the uterine lining than women who do not use the estrogens.

Dr. Allemang claims that the reports are difficult to analyze. He goes on to say, "If I were a woman, I would use ERT if I had menopausal symptoms." He claims that 20 to 25 per cent of the women he sees are so symptomatic that ERT is indicated. He believes that the benefit is greater than the risk.

Professor Harding LeRiche flatly asserts, "menopause is not a disease.... The physical symptoms are not that common. Most responsible gynecologists will say no to ERT." He concludes that, "there are tremendous changes in attitudes about menopause and that the trend is definitely against the use of ERT."

Dr. Sheila Cohen, a prominent Toronto gynecologist at Sick Children's Hospital, believes that there should be considerable re-evaluation about ERT. "Gynecologists," she says, "are not adequately trained in endocrinology. If a woman comes in depressed or melancholic, it should not necessarily be attributed to menopause. You don't just hand out a hormonal pill. Besides," she says, "there is no evidence to suggest that ERT retards the aging process. Estrogens have been proven to be harmful and if prescribed at all, should only be used in low dosages and in a sequential manner, and really for specific *uses*—hot flashes, estrogen deprivation of the vagina."

According to Dr. Cynthia Carver, a Toronto general practitioner whose practice is primarily female, women are still requesting ERT even when they are advised of the risks. She says, "women are conditioned to the notion that as they age, they will be less desirable. In our society, you have to be young and beautiful to be desirable."

NATURAL CHILDBIRTH AND HOME BIRTHS
"Attitudes on the part of pregnant women and their spouses, influenced by the new wave of natural childbirth proponents, are definitely changing," says Terri Brown, an instructor at the Childbirth Educational Association of Toronto. "More women," she claims, "are preparing for childbirth in the sense that they are aware of the alternatives."

"Women," she continues, "are becoming cautious about drugs that cross the placenta. They are asking about side effects to the baby and to themselves. They are less willing to accept that a medicated birth is the only alternative."

Gena Corea in *The Hidden Malpractice,* compares Dutch women who usually give birth with the emotional support of their husbands and midwives as their only (and very effective) form of pain relief, to North American women who are often frightened into believing that they could not possibly endure childbirth without some drug or anaesthesia. Ms. Corea has researched the routine use of anaesthesia by American obstetricians, leading, she observes, to other interventions in childbirth, including the following common ones:

- placing the mother in the more dangerous lithotomy position (on her back), as opposed to semi-sitting, sideways, or squatting, because it is convenient, not for a medically valid reason;
- delivering by forceps and performing an episiotomy (an incision to enlarge the vaginal opening) because the numbed, drugged mother has lost her bearing-down reflex and becomes incapable of participating in the delivery;
- elective labour induction that can lead to cord compression, premature separation of the placenta, and narrowly spaced contractions;
- chemical stimulation of labour;
- tranquilizers—almost all of which enter the fetus' bloodstream shortly after administration to the mother and tend to depress the fetal respiratory system;
- analgesics (pain killers) that tend to inhibit a newborn's efforts to breathe;
- anaesthesia that can reduce the mother's blood pressure;
- early clamping of the umbilical cord that reduces the newborn's blood supply.

Despite these and other hazards, Ms. Corea's research indicates doctors sometimes prefer a drugged mother because it is easier to work on an inanimate object than on a responsive person.

A more disconcerting statistic is cited by Dr. Eugene Vayda of the University of Toronto's Faculty of Medicine in the May 1976 edition of the *Canadian Journal of Surgery* in relation to intervention by Caesarean section. According to Dr. Vayda, "the caesarian section rate increased approximately 30 per cent between 1968–1972 and the inter-provincial variation was greater than 200 per cent, between 1968–1972." Dr. Vayda maintains in his article that "the 30 per cent increase was due to closer fetal monitoring (a device strapped to the woman's abdomen, tracing fetal heart rate and uterine contractions) and more liberal use of caesarian section."

Terri Brown of the Childbirth Education Association of Toronto believes the increased use of Caesarean section in birth is the result of doctors trying to make the birth process easier for women who do not necessarily want it so. In her work she observes that doctors intervene too quickly. The decision to do a Caesarean section can influence the birthing process for the next twelve years, because the first Caesarean precludes a normal delivery in future pregnancies.

Ms. Brown's organization encourages women to go "doctor-shopping" if they do not like the answers they receive from their doctor. She fears that many doctors view birth as a disease, not a natural event.

Phyllis Curry, the director of CARES, a Toronto pregnancy and abortion referral centre, believes that birth should be a family event where the father is encouraged to participate.

Recently she has noticed increased interest in home deliveries. She concedes, however, that home births in Canada are a middle-class phenomenon. In Metropolitan Toronto, fifty-seven home births took place in 1977, an increase in 44 per cent in the last five years. Home births focus in on the needs of the baby—i.e., born without trauma in the family setting. Home births, says Ms. Curry, encourage "an immediate and natural bonding with both parents." This concept, Ms. Curry maintains, is very appealing to mothers concerned about medicalization of the birth process.

ABORTION

Phyllis Curry, the director of CARES, a Toronto pregnancy and abortion referral centre, says she often hears from women who have been misinformed about the legality of abortion by physicians. "Some are told abortion is not legal after twelve weeks. We had a call the other day from a woman who told us her physician said he could not get the consent of the therapeutic abortion committee unless the patient could demonstrate there would definitely be a marriage breakdown and divorce if she didn't get the abortion." Ms. Curry attributes some of this misinformation to the fact that "doctors themselves are confused about the law."

Among the group of women surveyed who were carrying their pregnancies to term, the *Report of the Committee on the Operation of the Abortion Law* (the Badgley report), commissioned by the Canadian federal government in 1976, stated a number indicated they had at one time considered having an abortion, but had not because of a lack of access to services for therapeutic abortion, or because of delays that had been involved in applications submitted on their behalf to hospitals.

One out of five of these women thought that getting an abortion was illegal under any circumstances.

The Criminal Code provides that therapeutic abortion may be performed when, in the opinion of a hospital therapeutic abortion committee composed of three doctors, the continuation of a pregnancy "would or would be likely to endanger the patient's life or health."

The Badgley report concluded that accessibility to the abortion procedure is unequal across Canada, stating, "What this means is that the procedure provided in the Criminal Code for obtaining therapeutic abortion is in practice illusory for many Canadian women."

The inaccessibility is attributed to a small number of hospitals and doctors doing the procedure and quotas set by each hospital on the number of abortions per week.

Dr. Sheila Cohen says in her opinion the problems are caused because "patients are being shunted from doctor to doctor, there are hospital-imposed limits on the number of abortions in demand—Toronto has to service a large region of northern Ontario where the procedure is unavailable. If every hospital and every doctor able to do abortions accepted their responsibility in that regard, no one facility would be overburdened."

The hospital quotas are in many cases very low. Sherran Ridgley, a member of the Women's Health Organization, who works as a family planning counsellor in Toronto, points out as an example that Women's College has a clinic quota of two patients per week.

Delay is also a major factor. Abortions can be done in the first trimester of pregnancy (up to twelve weeks) by a safe, relatively simple procedure. When the pregnancy has advanced to the second trimester (thirteen weeks to twenty-four weeks), the procedure is more complex and the possibility of complications is much higher.

Sherran Ridgley says, "Although there is no legal limit before which time the procedure must be done, hospitals set a policy fixing a cut-off time. In Canada, some hospitals used to do the procedure up to twenty weeks."

"But both hospitals and doctors are cutting back in terms of time limits. Getting a second-trimester abortion in Canada is always a problem. But more and more doctors are no longer doing the full range of first trimester procedures—they're cutting off at ten weeks."

This cutting-back of time limits has grave implications for women seeking therapeutic abortion. The most common pregnancy tests are not effective before forty-two days from the date of the last menstrual period (at which point the pregnancy has already advanced to six weeks).

On the average, the manner in which doctors and hospitals now process requests for abortion creates an eight-week delay between a pregnant woman's first visit to a doctor and eventual performance of an abortion, according to the Badgley report.

The report noted that while many attributed this delay to the socially irresponsible behaviour of women seeking abortions, "the findings were unmistakeable" that the factors that accounted for most of the delay were the attitudes of physicians and hospital personnel.

Dr. Cynthia Carver, a Toronto general practitioner, states that "it is tragic that due to unnecessary delays many women are pushed into the second trimester of pregnancy before they can obtain an abortion. The system in Ontario that causes this delay increases the risk of complications beyond what it should be."

"Physicians in Toronto are finding that a woman who is seeking an abortion at six weeks must wait until the eleventh or twelfth week before the procedure can be obtained." The solution, as she sees it, is "to set up an out-patient clinic where the therapeutic abortion committee meets frequently and appointments are set up on the basis of need."

Due to many of these roadblocks, pregnancy counselling and referral agencies admit that many Canadian patients are forced to turn to the US for assistance. The Badgley report determined that a number of the women going to the US to obtain an abortion said they did so because their doctors would not do the procedure and would not refer them to other doctors or hospitals. In a number of cases, they had been told by physicians that getting an abortion in Canada was illegal.

RAPE EXAMINATION

While not all rape victims are willing to report their assault to the police or to participate in the criminal justice process, those who are must go to a hospital emergency ward immediately after the rape for a medical examination.

Concern has recently been voiced over their treatment, especially in light of the rising numbers of reported rapes. (In Metropolitan Toronto, there were 189 reported incidents of rape and attempted rape in 1976. In 1977, this number rose to 263.)

Ilene Bell of the Toronto Rape Crisis Centre says there are still some hospitals that will not do the required examinations for rape victims.

"Queensway General Hospital, for example," she says, "will not take rape victims. If the woman has knife wounds from the rape, they'll treat those, but will send her to another hospital for the medical examination. Although we've asked this hospital why it has adopted this policy, they refuse to talk to anyone about it."

"Etobicoke General didn't used to take rape victims either. Now they tell us they will, but the police do not know this yet, so few rape victims are taken there," she added. "When we asked them why they didn't let the police know their policy had changed, their reply was that if they advertised this, they would have every rape victim on their doorstep."

Ms. Bell added that even in hospitals that do take rape victims, many doctors are reluctant to do the examination. "They don't want to be required to go to court. It's time-consuming and they make less money in court than they do in practice. Also they're often embarrassed on the witness stand because they made some mistake in the examination."

"A lot of the problem is attitudinal. Many doctors have doubts about whether the patient has really been raped. When they feel it isn't a *bona fide* rape case, they feel the examination is a waste of their time."

Questioned about this allegation, Dr. Allemang said, "Whether doctors are as cooperative as they might be, in view of the legal involvement, I don't know. I don't think the onus is on the medical profession. There's a bit of a tendency to avoid involvement unless there's a good, legitimate *prima facie* case. You would want to avoid the drunk weekend rape complainant."

Concern has also been expressed about the quality of the tests conducted. Ms. Bell says that although the examination takes about an hour, it is actually quite simple. "But because it's so long and involved, and the doctor must do every step correctly, mistakes are often made. Many doctors haven't done the examination often and don't know all the details."

Dr. Sheila Cohen says that in the teaching hospitals, the residents on call for emergencies are the ones who do these examinations. "Whether a resident can handle this depends on the resident's training. I hope the training has improved from the time when I was a resident. I would say that there is not enough supervision at night, when many rape victims require examination."

Mr. Elgin Brown, head of biology, Centre of Forensic Sciences, receives the rape evidentiary specimens collected by physicians. Providing the analysis services for police throughout the province, he sees three to four hundred cases a year.

Problems with the quality and completeness of the tests done by the examining physicians have existed for the twenty years Mr. Brown has been working at the centre.

"We sometimes get inadequate specimens, improperly packaged specimens, or the physician fails to get combings from the pubic area. When the specimens are inadequate, we can't do the range of tests we would normally do."

"On occasion, in a province-wide operation, the police do get lack of cooperation from the medical profession. But most of the time it is due to a lack of complete understanding as to what is required both on the part of the police and the doctor."

Mr. Brown does state, however, that the situation is improving. "We have been working for the past two years with police, hospitals, the Rape Crisis Centre and the Crown's office to work up a protocol—a checklist of material we require, in the form of a sexual assault kit."

The Provincial Secretariat of Justice did hold a two-day conference in Toronto to discuss rape—prevention, investigation, and the care and treatment of the complainant. A number of recommendations were made, including the need for a more uniform approach throughout the province in the use of sexual assault kits for emergency room examination of rape victims.

The Rape Crisis Centre also expresses concern that in many

cases, physicians fail to discuss the problems of potential pregnancy and venereal disease with the patient. Ms. Bell recalls, "I recently counselled a rape victim who had not been warned about VD—she ended up with secondary syphilis. In other cases, doctors will automatically give the victim penicillin—without even knowing whether she has been infected—that's no better."

The psychological and emotional needs of the rape victim and how the medical examination affects her are other factors that concern the Rape Crisis Centre staff. They have developed a booklet, "Emergency Room Care for Rape Victims," which recommends that the patient be seen without delay, and where a delay is unavoidable that she be placed in a private room but never left to wait alone.

They also recommend that the victim not be pressed to relate the entire story to medical personnel and that all examination procedures should be fully explained to the patient in advance.

Dr. Cohen shares some of their concerns: "I know it's difficult in the emergency ward to give the required tender loving care. Ideally, the Rape Crisis Centre should have their own physicians on call who are trained to do the examination. Every hospital should have a protocol."

"I don't know what it is about the medical profession that they don't take this as seriously as it should be taken. Once doctors are out of residency they don't see rape in the emergency wards and I guess they become over-complacent."

TIP OF THE ICEBERG

This shocking information was unearthed during one year's work in preparation to establish the Toronto Women's Health Clinic, a project which ultimately was rejected by the Ontario Ministry of Health. It is obvious that our findings constitute only the tip of the iceberg. Since the medical establishment appears to be indifferent to the crisis in women's health care, we as women must take the initiative. We must move on several fronts: exchanging information, making our concerns public, and organizing self-help groups. Misogynist health care endangers us all. By default the remedies for these abuses will have to come from us.

REFLECTING ON 1977:
HOW MUCH HAS CHANGED?

Constance Backhouse

Rereading the article that Leah Cohen and I wrote in 1977, "Women and Health: The Growing Controversy," brings back some intense memories. The women's movement was in overdrive and we were immersed in a remarkably exciting project to set up a feminist health clinic in Toronto. We were voraciously reading every book and article we could find that critiqued the health care system from the perspective of gender. Leah and I, both of us between paying jobs, were hoping to chart a new direction as investigative feminist journalists and we decided to embark on a series of interviews with leading Canadian physicians and medical researchers to ask some probing questions about what we were coming to characterize as sexist health care. We were aghast at how free Toronto physicians felt to utter misogynist commentary about women patients and their illnesses and how their views corroborated and explained the statistical evidence we were uncovering in the literature. We drafted an article that we hoped would shock readers as much as the evidence had shocked us.

We contacted *The Globe and Mail*, to ask if the paper would purchase our article, and were elated when the newspaper indicated that it would. Our spirits were crushed several weeks later when we were advised that the editors had changed their minds, for reasons that still remain something of a mystery. The paper offered us a "kill fee"—a reduced fee for purchasing the rights to an article that would never be published. We refused and began to search for a feminist publisher. *Upstream,* one of Canada's new feminist newspapers, published the article in August 1978 and it was eventually reprinted in *Canadian Woman Studies* in the summer of

1979. It reached a smaller audience than we had originally hoped, but we were just happy that the piece saw the light of day.

Looking back at this almost forty years later, the article still has the capacity to astonish me. Sadly, there is no opportunity to ask Leah how she would view it after the passage of so much time, due to her premature death from cancer in 2007. But I like to think she would remain as upset by the revelations as we both were so many years ago. I also imagine that she would have hoped that feminists would continue to challenge sexist (and racist, able-ist, heterosex-ist) medical practices wherever they remain. Have we really rooted out all of the practices and attitudes chronicled here? Have we moved into a gender-equal, racially equal, dis/ability equal, LGBT-equal health care system? How much has really changed?

THE VANCOUVER WOMEN'S HEALTH COLLECTIVE

MY EDUCATION

Karen Buhler

My experience with the Vancouver Women's Health Collective (VWHC) continues to impact my daily life over four decades later. Recently, I found myself instructing a family medicine resident physician on how to do a sensitive and respectful vaginal exam on a woman in labour. I also explained how to modify the technique in case of a history of trauma or sexual abuse, and then how to manage labour without any vaginal exams at all. These are now simple and well-honed skills for me, but revolutionary for the trainee doctor and received with much gratitude.

I am a family doctor, practising in Vancouver since 1980, and have a focused practice in maternity care that includes care of women with trauma and substance use. The VWHC taught me essential skills in caring for people, especially those who are marginalized, how to take action, and how to improve the health care system.

In 1972 I had just moved to Vancouver to attend UBC and was enrolled in sciences. Later that year my elder sister Lynn, who was one of the very early founding members of the VWHC, introduced me to the collective. The fit was perfect for me as a budding feminist at the age of eighteen looking for a way to make a difference and hungry for information about my own womanhood. I read *Our Bodies, Ourselves* by the Boston Women's Health Collective with relish and the same "aha" feeling that Germaine Greer's *The Female Eunuch* had given me.

I got educated really fast by the older group members and, in the true sense of a collective, shared my knowledge with women who came to the clinic. We dared to do self-exams of our genitals and taught women to do the same. I learned how to have a conversation with what is now termed "informed consent." I also learned how to listen to women and value their experience of their own bodies. I volunteered in the clinic where we took samples for Pap smears, screened for STDs, and gave health and contraceptive information. We worked in a comfortable old wooden house in Fairview with second-hand medical equipment and printed our own information sheets to hand out.

Our doctors, including Hedy Fry and Liz Whynot, amazingly trusted us to do all this. They worked alongside us diagnosing and treating medical problems and prescribing contraception. We were the first multidisciplinary health care team I had ever seen. I loved working there and gained far more than I think I gave. Those dedicated doctors, who did so much for women and broke down barriers in medicine, inspired me to become a family doctor.

Saddened by the lack of knowledge of the medical profession in how to perform a sensitive vaginal exam, the VWHC approached the UBC medical school and offered to be models to teach students. I did that for a few years, overcoming my modesty for the benefit of other women. This programme expanded and continues to this day. It started an important change in medical education where the patients' experience of care became valued and live models are employed to teach medical students. This health care was really very different. Through the Vancouver Women's Health Collective I began to understand woman-centred care and have continued to explore and champion it ever since.

STILL STANDING

Elizabeth Whynot

At 29 West Hastings Street in Vancouver, across from the famous Portland Hotel and an overdose prevention site, is the large front window and the front door of the Vancouver Women's Health Collective. Along the window, in a line at eye level, are posters and notices about all kinds of issues relevant to women in the neighbourhood and elsewhere. Inside the door is a bright and pleasant place. I visited recently during one of the nurse practitioner–run primary care clinics for women. There were several local women in the waiting area, both patients and volunteers, with access to reading materials and donated baked goods, as well as an obviously safe respite from the rough community outside. Behind a few modest offices for (the one or two paid) staff and volunteers is a meeting area for community and health collective use and a resource centre. Government funding for the collective is limited and so they rely on partnerships such as one with BC Women's Hospital, which supports the nurse practitioners—including their rent and supplies—and other community-based foundations. Many supports are "in kind," i.e. volunteers to do the work of the collective and to provide additional health services such as acupuncture. The total annual budget, including the value of donated services is probably about $100,000.

The Vancouver Women's Health Collective was incorporated as a society in BC in 1972. Through its forty-five years, it has weathered many changes including important political challenges to its identity as a women-serving organization and experiments with social enterprise as a way to compensate for loss of government funding. One way or another it has survived forty-five years and has in a way returned to its original form: the provision of woman-centred health services.

The VWHC grew out of a small women's health discussion group at A Women's Place, a feminist resource centre created by women students at the University of British Columbia. Officially adopting their name in 1972, the VWHC morphed into a separate organization, attracting members from outside of the university community. In 1974, the collective received its first government funding, a Government of Canada Demonstration Grant.

In *The Pedestal* (Vancouver's Women's Liberation Newsletter), October 1971: "There is a meeting planned for Sunday October 17 at 2 p.m. at Women's Centre at 511 Carrall (just around the corner from 29 West Hastings) for any women who may have suggestions."

The collective operated their own laywoman-run women's health clinic (the first of its kind in Canada), created and distributed their own booklets and pamphlets on difficult-to-find women's health information, ran workshops, and dedicated themselves to learning about their bodies through texts, as well as through interactions with other women.

The VWHC emerged in a time of heightened political activity in Vancouver, as well as in the rest of North America. The eruption of social movements—the civil rights, student and new left movements, women's and gay liberation, and environmentalism—provided the broad background for the VWHC's birth. The organization was directly connected to the women's liberation movement, which was rising to its peak in the early 1970s just as the student and new left movements were beginning to decline. In 1970, while a handful of UBC students were putting together A Woman's Place, another group of feminists set off from Vancouver on the nationwide Abortion Caravan, a travelling demonstration for abortion rights. The massive protest was organized by the Vancouver Women's Caucus (VWC), a women's group that grew out of the new left and student movements at Simon Fraser University in Burnaby, British Columbia.

While VWHC members saw their work as part of the larger Canadian women's movement and the collective maintained connections with other women's groups, the VWHC was primarily inspired by feminist self-help politics and the work and publications of the American women's health movement. The women of the VWHC saw themselves as members of a self-help, or "mutual aid" group.

The Pedestal (June 1973) "Sickness and Health Issue": "Our beginnings as a Health Collective focused on the frustration (and often humiliation) we commonly experienced as women in our doctor's offices."

The VWHC practised and preached feminist self-help politics within a Canadian context where most women's health movement activists, while perhaps inspired by some aspects of feminist self-help, ultimately worked toward legal reform. Feminist self-help politics coming out of the United States spoke directly to the women of the VWHC because of the way it addressed issues that legal reform strategies could not adequately resolve. The emergence of the VWHC demonstrates that there was a need for a new kind of feminist practice in early 1970s Vancouver.

In the *Vancouver Women's Health Collective Newsletter* (Summer 1973), reporting on a workshop at the Society of Obstetricians and Gynecologists of Canada, Morgan Fox wrote, "Clearly the doctors were bewildered and threatened by the revolution of women.... The idea that we as women are capable of saying, 'If you don't give us what we want, we'll do it ourselves'...is shocking to many doctors."

The critiques of the medical system and the specific priorities of feminist self-help groups including the VWHC were shaped by the identities of their members. Self-helpers had a tendency to refer to "women" generally and to highlight commonality of experience rather than difference, despite the fact that in the United States, the early women's health movement was populated by overwhelmingly white, typically young, middle-class, well-educated women. Though there were some exceptions to the rule, VWHC members too, were almost all young, white, generally well-educated middle-class women. Like most American self-help groups active in the 1970s, many VWHC members were heterosexual, but unlike the majority of American feminist self-help organizations, lesbian and bi-sexual women were also well represented within the VWHC. Nonetheless, the VWHC's work centred on the health care concerns of heterosexual women and tended to marginalize lesbians. Some discussion at the collective emphasized the possible negative repercussions to the work if lesbian participation in the collective was more widely known in the broader community.

Before practical change is possible, it must be imaginable. For many women, the women's health movement made the concept of women's health as a particular and specific priority imaginable. Further, the movement was a major contributor to the idea that health is socially and culturally determined. In this way, feminist health activists participated in a project of what Canadian historian Ian McKay has described as "living otherwise"—the important work of first imagining that other ways of living are possible, followed by the daily work of making that change a reality. Indeed, the radical feminist practice of consciousness-raising—in which women came to recognize their personal experiences as political problems—was the first step in deconstructing gender-based injustices that had seemed natural and inevitable for so long. By living otherwise, the women's health movement successfully altered the terms of the dominant discourse within the health care system as well as contributed to practical changes.

THE DIAPHRAGM FITTERS COLLECTIVE

Jeanette Frost

The Diaphragm Fitters Collective was a sub-group of the Vancouver Women's Health Collective. At some point in the 1970s, early on in the Health Collective's history, staff and volunteers realized that there were few birth control options available for women from the medical profession other than the IUD and the pill. The diaphragm was available but doctors had received little if any training during medical school, and if they did, many were not comfortable doing a proper "fit" or felt that the time to do a proper "fit" would exceed a standard doctor's allowable visitation time period.

Given the many calls the Health Collective received from women looking for a safe and reliable method of birth control we decided to provide diaphragm fittings at the collective. Some of the women had previous fitting experience and early training involved practising on each other and then transitioning to fitting new clients. As the calls for fittings increased, the number of fitters grew, and eventually the Diaphragm Fitters Collective was formed.

The fitters were an eclectic group of women with a common interest in offering women a safe birth control option with proper education and fittings in a comfortable environment. The fitters came from a variety of occupations including health care workers, teachers, artists, engineers, and "stay at home" moms. They were heterosexual, gay, or bisexual—we welcomed all! In order to accommodate both the clients and the fitters' schedules, fittings were done not only at the Health Collective but also at the fitters' homes. Over the years our roster of fitters came and went, but we typically had an active group of twelve at any one time.

Following the collective process we developed a flexible system for scheduling, instruction, and fittings. Eventually the phone message machine (a tape, of course!) ended up at one of the fitter's homes, where she recorded the requests for fittings and answered any questions. We held monthly meetings at rotating homes. The meetings allowed us to schedule in the appointments for the month, talk about unusual or problem fittings, order more supplies, and get caught up on any other issues women wanted to discuss.

Whether the fittings were at the Health Collective, or at a home, during the day or evening, they all followed a set routine lasting about two to three hours. We typically had two fitters—sometimes they were both experienced but at other times there was one experienced fitter and a trainee—and would fit a maximum of two women per visit. The first part of the fit was a talk about responsible birth control, why we promoted the use of diaphragms with spermicidal jelly, and their effectiveness if used properly. This was followed by a demonstration of a proper diaphragm fit with a plastic pelvic model including the insertion of spermicidal jelly. We finished by informing women how long to keep the diaphragm inserted and its proper care. We also mentioned the added benefit of using a spare diaphragm as a menstrual cup.

The second part was the "fit," fitting one woman at a time. The process included a cervical self-exam, using a speculum and a mirror. The actual fitting followed this. Once a size was determined with fitting rings, the women were then shown with a diaphragm how a proper fit allowed it to cover the cervix and be held in place by the pelvic shelf. The women then practised with us to ensure they could insert the diaphragm properly. At the end of the fit we had a stock of diaphragms and spermicidal jelly that the women could buy at cost. Women were encouraged to call us or schedule another fitting should they have questions or experience any problems.

No doubt, doing fittings at home sometimes brought on the unexpected. The long-lost friend who appeared at your door for a fitting, the awkward moment of meeting a past "fittee" in a social setting—oh, I remember you; you fit me with a diaphragm in your apartment!—or the four-year-old son of a fitter who was wandering in and out of the exam room during a fit, finally pulling down his pants and trying to fit a sample diaphragm under his balls! We all loved the camaraderie, doing the fittings, the process, empowering women, and knowing that what we were doing was the right thing. It was wonderful how comfortable and trusting the women were by coming to our houses, meeting the two fitters and another fittee, having frank discussions, and being fitted in our homes.

By the mid-1980s we were getting fewer calls and our team of fitters was moving on to other adventures and The Diaphragm Fitters Collective ended. In retrospect, it would have been so beneficial to have followed up with our past "fittees" to find out whether this had been a good birth control option for them. We were curious about whether they continued to use the diaphragm as a method of contraceptive, or why they may have stopped using it, as well as any other feedback. Forty years on there is little discussion or use of diaphragms as a safe and effective method of birth control. Alas, it seems that diaphragms are no longer considered an option for birth control among a younger population, where Instagram is better understood than the diaphragm.

AT THE HEART OF IT

Melanie Conn

The Vancouver Women's Health Collective was my first practical experience of the personal as political, and it changed my life. Here's how it started. In 1971 I was twenty-nine and visiting a friend in California following a humiliating and painful experience with a gynecologist. Maggie listened carefully to my story, reached into her bookshelf, and handed me the original newsprint version of *Our Bodies, Ourselves* from the Boston Women's Health Collective.

I devoured it, and upon my return to Vancouver a week later I wrote a letter to *The Pedestal* (one of the two women's newspapers in the city at the time) calling for women to get together and talk about taking the care of our bodies into our own hands. Almost thirty women attended the meeting. It evolved into a weekly women's self-help health education group, and became the core of the Health Collective and all its future services. Within two years we had started the women's self-help clinic, a diaphragm fitting group, birth control, abortion and sexual health counselling, and an impressive collection of resources about pharmaceuticals and local doctors.

At the heart of the collective was our commitment to sharing experience and expertise on an equal basis with each other and with the women, who were never called clients or patients. We worked in teams as health group facilitators and at the clinic, inviting full participation by the women who came to the collective for services. The doctors who attended our clinic were members of the team, not its leaders.

Although we eventually (and wisely) abandoned the practice of rotating the bookkeeper role each month, our internal organization reflected the same commitment to sharing power and knowledge. Daily and weekly meetings to discuss operations and plans ensured we were all in the loop and provided a structure for us to make decisions from a solid foundation.

In thinking back to this time, what strikes me is the depth and intensity of our debates about how to best address the power and impact of the health care system on women's lives. Should we put our energy into creating a process for women to work around the restrictions on access to abortion or should we focus on advocacy at the policy level to change those laws? Could we do both? How could we be sure that working with doctors would not compromise our analysis of the health care system? Should we partner with doctors only on our terms and in our space? Or should we go into their world and participate in the education of medical students?

Two situations illustrate our struggles about how to make change. The first was when one of our members spoke at a conference about women's health and her collectively written presentation was reported in the local newspaper. At the time our self-help clinic was operating one evening a week in a group medical practice facility where a supportive doctor worked. The partners in the practice demanded that we retract the statement that "physicians profit from the system." It didn't take long for us to draft a response reiterating our analysis: The narrow focus on funded health care by physicians and drug companies benefitted doctors more than women because it excluded midwives, nurse practitioners, complementary health practitioners, and the use of natural medicine. The result was that we moved the clinic to another location operated by the City of Vancouver.

The resolution of the second situation was longer in coming and also focused on the self-help clinic. After three years we were seeing many women at the clinic who had been referred by their doctors for diaphragm fitting and other health education. We loved the clinic and we knew many women counted on it. At the same time we were frustrated about our lack of impact on the health care system at the local level. Instead of physicians changing their practices and, for example, spending more time with women to review birth control options, the mainly volunteer collective members were filling the gap in the system, not changing it. We temporarily closed the clinic and other services to give us time to research and discuss our options. After three weeks and many meetings, we decided to stop operating the clinic and instead to expand our educational presentations to include a more explicit analysis of the health care system. Was it the right decision? Did our education campaign make a difference? As I consider the erosion of health care today and the domination by drug companies, I am not so sure.

Looking back, I am still amazed at our determination to maintain our integrity. That lesson has stayed with me throughout the work I did that followed as a teacher, a consultant, and a co-op practitioner. At the Health Collective I learned that we need to understand the context in order to decide what lines we would or would not cross. Today as I consider what actions to take in the surge of hateful and divisive politics, the process still works for me.

RACISM, SEXISM, AND COLONIALISM: THE IMPACT ON THE HEALTH OF ABORIGINAL WOMEN IN CANADA

Carrie Bourassa, Kim McKay-McNabb, and Mary Hampton

Reprinted from Canadian Woman Studies/les cahiers de la femme, *Volume 24, Number 1 (Fall 2004), 23–29.*

Aboriginal women in Canada carry a disproportionate burden of poor health. Aboriginal women have lower life expectancy, elevated morbidity rates, and elevated suicide rates in comparison to non-Aboriginal women (Prairie Women's Health Centre of Excellence, 2004). Aboriginal women living on reserves have significantly higher rates of coronary heart disease, cancer, cerebrovascular disease, and other chronic illnesses than non-Aboriginal Canadian women (Waldram, Herring, and Young, 2000). A significantly greater percentage of Aboriginal women living off reserve, in all age groups, report fair or poor health compared to non-Aboriginal women; 41 per cent of Aboriginal women aged fifty-five to sixty-four reported fair or poor health, compared to 19 per cent of women in the same age group among the total Canadian population (Statistics Canada). In addition, chronic disease disparities are more pronounced for Aboriginal women than Aboriginal men. For example, diseases such as diabetes are more prevalent among Aboriginal women than either the general population or Aboriginal men (Statistics Canada).

Epidemiologists suggest that many of these chronic health conditions are a result of the forced acculturation imposed on Aboriginal peoples (Young 1994). Yet, for Aboriginal women, low income, low social status, and exposure to violence also contribute to poor health. Aboriginal women face the highest poverty and violence rates in Canada. Joyce Green (2000) notes that in 1991 eight out of ten Aboriginal women reported victimization by physical, sexual, psychological, or ritual abuse; this rate is twice as high as that reported by non-Aboriginal women. These issues are evident in Saskatchewan where the Saskatchewan Women's

Secretariat (1999) determined that at least 57 per cent of the women who used shelters in 1995 were of Aboriginal ancestry, yet they comprised only 11 per cent of the total female population. These numbers reflect the magnitude of the problem. Redressing these injustices requires awareness of the processes that create negative health consequences and mobilization of action to correct these processes. The Saskatchewan Women's Secretariat notes: "Studies have shown that health differences are reduced when economic and status differences between people, based on things such as culture, race, age, gender and disability are reduced" (44).

Gender and ethnicity have been shown to be influential determinants of health across populations. Conceptual distinctions between definitions of *gender* and *sex* have led to our understanding that the processes of sexism (such as increased exposure to violence) are more likely to contribute to women's poor health than biological or genetic differences between women and men. Similarly, conceptual distinctions between definitions of *ethnicity* and *race* in population health research suggests that *race* is used to describe natural units or populations that share distinct biological characteristics; whereas ethnic groups are seen as being culturally distinct (Polednak). In population health research, these two terms are used interchangeably, often leaving out a discussion of the processes by which racism creates conditions of poor health for certain ethnic groups (Young 1994). Racism is a biopsychosocial stressor that has severe negative health effects on racialized individuals (Clark, Anderson, Clark and Williams). Sexism is blatantly dangerous to women's health in many ways (Lips). Racism and sexism have this in common; they operate via external power structures to contribute to poor health in certain disadvantaged groups. Research suggests that culture and cultural differences also have an impact on health (Amaratunga; Wienert). However, little is written about how what we describe as culture can be the outcome of colonial processes. Cultural groups that have lived under colonization experience a legacy of oppression that adds another level of threat to their health. Indigenous Peoples as distinct cultural groups have been exposed to genocide to further the interests of colonization (Chrisjohn and Young; Tuhiwhai Smith). We will illustrate that this colonization and its contemporary manifestations in the policies and practices that affect Aboriginal women create unique threats to their health status. Our analysis will demonstrate that the process by which the definition of "Indian" is imposed by colonial legislation in Canada constitutes a form of multiple oppressions that differentially disempower Aboriginal women, conferring particular risks to their health.

LINKS BETWEEN SEXISM, RACISM, COLONIALISM, AND ABORIGINAL WOMEN'S HEALTH

Sexism, racism, and colonialism are dynamic processes rather than static, measurable determinants of health; they began historically and continue to cumulatively and negatively impact health status of Aboriginal women. Colonialism depends on the oppression of one group by another, beginning with a process described as "othering" (Gerrard and Javed). The process of "othering" occurs when society sorts people into two categories: the reference group and the "other." Women who bear their "otherness" in more than one way suffer from multiple oppressions, leaving them more vulnerable to assaults on their well-being than if they suffered from one form of oppression. The cumulative effects have painful material, social, and health consequences. We offer an example of the process of "othering" imposed on Aboriginal women through colonial legislation defining Indian identity between the years 1869–1985; these policies continue to influence women's health and well-being today. Using this example, we will deconstruct the process of colonialism and reveal its consequences for Aboriginal women and their health.

We describe ways in which the *Indian Act* differentially affects Aboriginal women and men in Canada; it is a case example of multiple oppressions. Colonial discourse has historically represented non-white populations as racially inferior. These assumptions have been used to justify social treatment of these populations that fosters inequality and social exclusion in all areas, ultimately contributing to poor health conditions in the oppressed group. Linda Tuhiwai Smith notes that racism, sexism, and colonialism (through the process of "othering") serve to describe, objectify, and represent Indigenous women in ways that have left a legacy of marginalization within Indigenous societies as much as within the colonizing society. She points out that racist and sexist notions about the role of women were imposed upon Indigenous communities by white, European settlers with patriarchal consciousness. "Colonization," she notes, "is recognized as having had a destructive effect on Indigenous gender relations which reached out across all spheres of Indigenous society." Sexism, racism, and colonialism have had a negative impact on Aboriginal women's identities, our sense of who we are, and where we belong. We argue that gender differences in the process of "othering" have forced Aboriginal women to challenge the racist, sexist, and colonial policies within and beyond our communities. We further suggest that accumulated disadvantage from past colonization and contemporary processes of ongoing colonization have a direct effect on Aboriginal women's access to social determinants of health and impedes their ability to develop a healthy sense of identity that can contribute to personal well-being.

IMPACT OF ABORIGINAL IDENTITY ON HEALTH AND WELL-BEING

An insidious result of colonialism has been the externally imposed definition of Indian identity through processes that create cultural ambiguity for Aboriginal women (Mihesuah). Bonita Lawrence (1999) argues that although Euro-Canadian legislation has affected what she terms "native identity" across gender lines, it has had greater impact on Aboriginal women. Consequently, significant gaps exist between material, social, and health outcomes for Aboriginal men and Aboriginal women. However, racist underpinnings of colonialism have also produced gaps amongst and between Aboriginal women themselves (Saskatchewan Women's Secretariat). For example, Métis women in Saskatchewan are more likely to be employed than status Indian women but less likely to be employed than non-Aboriginal women. Hence, sexism, racism and colonialism have converged to create a matrix of oppression that differentially affects specific Aboriginal groups and men and women within those groups.

Cultural identity evidently has implications for the status that women have in the external world and this has an impact on health. However, identity also has implications for feelings of self-worth and belonging, and this has an impact on health as well. A recent study conducted with Aboriginal women in Manitoba by the Prairie Women's Health Centre of Excellence found that Aboriginal women endorsed important links between health and wellness and their cultural identities. Cultural identities were inseparable from their family, history, community, place, and spirituality and all of these elements were integrated into a broad and holistic understanding of health and well-being. The women acknowledged that many factors shaped their health and well-being including poverty, housing, violence, and addictive behaviours. However, cultural identity served as a potential anchor to help them deal with these issues and promote health. Accordingly, they made recommendations for health practices that integrated holistic solutions that included "traditional cultural practices and understandings with respect to health and wellness" (24). This suggests that women who are Aboriginal can look to cultural identity as a foundation on which they can build healthy lives. However, for women who cannot draw on a firm sense of cultural identity, maintaining and promoting health could be more difficult. Unfortunately, there are large numbers of women who are in the latter position. It is through this removal of cultural identity and status within Aboriginal groups that Canadian legislation has produced a significant threat to the health and well-being of many Aboriginal women.

COLONIZATION AS AN INSTRUMENT OF MULTIPLE OPPRESSIONS FOR ABORIGINAL WOMEN IN CANADA:
INDIAN ACT LEGISLATION

The Indian Act, passed in Canada in 1876, defined Indian identity and prescribed what "Indianness" meant. Because of the sexist specification inherent in this legislation, ramifications of the Indian Act were more severe for Aboriginal women than men, ramifications that continue to have severe impacts on our life chances today. Lawrence (2000) notes that the act ordered how Aboriginal people were to think of all things "Indian" and created classifications that have become normalized as "cultural differences." She argues that the differences between Métis (or mixed ancestry people), non-status Indians, Inuit, and status Indians were created by the act and those differences became accepted in Canada as being cultural in nature when, in fact, they were social constructions imposed by legislation. It should be acknowledged that cultural distinctions did and do exist within and amongst Aboriginal people; however, those cultural distinctions were never categorized nor embedded in legislation prior to 1876 and did not have the same impact until commencement of the act. Indigenous scholars agree that the Indian Act has controlled Aboriginal identity by creating legal and non-legal categories that have consequences for rights and privileges both within and beyond Aboriginal communities (Lawrence 2000; Mihesuah).

One important consequence of the Indian Act is that status Indian women (hereafter referred to as Indian women) who married non-Indian men lost their Indian status and their band membership under this act. Prior to 1869, the definition of *Indian* was fairly broad and generally referred to "all persons of Indian blood, their spouses and their descendants" (Voyageur 88). After 1869, Indian women who married non-Indians were banished from their communities since non-Indians were not allowed on reserves; this was true even if a divorce occurred (McIvor). From the government's perspective, these women had assimilated and had no use for their Indian status. The goal of assimilation was a central element of the Indian Act 1876 because it would advance the government's policy of genocide through the process of enfranchisement: the removal of Indian status from an individual. Section 12(l)(b) of the act specified Indian women would lose their status if they married a non-Indian man. Further, Indian women could not own property, and once a woman left the reserve to marry she could not return to her reserve so she lost all property rights. This legacy of disenfranchisement was passed on to her children (Wotherspoon and Satzewich). In contrast, an Indian man who married a non-Indian woman not only retained his Indian status, but the non-Indian woman would gain status under the act, as would their children. Even upon divorce or the death of her husband, a non-Indian woman who gained status under the act through marriage retained her status and band membership as did her children (Voyageur). Only the identity of Indian women was defined by their husband and could be taken away. The imposition of this Eurocentric, sexist ideology on Aboriginal families was a direct disruption of traditional Aboriginal definitions of family. Under Indian Act legislation, enfranchised Indians were to become Canadian citizens and, as a result, they relinquished their collective ties to their Indian communities (Lawrence 1999). However, Indian women were not granted the benefit of full Canadian citizenship. Lawrence notes that until 1884, Indian women who had lost their status could not inherit any portion of their husband's land or assets after his death. After 1884, widows were allowed to inherit one-third of their husband's land(s) and assets if "a widow was living with her husband at his time of death and was determined by the Indian Agent to be 'of good moral character'" (Lawrence 1999: 56). Furthermore, if a woman married an Indian from another reserve, the act stated that she must follow her husband and relinquish her band membership in order to become a member of his band. If her husband died or if she divorced him, she could not return to her reserve, as she was no longer a member. These policies governing marriage and divorce were just one of several ways that Aboriginal women were stripped of their rights. For example, from 1876 to 1951, women who married Indian men and remained on the reserve were denied the right to vote in band elections, to hold elected office, or to participate in public meetings. However, Indian men were eligible to take place in all of these activities (Voyageur). Therefore, colonization was an instrument by which sexism and racism were created and reinforced on and off reserve lands, converging in diminishing power and resources available to Aboriginal women in Canada.

Passage of the *Charter of Rights and Freedoms* made gender discrimination illegal and opened the door for Aboriginal women to challenge the *Indian Act*. In 1967, Aboriginal women lobbied both the federal government and Indian bands for amendment to the act. Sharon McIvor notes that in *Lavell v. Her Majesty (1974)*, Aboriginal women challenged the government based on the argument that the government had been discriminating against Indian women for over one hundred years via the *Indian Act*. The Supreme Court of Canada, however, ruled that since Canada had jurisdiction over Indians it could decide who was an Indian and that the act was not discriminatory. Continual lobbying by Aboriginal women finally resulted in action and the act was amended in 1985 through passage of Bill C-31.

However, despite the amendment, long-standing implications of the *Indian Act* for Aboriginal women in Canada are still evident. As Lawrence notes, the government's "social engineering process" (1999: 58) via the act ensured that between 1876 and 1985 over 25,000 women lost their status and were forced to leave their communities. All of their descendants lost status and were "permanently alienated from Native culture, the scale of cultural genocide caused by gender discrimination becomes massive" (Lawrence 1999: 59). She notes that when Bill C-31 was passed in 1985, there were only 350,000 female and male status Indians left in Canada. Bill C-31 allowed individuals who had lost status and their children to apply for reinstatement. Approximately 100,000 individuals had regained status by 1995, but many individuals were unable to regain status. Under Bill C-31, grandchildren and great-grandchildren were not recognized as having Indian status and, in many cases, no longer identified as Indian (Lawrence 1999; Voyageur). In addition, legislative decision still blocked Aboriginal women from full participation in their communities. For example, the Corbiere decision in 1999 *(John Corbiere et al. v. the Batchewana Indian Band and Her Majesty the Queen)* specified that Indian women living off-reserve could not vote in band elections because the *Indian Act* stated that Indian members must "ordinarily live on reserve" in order to vote. Thus, reinstated Indian women and their children were still at a disadvantage despite having legal recognition under the act.[16]

In the end, the amendments did not repair the damage of previous legislation. Kinship ties, cultural ties, and participation in governance were significantly disrupted. Long-term consequences for these women and their children would include the erosion of connections and rights that may have enabled them to work collectively to address social disparities.

It is ironic that the only recourse Aboriginal women have is to appeal to the federal government and judicial system—the same government and system that instituted and upheld the sexist, discriminatory, and oppressive legislation for over one hundred years. This government holds different principles of justice than traditional Aboriginal government, leaving women once again vulnerable to multiple oppressions. As Jan Langford writes, "If First Nations governments are built on the traditional Aboriginal way of governing where equity is built into the system, there wouldn't be a need for the 'white' ways of protecting rights" (35). However, band governing bodies are not working according to the traditional Aboriginal way, instead using legislation to exclude women and protect male privilege.

After fighting for the recognition of Aboriginal rights, Aboriginal women have found themselves at odds with some of their own community leaders. Indian women and their children have not been welcomed back to their communities. Since the 1980s, when the federal government began the process of devolution of control to Indian bands, band governments have been able to refuse band membership. It should be noted that there has been an influx of status Indians going to their bands to seek membership. However, the government has consistently refused to increase funding to those bands. Cora Voyageur notes that some bands have not given band membership to people given status by the federal government because they do not have the resources or the land base to do so. Most reserves are already overcrowded, and many feel that conditions will worsen if a rush of reinstated Indians want to return to the reserve. Some reinstated Indians are referred to as "C-31s," "paper Indians," or "new Indians" (Voyageur). In addition, many of these individuals may have previously been identifying with Métis or non-status Indian communities and were rejected not only by their Indian communities but also by the communities with which they had identified. As Lawrence (1999) reports that resistance to acknowledging the renewed status of those reinstated under Bill C-31 has been expressed throughout the Native press.

Furthermore, women have been formally excluded from constitutional negotiations as a result of patriarchal legislation that was applied in the federal government's decision to exclude them. The Native Women's Association of Canada (NWAC) has argued that the interests of individual Aboriginal women should not be overshadowed by collective social values and operational mandates that may be enshrined in customary law (Jackson 2000). However, Aboriginal women find themselves caught between bands who appeal to traditional practices to avoid action and a federal government that avoids involvement in deference to self-government (Green 2001). In this way, government intrusion has succeeded in ensuring that divisions among Aboriginal people are maintained, if not more firmly entrenched.

Finally, as Lawrence (1999) argues, "Who am I?" and "Where do I belong?" are common questions among what she calls "people of mixed-race Native heritage." She examines the impact of the *Indian Act* and Bill C-31 on Métis people in addition to Indian people and argues that the act has externalized mixed-race Native people from Indianness and that this has implications for Native empowerment. What this discussion reveals is that other Aboriginal peoples have also been affected by these policies and this has likely had consequences for identity, empowerment, and quality of life of all Canada's Indigenous peoples.

IMPLICATIONS FOR THE HEALTH OF ABORIGINAL WOMEN IN CANADA

A review of the post-contact history of Indigenous peoples in Canada clearly demonstrates that direct practices of genocide have transformed into legislated control of Aboriginal identity and colonization-based economic, social, and political disadvantage that disproportionately affects Aboriginal women. The government's definition of who can be called Indian, who cannot, and who must exist in liminal spaces where they are outsiders both on and off reserve lands clearly has implications for citizenship, but it also has implications for access to health services and ability to maintain health and well-being. With this knowledge, we must re-examine data that suggests Aboriginal women are excessively vulnerable to cerebrovascular disease, coronary heart disease, diabetes, suicide, cancer, depression, substance use, HIV/AIDS, and violence/abuse in light of how colonization and postcolonial processes have conferred risks to the health of Aboriginal women, and barriers to accessing quality health care. It is these risks and barriers that contribute to rates of morbidity and mortality that are well above those of the average Canadian woman.

At a fundamental level, we understand that the colonization processes that began many years ago and continue today have material and social consequences that diminish access to social determinants of health for both Aboriginal men and Aboriginal women. Yet, as we have discussed, women have been especially marginalized through these processes and their lower social status is reflected in diminished resources and poor health. Health consequences for women have been identified, but largely within a western model of equating health with the absence of disease or illness (Newbold). The wounds that result from the cultural ambiguity imposed on Aboriginal women are harder to catalogue. They are perhaps demonstrated to us in the plight of the Aboriginal women of Vancouver's Downtown Eastside. This neighbourhood is home to thousands of Aboriginal women who have been displaced from their reserve communities and extended families (Benoit, Carroll, and Chaudhry). They are socially and culturally isolated, living in poverty, and often driven to substance use, violent relationships, and the street sex trade to survive and provide for their children (Benoit et al.). Their material circumstances force acts of desperation, but the damage that has been done to their cultural identities can leave them without the foundation to cultivate health and well-being in their lives. Recent initiatives that have arisen out of results from the First Nations and Inuit Regional Health Survey (National Steering Committee) may offer some hope for these women, but they are still disadvantaged in benefiting from them. First, the development of culturally appropriate services will not be useful for women who have been excluded from the definition of that culture and excluded from the decision-making structures that will determine how Aboriginal health resources are to be designed and distributed (Benoit et al.; Grace). Second, the research that serves as the foundation of these initiatives has not included many Aboriginal women, both because women and children have been overlooked in the work (Young, 2003), and because women who do not fit into research-defined categories of "Indian" (derived from Federal categories) have not been included in the data collections.

CONCLUSIONS

In conclusion, we reiterate the fact that in Canada, Aboriginal women have faced destruction in our communities, in our families as a result of multiple oppressions. Articulating the process by which the *Indian Act* differentially marginalizes Indian women is important for our empowerment. Devon Mihesuah notes that there has never been a "monolithic essential Indian woman... nor has there ever been a unitary world view among tribes" (37). She argues that this never created problems for people until after colonization and resulting genocide of Indian peoples (Chrisjohn and Young). Prior to the sexist specification of the *Indian Act* Aboriginal women were matriarchal in their families. Families thrived with their Aboriginal women's strength and support. Today, Aboriginal women suffer from poorer health than non-Aboriginal women in Canada; they suffer from more chronic diseases than Aboriginal men.

Our goal in writing this paper was to clarify our understanding of the externally imposed oppressions facing Aboriginal women: to know where to focus our fight and our healing and to show the impact on the health of Aboriginal women. This paper has not examined the impact on Métis women specifically, but they too, face similar challenges as a result of colonial policies. Today we find ourselves at peace with our identities, but vigilant against the ever-present social constructions of our identities. We can see the implications this has on our well-being and the well-being of our children. As long as we buy into the arbitrary, patriarchal, sexist, racist, socially constructed labels, we will continue to struggle not only as individuals but also as families and communities.

This article has been reprinted from Canadian Woman Studies/les cahiers de la femme, *Volume 24, Number 1 (Fall 2004), 23–29.*

REFERENCES

Amaratunga, C. *Race, Ethnicity, and Women's Health*. Nova Scotia: Atlantic Centre of Excellence for Women's Health, 2002.

Benoit, C., D. Carroll, and M. Chaudhry. "In search of a healing place: Aboriginal women in Vancouver's Downtown Eastside." *Social Science and Medicine* 56(2003): 821–33.

Chrisjohn, R. D. and S. L. Young. *The Circle Game: Shadows and Substance in the Indian Residential School Experience in Canada*. Penticton, BC: Theytus Books Ltd., 1997.

Clark, R., N. B. Anderson, V. Clark, and D. R. Williams. "Racism as a stressor for African Americans: A biopsychosocial model." *American Psychologist* 54 (10) (1999): 805–16.

Gerrard, N. and N. Javed. (1998). "The psychology of women." *Feminist Issues: Race, Class, and Sexuality*, 2nd ed. Ed. N. Mandell. Scarborough, ON: Prentice Hall Allyn and Bacon Canada, 1998, 103–31.

Grace, Sherryl L. "A review of Aboriginal women's physical and mental health status in Ontario." *Canadian Journal of Public Health* 94 (3) (2003): 173–75.

Green J. A. "Canaries in the mines of citizenship: Indian women in Canada." *Canadian Journal of Political Science/Revue Canadienne de Science Politique* 34 (4) (2001): 715–38.

Green, J. A. "Constitutionalizing the patriarchy." *Expressions in Canadian Native Studies*. Eds. R. F. Laliberte, P. Settee, J. B. Waldram, R. Innes, B. Macdougall, L. McBain and F. L. Barron. Saskatoon: University of Saskatchewan Extension Press, 2000.

Jackson, Margaret. "Aboriginal women and self government." *Expressions in Canadian Native Studies*. Eds. R. F. Laliberte, P. Settee, J. B. Waldram, R. Innes, B. Macdougall, L. McBain, and F. L. Barron. Saskatoon: University of Saskatchewan Extension Press, 2000.

Lawrence, B. "'Real' Indians and others." Unpublished PhD dissertation. Toronto: UMI Dissertation Services, 1999.

Lawrence, B. "Mixed-race urban Native people: Surviving a legacy of policies of genocide." *Expressions in Canadian Native Studies*. Eds. R. F. Laliberte, P. Settee, J. B. Waldram, R. Innes, B. Macdougall, L. McBain and F. L. Barron. Saskatoon: University of Saskatchewan Extension Press, 2000.

Langford, Jan. "First Nations women: Leaders in community development." *Canadian Woman Studies/les cahiers de la femme* 14 (4) (1995): 34–36.

Lips, H. M. *A New Psychology of Women: Gender, Culture and Ethnicity*, 2nd ed. Toronto: McGraw Hill, 2003.

McIvor, S. D. "Aboriginal Women's rights as existing rights." *Canadian Woman Studies/les cahiers de la femme* 14 (4) (1995): 34–38.

Mihesuah, D. A. Ed. *Natives and Academics: Researching and Writing About American Indians.* Lincoln: University of Nebraska Press, 1998.

National Steering Committee. *First Nations and Inuit Regional Health Survey: Final Report.* Akwesasne Mohawk Territory, 1999.

Newbold, K. B. "Problems in search of solutions: Health and Canadian Aboriginals." *Journal of Community Health* 23 (1) (1998): 59–73.

Prairie Women's Health Centre of Excellence. *Living Well: Aboriginal Women, Cultural Identity and Wellness—A Manitoba Community Project.* Winnipeg: Prairie Women's Health Centre of Excellence, 2004.

Polednak, A. P. *Racial and Ethnic Differences in Disease.* New York: Oxford University Press, 1989.

Razack, S. *Race, Space and the Law: Unmapping a White Settler Society.* Toronto: Between the Lines, 2002.

Saskatchewan Women's Secretariat. *Profile of Aboriginal Women in Saskatchewan.* Regina: Saskatchewan Women's Secretariat, 1999.

Statistics Canada. *Aboriginal Peoples Survey 2001: Well Being of the Non-Reserve Aboriginal Population.* Ottawa: Cat. no. 89-589-XIE, 2001.

Tuhiwai Smith, Linda. *Decolonizing Methodologies: Research and Indigenous Peoples.* New York: Zed Books Ltd., 2002.

Voyageur, C. "Contemporary Aboriginal women in Canada." *Visions of the Heart: Canadian Aboriginal Issues.* Eds. David Long and Olive P. Dickason. Toronto: Harcourt Canada, 2000.

Wienert, D. *Preventing and Controlling Cancer in North America: A Cross-Cultural Perspective.* Westport, CT: Praeger, 1999.

Waldram, J. B., D. A. Herring, and T. K. Young. *Aboriginal Health in Canada: Historical, Cultural, and Epidemiological Perspectives.* Toronto: University of Toronto Press, 2000.

Wotherspoon, T. and V. Satzewich. *First Nations: Race, Class and Gender Relations.* Regina: Canadian Plains Research Centre, 2000.

Young, I. M. *Inclusion and Democracy.* Oxford: Oxford University Press, 2000.

Young, T. K. "Review of research on Aboriginal populations in Canada: Relevance to their health needs." *British Medical Journal* 327 (2003): 419–22.

Young, T. K. *The Health of Native Americans: Toward a Biocultural Epidemiology.* New York: Oxford University Press, 1994.

ORGANIZING ON THE ROCK

Wendy Williams

The first time we used the words *women's health* was at a one-day conference held in St. John's in 1975. Cecilia Benoit and Jill Schooley were members of the organizing committee. With federal funding from Manpower and Immigration (Local Initiatives Programme), we presented workshops on topics such as sexuality, birth control, and menopause. Memorial University of Newfoundland (MUN) had a wonderful community-based division called Extension Services, which videotaped the workshops (now available online at MUN NL Collection). The videos neither name the presenters nor give credit to the organizers, the Newfoundland Status of Women Council (NSWC).

As feminists in St. John's in the early 1970s, we put much of our energy into making safe places for women. We spoke about women being beaten, child abuse in our homes, and rape. How did we do it, especially given that the 1970 Royal Commission on the Status of Women report had virtually no mention of violence against women? Barbara Doran and Diane Duggan were two of the pioneers who raised the issue of violence against women. The other pioneers in naming violence were members of the Woman's Place. We believed them. We worked hard to make decision-makers acknowledge these truths and to develop services to address our needs. It was a long time before I understood violence as a health issue, but I do remember a feminist family doctor saying that if she did not have to deal with the results of violence against women her medical practice would be much smaller.

There were two feminist groups in the early seventies in St. John's: the Woman's Place and the NSWC, which ran the Women's Centre. Cathy Murphy and Liz Genge were two of the early members of Woman's Place. Another founder of Woman's Place, Sharon Grey, who owned the Second Story Book Store, provided their meeting space at 144 Duckworth St. rent-free. Woman's Place was the first group to provide services for women who were victims of violence. Cathy Murphy remembers, "In 1976 or 77 I brought a woman into my home only to have her husband break into my home in the wee hours to attempt an assault."

Shortly after that incident Liz, Alice Brown, and I obtained funds to rent a boarding house that operated for a year to demonstrate the need for permanent services. The police, courts, and social services referred women to our project. Social services paid a daily fee for us to house women and children in the boarding house on Victoria Street. That project was called Family Crisis Service and provided transition house services for the one-year project. Woman's Place later moved to Prescott Street where we more openly provided abortion referral services and advice. Woman's Place closed in the late 1970s.

The Women's Centre was where women came to implement the recommendations of the Royal Commission on the Status of Women. I was a founding mother. We were lucky in that when the YWCA in St John's amalgamated with the YMCA some strong women left the "Y" in protest and joined the NSWC. These women had organizational experience and knew the value of a room of their own.

As every feminist knows, language is important. Names are important. The NSWC only operated in St John's, so when other independent Status of Women Councils were established, the new councils objected to our name because Newfoundland in our name implied a formal connection between the councils where none existed. We were the only Council that was formally pro-choice and spoke about abortion. While none of the councils were anti-choice, they worried that if they spoke in support of abortions, their community's response might be more than they could survive. In 1984 we changed our name to the St John's Status of Women Council (SJSWC).

SJSWC rented space for several years, first on Rawlins Cross then at 77 Bond St. When it looked as if we would have to move again, we decided to buy a house. The city was involved with a federally funded programme to revitalize the older part of the city. Good mortgage rates were available if an older house was refurbished and at least part of the building was used for housing. We found a suitable building and needed $2000 for a down payment. We thought if we could get $100 from twenty women, we would have our down payment. If there ever was a list of who those women were, it no longer exists. At the time we thought all work was to be credited to a group, that individual women should not be named. But how wrong we were, as so many women's work was lost. The following is a list of the names of the women who donated the money for the mortgage down payment that I have reconstructed from many emails: Susan Flynn, Sandra Penrose, Jill Schooley, Fran Baird Innes, Jane Crosbie, Diane Duggan, Pauline Bradbrook, Shirley Goundry, Lillian Bouzanne, and myself. Susan Flynn donated the final amount needed to make up the $2,000. Our Women's Centre in our own building opened in June 1978.

SJSWC accomplished many things. It started the first permanent transition house in the province and the rape crisis centre operated out of our space for years. Marian Atkinson and Kathy Coffin made sure that we set up a branch of the Canadian Association for the Repeal of the Abortion Law so that we spoke publicly about abortion.

The Council executives met weekly. Looking back, having weekly executive meetings was an example of the unhealthy practices we had as a volunteer organization. Unfortunately making our organizations good places to work was not high on many feminist organizations' agendas. Self-care was a challenge for many of the women, and feminist organizations had to get better at becoming excellent places to work.

The eight Status of Women Councils in Newfoundland not only still exist, but are funded by the provincial government's Women's Policy Office to advance the status of women based on specific needs. The councils operate women's centres in Grand Falls-Windsor, Stephenville, Corner Brook, Gander, Port Aux Basques, Labrador City, Happy Valley-Goose Bay, and St. John's.

The Newfoundland and Labrador Sexual Assault Crisis & Prevention Centre began as the St. John's Rape Crisis and Information Centre in 1977. Diane Duggan was the leader of this service. It initially serviced the St. John's region and later expanded to include the entire province. In the first two decades there was ongoing discussion about the risks of taking government funding, which would allow the government to have access to our files and define the programmes we delivered. With changes in the volunteer members, opposition waned, and government funding was sought and obtained. The operation of a toll-free crisis line was the first important step in making the services more accessible. In 1999 the Centre incorporated and received charitable status.

The first permanent transition house in the province opened in St. John's and was sponsored by the SJSWC. I remember meeting (in 1979 or early 1980) with Minister of Social Services, Charlie Brett, to get operating funds for the house, a place where battered women and their children could be safe while they planned their next steps. The minister was horrified that we thought Newfoundland men beat their wives. He was very clear that Newfoundland men did not do this so there was no need to give us money for a transition house.

Nevertheless, we started looking for a house. A house located at 9 Garrison Hill was sold to the SJSWC by Sister Amen, an Anglican sister who had been operating the house as a home for young unwed mothers, with the promise that the house would always be used to house women and children. We secured funds from both the federal and provincial government and bought the building with no funds of our own. The transition house, which opened in 1981, was later named after Iris Kirby, a deceased feminist who had worked at the federal secretary of state's office.

The Christian churches were a major player in health, education, and social services in Newfoundland. In 1984 the Salvation Army opened a transition house for battered women in St. John's. It operated on the basis that the family unit was to be preserved and the goal was to reunite the family. Thus husbands could visit the wives they had battered and the women were told to return to the violence they had fled. Not only did we operate feminist transition houses, but we also worked to get this service shut down. We did.

As of 2016 there are eleven transition houses in Newfoundland. The ten houses funded by the regional health authorities are Iris Kirby House in St. John's, O'Shaughnessy House in Carbonear, Grace Sparkes House in Marystown, Cara Transition House in Gander, Transition House (Committee on Family Violence) in Corner Brook, Libra House in Happy Valley-Goose Bay, Hope Haven in Labrador City, Safe House in Nain, Selma Onalik Safe House in Hopedale, and Rigolet Safe House in Rigolet. The Sheshatshiu transition house is federally funded.

By 1989 the Provincial Advisory Council on the Status of Women members saw a need for improved communication and understanding among groups, individuals, and agencies delivering services to women who were victims of violence. We decided to host a meeting, but we had to decide whom to invite. We knew that many women went to their clergy for support as they were the only listeners available in small communities. So we invited

the provincial bodies of all Christian denominations to send representatives to the founding meeting of the Interagency Committee
on Violence Against Women. Ministers and priests came. St.
John's is so small that we had to work with people on one issue
while working against them on another. I remember sitting next
to a Roman Catholic priest at one meeting of the Interagency
Committee, knowing that the man had recently condemned me
from the pulpit for my pro-choice stand on abortion.

The next work we did that we named as health work was a
joint project with the Newfoundland and Labrador Women's
Institutes (NLWI). In 1979 several members of SJSWC wondered
if a conference on women's health would be a mechanism for
raising women's health issues. Other members thought we should
be looking at a longer project with workshops across the province. When we approached the Health Promotion Contribution
Programme of Health and Welfare Canada for funding, their staff
wanted us to work with the largest women's organization in the
province, the NLWI.

It took two years from the time we started discussions until the
project was funded. We first had to develop a trusting relationship
with NLWI, as we had never worked together. We produced a
joint proposal and were funded from January 1981 until August
1984. Both groups wanted the project to respond to expressed
needs of women in Newfoundland. A great deal of time went
into developing a structure and programme that required the
active participation of women. Frances Laracy, a recipient of a
Person's Medal, was one of NLWI representatives on the board. I
chaired the board for the entire project and chaired the developmental meetings. Other members were Susan Felbsberg (Mud
Lake Labrador), Billie Thurston (St. John's), Kathy Sheldon
(Summerford), Rosalind Cross (Port Aux Basques), Penny
Alderdice (St. John's), and Wilhelmina Giovanni (St. Lawrence).

Under the strong leadership of Frances Ennis, the project used
a participatory approach to define the issues and deliver workshops
on women and stress, mothers and teenagers, various services
(both medical and community), women and food, reproductive
health, alcohol and tobacco use, and organizing for change. As
I reread the final report years later, I noted once again that we
did not name the women who volunteered as board members or
served on committees or acted as community contacts. But we were
very successful. We held a provincial consultation in June 1982 to
discuss our survey findings. In early 1983 we presented sixty-two
workshops to 1,141 women. Later that fall we delivered another

fifty-eight workshops to 1,011 women. It was an ambitious project that covered a large area using a participatory approach and the expertise of the women. Those who attended the events gave very positive feedback about their personal growth and the benefit to their communities.

Building and maintaining relationships in volunteer groups is time consuming. Women's groups do not have secure funding and when they undertake joint projects it takes resources away from their original programmes. Once the funding ended there were no ongoing projects between these groups even though friendships were maintained.

On August 15, 1984, the National Action Committee on the Status of Women hosted a two-hour debate among the three party leaders on women's issues. The leaders were Ed Broadbent (NDP), Prime Minister John Turner (Liberal), and Brian Mulroney (Progressive Conservative). The debate was in Toronto and broadcast nationally. I invited people to my home to watch the debate and to provide comments to the attending journalists. The largest newspaper, *The Evening Telegram*, sent a journalist to cover the debate. During the post-debate discussion the reporter said some women deserved to be beaten. I told her to leave my home. We wondered what her coverage in the next day's paper would be like. Had I just blown getting coverage for feminists and our work from the largest paper in the province? No, her article was on the front page of the paper with no mention of being asked to leave. Years later she told me she changed her mind and no longer believed some women deserved to be beaten.

Based on the National Action Committee on the Status of Women's annual lobby day in Ottawa we organized three provincial lobbies in 1984, 1987, and 1989. MUN had a wonderful system of teleconferencing in place from the early seventies. There were sites in all hospitals, community health clinics, town council offices, and at MUN. While I do not remember the rates I know they were cheap enough that the cost of a call was never a problem and we could use the network any time outside of business hours. This system, the first of its kind in Canada, allowed women's groups to organize easily and cheaply. For each lobby day we held monthly teleconference meetings for ten to twelve months before the lobby and spent a full day in St. John's before we met the members of the House of Assembly, both government and opposition.

The groups who participated had no formal ties but we shared common concerns and were highly aware that political action was necessary if remedies were to be found. Participating groups included Planned Parenthood, transition houses, first nations groups from Labrador, and women's centres. The teleconferencing calls were voice only, but they allowed us to build relationships with groups we had never worked with, to define the issues, and to hone the questions for the government and the opposition. Women were often reluctant to ask one of the questions so we provided training to the speakers at the day-long session before the lobby. Health issues were addressed at each lobby. In the second lobby women living on the coast of Labrador asked for sewer systems that did not freeze in the winter. Under housing we asked for emergency shelters that were virtually non-existent in Labrador for women escaping violence.

In 1978 the female staff of the Labrador Inuit Association organized the first Northern Women's Conference in Nain, Labrador. The conference had lasting impacts for the women of Labrador. One resolution discussed the feasibility of a Northern Labrador Women's Association. This resolution was realized in 1983 with the establishment of the Labrador Native Women's Association, an umbrella group for Innu, Inuit, and Southern Inuit of NunatuKavut. The report was written in Inuktitut and English and spoke about the need for books and other materials in Muchuau Innu and Inuktitut.

Another result from this conference was the formation in 1979 of the Nain Women's Group, which became a significant presence in the community by providing services such as a daycare centre, a shelter for battered women, and a thrift store. Other native women's groups were established later, at Sheshatshiu, Hopedale, North West River, Happy Valley-Goose Bay, Port Hope Simpson, and Davis Inlet.

In 1991 the deputy minister of health established a working group on women's health as part of the government's slow response to the 1988 Federal/Provincial/Territorial Working Group on Women's Health. The group met for three years and published their work as the Working Group on Women's Health: *A Profile of Women's Health in Newfoundland and Labrador* (St. John's, Government of Newfoundland and Labrador 1994). The report used a health promotion framework with detailed sections on reproductive health, chronic diseases, occupational health, environmental health, mental health, violence against women, women and addictions, and healthy and active living. In 1992 the first piece of research on lesbians in the province was published by the Provincial Advisory Council on the Status of Women and the 1994 report expanded on that work. The 1994 report included a women's health timeline from 1794–1993 and twenty-six recommendations (e.g., legalize midwifery and require that the Department of Health have 50 per cent female representation on all boards).

In January 1995 the Women's Health Network was established. Both academic researchers and community activists worked together. It was the first organization to specifically address women's health in Newfoundland, but it was short-lived and disbanded in the early 2000s. Midwives had practised in Labrador and parts of the Island from 1892 until 1963. Work to re-establish midwifery started in 1979 with courses being offered by the MUN School of Nursing. A detailed history exists on the Association of Midwives of Newfoundland and Labrador website. In September 2016 the regulation governing midwifery came into force.

The work of feminists organizing for better health for women in Newfoundland and later Labrador was extensive. It made a huge difference to the lives of women and girls on a range of issues. And years later, while there are now many publicly funded safe spaces for women, there is still violence against women. And activists and researchers continue to work together to keep an inclusive perspective in their work and keep feminism in the public's eye. Feminists continue to work to ensure that all health research, policy, and programmes are inclusive. There remains much to be done, but a sound base was built on the Rock by the incredible and determined feminists of the "second wave."

From: *Healthsharing*/Immigrant Women's Centre

SECTION TWO:
CLAIMING OUR BODIES

Nothing is more fundamental than the body we live in. How does it work, how is it working, how do others see it, how do we learn about it, how do we get better treatment, and how do we get to direct what happens to it? And in this realm, nothing, perhaps, was more fundamental to women of the second-wave than reproductive freedom. How would we control sexual health, conception, pregnancy, and abortion? These issues dominated the second wave.

It was no surprise that a key document of these years was the 1970 *Our Bodies, Ourselves*, perhaps the best self-help manual for women ever. Published by the collective of the same name, located in Boston, Massachusetts, this book was the leader in a wealth of documents that aspired to increase our health literacy. Women in the early second wave devoured these books, pamphlets, and self-help books, learning bodily mechanics, self-exam skills, home birth, and information to use in confronting sexist doctors. Again, though, perhaps nothing was more fundamental than finding contraception and procuring abortions for each other until the laws changed in Canada.

Zingaro documents that underground world in Vancouver in the 1960s. Her account takes us into a world of desperation, risk, and trauma and highlights the limits on choices that confronted girls and women in that decade. Woodsworth describes the grass-roots, confrontative, wild, and jubilant Abortion Caravan that worked its way from Vancouver to Ottawa, ending up with some activists chained to the gallery in Parliament. Bazilli relays her individual, lonely, and anonymous journey to an abortion provider in Buffalo, leaning on one of the many intricate, caring networks of women (and some men) who hustled girls and women needing abortions to the right places, namelessly and quietly. These networks were word-of-mouth triumphs and existed across Canada.

Whynot described the local hospital politics that played out at the Vancouver General Hospital in the midst of the abortion access battle long before the Supreme Court ruled in 1988. Desmarais and MacQuarrie et al. describe the long and painful details of getting reproductive freedom in place in Quebec and Prince Edward Island, respectively. These were very different stories decades apart, but all three of these stories detail the tedious, relentless, wily, and unpredictable politics of abortion services. Finally, Knight describes the front line. The horror and drama of the police raid on the Morgentaler clinic in Toronto, and her very personal role in that event.

As preoccupying as abortion access was, claiming our bodies back was a fight with many fronts. Contraception was illegal and unavailable until 1968. Landsberg describes a condescending and likely typical encounter with a Toronto gynecologist when she went asking for contraception as a young single woman in 1963. And Williams describes the multiple challenges in establishing Planned Parenthood in Newfoundland, including finding ten donors to hold a mortgage and going to court to resist the Catholic Church. Nayar describes the essential and amazing grassroots initiatives of Filomena Carvalho in bringing health information to immigrant women working in Toronto factories.

All bodies and body parts mattered to feminists of the second wave, including ovaries and breasts. Batt assesses breast cancer activism and her ambivalence about its record of success, and its engagement with medical and pharmaceutical interests. Prior describes the relentless effort in keeping a Vancouver research centre going to develop an entirely new view of the menstrual cycle. Finally, Odette addresses how women with disabilities are "othered" by the gaze of other women and society at large, and experience body image pressures. All of our bodies, and all of their parts, matter.

ABORTION

SECRETS, LIES, AND SILENCE:
PROCURING AN ABORTION IN THE 1960S

Linde Zingaro

SECRETS

In 1962, she knew she was pregnant several months before her sixteenth birthday. That secret was impossible to keep, though she took a job for the summer on an island outside the small community where her family lived. So at the end of the summer her mother bought her a brown corduroy maternity smock to wear for the first day of Grade 11, where, within a few days some of the mothers of other girls in her class insisted that she not be permitted to attend. Her mother would not allow her to marry her fifteen-year-old boyfriend, and her family did not want another baby, so she was sent to the city down south to a Salvation Army Home for Wayward Girls, one of many such institutions being operated across the country.

As was policy in those days, she was sent for the birth to the Grace Hospital, where, without any prenatal education, she laboured alone, delivered a child she was not allowed to see or touch, and remained for a week in a maternity ward with other (good) mothers who were learning to feed and care for their babies. Her breasts were bound to limit the production of milk. After she signed the papers giving the child up for adoption she went home to go back to school, to carry the public shame of the local girl who got herself "in trouble" and couldn't get married. The secret that the child could have been her father's was kept for almost thirty years.

In 1964, she had won a scholarship that would help her escape to the college that she had chosen, but she was pregnant again. Her desperate need to get away led her to try all the solutions that her friends knew about—taking many aspirins, drinking vodka until she passed out, staying in a scalding bath for hours, hitting herself in the stomach, throwing herself down the stairs. Nothing worked. A man told her ex-boyfriend about a woman who lived thirty miles down the highway. A week after graduation, when her brothers were gone to work for the summer on fishing boats, and her mother had taken her father out of the psychiatric hospital to drive to the prairies for a visit with his family, she arranged to see the woman.

But once again, the secret of what that woman did to her could not be kept for long. Thirty-six hours after that meeting, her ex-boyfriend had told the doctors at the small local hospital what had happened and she was emergency air-lifted to a city hospital to give a typical dying statement to the nurses and the police.[17] She did not know the woman's name, but she knew where she lived, and could describe the procedure. The woman had used a common rubber douche-bag with a long tube, and had pushed the anal attachment into her vagina. The woman had said she had to push until she could feel something break inside, and then she emptied the bag, filled with a warm solution of Castile soap, into her body. The statement that she signed with an X, barely conscious, became part of a court case. She had to leave her school to travel back up the coast to give testimony, after more than a month in the hospital and having finally moved away from home. The woman was convicted and the girl went back to school and her new life.

In 1965, living in Vancouver, she once again found herself pregnant, even though she had been told by the gynecologist at the hospital that she had ruined her body—with a perforated uterus and the level of infection that she had suffered, he warned her that she would never again conceive a healthy child. One of the solutions available to her at that time involved a trip to an undisclosed location in Washington State, but the amount of money required was beyond her. People knew about a doctor in Vancouver who had been known to do abortions, but he had been sentenced and his office would not take any new patients. Somebody gave her an envelope of tiny pills from Chinatown, but they just made her vomit.

Finally, a friend introduced her to a man who had, years before, learned a safer method for termination after his girlfriend had died as a result of an illegal abortion and he agreed to help her. He was kind, careful, and sanitary, and though the procedure required her to labour to expel the fetus, she recovered quickly. Though his name and his movements were kept secret, within the group of people who were her new community it was not a secret that she had had an abortion. As a result, for those around her, she now represented a point of access to safe abortion.

The first young woman who approached her to be introduced to the man was a friend. She had a job she liked and a boyfriend who was not serious. The second was a slightly older friend who was seeing a man who was already married. For each of those women, she arranged for the man to come to the communal house where she lived, bringing his sterile equipment with him. There, in the anonymity of many people coming and going, he could see the women in private for only a few minutes, and then leave the young woman to take care of her friends while they laboured. They agreed that she would be responsible for taking them to the nearby hospital if anything went wrong. The next woman had approached the man through a different connection, but did not want anyone where she was living to know what she was doing, so he suggested that this arrangement would be best for her too. He had learned that she could keep the women safe and comfortable, that she would keep their secrets, and his.

For the next four years there were dozens of young women and girls who did not go to the Salvation Army, but instead they stayed a day or two at a big house in the West End. There were married women who already had more children than they could manage, young women with hopes and opportunities that would be lost if their pregnancy was known, women who felt threatened by the possibility of dependency on an unwilling partner or their families. Each woman had her own secrets, her own particular pain and loss, her own specific fear and shame, and some came more than once. Some of those feelings were shared during the process, but most went unspoken. When her sixteen-year-old sister came to stay with her to meet with the man, she did not ask whether that pregnancy, too, could have been their father's.

Most of the time the physical part of labour went smoothly, waiting and crying through the pain of passing what usually just seemed like heavy menstrual clots. But on one occasion the woman had not known or admitted how far advanced her pregnancy was. Her labour was long and difficult, and the product obviously more developed. The shock of seeing what could only be a tiny baby dead in her hands was deeply disturbing, but only once in all those years was it necessary to help a woman to the emergency room of the hospital down the street when her bleeding was too extensive after the fetus was passed.

Far more complex was the emotional response, both for her

and for the women she supported. The prevailing social attitude toward abortion made it not only illegal but reprehensible. Part of the experience for every woman in this situation was the fear of being caught, the worry about who would find out, how anyone would react if they knew. For some women, the idea that they were also committing a sin was terrifying and traumatizing, even beyond the physical struggle and the emotional pain of loss.

She knew nothing then about feminism or the history of women's fight for reproductive rights. She knew nothing about the government nation-building policy that was driving church and agency practice, justifying the humiliating treatment she had experienced in the Home for Unwed Mothers. She had no idea of the theorizing that went into these structures—all calculated to ensure that (white, healthy) children, born to unmarried women, would be available for adoption by "good" families.[18] She only knew that a woman, desperate to be rid of an unwanted pregnancy could, and would have to, put her health and her life at risk.

In almost five years of assisting an unrecorded number of women, she never received any money or compensation of any kind. In late 1969, hearing that the law had been changed to allow (limited) access to therapeutic abortions, she and the man agreed that they did not have to do this anymore. She did not think of her part in this as activism and, even in the many feminist conversations that she was part of for decades afterward, her experience as a provider/supporter of illegal abortion remained a secret. In 1974, ten years after that first disastrous abortion, she gave birth to a much wanted, perfect child.

LIES AND SILENCE

In the years since 1969, we learned much that transformed those attitudes we took for granted—that changed what was then seen as unassailable truth into myths, or even lies. Indeed, the work of contradicting some of the grounding assumptions of those times has informed many of the central arguments of and for feminism.

The first "truth" to be challenged was the question of who needs or wants an abortion. The assumption that women who terminate a pregnancy are bad and dangerous was based on the belief, supported in court processes and popular discourse, that women who are raped or sexually abused as girls must have somehow "asked for it," and that women and girls have full responsibility for their own sexual experience or exploitation. Without acknowledging the possibility of rape, abuse, or coercion, the lack of access to birth control outside of marriage was, in the 1960s, not only unquestioned, but in fact morally justified as not encouraging promiscuity.

In the double bind of the times using birth control was evidence of a lack of innocence. At the same time it was understood that women would choose to have sex without protection because of unhealthy desire or a lack of self-control. With pregnancy being the strongest evidence that a girl or young woman had been sexual it was also proof that she was promiscuous, careless, or not very smart. Women and girls "got themselves into trouble." Often.

The second important lie about abortion was the prevailing story about who was willing to perform or procure an abortion. This lie was sustained by the invisibility of class difference in access to the procedure. In the hush that accompanied any talk of being "in trouble" there was always innuendo about the possibility of "getting rid of it"—about the risks and the dangers, but even more about the unsavoury, even criminal, character of any person willing to perform a termination. A woman was putting herself into the hands of murderers who, for money, would be willing to do something vaguely sexual, which, if it did not kill her outright, would damage her for life. But at the same time, while rural, poor, or working-class women really were facing those risks, there was always a clinic somewhere, available to those who had the ability to pay for it. The myths had those clinics somewhere in the US, in Bellingham or Seattle for those of us in Vancouver, across the line somewhere in Maine, for those in Halifax or St John's.

It was never part of the story that access to safe abortion might be something organized by women or provided as a commitment to women's health. But in a conversation with a friend who was a young teenager in Vancouver during the early sixties, I learned that even then there were other women who were engaged in providing abortions as a kind of activism. My friend's mother was a social worker with a commitment to social justice, who had contacts in her professional community with direct and immediate access to a local clinic when her daughter's fifteen-year-old friend disclosed that she was pregnant. Though still cloaked in the need for secrecy, her sense was that the address on Broadway was a safe place and that the decision to abort was difficult but justified.

The most destructive lie of all is still part of the rhetoric of the anti-choice lobby: the belief that if women have access to abortion on demand they will simply use termination as an alternative to birth control—that lazy or careless women are thoughtlessly capable of killing their children rather than managing their somehow shameful, questionable sexuality. And there is still a secret that so many of us (responsible, credible, respectable women) keep to ourselves: that in some painful time, with deep sadness or immense relief, we have been in a position where we needed to end a pregnancy. This secret allows the lies to continue and keeps the so-called "abortion debate" active enough to risk a return to the dangerous times of no access, especially for rural, poor, or victimized women and girls.

ROLLING INTO OTTAWA ON
THE ABORTION CARAVAN

Ellen Woodsworth

The idea of the Abortion Caravan and the caravan itself started in the Vancouver Women's Caucus. In 1970 we drove across Canada to Ottawa, where we were met by women from coast to coast to coast, to demand that the prime minster of Canada and members of Parliament decriminalize abortion. It was an amazing adventure and a powerful statement by women who had had enough of being the second sex in the days when abortion was not available

It was an exciting time. People all over the world were rising up and gaining understanding and strength from others like activists in the student, civil rights, anti-poverty, First Nations, and anti-Vietnam-war movements. Women were part of all of these movements in some way and were gaining a voice. We found we had a lot to say. We felt that women must be part of creating a new world that would work for women and girls. But we very soon learned that to be heard we had to start our own movement and define our own issues.

In 1968, I was elected head of the Speakers Bureau at the University of British Columbia and had an office in the Student Union building. I turned it into a women's centre but we had no organization. I wanted to be part of a women's organization so I decided to join the off-campus Vancouver Women's Caucus. The majority of us were in the student movement and, in our late teens, were very aware of the importance of birth control and abortion. Women were getting pregnant and unless you had money to go to Japan for an abortion, it would spell the end of university, family support, social acceptance, and an immediate drop into poverty with a child that was not intended, or having to give up the child or having a back room abortion in Canada. It was a time of "free love" but it wasn't "free" for women.

Women's Caucus members were helping women gain access to abortions that were then totally illegal, difficult, or impossible to access in Canada. Others were active in the student movement, while some were fighting for child care. Some were involved in supporting low-income women issues such as the need for an overpass of the railway tracks by Raymuir Housing and others were fighting for equal pay. Our organization was working on many issues but when the federal government brought in new laws on May 14, 1969, that legalized contraception and allowed women to have abortions if recommended by two doctors, the Women's Caucus confronted the BC government in the legislature, the BC Medical Association, and the prime minister. The fact was, most women could still not access affordable contraception or abortion on demand.

We decided that abortion was the issue most women could unite behind, the issue that would give strength to the women's liberation movement and really change women's lives. We were already addressing the broader need for expanded social programmes like health care to give women control of their own lives. We knew that women were facing unwanted pregnancies and having unwanted children, and that Aboriginal women were being forcibly sterilized and others were being butchered by untrained abortionists. Women were dying.

WHY A CROSS-COUNTRY CARAVAN?

Many people in Canada were aware of the "On to Ottawa Trek" of the unemployed during the depression. Unemployed, desperate workers from across Canada had climbed on trains and headed to Ottawa to raise the issue of jobs. That movement led to the largest confrontation of workers and the police that Canada has ever seen. Several supporters were elected to Parliament and they formed a new party called the Co-operative Commonwealth Federation that was to change history by fighting for and winning a national health care programme.

We also knew the herstory and courage of the suffragists who had to march on the House of Commons and not be afraid of being arrested. We thought that if we drove across Canada we could talk to women in small and large communities in order to learn from them and share our experiences of organizing for women's liberation. We wanted to work with them to change Canadian laws so women would have the right to safe, affordable, accessible abortions when women wanted them.

The first thing we did was to talk to women and women's organizations and to our allies across Canada to ensure that we all agreed on the issue and the strategy. We wanted to build support for the caravan and needed groups all across Canada that would host events and join us along the way or in Ottawa. Together we mapped out a strategy for the campaign. What needed to be said? What literature needed to be written? How would it be distributed and which cities would do what part of the work and how many we could count on to join us in Ottawa? The plan emerged. Some women would bus in from the East Coast, Quebec, and other parts of Ontario. We planned to drive from Vancouver to Ottawa, stopping along the way to talk about the issues and gain support. We decided who would lobby their MPs, who would speak, how to announce our arrival, how to write media releases, perform in plays, and sing songs.

We found friends in the YWCA, the churches, the universities, the unions, and other social movements that wanted to host our meetings, organize and advertise the event, and provide beds. Then we planned a route that included ten cities and involved five vehicles. We worked hard and were very excited with our plans. I was looking forward to the trip and the chance to really stand up for women. Finally we had enough women who could take the time off and found vehicles that could make the trip. The plan was to let the media and the local groups know we were coming, hold a meeting, do some theatre and songs, and talk about the issue with a focus on the local concerns.

In the early spring of 1970, we gathered hundreds of supporters on the steps of the Vancouver Art Gallery holding signs like "Illegal Abortions kill 12,000"; "Women Demand Safe Abortions"; "Abortion Is Our Right"; "We Are Furious Women"; and "Free Abortion on Demand." Eighteen women loaded into five vehicles, one of which had a coffin on top, and headed to Ottawa. Although we had basic guidelines for our work and the politics that we stood for, there were some glitches. On the first night, dressed in our pyjamas and sleeping on the floor of a centre in Kamloops, we began a long argument about the "Smash Capitalism" slogan on the side of the VW van. We finally decided to erase it so it wouldn't distract from the immediate issues.

Bonnie Beckwoman brought her guitar and rewrote songs to feminist lyrics like "Hold the fort for we are coming, sisters all be strong, side by side we battle onward, victory will come" or "Bella

Ciao" from the Italian anti-fascist resistance movement, "Down by the Riverside" from the civil rights movement, and "Solidarity Forever" from the union movement. Just imagine five vehicles — one with a coffin on top that was full of coat hangers to symbolize the women who had died from illegal abortions and one a convertible full of women singing — driving into a little town. Once we had parked in a key public location, we jumped out and started talking to people, then, led by Margo Dunn, performed street theatre about abortion. We would listen to horrendous stories from women and girls about their experiences with abortion. In the evening we held a public meeting at which Marcy Cohen, Betsy Wood, and others spoke as we became more confident of the issues. Though we didn't get any media attention at the beginning, we talked to many women and learned a lot about the terrible powerlessness of women and girls across the country. We also had fun singing and learning how to do street theatre. We never knew where we were going to stay each night. Little did we know that the Royal Canadian Mounted Police who took note of all our work all the way to Ottawa, had infiltrated the Caravan.[19]

Women from across Canada shared their experiences of the power of doctors to do good or evil; of the power of private men's organizations and clubs that allowed violence against women and protected their own from any charges; of racism toward Aboriginal women that included sterilization; of the forced incarceration of women in mental hospitals and their involuntary sterilization; of graveyards with the unmarked graves of hundreds of women who had died from abortions and difficult births; and of the amazing untold courage of doctors and others who quietly performed abortions illegally.

Day after day we met incredible women who had had their lives destroyed because they couldn't get a safe, affordable, accessible abortion. These women gained strength from our public campaign and many were able to speak out for the first time in their lives. Some of them even came to Ottawa. Finally the situation was out there for all to see. We met ferocious opponents who were bigoted, moralistic, and powerful, but we were not alone. We were organized and we were on the move, building strength and numbers day after day as we drove across this huge country.

It was intimidating to drive into the big city of Toronto where we joined the Toronto Women's Liberation movement, a well-organized group with which we were planning the confidential details of what we would do in Ottawa. We all ended up staying at my mother's home. Though she hadn't expected all eighteen of us, she supported what we were doing because as the executive director of a YWCA, she had heard women and girls tell their stories about abortion. There was a large meeting in the St. Lawrence Centre for the Arts, a parade, a rally, and a "Declaration of War" that was sent to the prime minister.

The main rally was held in Ottawa on Mother's Day, May 10, 1970. Hundreds of women arrived by bus, train, car, and plane from across Canada to gather in front of the Supreme Court. We requested to meet with the prime minister and the members of Parliament, but only four MPs attended the meeting. The only MP that completely supported our call for removal of abortion from the Criminal Code and for the decriminalization of abortion was Grace MacInnis, then the only woman in the House of Commons.

We were outraged that the government was refusing to meet with Canadians who had made such an effort to come all the way to the nation's capital. We marched to the prime minister's house with the coffin that we used in our theatre piece. We almost went right into his house as it wasn't guarded, but decided that we wanted the focus on the issue of access to abortions not on the fact we had occupied the PM's official residence. The media were finally paying attention and doing some stories, which gave us the confidence that we were being heard. We regrouped at the school where we were staying and decided that we had to do something to get the attention of the government. We wanted them to listen to what was happening to women and acknowledge that it was their responsibility to change the law. We wanted them to know that we were not going to go away until we were heard.

Finally, after hours of discussion, when many of the women who were exhausted after long trips to Ottawa had gone to sleep, we decided that some of us would chain ourselves inside the House of Commons while the others would demonstrate outside the main entrance. We chose a small group of women representing every area of Canada. These were women who could both speak strongly to the issue and could afford to get arrested. Some local women and men secretly got us passes from their local MPs so we could enter the Parliament buildings. We dressed up, with chains in our purses and a strategy of how we would enter, with whom, when, where we would sit, and what we would chant. We also discussed what we would do if we were arrested and shared the phone numbers of supportive lawyers.

We were afraid but not alone. I remember feeling terrified that they would sense our tension and stop us before we were able to speak. Some of us had to borrow clothes that looked middle class and unobtrusive. Two by two we moved up the steps of the House and were able to get into the Parliament buildings. There we headed off into the various galleries to quietly chain ourselves to our seats. The moment had arrived.

We looked down at the debate going on below us in the House of Commons. Slowly, one at a time, we stood up and shouted, "Women's right to choose," "Abortion is our right," and other slogans that made our point. As one woman was grabbed a woman from another area of the gallery would stand up and start shouting, which was the only way they could hear us. The members of Parliament slowly stopped debating. There was chaos as they tried to figure out where we were, what we were saying, and how to stop us. They shouted, "Silence! Silence in the House!" They demanded that we stop speaking, but we wouldn't and we were speaking out from all directions. "Canadian women are dying," we shouted. When they couldn't silence us they tried to get security to pull us out of our seats and throw us out of the House, but we were securely chained in place. We kept shouting out the issues that they didn't want to hear, about women's lives being destroyed, women dying, and women being sterilized. We wouldn't stop because women across Canada needed to be heard.

Security finally found some wire cutters and started grabbing one woman at a time and cutting her chains, hauling her out of the gallery still shouting. Then another woman would stand up and start speaking. They had to drag us out of the House of Commons one by one and push us out a back door. We were very afraid that we would be arrested. Instead we were allowed to go around to the front of the House of Commons and join our sisters who were walking around the flame. We received a huge amount of media coverage in every major news outlet in Canada.

The issues around abortion were finally out in public all across the nation. From then on, wherever the prime minister went in Canada women and allies were able to put pressure on him and on other MPs to decriminalize abortion. The issue of abortion became a key issue for women's rights and a number of organizations formed that focused solely on abortion. However, it wasn't until 1988 that the Supreme Court finally ruled that limiting abortion was unconstitutional.

We take all of these things for granted today. Many younger women don't seem to feel the need or the pride or the anger to call themselves feminist or to see the necessity of being part of the women's movement. Even in the context of the election of the misogynist Donald Trump for US president against the feminist Hillary Clinton, making it clear that the fight is not over. What have we learned that we can apply to the new times we live in today? We have learned that through organizing together we can change history and create herstory. We have learned that we need a plan and an organization to be able to relate to a wide base of the population and we need media strategies. We must always share knowledge and educate each other.

We have also learned that we have achieved rights by building on the movements of those who fought before us such as our mothers and fathers, our grandparents, the suffragists, the Women's International League for Peace and Freedom, the Chinese women's movement, and many, many others. We understand that whatever power we now have we have because of the work of those women and those organizations. We have to work with and mentor the youth. We must learn from the past and build for the future in order to hold on to what we have in the present. What we won yesterday we may have to fight for again tomorrow. We have learned that we have a responsibility to be role models. We have learned the power of using media. We have learned the importance of bread and roses.

OAKVILLE TO BUFFALO ON THE UNDERGROUND RAILROAD

Susan Bazilli

Given my years as an advocate with survivors of violence (and some who did not survive), I know that trauma can repress memories, but I did not realize how much until I was asked to write a piece for this book. I used social media to track down friends from high school to help me reconnect with my experience. Most of us had not spoken for forty-seven years about this or anything else, and so I am grateful to them for helping me to remember and to verify my experience.

I got pregnant when I was sixteen. It was not planned. I had been to a doctor to try to get contraception. I did not go to our family doctor at the time as I was too embarrassed to ask him for birth control and I did not want my mother to find out that I was asking for it. I had not yet had sex, and in fact had very little information about sex, but I knew that I needed to get something. I remember my mother took me to see a film about menstruation at the school when I was around eleven, but neither she nor the film provided me with many details. I had no idea if any of my friends were actually "doing it" yet and I did not feel comfortable asking them.

I do not remember who the doctor was, but I vividly remember him asking me questions about orgasms. I did not understand why he was asking me these questions. I probably did not even know what he was talking about; I just know that it felt creepy and did not seem to have anything to do with why I was there. He did not give me the birth control I had requested. I guess I did not answer the skill-testing question correctly. Knowing what I know now, I was lucky that I was not sexually assaulted by him and I often wondered how many other women and girls ended up pregnant because they could not get birth control in Oakville, Ontario in 1970.

I had a boyfriend. He was five years older than me and not in high school like I was. He worked as a logger in the bush and wore those checked logger shirts. I had met him at the cottage in the summer where he was living nearby with his grandmother. He was very kind and he was also a virgin at the time. So neither of us had any experience. We had very limited knowledge about sex, but we knew about condoms. And he had heard this tale that if you took saltpetre (potassium nitrate) it would reduce libido. He tried it. It didn't work. I got pregnant the first time we had sex, with a dysfunctional condom, lack of experience using them, or just bad luck.

Having an abortion was the best option for me. I do not recall thinking there was any other option—but how I even knew it was possible is still a mystery. As a high-school student how would I do that? In 1970 abortion was illegal in Canada. I do remember finding out that even with parents' consent and a medical opinion, I was not going to be able to obtain one. And since I was not going to tell my mother anyway, that was not an option. By this time my mother was a single parent with four children and working incredibly hard to support us all. I could not disappoint her or give her even more to deal with than she already had. We had no money and no connections.

Oakville had acquired a lot of notoriety in the early 1970s as a drug capital of Canada, a middle-class town supposedly full of bored and disaffected youth. There had been a scare involving LSD that had been cut with something like strychnine and several young people ended up in hospital. The LSD was called "Orange Sunshine" and the incident became known as "The Oakville Orange." Out of this experience, youth activists became involved with the city council, forming a youth council and working with the Addiction Research Foundation and Queen Street Mental Health Centre (Dr. Bill Clements) in Toronto, along with local mental health organizations. I remember going to many community meetings and ultimately a group of volunteers set up a house to work with youth on drug and other issues.

There was a group of women who were part of this project focusing on mental health. They were feminists who were very concerned about reproductive rights issues. They had informed themselves about access to legal abortions in New York state. Fortunately for me, I had met them through my peripheral involvement with the youth council work. They helped girls like me get to Buffalo, New York, where clinics would take Canadian girls who needed abortions. I remember a meeting in someone's living room. I cannot recall their faces or names, but I do recall that while I was very scared, I knew that these women were going to help me. I have no idea where the money came from to pay for the abortion, but likely the boyfriend, who was employed, gave me the money.

A friend of mine was pregnant at the same time and somehow appointments were made for us to go to Buffalo, conveniently on a school holiday. She miscarried the night before we were to go. All these years I have felt badly that she had to go through that on her own with no one knowing, and I now know that she has felt badly that I had to go to Buffalo on my own. But I was not alone—one of the women from the network drove me to Buffalo in a Volkswagen Beetle. I had the procedure at a licensed clinic with caring and professional staff. I remember very little, but I do remember that in my groggy state during the procedure the radio was playing Crosby, Stills, Nash and Young's "Teach Your Children Well." That music haunted me for years. I always felt it was a deliberate selection.

I was driven back to Oakville. I remember little except that I was still dopey from the anesthetic when we came back across the border and I was questioned quite aggressively, it seemed, about where I had been. I remember being quite frightened by the border guards' authority and attitude. But we made it back and I went home with the excuse that I had spent the day with a friend. To this day the worst thing about the whole experience was lying to my mother, a guilt I have carried all my life. She has been gone for almost a decade now, but I was never able to tell her.

Now, forty-seven years later, I am writing about this for the first time. There had been violence at home preceding my parents' divorce and that, coupled with what happened to me, left me quite traumatized and not able to remember all the details. But it has always given me extreme comfort to know that such a group of women existed in the early 1970s. I have always thought of them as members of a feminist underground railroad who helped to save my life.

I left home not long after this experience, without finishing high school. When I was seventeen I moved to Australia. My first feminist political action was becoming involved in the pro-choice movement in Melbourne, in the Women's Abortion Action Coalition where I participated in my first demonstration. Much later, when I moved to Toronto to go to university and then to law school, I became an active member of the Ontario Coalition of Abortion Clinics (OCAC). I was involved in the advocacy in the early days of the Morgentaler Clinic on Harbord Street, which opened in 1983. I vividly remember the fire bombing of the clinic in 1992. I was very lucky to have been able to work with such stalwart activists as Judy Rebick, Carolyn Egan, Norma Scarborough, and others.

But I was even more fortunate that this group of early feminist activists in Oakville were able to find me, or I them, and get the help that I needed, choices that should have been available to me in my own country. They all took courageous risks for me, and presumably for many others, and I have been grateful to them for my entire life. The best way for me to acknowledge their courage and support was to have worked in the movement for women's equality for my entire life. I have always identified my abortion experience as the moment that I became a feminist.

I am writing this account in a somewhat dispassionate way to protect myself; I actually do not want to go back and recall what I felt at the time. But I do realize how very, very fortunate I was. I know the global statistics. Almost 22 MILLION women have unsafe abortions each year and according to the World Health Organization over 50,000 die every year. Forty-seven years later, we still do not have fully equal access to abortion rights and reproductive choice in Canada, and pro-choice activists, doctors, and the girls and women who need assistance are still at risk in many places across the country. The struggle continues and without brave determined women activists, young women today can be caught, just as I was decades ago.

HOLDING THE LINE: ABORTION AT VANCOUVER GENERAL HOSPITAL

Collated by Elizabeth Whynot

What I remember most is meeting with many, many other volunteers in a downstairs room at the Vancouver Status of Women offices on West 4th Ave and developing plans to support continued abortion access at the Vancouver General Hospital. We were vocal. We spoke out when asked, on local radio and TV shows hosted by guys like Jack Webster and Bill Good, took every opportunity we found to publicize and debate the issue. And we sold memberships for the hospital. We sold them everywhere: on street corners, parking lots, college and university campuses, and at the beaches, including Wreck Beach, the famous nude beach near the University of British Columbia campus.

The last annual general meeting of the VGH Society was in the fall of 1977, where a few thousand people packed the Hyatt Regency Ballroom for speeches and the all-important vote. The vote was ultimately won by the candidates recommended by the board of trustees (who were pro-choice).

This was a much-beleaguered board, which was struggling not only with this issue but also significant unrest among the hospital's nursing staff. The following few months saw intense conflict and activism surrounding the board membership. Both pro-choice and anti-choice groups were organizing to buy memberships to acquire voting rights at the next annual general meeting. The UBC newspaper, *The Ubyssey*, was heavily involved in generating support among students.

EXCERPTS FROM "VGH ABORTION BATTLE LOOMS" BY KATHY FORD, THE UBYSSEY, MARCH 18, 1977

Laurie Flynn, a volunteer at the Pine Free Clinic, said Thursday members of the Pro-Life Society have staged a massive corporation membership drive in an attempt to railroad anti-abortionists onto the VGH board of trustees. The 18-member board—12 elected and six appointed—must approve all abortions performed at the hospital. "They (Pro-Lifers) have been going around to all the churches and getting people to join the corporation," she said..... "We (the clinic) and other groups have been trying to get people who do not support the Pro-Life campaign to join.... The issue is...whether you feel that women should have the right to say what is done to them or have that right taken away."

***

Dr. Chapin Key, VGH executive director, said Thursday the hospital is not where the abortion issue should be disputed. "This is a political battle, and the hospital is not the place for that," Key said. "Things are more complex than these people realize. They are fighting on one issue, but the board doesn't just control one programme in the hospital." The feeling on the present board is VGH is meeting a legal need in the community. Key said the corporation, formed in 1902, had less than 10 members each year until 1974. Last year there were about 400 members, and he said membership will be nearly 1,000 this year. (In fact, membership ballooned to 2000+).

***

People can join the corporation by signing forms available at a table in SUB mall today, set up by Flynn and the UBC women's committee. Annual membership costs $2 and the deadline for joining is 5 p.m. today.

***

By the following spring, the dispute had reached the BC Legislature. Rosemary Brown stood and addressed the legislature, asking for the Minister of Health to intervene to prevent looming chaos at the next Annual General Meeting. The Minister of Health, Bob McLelland, replied in a most unsatisfactory manner, reiterating a "wait and see" position.

EXCERPTS FROM HANSARD, 1978 LEGISLATIVE SESSION: 3RD SESSION, 31ST PARLIAMENT (BC)

Monday May 29, 1978

Rosemary Brown (MLA Vancouver Burrard): I'm wondering what the minister is going to do about Vancouver General Hospital and the fiasco we go through every year when they have to elect a new board. It's coming up again in September, and I understand that the membership of the hospital association is now over 10,000. This is a hospital which a couple of years ago could hold its annual meetings in a telephone booth. Its membership is now over 10,000, and all because those who are against women having the choice about whether they should or would have an abortion or not are mobilizing to change the board, and those who have worked for years so that women can have this choice are mobilizing to protect the board....

***

According to the law of the land, the general hospital, if it has a board, if it has an abortion committee, makes a decision about whether a woman meets the criteria established by law, which is that her health is in some kind of danger. That's all that VGH does; it has a committee which rules on these decisions. In addition, it has chosen to accept the United Nations' definition of health rather than the very limited and confining definition of health which some other hospitals use. Because of this, Vancouver General Hospital is under attack. Is the minister going to intervene or are we going to have to go through this battle year after year to ensure that the one hospital in this province which makes it possible for women to have a choice is going to continue to deliver that service? Once the board is elected, the board has the right to decide, as the board at St. Paul's Hospital and Grace Hospital and other hospitals have decided, that they will not allow women this choice. And the forces who are against choice, the anti-choice forces, are now mobilizing their resources to change the board of the Vancouver General Hospital.

***

There is no such thing as abortion on demand, or everybody having a right to have an abortion if her doctor decides that is best for her—or the woman and her doctor and her husband or whoever making that decision. The choice still rests with the hospital; they still make that decision. Despite that there is only one major hospital in this province which uses the United Nations' definition for health, which makes it possible for women to enjoy some degree of choice in this area. And the chances are that when the elections are fought this year, the forces on behalf of choice will win again; but there is also the possibility that they may lose. Then what happens if they do? If Vancouver General Hospital ceases to permit the performance of abortions, what happens to the women in this province who have decided for one reason or another whether through health or age or whatever that they would like to have an abortion? Are we going to go back to the kitchen table abortions? Are we going to go back to the clothes hangers? Is that the only option that's going to be open to the women of this province?

* * *

What is the minister going to do about that? The minister has the option to say that a hospital which presently delivers such a procedure cannot cease to do so regardless of what its board may decide; the minister has that option. But is the minister sufficiently concerned to exercise that option on behalf of VGH...?

Hon. Bob McClelland (Minister of Health): ...I am not looking forward, nor is the administration of Vancouver General Hospital looking forward, to their annual meeting, because we have had some indication that there are going to be a tremendous number of members at that meeting and we'll have to deal with that in one way or another.

* * *

I think that what I have to do as minister is just wait and see. If it proves at any point down the line that a hospital board is being operated on narrow interest lines, then I suppose the Ministry of Health has to take some action. But I don't see in any way how I can take action at this point when most of what we are talking about is speculation. I have talked with the board, and I've talked with the people involved on both sides as well, and I have appealed to them... to really take a look at what they are doing and make sure that...they...provide a total spectrum of health care for our people who are served by those hospitals. I can't do anything else, and I don't intend to do anything else...until we see what happens.

Despite this exchange and perhaps as a result of our intense activism in selling memberships, on August 11, 1978, the BC government dismissed the VGH board of trustees and appointed Peter Bazowski, a retired RCMP commanding officer for BC and the Yukon as public administrator for the hospital. For the BC government this appointment served two purposes, averting the potentially disastrous AGM and providing a mechanism for addressing the serious quality of care and training issues raised by nurses working at the hospital. To this day, abortion access is available at the Vancouver General Hospital.

QUEBECOISES DEBOUTTE![20]

Louise Desmarais
Translated by Martin Dufresne

No one could have foreseen that, on May 14, 1969, by enacting amendments to the *Criminal Code* that authorized abortion for therapeutic reasons, the Canadian Parliament would trigger a major conflict that arouses passionate debate to this day. As the results of a compromise aimed at protecting doctors already practising such abortions in hospitals and at countering the scourge of clandestine abortions, these amendments satisfied no one, neither those who consider abortion murder, nor those who see the law as a hijacking of their body. Thus, while anti-abortion activists set off on a "holy war" to have fetal rights acknowledged and protected from the moment of conception, feminist activists undertook a protracted struggle in favour of the right to "free and on demand" abortion. Despite being carried out in collaboration and solidarity with the Canadian pro-choice movement, Quebec's struggle was characterized by the primacy of its political dimension and its focus on quality and free abortion services throughout the province, delivered in the public health network and in women's health centres. Women activists managed to make abortion the basis of a feminist political discourse.

IN FAVOUR OF WOMEN'S POLITICAL RIGHT TO CHOOSE

From the early days of this struggle, while supporting Dr. Morgentaler in his legal disputes, women's activists from the non-mixed autonomous feminist groups, i.e., the Front de libération des femmes du Québec (FLFQ), the Centre des Femmes and the Comité de lutte pour la Contraception et l'avortement libres et gratuits (hereafter, the *Comité de lutte*), distanced themselves from him because they refused to reduce this battle to its legal dimension alone. Their analysis, both anti-patriarchal and anti-capitalist, acknowledged maternity and domestic work as the basis of women's exploitation. This entailed that they did not want to fight for the right of doctors to perform abortions, but for the right of women to abort. Adopted in 1974, this position proved decisive in guiding the Quebec struggle for the next decades. While denouncing the federal abortion law and demanding its removal from the *Criminal Code*, the Comité de lutte felt that it was of utmost importance to convince women that this struggle was political and that this right was not incidental, but an initial step and an essential condition for their liberation. It published a first manifesto in 1975, followed by a second in March 1977: *Nous aurons les enfants que nous voulons* (We will have the children we want). In April 1977, more than 2,000 women marched in Montreal streets. On the strength of this success, the Comité de lutte noted the urgency of delocalizing the struggle from Montreal and extending it to the whole of Quebec. In 1978, approximately one hundred women, including representatives of women's groups, as well as individual activists and trade union and community groups, heeded the call of the Comité de lutte and created the Coordination nationale pour l'avortement libre et gratuit (CNALG).

AN ADVANTAGEOUS JUDICIAL LULL

Following three acquittals of Dr. Morgentaler, the PQ government decided to stop all legal proceedings against him and not to apply the federal legislation in Quebec, which meant that doctors who practised illegal abortions (outside of hospitals and without the approval of a therapeutic abortion committee) could now do so with impunity. This judicial lull allowed the Comité de lutte and then the CNALG to concentrate their efforts on the political struggle and on access to abortion services. Concurrently, Quebec society, having broken with the Catholic Church, was experiencing an unprecedented period of social and political challenges, among which was the emergence of a new feminism whose fight for the right to abortion would become the priority.

From its inception, the CNALG intensified women's mobilization, with numerous demonstrations and public declarations. It denounced the shoddy state of abortion services and the inertia of the PQ government, accusing it of turning a deaf ear to women's demands. Following the partial failure of the Lazure clinics,[21] five local community service centres (CLSCs)[22] and the Montreal Women's Health Centre (MWHC) defied the government and began in 1981 to practise illegal abortions on MWHC premises. This act of disobedience facilitated a major breakthrough in access to abortion services in Quebec. The Comité de vigilance (Vigilance Committee),[23] which replaced the CNALG when it folded at the end of 1982, chose as its priority the development and consolidation of "free and on demand" abortion services in CLSCs and women's health centres. Thus, it refused in 1983 to campaign and raise funds for the opening of Dr. Morgentaler's clinics in Winnipeg and Vancouver.

A REGROUPING OF FORCES

Following their attendance at a meeting of the Ontario Coalition of Abortion Clinics in May 1985, and given the rise of the right in Canada and the United States, women activists from Quebec student associations, trade unions, political groups, and women's organizations acknowledged the urgency of retaking the offensive. They founded, in early 1986, the Coalition québécoise pour le droit à l'avortement libre et gratuit (CQDALG) (Quebec Coalition for the Right to Free and On Demand Abortion). The coalition immediately had to intervene against a judicial offensive of the pro-life movement levelled at the illegal practice of abortions in CLSCs. With local branches in most parts of Quebec and over two hundred members, it launched a vast mobilization to defend abortion services at the Saguenay-Nord, Le Norois, and Sainte-Thérèse CLSCs. Finally, bowing to these pressures, the provincial Liberal government's minister of justice, Herbert Marx, invoking the precedent established in 1976, ordered the cessation of court proceedings against CLSC physicians, as well as Dr. Morgentaler and Dr. MacHabée. The ensuing improvement in services offered within the public and community networks during the 1980s was due in large part to the willingness of abortion rights movement activists to collaborate in broad coalitions (CNALG and CQDALG) despite ideological and strategic differences. Building on the women's movement, which was then spreading like wildfire throughout Quebec, these coalitions succeeded in establishing a balance of power with the Quebec government. The radical nature of their political discourse, far from "scaring folks," spoke to women and rallied public opinion to their demands.

In the late 1980s, a first cycle of twenty years' struggle ended with three decisive victories. First, the historical Morgentaler decision of the Supreme Court of Canada, in January 1988, decriminalized abortion. This decision did not, however, change the situation in Quebec since abortion had been freely practised there since 1976. Then, in the summer of 1989, Quebec society mobilized in support of Chantale Daigle, who defied a court injunction forbidding her to have an abortion. Ten thousand women took to the streets, chanting, "No pope, no judge, no doctor, no spouse, it's up to women to decide." The Supreme Court vindicated this young woman by finding no basis for rights of the fetus nor of the father. Finally, the Canadian and Quebec pro-choice movement rose to the barricades in 1991 to prevent a recriminalization of abortion by the federal government, a wager it won against all odds through an equally split vote in the Senate. The early 1990s inaugurated a second twenty-year cycle, characterized by a defensive mode, in a political context increasingly dominated by a conservative, moral, and religious right. However, this failed to prevent a few additional victories.

SOMEWHAT OF A DEMOBILIZATION

Out of breath and still feeling the shock of the December 6, 1989, École Polytechnique Massacre, but above all convinced that the problem was resolved, Quebec's pro-choice movement experienced something of a demobilization. It devoted most of its energy to monitoring the accessibility of services, which were declining in the public health network; in 1992, more than one-third of all services were being provided by community and private resources, for which women had to pay. The debate surrounding the introduction of the RU-486 abortion pill in Canada sharply divided Quebec's pro-choice movement, which predominantly opposed it, while doctors practising abortions were rather supportive. In 1995, a coalition of some sixty organizations alerted the population by strongly denouncing Human Life International, a US anti-abortion, homophobic, racist, and antisemitic organization that was holding a convention in Montreal. This response, supported by media pundits, proved a major blow to anti-abortion forces in Quebec. For their part, five private clinics, under the leadership of Dr. Morgentaler, ceaselessly lobbied Quebec's various ministers of health and social services between 1995 and 2000 for a full reimbursement of abortions performed in Quebec, but to no avail. The dissolution in 1997 of the CQDALG marked the end of the broad permanent coalitions, and also that of major feminist debates around abortion.

SOME OTHER VICTORIES

During the 2000s, the Canadian anti-abortion movement expanded, while that of Quebec was almost moribund. In Ottawa, MPs of a "pro-life caucus" undertook a legislative offensive, tabling seventeen bills in the House of Commons between 2001 and 2010. Of these, Bill C-484 produced a significant mobilization of pro-choice forces, with media and medical corporations joining in to denounce the proposed legislation. Activists distributed leaflets, held press conferences, signed petitions, and organized a demonstration that was attended by more than 5,000 women. The bill died on the order paper because of a federal election call. In 2001, the Quebec government significantly funded abortion services, which made it possible to catch up and ensure their consolidation. Then, in 2006, the Quebec Superior Court upheld a class action suit against the Quebec government by the Association pour l'accès à l'avortement (AAA) (Association for Access to Abortion), which brought together private clinics and the MWHC. Abortions practised in Quebec private clinics and women's health centres would now be free of charge, ending thirty years of inequity for women.

In 2009, Quebec women's health centres refused to privatize and transform into specialized medical clinics (SMCs). They fiercely defended their autonomous practice, their feminist approach, and their status as non-profit community organizations. Finally, with the support of the official opposition in the national assembly, the Council on the Status of Women, and the labour unions, they were successful. During the 2000 decade, the pro-choice movement benefited from the leadership of the Fédération du Québec pour le planning des naissances (FQPN) (Quebec Federation for Family Planning), in conjunction with the Fédération des femmes du Québec (FFQ) (Quebec Women's Federation), who monitored the accessibility of abortion services. They now enjoy a balance of power established with the state by the feminist and pro-choice movement in the 1980s, a public opinion favourable to free choice and a marginalized anti-abortion movement.

Thus, for more than forty years, Quebec activists led this political struggle, without ever planting a bomb at the national assembly, nor murdering a single anti-abortion activist, with only their pencils and the force of their convictions as weapons. Today we have every reason to be proud because we have achieved the objectives we set for ourselves in 1970: abortion is decriminalized, women no longer die in Quebec from clandestine abortions, and they can decide to freely interrupt a pregnancy and abort in full safety, free of charge, throughout Quebec's forty-eight service delivery points.²⁴ This record is impressive, but although the situation is enviable, it remains fragile: history teaches us that our gains are not irreversible and that it is better for our health never to forget that!

This article is an excerpt from the conclusion of La bataille de l'avortement. Chronique québécoise *(The Battle for Abortion: A Quebec Chronicle) (Montreal: Les Éditions du remue-ménage, 2016) with some modifications.*

POLICE! THE RAID ON THE TORONTO MORGENTALER CLINIC

Andrea Fochs Knight

We all knew that this was going to be the day. I arrived early that morning, but early as I was, the media were already there. The air was filled with a mixture of tension, excitement, anticipation, and dread.

It was July 5, 1983, and the Toronto Morgentaler Clinic had only been operating for three weeks. My job, as a member of the Ontario Coalition for Abortion Clinic's Clinic Defense Committee, was to get to a phone as quickly as possible in the event of a police raid and activate the emergency phone tree. There were no cell phones then.

The clinic occupied the second and third floors of the narrow semi-detached red-brick house at 85 Harbord Street. On the ground floor was the Toronto Women's Bookstore.

I had gotten there at 9:00 a.m., even though the clinic wasn't due to open until 11:00. As time passed, the media started to get restless. I had butterflies in my stomach but I was calm. A few other members of OCAC showed up and we sat on the steps of the house next door, waiting. No e-mail to check, no Twitter feeds, no Facebook.

We didn't see any of the staff or patients arrive—they went in through the back entrance off Robert Street to avoid any scrutiny. There were no protesters then since the anti-choice organizations were still confident that the police and the courts would shut down the clinic for them.

"Maybe our information was wrong," one of my comrades said. "Maybe it isn't going to happen today."

"Well," I replied, "the media clearly got the same memo or they wouldn't all be here."

A few minutes before noon, a tall, good-looking, conservatively dressed, thirty-something couple hurried along the sidewalk and up the five wooden steps to the front entrance of the clinic, their faces filled with tension and resolution.

"I guess that they didn't know to go in the back," I said.

In response to the doorbell, the clinic receptionist opened the door just a crack and carried on a low, urgent conversation with the man. I couldn't hear what they were saying, but a few moments later she opened the door and let them in. When the door closed behind them, we all went back to our vigil.

About twenty minutes later, Harbord Street erupted. The street turned into a canary yellow river as police cars streamed toward us east and west along Harbord Street and south down Spadina. There must have been hundreds of them, along with three ambulance buses. Not ambulances—BUSES. Not one but three.

What the hell were they expecting? I thought as I dove into the women's bookstore, hurtled past startled customers, and ran into the office to use the phone. When the first person on my list answered, I yelled, "It's happening! Make your calls and get down here!"

All around me I could hear the deafening tread of police boots as they charged up the inside stairs and thundered up the iron fire escape just outside the office window. CLANG! CLANG! BANG! THUD! The din seemed to go on forever as they swarmed the building.

I finished making my calls and then pushed my way back out onto Harbord Street. At least a dozen cops were blocking the front of the building but I was able to slip through. There were already fifty to a hundred pro-choice supporters out front. Soon there were two hundred and then five hundred—the crowd just kept growing until the street was full of people singing and chanting, "NOT THE CHURCH AND NOT THE STATE! WOMEN MUST CONTROL OUR FATE!"

For a while it was hard to tell what was happening inside. After about an hour, the cops started coming out the front carrying boxes, removing everything that wasn't nailed down—files, medical supplies, and equipment, even office supplies. The pro-choice crowd had completely blocked their path so the cops had to pick their way through, carrying their "evidence" high above their heads.

"We may not be able to stop you," we shouted at them, "but we're sure as hell not going to make it easy."

Dr. Morgentaler wasn't in the clinic that day, but about three hours after the raid started, the police hustled Dr. Robert Scott, the operating physician, out the front door and into a police car. Most of the police left then—as did the ambulance buses and the media. Dr. Scott was being taken to 51 Division to be formally charged and all the pro-choice supporters decided to move the demonstration there.

Suddenly, the street was empty. A few cops were still inside looking for evidence and I didn't feel right about abandoning the clinic to them. Two other women—Linda Gardiner and Sandy Fox—stayed behind with me.

We learned later that the couple we had seen go in the front door had been undercover cops. They had begged the receptionist to let them in without an appointment and once inside, they had triggered the raid.

The patients had been allowed to leave down the back fire escape almost as soon as the raid began. One woman had been on the operating table but the nurses had barricaded the door until everything was safe for the patient. One of the nurses almost got pushed over the third-floor railing in the process.

The staff was held for about three hours and then allowed to leave by the back. None of them was charged.

When the last of the cops finally came out, it was close to six in the evening. There were still only the three of us left outside the clinic then. One of the cops approached us and said, politely, "Excuse me. We're required by law to turn the keys to the building over to someone in charge. We cannot leave the building unsecured."

How ironic.

I took the keys from him without a word, planning to return them to the staff the next morning. But the staff never returned and the clinic didn't resume operations until Dr. Morgentaler and Dr. Scott were acquitted by a jury eighteen months later.

I still have those keys.

THE LAST BASTION: ABORTION ACCESS
IN PRINCE EDWARD ISLAND

Colleen MacQuarrie, Ann Wheatley, and Anne Mazer

Reproductive justice has long included abortion as part of women's ancient history. In every culture and corner of the world, women have been helping women with pregnancies—wanted and unwanted—with giving birth, with miscarriages, with raising children, their own and others', and with raising their children's children. Abortion has always been as much a part of the fabric of women's lives as any other aspect of reproductive health and care. The long road to abortion access and reproductive justice in Prince Edward Island (PEI) is a story of women's struggle for human rights and dignity, for voice, and for freedom from control from patriarchal systems of church or state in Canada.

Canada's only island province is also the smallest and most densely populated one with approximately 145,000 people living in small towns and villages on approximately a million acres of land. PEI is remarkable not only for its agricultural and fishing traditions but also for its picturesque landscape that seems to be marked with a church every few kilometres. More than 95 per cent of the population is religiously affiliated; half are governed under the Roman Catholic Diocese of Charlottetown, which comprises the entire province and is the second oldest English diocese in Canada. And, of course, it also promotes traditional heterosexual roles for women. The geography and politics of PEI created a climate ripe for anti-abortionists to assert power over women's reproductive lives, and they were especially prominent in the 1970s. Anti-abortion powers remained impervious to the 1988 Morgentaler ruling that decriminalized abortion in Canada. PEI illustrates how a province can frustrate a federal law to subvert the constitution, since provinces have the authority to regulate abortion access through their jurisdiction over matters of health. So while the Morgentaler ruling was meant to, in the words of Justice Bertha Wilson, ensure women's right to "life, liberty, and security," PEI shirked its responsibility for women's human rights, and women's health care, through their denial of abortion access within the province.

The lack of attention to human rights for women is exacerbated by intersecting lines of oppression through class inequality and class privilege. In PEI, those with connections and money were able to secure abortions by leaving; those without money or connections were harmed further by the barriers to abortion access. A lack of knowledge about where or how to secure a pregnancy termination combined with a lack of resources and supports so that poorer, rural, isolated women were most at risk from unwanted pregnancies.

THERAPEUTIC ABORTION COMMITTEES — THE SITE OF CONFLICT

Prior to 1988 the Prince County Hospital in Summerside and Prince Edward Island Hospital in Charlottetown had both established Therapeutic Abortion Committees (TACs) after an amendment of the *Criminal Code* in 1969. At the time of the Morgentaler ruling, the PEI Hospital and Health Services Commission was vested under public law with broad authority to determine what types of care and procedures qualified as fundable Medicare services as stipulated in their *Health Services Payment (HSP) Act* Regulations of PEI. However, individual hospitals acting through their elected boards had the authority to determine which specific services they would provide.

It was at these individual hospital boards that the PEI Right to Life Association, in the early 1980s, targeted women's access to abortion. The construction of a single hospital in the capital city of Charlottetown resulted in the amalgamation of the Catholic and Protestant hospital boards (the Catholic hospital had not permitted the establishment of a TAC while the Protestant hospital board had). A rancorous, protracted public battle over the establishment of a TAC and provision of abortion services ensued, threatening the viability of the equipment drive for the new hospital. In April 1980, the chancellor of the Roman Catholic Diocese of Charlottetown, Reverend Eric Dunn, announced that he did "not intend to contribute to the fund until the board of Queen

Elizabeth Hospital (QEH) made known its decision about the abortion committee."

Many Islanders agreed with this tactical measure and either withheld support from the equipment fund or added a condition to their financial pledges that stated if the QEH went ahead with the TAC, these pledges would not be honoured. The anti-choice strategy was to eliminate the pregnant woman and her reproductive health concerns from consideration while using emotive and sensational language to inspire a misogynist climate where reproductive rights were cast in a criminal light. Women active in the movement for choice often recall how vilified they felt during this time.

After more than a year of debate over the issue of implementing a TAC at the new hospital in the provincial capital, the board of directors released the set of proposed bylaws that supported the formation of a TAC. On June 25, 1981, the hospital held its annual general meeting (AGM) where the membership of the hospital corporation was given the opportunity to vote to accept or reject the proposed bylaw. Because of this controversial issue, the membership of the new hospital corporation had exploded from two hundred in the spring of 1980 to more than 3,000 by the date of the AGM. The cost to join the corporation was set at $1 to ensure that individuals interested in this issue would be able to participate and groups from all sides of the debates urged Island residents to become voting members of the corporation through letters to the editor, newspaper advertisements, and word of mouth. The local chapter of Canadian Abortion Rights Action League (CARAL) ran a candidate for the board who was not elected.

Women who supported the formation of a TAC attended the meeting to speak up about the importance of this service. Anne Taylor-Murray recalls that meeting:

> I was there at that first meeting. The original idea was to offer abortion services. But, when the Roman Catholic Church got wind of this they mobilized all their parishes to send busloads of people. The public meeting had to be moved to the old Forum hockey arena to house everyone. I was fairly new to the Island at that time so didn't know the women who had planned to speak up for the inclusion of abortion services. But what I do remember was my horror at the behaviour of those who later called themselves the "Right

to Life" movement. They shouted down the women who were trying to speak in favour of abortion services. I felt as though I was attending a gathering of fascists in Nazi Germany. I went home quite shaken wondering what kind of a society I had chosen to live in. My whole British training of "fair play" had been trampled upon! What an about-face for a church whose doctrine had always been that babies were born in "sin." Only baptism by one of their priests could rescue them from a life of hell. Suddenly these fetuses were sacred!

ONGOING CONFLICT

Katrina Ackerman, a historian of abortion, notes that the 1970s and early 1980s was a time of struggle within many mainstream women's organizations. Many remained silent on the abortion question in an attempt to remain neutral, which impeded the efforts of CARAL and other local pro-choice organizations to improve access to abortion services. Indeed, the Planned Parenthood chapter in PEI faced relentless struggles to keep its doors open and eventually closed in 1983.

The PEI Advisory Council on the Status of Women Council (ACSW) president, Margaret Ashford, was not able to take a stand due to different views within the organization. In a letter to Patricia LeGraw, president of Planned Parenthood Association of PEI, on April 8, 1980, Maureen Malloy, executive assistant of the PEI ACSW explained with "regret" that "since the Council cannot reach a general agreement on this issue, the Council will not write a letter to the Board of Directors of the new hospital in support of or against the establishment of a therapeutic abortion committee." She continued to explain how the "issue was discussed and debated at length but the personal convictions of the members were expressed as unalterable." She concluded that it was up to individual "members of the Council who support the establishment of a therapeutic abortion committee" to "write letters of support to the Board of Directors of the Queen Elizabeth Hospital." Thus a key leader in women's equality rights was muted on the issue.

The 1981 vote at the AGM of the QEH marked a major turning point in PEI abortion access. Motivated by their victory, opponents of abortion were keen to completely eradicate provincial abortion access by targeting the last remaining TAC in the province. Largely represented by the Right to Life Association, they lobbied relentlessly for the Summerside hospital to abolish its TAC. Over a span of approximately five years, the Right to Life Association used varied tactics including detailed profiling of bylaws and membership procedures of the hospital, showing emotive films depicting the horror of abortion to schools and in church groups, circulating briefs and eliciting the support of prominent politicians to promote their perspectives. The Right to Life Association focused on the anti-abortion vote within the Prince County Hospital corporation, where hospital membership and board of directors held jurisdiction over the maintenance of a TAC.

At the annual meetings of the Prince County Hospital from 1982 to 1986, the PEI Right to Life Association raised the issue of the TAC, forcing a vote on whether the committee should be disbanded. The organization actively recruited anti-abortion Island residents to join the Prince County Hospital's membership by launching a series of newspaper advertisements entitled "Let the Unborn Speak for Themselves." Not surprisingly, this attempt to dislodge the remaining TAC was challenged by abortion rights advocates across the province.

ORGANIZING RESISTANCE

In 1985, in the midst of the blitz by the Right To Life Association, three women—Alice Crook, J'Nan Brown, and Jennifer Brown—created a provincial chapter of the Canadian Abortion Rights Action League (CARAL). Working collectively they built a resistance movement to challenge the RTLA by writing letters to the editor of local newspapers and publishing articles in women's magazines. They, together with several of their membership, attended the Prince County Hospital AGM in 1986. Alice Crook recalls:

> I certainly remember June 3, 1986, at the PCH. I was 7 months pregnant when I spoke that night in favour of keeping the TAC. It was the only TAC on the Island—because none was established at the new QEH (a bitter fight during the merger). The vote at PCH was to get rid of the TAC, and the vast numbers of people bussed in were entitled to vote because they (or their parishes) had paid a small membership fee ($5 I

think) as had the small group of "us" who had
also paid so as to vote.

The PEI ACSW was able to weigh in with a more pro-choice
opinion at this time. ACSW chair Dianne Porter's September
25, 1985, memo to Premier Ghiz informed executive council of
their position paper on therapeutic abortion and their interest in
moving away from "polarized views." In the memo, ACSW reiter-
ates "that therapeutic abortion is a complex issue, one that involves
personal, moral, religious, judicial, and medical implications." The
PEI ACSW was still not advocating for abortion on demand in
these pre-Morgentaler years, however they put forward five clear
position statements in this memo including the clear need for
"medically approved, therapeutic abortion in PEI" and the need
"for the Premier to discuss with the Federal Government possible
changes to the *Criminal Code* and the *Canada Health Act* to ensure
access for all PEI women to this medical service." This significant
shift toward more pro-choice advocacy marked a turning point in
abortion politics within the PEI ACSW.

Despite the abortion rights activism, the Prince County
Hospital 1986 Annual General Meeting voted to remove the TAC.
PEI officially became the only Canadian province without a legal
capacity to perform abortions.

Two years later hope surged among abortion activists with the
1988 Morgentaler Supreme Court of Canada ruling: The law governing abortion in the *Criminal Code* was unconstitutional. The
local news filled with confident declarations that abortions would
be available in PEI. Alice Crook, a member of the PEI chapter of
CARAL, stated that if a woman wanted to have an abortion on
the Island and had a doctor willing to do the operation, there was
nothing that could stop it from proceeding. The 1988 decision may
have opened possibilities for abortion services across the country,
but it never resulted in legislation guaranteeing access to abortion
services for Canadian women.

In February 1988, the PEI government announced it would
fund abortion services only in Island hospitals and the abortion
must be declared medically necessary. The government coyly left
the decision to perform abortions up to the hospitals' boards of directors. Justice Minister Wayne Cheverie was unconcerned about
what hospitals would do but that they would govern themselves.
In the end the province's hospitals chose to keep their anti-abortion
policies since it was the path that appeared less divisive. Illustrative
of this is the sentiment from Wayne Carew, executive director

of the Prince County Hospital, that the history of the abortion debate had caused more conflict than it was worth to reinvigorate the issue and upset community interests. One might wonder if this was the provincial government's strategy from the outset. Certainly a provincial government could have created access to abortion through requiring the hospitals to provide these services, but they abdicated that responsibility and completely ignored women's right to accessible abortion services within the province.

In the week following the Morgentaler ruling, PEI's attorney general stated he had not received a lot of calls from Islanders pressuring the government to take a stand one way or the other. Within a month, on February 25, 1988, the Charlottetown *Guardian* published a half-page letter signed by 167 "Islanders for Choice." It read:

> We, the undersigned, wish to express our support for the recent Supreme Court Decision on abortion, which states that abortion should be a private matter between a woman and her physician. Our provincial government's recently announced intention to set up a committee, to evaluate a woman's request for an abortion with regard to payment, defies the spirit and the letter of the Court's judgement, in addition to the principle of universality of health care in this country. We deplore the efforts of the Queen Elizabeth and Prince County Hospital Boards to block access, by refusing to grant hospital privileges for this medical procedure to physicians who wish to act in accordance with the Supreme Court of Canada.

The committee referred to by the petitioners was a committee of five physicians who would be appointed to review claims made by women for reimbursement of the costs of abortions obtained in hospitals outside Prince Edward Island.

At the end of March and continuing into April of 1988, the members of the PEI legislative assembly publicly formed a resolution on abortion calling for legislation to protect the fetus. Although the accompanying debate and deliberation was not included in the *Journal of the Legislative Assembly of Prince Edward Island*, Resolution 17 itself was revealing in that it clearly valued the life of the fetus above that of the pregnant woman. An amendment was added as almost an afterthought wherein under rare circumstances might abortion be allowed to save the life of the woman. Resolution 17 on abortion made clear to the residents of Prince Edward Island as well as to the entire country that the legislative assembly in its entirety, the provincial government and the opposition, agreed that PEI should remain an anti-abortion province. Further they believed this resolution should be embraced at the federal level. Members from CARAL sat in the balcony of the legislative assembly to bear witness to the proceedings. Anne Mazer recalls the anger in the face of one MLA. "She was totally unsupportive and we were very disappointed, being that she was a woman."

The feminist community was creating significant momentum post-Morgentaler. When the PEI Standing Committee on Health and Social Services held public consultations, Women's Network organized a mass presentation. On April 12, 1988, carloads of women descended on the Coles building to present their realities. As Anne Mazer explains,

> I told my story. In great detail. It was very empowering, looking at all these men's faces around that room, and using words like "vagina" and so on. It was very empowering, looking them right in the eye, and saying, "There are women in your lives who have had abortions; you just don't know about them." So we gathered, I think, 23 women that day who had had an abortion for all kinds of reasons, or knew of women who had had one, and sat in the audience and said, "There's a woman in this room who had an abortion after being raped, there's a woman in this room who had an abortion for—" you know, listed all of those. And then I told my story in detail, and their faces were just...(stone-faced)... but we all went out holding our heads up and felt empowered by that, so even though votes weren't changed, women were strengthened by it, and probably told their story again, and the world doesn't fall apart when you tell your story, and I don't think we were disheartened by it; it was just predictable. And almost laughable, you know, you look up there and there's a whole horseshoe of men in suits.

The PEI ACSW became vocal in its dissent from the PEI gov-ernment. On May 5, 1988, the council approved a new position paper on abortion, which aligned with the Morgentaler decision that abortion services must be free and accessible to women in PEI, and they affirmed the Canadian Medical Association policy that abortion is a decision between a woman and her doctor and recognized the World Health Organization's definition of health. They recommended that all elected officials, at the provincial and federal levels, receive information and education in the various complexities of the abortion issues.

But the women of the ACSW also understood that polarizing the issue was harming women and they needed more evidence to show the complexity of thought in the PEI populace. To facilitate knowledge and discussion, the ACSW commissioned a survey to measure attitudes toward health and social services provision in the province with a particular focus on AIDS, domestic violence, family planning, and abortion. They hired Baseline Market Research (BMR) to create and conduct a telephone survey of five hundred households across the province. This initiative created the first substantial opinion data in the province on issues as health care funding for abortions, freestanding abortion clinics, and correlations between positions on abortion and religious beliefs, age, education, and residency in the province. Not only did a majority of PEI residents support a woman's access to abortion in certain circumstances, but the general population did not see their opinion adequately reflected by anti-abortion nor pro-abortion ideas. Most residents stated they were neither pro-choice nor anti-choice in their views—however they recognize that certain situations may require the use of abortion services. It was a common refrain of contentious issues that the nuances were lost in the news coverage. A simplistic binary argument had been created through media and perhaps perpetuated in provincial government circles, but the evidence showed a much wider diversity of opinions on abortion in the population.

This simplistic conversation rippled into conversations with elected officials and cabinet ministers. At various moments throughout the late eighties and continuing through to the 2000s, politicians, elected representatives, and key government officials would declare and whisper to pro-choice groups that they were personally pro-choice but they could not act in congruence with that as a public figure. It was insulting and negligent behaviour that was repeated any time someone who was responsible for upholding women's rights acted to undermine them. Personal

opinions could not substitute for political actions. One stunning
example, as the ACSW gained voice in opposing PEI's anti-abortion position, the minister responsible for the status of women
took the unprecedented move of assigning a seat on the council
for REAL Women, a vocal anti-abortion group. In response, the
incoming chair of the PEI ACSW, Colleen MacQuarrie initiated
a council policy discussion that resulted in an official unequivocal
pro-choice policy enabling the ACSW to work ever more openly
and actively toward re-establishing abortion care in the province.

WHAT WERE WOMEN DOING?

Since the eradication of abortion access in PEI, each year at least
170 women were forced to leave the province for safe surgical
abortions and to sustain large bills as a result. Depending on the
era examined, travel varied and it was not unusual for women
to travel to Boston, Montreal, Toronto, or as far as Vancouver.
Hundreds went to Halifax to either the Victoria General Hospital
or to the private Morgentaler Clinic while it was operating (1990–
2003). Hundreds journeyed an equal distance to the Fredericton
Morgentaler Clinic until its doors closed (1994–2015). Travel was
a choice unavailable to low-income or younger women without
family support. A provincial policy approved an average of just
six women per year from 1991 to 1995 for reimbursement of the
costs of their abortions performed at the Halifax Victoria General
Hospital. At no point in this history have Atlantic regions provided later term access; women were required to travel to Ontario
and Quebec for later-term abortions at their own expense.

During the 1980s a Planned Parenthood office operated in
PEI. Planned Parenthood Canada underwrote this service, but as
one of their former employees recounts:

> There was no way for Planned Parenthood PEI
> to get its own money, and money was a con-
> tinuous problem. Finally, Planned Parenthood
> Canada fell on hard times so they didn't have
> any money to offer...unless there was a lot of
> support in the community already, they [offices]
> closed. And that's what happened here. So, there
> was no support or anything from the Province,
> there never ever would have been. Sometimes we
> got little contracts—like when I developed the
> sex education for people with mental challenges,

we got paid for that, and there was an attempt at one point for Planned Parenthood to actually do something to raise its own money, and so they opened a flower shop, which still exists! It's called Hearts and Flowers...the idea was that they would be this business, and the profit from the business would go into supporting Planned Parenthood.

Loss of funding spelled the end of the service but while they operated, they were a key part of how women gained information. This former employee described how abortion at the time involved a flight to Montreal.

We provided all the information, but they had to come up with the money. I just remember this one really distinctly. She just didn't have any money and I remember her so clearly, when I told her what she had to do, she just burst into tears. She was young, maybe eighteen, maybe not even that much. I knew some people here in the province who were kind of friendly toward this struggle, and so, they had said, "If there's ever anything we can do to help..." and so I said, "Oh, here you go, here's something you can do." I had a friend in Montreal at that time who went and got her, and took her to the clinic, stayed with her, and took her back made sure she got on the plane. And she came back. You know, she was very, very, very grateful, and I was very pleased that everything conspired to work out for her.... But generally, you know, you'd go through the whole thing and explain to people what it was going to cost, you know, the cost of the plane and everything like that, and they just did it, because it was important to them, they needed it, or they wanted it, or—so, that's just how it went.

From their inception throughout the long struggle of losing abortion access, pro-choice activists continued to work toward re-matriating abortion care to PEI. A chapter of CARAL counted among its membership over one hundred paid supporters from PEI. Ann Wheatley recalls, "In the early days, we were a real community of pro-choice activists, with purpose. Over the years, there were fewer people involved. But at the beginning, it was a true collective." The efforts of the (CARAL-PEI) group were divided between advocacy and public engagement, and supporting women who were travelling off-Island for abortions. CARAL-PEI regularly communicated with policy-makers about the crucial work they were doing to support women's access to safe abortion. They repeatedly asked the province to provide better public access.

During federal and provincial election campaigns, CARAL-PEI sent surveys to candidates. They compiled responses to share with the public through newsletters and media releases. On a regular basis, CARAL collected up-to-date information about abortion services in other provinces and sent it to Island doctors, whom they also canvassed to determine their willingness to make referrals to off-Island hospitals, and to see women for post-abortion check-ups. Members of CARAL ran an Abortion Information Line (telephone service) from prior to 1990 through to 2006. Ann Wheatley recalls this essential work.

> I responded to many calls for many years. Women would call the information line to ask for information about abortion services and also to ask for financial help. Backed by several dozen very generous Islanders, we raised a lot of money for women to travel off-Island and pay for their abortions. That became a really important function of our group. Many of the women felt they couldn't talk about their decision with anybody else. They felt so alone. It was always an important conversation; something they didn't want to talk about with their families or with their friends.
>
> But, I found that on occasion a woman would decide at some point to talk to a friend or talk to a parent, and would be surprised by the reception they got. They felt supported, when they expected to be rejected. They were so afraid, so fearful of telling somebody, when they finally did they were quite surprised. When people who might have been publicly anti-choice were called on to support their daughter, their sister, or their

friend in this decision, they were able to suspend their opposition and be supportive.

Alice Crook described CARAL-PEI's Day of Action in October, 1989, in response to the PEI RTLA's demonstration. She documented that sixty-five women, children, and men gathered on the steps of Province House, where an Australian visitor sang, "The Backyard Abortion Waltz" by Robyn Archer. The CARAL group marched through downtown Charlottetown and through the anti-choice gathering, singing, "Choice is the right of every woman, and we are singing, singing, for our lives." Afterward, they circulated a petition calling for safe abortion access for PEI residents and sent it off to Prime Minister Brian Mulroney, MP Catherine Callbeck, and Premier Joe Ghiz.

An April 10, 1990 newsletter illuminates the ongoing efforts and the toll it was taking on the activists at the forefront. We learn that "On February 27th Carol Chapman and J'Nan Brown made a submission to the Hospital Role Panel which resulted in the 1990 Rossiter Report. In the submission they emphasized that women on PEI should have access to abortion within their own medical community." A letter written to PEI ACSW from the Victoria General Hospital in the adjacent province of Nova Scotia says that 142 women from PEI had abortions there from 1986 to 1990. CARAL documented that women were also travelling to Montreal, Boston, and Toronto.

PEI CARAL activities included fundraising but also organizing and training activities. For example on March 31, 1990, they participated in a day-long meeting in Halifax in collaboration with their sister organizations in New Brunswick and Nova Scotia, where Kit Holmwood, national coordinator for CARAL spoke about Bill C-43. In 1990, after much resistance and court action by the NS government, Dr. Morgentaler had opened a clinic in Nova Scotia to which Island women had been journeying. CARAL member J'Nan Brown writes of a journey she took to support Dr. Morgentaler's Clinic in Nova Scotia:

On June 4th, 1990, the day the court case against Dr. Henry Morgentaler reopened, my daughter, Jennifer, my eight-month-old grandson, Alyre, and I travelled to Halifax. We were going to present a blanket to Dr. Henry Morgentaler on behalf of Island women. We drove through heavy rain showers on the way there. It was a cool, damp, and drizzly day when we arrived in Halifax. A group of about 25 pro-choice supporters were on hand for the presentation that took place on the steps of the Nova Scotia provincial courthouse. Dr. Morgentaler expressed his thanks, made a statement to the media and left the courthouse with his lawyer, Anne Derrick. Walking away from the courthouse in the rain, Dr. Morgentaler unfolded the blanket and wrapped it around his shoulders. Moments later he took it off and wrapped it around Anne's shoulders.

The blanket, woven by Island weaver, Lynn Douglas, is a gift to the Morgentaler Clinic in Halifax. It is a symbol of the care and compassion that Morgentaler and his clinics' staff have given to women. It is also a symbol of CARAL PEI's continuing support for the opening of a clinic in Halifax. Historically, Island women have had to travel to Montreal or Boston to have an abortion. The clinic in Halifax will provide access to this legal medical procedure within an easier travelling distance. Until we can have access to abortion within our own medical community the clinic in Halifax offers the best option.

During the drive back to PEI my daughter and I reflected on the day's event. We talked about how grateful we were to Dr. Morgentaler, grateful that he has been willing over the years to take the issue of choice for women through the courts. We agreed that despite Justice Minister Kim Campbell's assurance that with the passing of bill C-43 the problem of access would be solved, it would probably be necessary to take our provincial government or the PEI hospitals to court. And we smiled at the thought that Alyre had attended his first demonstration.

This illuminates how passionate the CARAL members were in their purpose to support women and their reproductive rights, but also their sense of reproductive justice as women connected to supportive communities. A strong community advocate for women's health and dignity throughout this time, Women's Network of

PEI claimed an urgent need for Planned Parenthood's birth control information "because PEI has one of the country's highest rates of teen pregnancy." The network published a magazine called *Common Ground*; this magazine was a way to create ongoing community support and was an effective tool for abortion and reproductive justice theorizing, organizing, and advocacy.

Among the many supporters of choice in the PEI community was Jean McKay, who periodically sent letters of thanks to CARAL and letters of protest to various government representatives. In one of those letters, written in 1996, Ms McKay addresses Premier Keith Milligan (copies were sent to opposition leaders). "At the age of 76 I have no need for the service but I am strongly pro-choice and believe that women must have the freedom to make the choice that will impact on their whole future lives."

CARAL PEI met with Dr. Morgentaler's lawyer, Anne Derrick, in 1994 to support the return of abortion services. The numbers of Island women journeying to his clinics in other provinces prompted the abortion hero, Henry Morgentaler, to act. In 1994 Anne Derrick argued on his behalf that the *HSP Act* Regulations of PEI denying payment for therapeutic abortions unless the Health and Community Services Agency "determined that such abortion was medically necessary and performed in a hospital" overextended the province's jurisdiction, and that doctor's fees in his clinics should also be covered. The judge ruled in favour of Morgentaler, pointing out that the regulations "severely restricted payment for a necessary medical service and effectively prohibited abortions." However, celebrations were cut short in 1996 when the case was overturned on appeal at the PEI Supreme Court when it ruled that the *HSP Act* could restrict payment for abortion services if they failed to meet the requirements of the regulations.

In 1995, as the appeal was making its way to the high court, quietly behind closed doors, the PEI government negotiated an agreement to pay for abortion procedures when women were referred to the Queen Elizabeth II Health Sciences Centre (QEII) in Halifax, Nova Scotia. Under the new policy, women needed referral by an Island physician to a physician in QEII, be less than fifteen weeks pregnant, have had an ultrasound, and not have a previous referral for abortion. It was a small victory for choice, but it was kept hushed. Women had been referred there for years, but this was an agreement to cover procedure costs without women having to request reimbursement. Unconscionably, the government refused to educate the public on how they could access abortion services through the public health system. Throughout the years, pro-choice advocates petitioned government to make this information public but were ignored.

This era was critical in Canadian and Island history. The activism was directed predominantly by citizens, mostly women, toward governments whose positions on abortion were against our human rights. Federally, there have been numerous anti-abortion bills introduced in Parliament. For example, in 1990, Progressive Conservative Prime Minister Brian Mulroney introduced and passed Bill C-43 in the House of Commons—this would see a two-year jail sentence for doctors performing abortions where a woman's health was not at risk. The bill was defeated in the Senate after a tie vote.

PEI politicians have been spectacularly united against women's demands for abortion access. In 2010 a new *Health Act* reorganized PEI's health system and abrogated the ability of individual hospitals to determine which services they would provide, thus cancelling their authority to formally adopt a no-abortion policy. As a result, at least in theory, it seemed possible that an individual physician could terminate a pregnancy in PEI since no individual hospital policy formally prohibited it. However, the premier and the health minister stated publicly that they wanted to preserve the "status quo" on abortions, meaning that they did not want abortions available within the province. Taking their cue from the government's anti-abortion position, the newly formed Health PEI refused to allow re-matriation of abortion care despite legal, economic, and health arguments supporting the provision of this service within the province.

POSTSCRIPT AND VICTORY

The year 2010 marked a major turning point in PEI activism. In September 2010, "Understanding for a Change" launched as a community-based collaborative research project led by Colleen MacQuarrie at the University of Prince Edward Island to address the policy prohibiting abortion access in the province. This project drew from women's experiences trying to access abortion in order to provide critical insights into the violation of women's human rights in PEI. The evidence from this project contributed to societal and political change and formed key evidence for a court case challenging PEI's abortion policy and a victory for abortion access in the province.

On March 31, 2016, the PEI government committed to re-matriating abortion care and announced plans to open a new women's reproductive clinic in Summerside at the Prince County Hospital; by all appearances they have decided to embrace abortion rights. Ending this oppression was the result of a dogged commitment to exposing violations of human rights and using every possible avenue to educate the population about injustice. What changed in PEI politics from the Resolution 17 response to the 1988 Morgentaler ruling through to the determined denial of abortion access up until the eventual shifting of regulations to allow local access to abortion? It took a community of activism to expose the injustices so relentlessly and so effectively that there was little political will to fight against Abortion Access Now PEI when they partnered with Legal Education Action Fund Canada. Ultimately, it was a fight the politicians recognized that they could not win in the courts or in the court of public opinion. Decades of activism and education endured in the struggle against oppression and finally brought PEI into line with the rest of Canada.

CONTRACEPTION

WHAT IT WAS LIKE BEFORE THE PILL

Michele Landsberg

Cold. Hard. Humiliating. Any young woman's first introduction to the gynecologist's stirrups is bound to be unpleasant, but in 1960 my mother's gynecologist contrived to make my first experience as mean and ugly as possible. I needed a gynecologist because my periods were viciously painful; each month I would miss a day or two of university classes, trapped at home and moaning (not to mention writhing) with a heating pad clutched to my stomach. Hopeful that a specialist could prescribe a magical remedy, I made an appointment with my mother's gynecologist, Dr. Roland Suran, who had fancy offices on Avenue Road.

The initial interview was unsettling enough. He demanded to know if I had a boyfriend. "Yes." Was I having intercourse with said boyfriend? "Yes." And just when was I planning to get married? I was taken aback; although this was 1960—and it is important to note that the "real" sixties, legendary for that era's supposed liberation, did not begin till at least 1968—and puritanical mores still prevailed, I did not expect a doctor to proselytize for premarital chastity.

I told him I had no plans to marry. I still had two more years to complete before graduation—and anyway, although I didn't say this out loud, I didn't believe in marriage. Dr. Suran looked annoyed; he pressed me a bit more about the wisdom of marrying soon if I were already having intercourse. He asked me about contraception and I told him about the diaphragm I'd been prescribed as an eighteen-year-old on a year's adventure in Israel. The diaphragm was unreliable, he warned. He then gave me his medical opinion: the severity of my cramps was due entirely to the guilt I felt at indulging in premarital sex. The sooner I married, the more quickly I would experience relief from that grinding pain. I must have looked baffled; never for a moment had I felt guilt about sex. (Anxiety about pregnancy—yes, which I told him.) I had despised the whole concept of virginity and "saving it" since I'd begun thinking rebellious and feminist thoughts at around the age of twelve. My lack of contrition must have goaded him. Looking even more disgruntled, he ordered me into a paper gown and onto his examining table.

Paper gowns scritch and rattle and don't properly cover your body. Once he had my feet in the stirrups, he told me to wait and left the room. Lying there, with my legs splayed and my vulva exposed to the empty room—feeling the helplessness, vulnerability, and mortification of a bodily violation that comes close to an assault—I could hear Dr. Suran's voice on the telephone down the hall. He was talking to his stockbroker, at some length, about shares to buy and sell. It must have been a pleasing power trip for him, to leave a woman exposed on a table while he flaunted his wealth and indifference.

After an excruciating internal examination, Dr. Suran told me to get dressed. When he returned, he was holding a little package labelled "Enovid. Caution. Experimental Use Only." He explained that if I took this pill daily for a prescribed three weeks each month, I would have much less cramping.

It worked like magic. Several months passed and I forgave Dr. Suran's hateful behaviour as I experienced overwhelming relief from the dreaded cramps.

I might have forgotten this whole episode as I forgot so many others had it not been for one startling moment a few months after that visit to Dr. Suran. Leafing through a copy of *Time* magazine, I was jolted in astonishment to see a headline hailing the market debut of Enovid—the miraculous new birth control pill.

It sank in gradually: Dr. Suran had given me birth control without letting me know that I was now protected from pregnancy. Whether he wanted me to be under pressure to marry, or maliciously hoped I would go on suffering needless pregnancy anxiety, I will never know. But the shock of learning how he had deceived me sealed this incident into the amber of memory.

It's a valuable nugget of memory, bringing into harsh light the uncertainty, the anguish, the fear that young women lived with before the feminist (and contraceptive) revolution: having sex—if an accidental pregnancy occurred—could disgrace your family, derail your education, and maybe even end your life in the den of a backstreet abortionist. And even when a doctor could save you from that haunting dread, he might easily choose—as Dr. Suran did—to let you suffer, all in the name of perpetuating patriarchy and its control over women's bodies.

GOING TO COURT:
CONTRACEPTION IN NEWFOUNDLAND

Wendy Williams

In 1972 the Canadian Public Health Association sponsored a public meeting in the St. John's City Hall, the founding meeting of the Family Planning Association (FPA) of Newfoundland and Labrador (NL). Early members Fran Baird Innes, Dr. Al Mercer, David and Monica Kirby, Connie Crutcher, Pam Kipnis, Elaine Frederiksen, and Dr. Helen McKilligan knew that more birth control education was needed in NL. Fran Baird Innes became the first president (1972–1974). Dr. Mercer, the first urologist in NL, was on the first board. He was so proud of his role that his family mentioned his commitment to the FPA in his obituary.

The FPA opened its offices on Church Hill, where it provided confidential pregnancy tests, counselling, a speakers' bureau, information on birth control, and—another first for NL—anonymous pregnancy tests. This was long before drugstore tests were available. Two nurses were hired, one in St. John's and the other in Stephenville. The focus of their work was education. The nurses expanded the services to include a lending library and educational conferences such as a 1977 conference on sexuality for physically disabled women and men. The west coast director, Viola Day, worked part-time with branches in Stephenville and Corner Brook. In 1978 the west coast programme ended due to lack of funds. On the east coast, Barbara Collier worked as the education director until she left the province in 1978.

By 1975 the organization identified the need for them to provide clinical services. A 1976 application to the Federal Health Promotion Directorate for a demonstration birth control clinic was approved for three years and the clinic opened in June 1977 at 21 Factory Lane. I was the first clinic coordinator. In 1978 the board changed the name to Planned Parenthood Newfoundland and Labrador (PPNL). Branches of the organization opened in Corner Brook, Grand Falls, Bay St. George, and Grand Bank/Fortune, but all later closed. The St. John's office is the only one operating now.

When we opened, we sent a letter to general practitioners working in the St. John's area inviting them to work in our clinic. However, the Newfoundland Medical Association responded by sending their members a letter advising them to not work with PPNL, as we would be competing with them to provide services. Nevertheless, physicians did work with us, notably Dr. John Ross; indeed, in the beginning all the physicians were male. We offered weekly clinics with a physician who prescribed birth control pills, inserted IUDs, fitted diaphragms and cervical caps, and made referrals for therapeutic abortions.

The other services we offered included pre- and post-natal support groups for single women sponsored by the Kinette Club of St. John's, a baby-car-seat rental service, and a theatre programme called Focus Theatre. Memorial University of Newfoundland (MUN) assigned nursing, social work, and medical students to our clinic as part of their education. Our physicians saw women who had a positive pregnancy test and wanted an abortion. Many women who could, opted to leave the province for their abortions; teachers had to leave the province for theirs.

A bit of constitutional history is needed in order to understand the problem for teachers. There are constitutional differences between NL and the rest of Canada because of the 1949 Terms of Union with Canada. One of the terms ensured the continuation of an education system that allowed Christian churches to be the only providers of public education. This had implications for women. Teachers worked in the school board of their respective Christian denominations and required a letter of good moral standing to secure their positions. Roman Catholic priests wrote these letters for Roman Catholic teachers in the Roman Catholic school boards and Anglican clergy wrote the letters for Anglican teachers working for the Consolidated School Boards. Therefore, a pregnant Roman Catholic teacher who wanted an abortion had to ensure that no one at her school knew she was pregnant and had had an abortion. If her employer found out, she could not only lose her job but then other school boards would not hire her. Roman Catholic school boards only hired Roman Catholic teachers, with some rare exceptions. For example, a school board of a different denomination might hire a teacher with a skill set such as music credentials. This situation did not change until December 18, 1997, when, after a long legal political battle in NL, the Senate of Canada passed a constitutional amendment to eliminate church-run school boards. The province adopted the non-denominational system in September 1998.

Confirmation of early pregnancy by physical examination is very difficult. PPNL had no access to ultrasounds so women were flying off for early abortions on the basis of a pregnancy test alone. While one gynecologist did abortions weekly at the General Hospital in St John's, women with resources went to Montreal as you could leave St. John's on the early flight and arrive back around midnight. A very long day. I told every woman to have a story ready explaining why she was on a flight from Montreal. It was amazing how many women met family or friends on the flight home. The services in Toronto included later abortions. Toronto required a more expensive overnight stay and it was more difficult to explain a two-day absence. Some women went to the USA for later abortions, but that was always a nightmare. The women travelled alone, had to be in New York for many days, and, in case there were complications, the health facilities required cash up front.

For some women it was their first plane trip. I recall one woman who lived in a community with one traffic light. I would tell women going to Montreal that people spoke French and that the cab drivers would likely be black. One young woman almost missed her plane home as she was amazed at all the ice-cream choices in the airport and could not decide what to buy.

We also participated in research, such as a study sponsored by the Canadian Association for Fertility Research to see if cervical caps were a reliable method of contraception and if women were interested in using them. Once the research showed that they were reliable, our physicians fitted them and women purchased them at our clinic. Cervical caps were not manufactured in North America, so we had to import them from the Marie Stopes UK clinic.

May Johnson, our second clinic coordinator, heard about a theatre programme at Boston Planned Parenthood and in 1980 May and Diane Siegel visited there. Diane recalls that the programme used theatre to raise such topics as teenage pregnancy, sexuality, venereal disease, and even gender identity and homosexuality, issues not often discussed at that time. PPNL developed our own programme, called Focus Theatre, and actor Beni Malone was hired as the theatre consultant. We recruited students from schools, ending up with ten students age fifteen and sixteen, including Diane's daughter Elizabeth, which delighted Diane.

In the summer of 1981 Focus Theatre travelled across the island performing in four small towns, sleeping on the floors of church basements and in private homes. Diane recalls "being served a wonderful meal on fine china at a picnic table in the yard of the mayor of Deer Lake. We were well received and it was a wonderful experience travelling with such a lively, intelligent, interesting group of teenagers."[25]

In 1980 Cheryl Hebert began working part-time as a social worker providing counselling to patients on birth control, pregnancy, and sexual assault. She describes her experiences:

> This was an exciting and formidable time to be working as a young health professional in the field of reproductive health and rights. The knowledge of birth control methods was rapidly growing and changing and women were becoming better informed about their sexuality, long considered a taboo topic. PPNL was a leader in this movement to provide non-judgemental professional advice on the methods of birth control and to support women who were pregnant and unsure of what direction to take. The organization was exceedingly professional and set a high standard by the nurses and doctors working there to treat all patients with the utmost respect and to tackle the continuous array of ethical dilemmas with an open mind.[26]

In the spring of 1980 we received a fourth and final year of federal money. The board worked hard to ensure that the clinic stayed open. They adopted two strategies: 1) ask the province for funding as the provision of health care services is a provincial responsibility; and 2) expand fundraising activities. PPNL board members were aware that both of these would be difficult strategies to implement. There were two main reasons for this. First, the Christian churches played a big role in political life and politicians would be reluctant to support PPNL over opposition from them. Second, ongoing public attacks by the Right to Life Association and by a woman named Vera Fedorik, who identified herself as a spokesperson for the Right to Life Association, deterred supporters. Nevertheless, in the fall of 1980 PPNL prepared a funding application for the provincial department of health. On December 4, Premier Brian Peckford signed the letter denying PPNL funds.

The board's fundraising programme included monthly advertisements in *The Evening Telegram* saying our clinic would close unless additional funds were raised. Advertising works. In September 1980 Ross McKee, an American with ties to NL, visited the clinic and introduced himself to May Johnson. He asked many questions and said he might be able to help. No one involved with PPNL knew this man. Eventually he told us his story. Late in life, he married a former Newfoundlander, Anne Hennessy Corbett, and thereafter spent summers in NL. Ross's mother, Christine Hayward McKee, had inherited money but died before receiving it. Ross was spending her money, which was in the New York Community Trust. He invited us to dinner at his home in Avondale so he could learn more about us. Our board sent three active members who were married to doctors (a physician, a dentist, and an orthodontist). Ross was very clear about wanting to know that we had good community support and competent people on our board. Carolyn and Gary Butler, Susan and Jim Flynn, and myself and my then-husband, Gordon Higgins, dined with Ross and Anne McKee. On the drive back to St. John's we did not know if we had passed the test or not. We did not hear from Ross for almost a year.

Early in 1981 our landlord told us the building we were in was to be demolished in 1982. We had to move and we knew it would have to be to more modest accommodations. We began our search for a new location. In December 1981 Ross got in touch with us; he would have money for us from the New York Community Trust via Planned Parenthood of America. In the meantime, he sent a personal donation. At that point there was $10,000 in the bank, enough to operate our clinic for three months. The news galvanized us into action. We could buy our own building! It would have to be commercially zoned so we could avoid the political battle of getting a zoning change through city council. It had to be affordable and be in the downtown area, where most high schools were. We found our building at 203 Merrymeeting Road, a great address for a birth control clinic. The purchase was to close March 1. Ross gave us $20,000 USD operating money, but we still needed the down payment.

The board members were "can do" people. In February 1982 we held our first of many auctions and raised $10,000, a huge amount of money for us. A bank approved a mortgage because three supporters (Dr. Gary Butler, Dr. Gordon Higgins, and myself) gave personal guarantees. We were mortgage-free in five years.

While we were changing our location and our funding sources, we were being attacked in print and on open-line radio shows by the Right to Life Association and Vera Fedorik. Our board believed that the latter's false and defamatory statements damaged our financial position and impaired our ability to operate. These are two examples of Fedorik's defamatory statements:

> In Newfoundland, pro-lifers vigorously lobbied to have the provincial government reject Planned Parenthood's request for funding on grounds that it provided abortion counselling. The government acquiesced. It's definitely an abortion referral centre, says Vera Fedorik, a consultant to Right-to-Life groups across the province. I've seen some of their sex educations films for teenagers and some of them could be considered pornographic.[27]
>
> I think that there is a way of teaching sex education as part of family life education that sort of anticipates it totally and there is a way of presenting it in such a way that it increases the problem and I very firmly believe that the way that Planned Parenthood goes about sex education in the schools increases the problem and I think even if we look at the statistics and in the early seventies when Planned Parenthood started getting gigantic amounts of federal money for them to assist them, it was at this point that the rate for teenagers and the abortion rate for teenagers started to sky-rocket.

Vera Fedorik was the executive director of Alliance for Life, the national coordinating body for the anti-choice movement in Canada, when she was engaged by the anti-choice foundation, Valade Vitae Service, as an educational liaison officer. In 1977, the foundation sent her to NL to encourage and coordinate the activities of anti-choice organizations. In response to her constant attacks on us, PPNL asked Vera Fedorik for a public apology. When she did not respond the board asked our lawyer, James C. Oakley, to start legal proceedings; he filed a statement of claim August 15, 1980, in the Supreme Court of Newfoundland. Our court date was March 17, 1982. We estimated that we would be in court three days. In fact, I myself was on the witness stand for three days and we were in court eighteen days.

The court case was exhausting, but the community and individual support was wonderful. Pro-choice groups sent telegrams, letters, flowers, and cheques. Each day people came to court to sit with us. The power of people bearing witness to your work is amazing. We were on the front pages of both daily newspapers every day that we were in court. Our court case was written into the script of the locally produced CBC radio drama called "Oil in the Family." The show started two days before our court case and the script was written daily with comments about PPNL. In court, the lawyer for the Right to Life Association objected to the show's content. Judge Noel dismissed his objections. Our case also included bringing in expert witnesses such as Maureen Orton, a social work professor at McMaster University, as well as local witnesses.

Ruby Dewling, a professor at the School of Nursing at MUN, testified and after she gave her testimony, she shared this story with me. She and Dr. Andy Wells, a family physician whose practice was located in the east end of the city, ran a small birth control clinic in St. Thomas' Anglican Church Hall. Reverend Rhodes Cooper was the senior priest of this parish. Ms. Dewling was a member of the parish and the public health nurse in the area. Dr. Wells prescribed birth control pills for married women in the parish. Ms. Dewling said they also had some married women patients from St. Joseph's Roman Catholic church, a few blocks away. This clinic, which operated some time between 1963 and 1969, was very cloak and dagger. Another connection to this story was that Reverend Cooper's daughter, Susan Adams, was on our board and came to court as a supporter.

Judge Noel at one point said to one of their witnesses, "You say Planned Parenthood is an evil influence, then you say Planned Parenthood is not worth going to. You have to have it one way or the other."[28]

On May 4, 1982, Judge Noel released his decision. He dismissed the case against the Right to Life Association, ruling that Vera Fedorik was neither an employee of the association nor a member. PPNL had shown that she publicly identified herself as their representative and had keys to their office, but that was not enough to find the Right to Life Association responsible for what she said. The Judge said that Ms. Fedorik made defamatory statements that were not fair comment. She was ordered to pay

PPNL $500 plus court costs, which she never paid. The more important outcome was that the false statements stopped. There is no opposition now.

PPNL believed in education, which we put into practice by developing educational materials including:

- Connie Crutcher, *Infertility: Facts and Feelings* (St. John's Planned Parenthood Newfoundland/ Labrador, 1981).

- Audrey Hurley, *The Teen Man's Sexual Survival Manual* (St. John's Planned Parenthood Newfoundland/ Labrador, 1981).

- Diane Siegel and Patricia Boyle, *Facing the Change of Life: a Resource Kit on Menopause* (St. John's Planned Parenthood Newfoundland/Labrador, 1984).

- Amy Zeirler, *In Touch: for Teen Women about Sex* (St. John's Planned Parenthood Newfoundland/ Labrador, 1985).

- A series by Debbie Redfern and Carmel Wyse, *Infertility: Treatment and Choices; Fertility Awareness; Nonparenthood, Adoption and Artificial Insemination* (St. John's Planned Parenthood Newfoundland/ Labrador, 1987).

- Annette Johns, *Adolescent Sexual Decision-making in Newfoundland and Labrador* (St John's PPNL and Women's Health Network, 2004).

We expanded our sexuality programmes when we could. In keeping with our board's awareness and concerns for people with fertility problems, we presented a brief to the Royal Commission on New Reproductive Technologies in 1990.

PPNL board members spent a lot of time raising money. Becky Roome, a board member from 1987 to 1995, remembers the summer crab fest with mountains of crabmeat and shells, and making gallons of seafood sauce in her tiny kitchen. Each February found board members wrapping bouquets of carnations in Catherine Dempsey's home. There was the work and fun of planning the annual PP auction, with board members wryly realizing how much they themselves spent on auction items. They would have been better off doing straight out donations! Each December there were the fabulously social and supportive Christmas fundraising coffee parties hosted by Debbie Fry and Lois Hoegg.

In 2005, PPNL added NL Sexual Health Centre to their name to reflect their expanded services, which included a toll-free sexual health line and their work with the LGBTQ community. We had fun, we made a difference, and Planned Parenthood continues to have a positive effect on women's lives.

Thanks to Catherine Dempsey for assistance in researching this article.

FILOMENA CARVALHO
AND THE IMMIGRANT WOMEN'S
HEALTH CENTRE

Radha Nayar

This article originally appeared on section15.ca, *March 11, 2003.*

Filomena walked into the Immigrant Women's Health Centre in Toronto, Ontario, on a snowy day in 1982. She felt scared and wondered if she should just turn around and go home. She had started a new job there three months earlier as the Portuguese sexual health counsellor and was still reeling from everything she was learning. She knew that applying for the job had been the right thing to do—she felt it in her soul.

She had asked the collective that organized the Immigrant Women's Health Centre if she could start a sexual health support group for women in the Portuguese community and had been given the go-ahead. She had wanted to do it because so many of the women had similar concerns and fears. Why not get them all together to chat? She wasn't sure if it was a good idea, but she wanted to try. Maybe they would hate it and feel shy. But five women had agreed to come to at least one meeting to see what it was all about. If it was a flop, at least she could say she had tried something new. She could never have known that she was about to start on an incredible journey of discovering who she was as an immigrant woman, a woman who has fundamental human rights and could support other women to realize their rights as well.

It was time to start the group. She sat down with the women. Everyone seemed nervous. They wouldn't look at each other. Some of the women looked older, others as young as early twenties. All looked a little scared.

Filomena took a deep breath. This was a new thing to be doing in her community. Had she made a horrible mistake? There was no turning back, so she began.

"Why don't we start by talking about who we are?" she said. "Maybe our stories of coming to Canada? Does anyone want to start?"

Nobody did, so she went first. She talked about coming from a village, about her parents deciding to leave Portugal so her brothers would not have to do mandatory army service. She talked about her parents getting jobs in factories in Toronto. She talked about going to school and experiencing racism. She talked about how she used to feel like a sexual object. Everyone called her "exotic" and she never knew if it was a compliment or not.

Slowly, the other women started to talk. And talk and talk and talk! The stories were soon coming out faster than Filomena could remember them. Everyone was animated. They nodded their heads, or smiled, or laughed, or sat still if someone shared something painful. Stories of first days in Canada, of having a child, of the first time they fell in love in this country, of the first time they realized that they were being discriminated against here. Stories about being new to this bizarre, cold place.

A woman told her story:

> We came here with two children and very little money. The Portuguese community was so helpful and kind. But still, I had to find a job, I had to feed my kids. I was trained as a nurse in Brazil, but couldn't find any job. Finally, I got work cleaning hotel rooms. And my husband, he got a job driving a truck throughout Ontario. He was hardly home at all, but we managed.
>
> About a month ago, I started to have some terrible things happening to me in my private place. I had itching and a terrible discharge. It hurt a lot. I tried to go to a walk-in clinic, but I didn't understand what they told me. The doctor spoke really fast and didn't answer my questions. I didn't want the medicine he gave me. Why would I take something when I don't even understand what it is? I was telling my friend about it and she told me to come here to the Immigrant Women's Health Centre. But I'm still scared about it. What's wrong with me? And is my husband okay? I don't even know what to tell him.

Another young woman started to cry.

> I didn't want to have sex without a condom. I
> was scared to say no, though, because I asked
> my boyfriend to wait for so long. When the time
> finally came that I was ready, I didn't want to
> put it off again. So I said okay, if just for one
> time only. Now I'm pregnant and I haven't heard
> from him since I told him. I'm scared and don't
> know what to do.

As the women told their stories, Filomena's life work slowly
came into view. This was what she was meant to do! This was
where she was meant to be! Supporting women like herself
to become strong in their health, empowered in who they are,
and what they need! She wanted to support women to ask the
tough questions and get answers! Questions around dealing with
relationships, being empowered in using birth control, talking to
doctors without feeling intimidated.

She looked into the faces of the women before her.

We can do this together, my sisters. We can make a new life
for ourselves, one where we are strong, where we get what we de-
serve, where we live our lives to the fullest. We can be the makers
of our destiny, and it is going to happen starting here, starting
now. Just by sharing our stories with each other, we are becoming
stronger! And now that we have shared our stories, we can explore
them and come up with ideas to help each other and ourselves.
Together, we are stronger than if we are alone.

The women looked at each other, full of hope and excitement.
They were glad they had come to the group after all. Things could
change for them, in ways they hadn't expected. Filomena took a
deep breath and said, "Flaviola, let's start with your story. Let's put
our heads together and come up with some solutions."

*Congratulations to Filomena Carvalho, winner of the $10,000 Marion
Powell Award for 2003. In making her destiny, she helped other women
make theirs. The award recognizes an individual who has demonstrated leadership, commitment, and dedication to the advocacy in women's
health over his or her career. The award is named for Dr. Marion
Powell, a woman committed to women who fought for access to birth
control and sex education for fifty years. Filomena donated the $10,000
she won towards a new mobile health clinic unit which, if the remaining*

$280,000 is raised, will visit factories where many immigrant women work. With all her advocacy on behalf of the centre and this generous gift, Filomena has really put her money where her mouth is!

ACTIVIST CHEQUE-MATE?
A LOOK BACK AT CANADA'S BREAST
CANCER MOVEMENT

Sharon Batt

I gave a plenary address to the World Conference on Breast Cancer in Ottawa in July 1999. It summarized my views on the breast cancer movement after a decade in which I had been actively involved as a leader in that movement, both in Canada and internationally. The talk also captured a critical moment for me personally, as I left the breast cancer community that month to take up a two-year university appointment in Halifax, in the Nancy's Chair in Women's Studies at Mount Saint Vincent University. As the talk suggests, I felt that the movement, ten years in, had strayed from its activist beginnings. I welcomed the chance to retreat from activism and reflect on what had gone wrong. That hiatus led me to return to university as a PhD student to study the alliances that many patient advocacy groups had formed with pharmaceutical companies.

I continued to write about breast cancer and women's health and have written two books about the breast cancer movement. I remain engaged with feminist health activists whose roots were in the women's health movement, including women from Breast Cancer Action Montreal, the group I had co-founded after my diagnosis (now called Breast Cancer Action Quebec) and Women and Health Protection (WHP), a national working group of women's health activists, university-based researchers, consumers, community groups, and health practitioners. WHP was founded in 1998 with funding from the Centres of Excellence for Women's Health, a programme within Health Canada that was concerned about the safety of drugs and medical devices used by women.

What follows is an adapted version of that talk. I have added some afterthoughts about how things have changed in breast cancer groups and breast cancer treatment in the seventeen years since I left the movement.

JULY 1999
BREAST CANCER ADVOCACY:
THE REALITY CHECK

What is breast cancer advocacy? I'm going to start with some definitions. What do breast cancer advocates do? There is a number of distinct approaches to breast cancer advocacy, and I want to both position myself among them and advocate for my favourite model.

One idea is that advocacy means that women, in our role as patients, should have a say in our own treatments. I do believe cancer treatments are most likely to benefit the woman when she and her doctor come to a mutual agreement that combines the physician's expertise with the women's personal values. But that sort of one-on-one negotiation is not what I mean when I talk about advocacy.

In the 1980s, cancer organizations in North America fought to give cancer patients a say in their treatment. But in the 1990s, something much more profound took place. For the first time in history, women with cancer mobilized as a political force. We brought breast cancer out of the closet—and out of the physician's office—and put the disease on the public policy agenda.

But that still doesn't end the confusion. Even after almost ten years of activism, most people still think what advocates do is lobby for more research money for breast cancer. And that has been one approach to advocacy. The tangible expression of this philosophy is found in the ever-popular runs and walks designed to raise money for treatment research, and often billed as a way to cure cancer.

To me, the pulse of advocacy is to provide a reality check. What is the view from the ground? Whether we are women living with breast cancer or citizens concerned about the disease, our task is to see our own interests clearly, to speak about breast cancer in a voice rooted in lived experiences and in our own system of values. We need to be alert to the turf wars and vested interests in the system, and we need to question. Who is making the decisions, and why? And are they really in the best interest of patients?

This business of the reality check strains relations between advocates and researchers. As advocates began to take part in meetings with researchers, the typical discourse has been a classic case of miscommunication. We were saying "reality check" and researchers kept hearing "really big cheque." But, before advocacy, that is what the public did.

Dr. Susan Love captured the transition when she described the mandate of the National Breast Cancer Coalition in the US. She said, "We're not the women's auxiliary of the American Cancer Society—we don't just say, 'here's some money, boys—come back when you have the answer.'" Today's advocates want a say in decisions about what research gets done and what policies are developed.

BACKLASH

This view of advocacy has generated some backlash among scientists.

The backlash came home to me at a breast cancer research conference in Toronto. The featured speaker at the banquet finale was the American researcher Dr. Bernard Fisher. Dr. Fisher is a senior, internationally known member of the breast cancer research community and many of you will be familiar with highlights of his career as head of a large, federally funded research programme of clinical trials that has evaluated the effectiveness of common breast cancer treatments.

Dr. Fisher is an entertaining speaker and he spoke that evening with considerable charm about his many decades heading this international programme in breast cancer research. Toward the end of his talk, I was astonished to hear him name my book, *Patient No More: The Politics of Breast Cancer*, as one of four books that had deeply hurt him and his family.

He went on to depict me, and a number of other advocate-writers, and the National Breast Cancer Coalition (NBCC)—the national US advocacy umbrella group—as part of an "anti-science movement." He even showed slides listing the books that offended him and parts of a letter from the NBCC, which said breast cancer treatments had not really advanced beyond the slash, burn, and poison of thirty years ago.

At the time this event took place, I had drafted an abstract for this talk in which I lamented the failure of the advocacy movement to live up to its promise. It seemed to me that after exciting beginnings early in the decade, breast cancer advocacy had foundered. I planned to talk about the need for renewal. But after being denounced from the pulpit by a high priest of breast cancer research, I had to rethink. If breast cancer advocates have spooked someone as powerful as Bernard Fisher to the point where he feels moved to give us and our work a tongue-lashing in his after-dinner talks—well, maybe we've had an impact after all.

Now, I'm not saying that our role as breast cancer advocates is to oppose scientific research or to antagonize scientists. I do believe we have a right—and an obligation—to question the directions science is taking and the way science is applied in the light of our own experience; in the light of our values and our political vision of the kind of society we want to live in; and in the light of common sense.

These actions seem to me quite moderate and reasonable, and consistent with the way democracies are supposed work. So when a prominent researcher describes advocates as "anti-science," we need to ask, "What's going on?"

The answer could take us down several paths. I've chosen today to explore pharmaceutical drug research in breast cancer. In the wealthy industrialized countries, drug development now dominates cancer research and policy to an unprecedented degree. We need to keep a hawk eye on this development and its special pitfalls for advocates.

Let me first return to the question of advocacy and what drove many of us who were diagnosed with this disease to form a movement for change.

I began meeting and talking to other women with breast cancer a year or so after my diagnosis in 1988, and have remained active in grassroots groups to the present day. From the beginning, I was struck by the fact that other women had many of the same questions I did. We noticed a gulf between our reality and what we heard from researchers and cancer agencies, and in media reports. The mythology about breast cancer was all high-tech medicine, breakthroughs, cures, genetic testing, and early detection as *the* solution to the disease.

As women who had gone through these treatments, we

had a different perception. We were shocked at how brutal the treatments were, even as they offered no guarantee of a cure. We worried about side effects, like lymphedema (a painful, incurable swelling of the arm after breast surgery), the long-term toxicity of chemotherapy, and radiation damage. We were dismayed at how common these damaging side effects seemed to be and at the scarcity of research on how to alleviate them. We searched the forbidden literature on complementary or alternative medicines for less toxic treatments.

I was treated in Montreal, a city with a large oncology research community. Like the other women I came to know there, I had treatments that were considered state-of-the-art; yet we felt our emotional and spiritual needs as patients had been ignored. Our (mostly male) physicians were technically competent but they had no idea how to talk to us.

And prevention! One of the first questions women diagnosed with breast cancer ask is, "Why did I get this disease?" When women began to compare notes and to research the scientific literature, we realized that research into causes of breast cancer got short shrift compared to the research on treatment. Only 5 to 10 per cent of breast cancer cases have a hereditary component; yet the search for genetic tests for breast cancer was fast-tracked in the early nineties, leading to the discovery of the so-called breast cancer genes and tests to determine who had them. These tests could identify women at high risk, but the only way for those women to reduce their risk was to have both healthy breasts removed.

There's a thematic thread running through all these issues. If enough people pull that thread, they could crack the very foundations of modern medicine. Many breast cancer advocates quite consciously question the biomedical model that underpins western medicine—the ideology that equates the human body with a machine. We question as well the faith in technology that draws western medical researchers to ever-more extreme experimentation in the name of "progress."

Rachel Carson, in her book *Silent Spring*, used the analogy of the superhighway versus the road less travelled. She was writing about the scientific search for ways to eradicate insects in the 1950s, but she could just as well have been writing about methods for eradicating cancer today.

I believe this is why breast cancer advocacy threatens many scientists—and governments as well. Advocates have proposed not only that breast cancer research be reorganized around a different scientific model, but we have also demanded structures that are open to public scrutiny and debate. We want processes that allow for public input and a place at the table for advocates.

DRUG COMPANIES: SPEED DEMONS ON THE SCIENCE SUPERHIGHWAY

Breast cancer treatment drugs illustrate some obvious problems with the modern, western view of medical progress in breast cancer. Only twenty years ago, surgery was the first-line treatment for breast cancer in industrialized countries. Drugs, when they were used at all, were an adjunct, to try to prevent spread of the disease in women at high risk of metastasis.

Today, the picture has a different focus. Surgery is less mutilating but its importance in the therapeutic picture has been downgraded—it's considered a minor part of treatment. Drugs are the main action. They still aren't all that effective. But, we're told, they will be. New kinds of drugs are held out as our hope for effective treatment and eventual cure of the disease.

Maybe so. But at what cost?

TAMOXIFEN

I'll talk first about tamoxifen, which is not a new drug—it's been used for twenty years. It's currently the most widely used breast cancer drug in the world.

About three weeks ago, an article appeared in the *Montreal Gazette* comparing the price of tamoxifen in Canada and the US. The story told of five Vermont women with breast cancer who crossed the border to buy tamoxifen in Quebec. In the US, they were paying (US) $156.42 for a three-month supply of the drug. In Canada, they paid (US) $12.80—less than one-tenth the amount back home.

Vermont congressman Bernie Sanders organized the delegation. Sanders wanted the US to adopt comprehensive public health insurance—which Canada now has and the US doesn't. His point was that drug prices are lower in Canada than in the US because of our public system of health care. He's right. When Canada's health care system was in its prime, we created a system that allowed generic drug companies to make inexpensive copies of certain drugs. This explains why tamoxifen can be purchased in Canada for so much less than in the US. Unfortunately for people who need medications, the multinational drug companies success-fully fought that system, so you would not see the same disparity between US and Canadian prices in newer drugs.

One interesting point about the story, though, was that the Canadian pharmacist was quite happy with his mark-up—50 per cent over the wholesale price. He thought that was fair—as far as he was concerned, he was selling at a just price, not a bargain price.

THEN CAME TAXOL

Taxol is a newer breast cancer drug and it's much more expensive than tamoxifen. The National Cancer Institute (NCI) in the US paid the research and development costs of Taxol but when the drug was approved in 1992, the NCI gave Bristol-Myers Squibb the exclusive right to manufacture and sell the drug. The company proceeded to price the drug at $4.87 per milligram, more than twenty times the cost of production.

The NCI, like government cancer agencies in Canada and else-where, sees no conflict between using taxpayer's money for drug development, and then allowing drug companies to sell those drugs at what the market will bear. This is part of the current ide-ology in which governments view industry as partners.

In *Dr. Susan Love's Breast Book*, she evaluates Taxol. She says it is not a miracle drug, though the media hyped it as if it were. It works well in some women for up to eighteen months, but can also have serious side effects, notably neurological damage to hands and feet. When Taxol was still relatively new, breast cancer advocates in the Netherlands and Australia successfully lobbied their governments to provide it as a second-line treatment under public health care plans. So did an advocacy group in Ontario.

Taxol got a boost in 1998 when a clinical trial showed that, administered after a cycle of the conventional chemotherapy drugs Adriamycin and Cyclophosphamide, it significantly reduced re-currence and death rates. As a result, Taxol is now being offered in the US as a first-line breast cancer treatment, in combination with the two older drugs, a combination treatment referred to by the shorthand AC+T.

TREATMENT ADVOCACY

A new Canadian group called Breast Cancer Advocacy Canada has just initiated a lobby to have the AC+T combination treatment made available as a standard treatment option for all high-risk, node-positive women in Canada. At present, Canadian oncologists can't offer this treatment to their patients under our medical insurance plans because of its high cost.

Taxol lobbies disturb me, not because I want to deny any useful treatment to women, but because I believe universal access should be an absolute principle of health care. And pressuring our governments to pay for drugs at inflated prices will only push our more democratic system into an American-style model. Why shouldn't drug companies be required to price their drugs at affordable levels—especially if they were developed at public expense, as Taxol was?

We're now layering one treatment on another because none of them do very well on their own: we've layered Taxol on conventional chemo, which is layered on surgery and radiation, which are layered in turn on mammography. These are all expensive interventions. When do we hit the wall of unaffordability?

The truth is, we already have, and we're nowhere near curing breast cancer.

At the World Conference on Breast Cancer two years ago, Gail Tishera, the minister of health from Guyana said, "We, in the developing countries, cannot afford the treatments that have been found." Women in her country, she said, needed appropriate and affordable treatments.

HERCEPTIN

Since Gail Tishera made that plea, the breast cancer treatment making waves in the industrialized west is Herceptin. The FDA approved this new drug last October. For a subgroup of women with advanced disease, Herceptin is effective at alleviating symptoms and probably extends life. Canada has just approved the Herceptin test and will soon consider approving the drug. The problem is, Herceptin costs $8,000 Canadian a month—in US funds, that's $5,333.

Researchers tell us Herceptin is just the beginning of the new therapies that exploit recent genetic discoveries. It makes you wonder.... Who are these drugs being developed for?

Again, to put this issue in a world perspective, I recall the physician from Cameroon who talked at an advocacy conference in Brussels about the plight of women with breast cancer in her country. A typical Cameroon woman with a breast lump, she said, can't even afford a biopsy to determine whether she actually HAS breast cancer—because a breast biopsy in Cameroon costs $10.

ROADS FOR ADVOCATES

At the outset, I mentioned the different visions of breast cancer advocacy. With the move to new, more expensive drug therapies, a basic division within the movement has become glaringly obvious. While some of us are pushing for fundamental change, other groups focus on promoting high-tech treatments, and insurance coverage for these treatments—whatever the price.

If we recall Rachel Carson's metaphor of the superhighway and the road less travelled, they are saying that we need to go even faster down the superhighway. This vision is in sharp contradiction to the paradigm shift others among us have promoted.

Accentuating this split in advocacy groups is the troubling trend towards industry funding of "health consumer groups." These industry-sponsored organizations are proliferating in the US, Canada, and Europe. In Canada, during the past year, the drug company Merck Frosst funded meetings to set up a "National Consumer Health Network." The environmental movement calls industry-funded groups that present themselves as green lobby groups "astroturf groups."

I'm not saying that all breast cancer groups that take money from industry are actively working as industry mouthpieces. That's not the case. Community groups are typically small, cash-strapped organizations with large ambitions. There's a lot of confusion in the community about how to handle drug company offers. But we need to recognize that pharmaceutical companies are actively wooing advocacy groups as partners and they are doing so because breast cancer advocacy can help their bottom line.

Last fall, the San Francisco–based group Breast Cancer Action became the first breast cancer group to draft a policy on corporate funding. BCA decided not to accept funding from six categories of corporations, and pharmaceutical companies led the list. A similar initiative, which arose from concerns in the women's health community in Canada, is a booklet by Anne Rochon Ford called "A different prescription: Considerations for women's health groups contemplating funding from the pharmaceutical industry." I urge any of you who belong to breast cancer advocacy groups to take a look at these two documents.

WHICH PATH?

To conclude, I want to address the accusation that advocates who question the scientific agenda in breast cancer are "anti-science."

The very foundation of science is to question, to debate, and to remain open to ideas from different perspectives. If anything, breast cancer advocates have pushed researchers to be more open and rigorous. But we do have qualms about medicine's love affair with the lab. If doctors want to keep their patients' trust, they can't permit science and technology to override the caring, ethical side of medicine. Our unease with the machine model in bioscience is well-grounded, not only in our personal experiences, but in the analyses of distinguished scientists and philosophers.

It's easy to cheer science along the superhighway. It's far more difficult to promote fundamental change. But I believe we must take that path. If we work together, following a global, ecological, socially just vision, we can lower breast cancer incidence. We can find humane, effective treatments and make them universally available to women in all countries.

The future of women with breast cancer depends on the choices we make.

POSTSCRIPT, NOVEMBER 2016

Rereading this speech seventeen years later, its message seems even more urgent. With few exceptions, breast cancer advocacy took the superhighway. Drug prices continue to spiral upwards, with new cancer drugs leading the pack; this despite research that shows these new therapies typically add, at most, a few months of life to patients who take them. Cancer specialists and policy-makers are now sounding the alarm because no health care system, public or private, can continue to pay hundreds of thousands of dollars for therapies for a single patient when that treatment adds little or nothing to the patient's health, and will cause some significant harm. The tragedy is magnified in cases when preventative strategies, non-drug remedies, or less expensive older treatments could provide as much benefit or more. And yet, most patient advocacy groups, the very voices one would hope and expect to demand the best system for all patients, continue to lobby for rapid approvals of these new medications and to pressure politicians to add them to provincial drug formularies.

I attribute much of this myopia to the phenomenon of drug companies' funding of breast cancer (and indeed virtually all) patient advocacy. In the past two decades, these partnership arrangements have gone from novel trend to accepted norm for funding health and patient advocacy organizations. In Canada, the main responsibility for this transformation, I argue, lies primarily with

the federal government, which once saw grassroots public advocacy as essential to Canada's democratic system and funded groups
whose advocacy mission was to bring the needs of marginalized
constituencies to public and government attention. Throughout
the 1990s and 2000s, this support was withdrawn. Advocacy
groups were branded the voices of "special interests" and were
told to find funding where they may.

In the health sector, the pharmaceutical industry filled the
funding gap, and patient group advocacy with drug company
funding became the status quo. A few breast cancer groups resisted
the pressure to seek pharmaceutical company funding. One, the
Toronto-based Alliance for Breast Cancer Survivors, was forced
to close its doors in 1999 for lack of money; Breast Cancer Action
Quebec (formerly Breast Cancer Action Montreal) has survived
and carries the cancer prevention banner high, but is a rare exception and is marginalized in the breast cancer movement. Groups
like DES Action Canada, Women and Health Protection, the
Canadian Women's Health Network, the Consumers' Association
of Canada, La fédération du Québec pour le planning des naissances, and the Réseau des tables régionals de groupes de femmes
du québec, all of which spoke to the importance of preventive
health and an approach to pharmaceutical policy that recognized
both harms as well as the benefits of drug remedies, were stripped
of their federal grants.

In this anti-advocacy policy environment, breast cancer stands
as a case study in distorted advocacy priorities. Within the movement, the voice for rational drug use in women's health and for
disease prevention has weakened significantly. Prices for cancer
drugs are now in the six-figure range. Yet advocacy groups still
push to have every new treatment put on drug formularies, arguing that patients have a right to maximum "choice." Unfortunately,
patients are vulnerable to persistent myths, such as the idea that
new treatments must be better than old ones—especially if they
cost more. Research soundly debunks this belief. Advocacy that
single-mindedly focuses on access to new drug treatments is not
only detrimental to the well-being of patients, it derails efforts
at public education and is putting our health care system on life
support.

Timely, evidence-informed treatment is certainly to be desired when we have a cancer diagnosis, but new drug treatments
have a surprisingly modest impact on reducing cancer mortality.
Cancer epidemiologists point out that the best way to reduce
cancer mortality is to reduce the incidence of cancer. Indeed, the

most dramatic drop in breast cancer in the past two decades is likely attributable to a drug women *stopped* taking. In July 2002, the Women's Health Initiative (WHI), a study undertaken in the United States to investigate the most common causes of death, disability, and impaired quality of life in post-menopausal women, concluded that long-term use of combined hormone therapy (estrogen plus progestin) after menopause increases the risk of breast cancer by 26 per cent. Prescriptions in the United States dropped from 61 million in 2001 to 21 million in 2004 and the age-adjusted incidence of breast cancer rapidly dropped an astounding 8.6 per cent. Similar declines were observed in Canada, Belgium, and elsewhere. It's worth noting that the WHI, a fifteen-year, multi-million-dollar research project that many in the research community opposed, was undertaken in large part because of pressure from American women's health activists, including the National Women's Health Network. The WHI, a study in preventive medicine, has long since proven its value.

And yet, advocacy in the breast cancer movement continues to emphasize access to expensive new treatments. Peter Wise, a cancer specialist and ethicist based in London, England, argues that patients and the public would be better served if the huge amounts of money spent on new cancer treatments were reallocated to intensified efforts at prevention, effective early detection (not necessarily by mammography, another overrated technology), prompt treatment of localized disease, and improved supportive care.

A subset of activists upholds the feminist tradition of promoting prevention research and policies, especially when it comes to toxins in the environment. Sometimes termed the green breast cancer movement, its adherents have long argued that prevention gets short shrift, particularly when it comes to toxic chemicals in the environment. Causal connections are difficult to demonstrate using conventional research methods and few corporations or government agencies support research and advocacy critical of profitable industries. Mainstream researchers and charities don't entirely ignore prevention, but they focus on behaviours like exercise, diet, smoking, and alcohol consumption. All of which do influence cancer risk, but they are typically framed as "lifestyle factors"—individual choices—as if we live in a social vacuum. In reality, societal forces (e.g., time, stress, poverty, advertising) strongly influence behaviour patterns; unless they are acknowledged, lifestyle prevention amounts to victim blaming and has limited effect.

In recent years, the efforts of the green breast cancer movement have gained validation, particularly with respect to workplace exposures to chemicals. Canadian researchers Jim Brophy and Margaret Keith studied women's exposures to Bisphenal A and phthalates in southern Ontario factories and found female autoworkers and women working in food-packing have a risk of breast cancer four times more than other workers.

And in British Columbia, in June 2016, a landmark court decision recognized that a different burden of proof makes sense when causal links to a disease are likely but difficult to prove scientifically. This case involved lab technicians working for the Fraser Health Authority who were exposed to a known carcinogen, formaldehyde, and who developed breast cancer. In the lab of sixty-three workers the rate of diagnoses was approximately eight times that in the general population (four other women had also developed breast cancer but were not appellants in the case). In a 6-1 ruling, the Supreme Court of Canada concluded that the evidence was strong enough to establish a causal link between the work environment and the women's breast cancer diagnoses, allowing them to seek compensation.

These important inroads to recognizing environmental cancers largely flew under the media radar and only one breast cancer advocacy group that I know of highlighted them; I can say with pride, it was Breast Cancer Action Quebec, the group I co-founded twenty-five years ago. More humbling is the state of the breast cancer advocacy writ large, a movement I once enthusiastically championed. After almost three decades of engaging with patient advocacy, as both an activist and a scholar, I now believe we need to rethink the whole concept. The idea of including patients in policy decisions that affect them sounds democratic and beneficial to patients' interests—but who decides which patients speak for patients? And is the pharmaceutical industry truly the most logical actor in the system to be educating patient advocates and funding their work?

I say it with sadness: rather than being agents for change, many patient advocates have become the voices for the worst features of status quo.

MAKING OVULATORY
MENSTRUAL CYCLES MATTER
IN WOMEN'S HEALTH

Jerilynn C. Prior

A few others and I founded the Centre for Menstrual Cycle and Ovulation Research (CeMCOR) in Vancouver on May 7, 2002. We had $40,000—half from the University of British Columbia (UBC) Department of Medicine and half from what became the Vancouver Coastal Health Research Institute—and little else. But we had a bold vision: To reframe scientific knowledge of the menstrual cycle and ovulation in a woman-centred context. A former patient later became a major sustaining donor for a number of years. Together, these contributions allowed CeMCOR to perform the first ever randomized placebo-controlled trial that documented that progesterone was effective for treatment of menopausal hot flushes.[29] Subsequently these donations also funded a participatory Perimenopausal Experiences Project in Victoria, British Columbia.

From day one, CeMCOR had a local community advisory council, that included Dorothy Stowe, a Quaker like myself and one of the founders of Greenpeace, and an international, multidisciplinary scientific advisory council that included Dr. Valerie Beral, an epidemiologist in England; Dr. Susan I. Barr, professor of nutrition at UBC; Dr. Janet E. Hall, a reproductive endocrine leader in Boston; and Dr. Susan Love, the famous breast surgeon and author of several women's health books. In the fall of 2003, we launched the CeMCOR website designed to provide information for adolescent, premenopausal, perimenopausal, and menopausal women, and for health care providers and for researchers. We began to answer individual women's questions and to anonymize and publish some of these in "Ask Jerilynn" postings. By 2016 the CeMCOR website (www.cemcor.ca) garnered 5,000–7,000 pageviews a day!

The gestation of the Centre for Menstrual Cycle and Ovulation Research took many years. Perhaps its seed was when I missed my period for nine months from the fall of 1961 as I first started university. I knew I wasn't pregnant; I told no one. I recall being puzzled about why—when I felt healthy, was well-fed, and even happy—my period had disappeared. In retrospect, I behaved as though I knew, even then, that what I was experiencing was an *adaptation,* not a disease. I now know that I would not have developed amenorrhea if I had had previously established normal ovulatory cycles, and neither would it have happened if I hadn't been struggling so hard to get to and succeed in university and become a physician.

Losing my period in my first year of university was likely when I first realized the strength and importance of the profoundly protective hypothalamic-pituitary-ovarian system that holistically assesses and integrates "threats" or "stresses," and, should they be high, temporarily either suspends menstrual cycles or allows regular cycles with ovulatory disturbances. As a first-year university student I was stressed by the challenges of a totally different world. I was a physically strong, independent, and resourceful late adolescent woman from a small, isolated fishing village in Alaska who found herself locked into a dormitory at night, eating in a cafeteria, and incessantly surrounded people whose life experiences and goals were totally different from mine.

In the following I review the *why* (including the personal and scientific ideas) and *how* of the founding of CeMCOR.

WHY?

"It was clear to me that the approach to menstrual cycles 'out there' was not helping women," I replied when asked by a journalist in 2015 why I founded CeMCOR. "Many of the things that I had already learned in research needed further investigation; and most of all, research results needed to be effectively shared with women. Hence CeMCOR became the unique combination of a centre that does primary research *with* women and also directly translates the research results *to* women."

It took a long while, however, to achieve the vision and the confidence to found CeMCOR. As a feminist physician from Alaska, I managed to work and earn scholarships to complete university and, after nine rejections, was accepted into the University of Oregon medical school, where the quota for women was six of, I think, eighty-eight students per class, in 1965. As I completed medical school (Boston University in 1969), I realized that the for-profit medicine practice pattern in the USA was something I could not accept. For me, medicine was first a service. I knew I would be both burnt out and broke if I didn't require—as I ethically couldn't—payment from those without adequate resources.

I was already a specialist in internal medicine and had one year of research training in endocrinology when we immigrated to Canada because of its universal health care system. After I had worked in the Alaska Native Health Service for two years, my husband got into a PhD programme at Simon Fraser University. He, our four-year-old daughter, and I then moved to Vancouver in the fall of 1976 on a "ministerial permit" and, because I was not yet qualified to practice medicine in Canada, I scrounged a $16,400/year "teaching fellow" full-time job for the University of British Columbia at Vancouver General Hospital (VGH). I was subsequently chosen VGH chief resident in medicine, took the required exams, and eventually earned my Canadian internal medicine credentials. During that period I also finished my endocrinology training by organizing informal apprenticeships since Canada did not have an official endocrinology sub-specialty training programme at that time. These were with Dr. Ho Yuen in gynecology/reproductive endocrinology and Dr. Bert Cameron in nephrology and bone metabolism, as well as various endocrine specialists. As soon as I was licensed, however, I was warned by Dr. Hamish McIntosh, then head of endocrinology, to not bother opening a clinical practice because, "We've already got enough doctors."

My second child was born soon after I completed my re-training in 1978. I got a half-time UBC assistant professor position, saw patients one day a week, and soon had more women patients who had previously not been satisfactorily helped than I could handle. To work within an academic system I realized that I needed to specialize even further, so I chose women's reproduction and bone health since these were areas within endocrinology that no one else covered.

I reflected whimsically one day that I felt like "A noiseless patient spider...on a little promontory it stood isolated...seeking the spheres to connect them."[30] I was trying to make relationships where the science of the time was (and still is) about moving in a linear fashion from A to B. But to do further research and disseminate the new knowledge that I was uncovering required many researchers to collaborate. It also needed more effective methods of knowledge translation than my public lectures and mimeographed handouts. I needed to gather like-minded scientists to share the challenges of changing the existing very paternalistic and gyn/authority-based "knowledge" about women's reproduction.

Looking back at the lead-up to CeMCOR, the day-by-day progression of new knowledge and concepts seemed ordinary. It was not. The newly discovered evidence-based concepts clearly shook the foundations of medical/gynecological power. The major idea, one that could lead to effective *prevention*, needed to be shared: *Silent ovulatory disturbances within normal menstrual cycles are the major, hidden risks for women's osteoporosis, heart disease, and breast cancer.*

Here I trace the ideas, their stimulae and events that brought the Centre for Menstrual Cycle and Ovulation Research into being within the Department of Medicine at the University of British Columbia in 2002. What follows is the genesis of the four discoveries that necessitated the formation of CeMCOR.

WOMEN'S REPRODUCTION ADAPTS TO ATHLETIC ACTIVITY

In the seventies and early eighties, women as well as men in Vancouver were enthusiastically training for and completing "fun runs" and following the "aerobics" fad that was sweeping North America. Almost immediately the medical literature began presenting "evidence" that exercise was bad for women's menstrual cycles and fertility. In the summer of 1980, associated with a Simon Fraser University (SFU) conference on "The Female Athlete," I ran my first fun run (in "runners" purchased from the local grocery store). In my Alaskan childhood I was required to be physically strong to survive and be socially accepted; I was offended by the concept that women could be disabled or diseased due to athletic activity.

The popular concept soon became: physical activity was *causing* diseases such as amenorrhea and infertility. Most published studies were cross-sectional (comparing runners with sedentary women at one point in time) and even those that were prospective didn't objectively assess women's baseline reproductive function, weight, stresses, and pattern of training. I tried and failed to publish a prospective year-long participatory study of menstrual cycles as women increased their running. I say participatory (although it was not in vogue then) because the two women who kept and shared their meticulous records became co-authors; it was eventually published as a now well-cited letter in the *Lancet* in 1982. I realized then, that we didn't even know how variable menstrual cycle lengths and ovulatory characteristics were in average women during the course of a year.

As I worked with SFU colleagues on a prospective study of menstrual cycle changes while women undergraduates increased their running exercise, I soon realized we needed better tools— non-invasive but validated ways such as quantitative basal temperature to assess ovulation and the luteal phase length (how long high progesterone levels were present at the end of a menstrual cycle)[31] as well as a menstrual cycle diary to track women's day-to-day experiences (both positive and negative) and cycle and flow lengths.[32] Using these tools, I showed that most mature, community-dwelling women runners had regular, normal ovulatory cycles. However, if they were doing longer training runs or increasing running in preparation for their first marathon, they might develop anovulatory or short luteal phases within regular, normal-length menstrual cycles called "silent ovulatory disturbances."

I reasoned that exercise training required conditioning or adaptive changes in our heart, lungs, and leg muscles so why shouldn't women's reproductive systems also adapt? Based on tracking my own and the cycles/ovulation of other women in their thirties, there was good evidence that women's menstrual cycles and ovulation could adapt to the undoubted stressors of exercise if they were initially normally ovulatory, trained sensibly, ate enough to cover their energy needs, and were not otherwise stressed. By the mid-1980s I had finally acquired funding to do a prospective observational study showing for the first time that 99 per cent of cycles remained of normal length and regular; the majority of women experienced silent ovulatory disturbances; and their exercise habits had no relationship with the menstrual cycle or ovulatory outcomes even in the nineteen women who trained for and ran a marathon, often their first, during that year, despite the fact that their body weight/body fat values were lower.

NORMAL PROGESTERONE EXPOSURE IS NEEDED TO PREVENT BONE LOSS IN REGULAR CYCLES

The same study also taught me about bone health. In 1984, I got National Health Research Development Programmeme funding. It was my second application; I now made bone change (a "hard," scientific end-point) the primary outcome rather than menstrual cycle and luteal phase lengths. Our purpose was to do a one-year study of the spinal bone changes, menstrual cycles, ovulation, weight, exercise, diet, and hormonal changes in healthy women ages 20–42. In addition to being non-smokers, taking no hormones for contraception or other reasons, of normal weight, and not having androgen excess, I decided we needed to study women who at study start were proven to have normal reproduction. Thus to be eligible, all women also needed have normal menstrual cycles (21–36 days long) and ovulation (10 days luteal lengths) on two consecutive cycles. The enrolled women fell into three different exercise groups: normally active (it was very negative in that era to call someone "sedentary"), recreational runners who ran for health and fitness, and runners who were training to run a marathon.[33]

As a participatory study women became co-researchers; study personnel considered their jobs were to support each participant; all women were given their own data and, at a pot-luck dinner party at the end of the study, we shared our collective results. This turned out to be three years before results were finally published. In the 66 women who completed the year-long study we additionally found: regular cycles and normal estrogen levels were not sufficient to prevent women's spinal bone loss; women also needed normal luteal phase lengths and normal progesterone levels for stable bone density.[34]

When the study results were finally published in 1990 we were able, through a fluke of changing assistant editors and my dogged persistence (in the days of paper copy, the assistant editor corrected every other word twice, once in green and once in brown ink), to get that article published as a lead article in the prestigious *New England Journal of Medicine*.[35] But even after acceptance, I had to demand (on threat I would withdraw permission to publish) that the editor, in proof, not be allowed to change the title from "Spinal Bone Loss and *Ovulatory Disturbances*" to "Spinal Bone Loss and *Menstrual Cycle* Disturbances."

Already, I had hypothesized that estradiol's job in women's bones was to prevent bone loss but progesterone's job was to stimulate formation of new bone. It was years before I realized *why* women lost bone if they weren't ovulating normally. That occurred because the normal downward swing of menstrual cycle estrogen levels from the midcycle peak to the normally low levels during flow caused a small increase in bone resorption (leading to bone loss) that progesterone's direct osteoblast bone formation-stimulating effect was needed to offset in order to prevent bone loss. CeMCOR has now confirmed that innovative observation in a meta-analysis of six international prospective studies measuring bone change and documenting menstrual cycles and ovulation.[36]

NORMAL PREMENOPAUSAL ESTROGEN LEVELS ARE NOT SUFFICIENT TO PREVENT WOMEN'S HEART ATTACKS

Perhaps because of my own dramatic adverse reaction to the high doses of estrogen in the birth control pill I unsuccessfully tried to take in 1967, I was suspicious of the prevalent cultural notion that "estrogen's what makes a girl, a girl." I also suspected its corollaries were erroneous: that menopause means "estrogen deficiency" rather than the normal low levels of that part of the life cycle; and that "estrogen replacement" therapy was needed to prevent menopausal heart attacks. I knew from our local research in healthy menopausal women that endothelial function, the fundamental cardiovascular action to control small blood vessel flow was at least equally related to progesterone as to estrogen[37] and that the evidence for "estrogen replacement" therapy preventing heart attacks was flawed and grossly inadequate. So I asked: Could normally ovulatory cycles prevent heart attacks? Perhaps, yes, because they required a woman to adapt to her exercise, to feel "at home" in her social environment and with her dreams, as well as to be well fed, rested, and healthy. Even the very early evidence said that ovulatory premenopausal cycles could prevent heart attacks, as I've now hypothesized.

PROGESTERONE AND NORMAL OVULATION COULD PREVENT BREAST CANCER

I had already learned that estrogen and progesterone are both essential for premenopausal health; and that they work together in every tissue complementing or counterbalancing each other. Two experiments in which women who needed a surgical breast biopsy had women randomly apply an estrogen, progesterone, estrogen and progesterone, or placebo gel to their affected breast for eleven days before the biopsy in which tissues far from the benign mass were removed and examined. Both studies showed that estrogen increased cell growth (proliferation—a cancer risk factor) and progesterone caused breast cells to mature and become more differentiated (an anti-cancer effect). Therefore I postulated that normal ovulatory cycles and progesterone to counterbalance the estrogen levels in the menstrual cycles were needed to prevent women's breast cancer. Some 1980s studies supported this idea.

I was able to publically summarize these ideas in the UBC Faculty of Medicine Clinical Research Lectureship I was awarded on September 10, 2002, just a few months after CeMCOR's launch on May 7, 2002. For that lecture I invited the public and was delighted with an overflow crowd in the old VGH Willow Pavilion B Lecture hall. I spoke about normal ovulation within regular, normal-length menstrual cycles as the "bellwether of women's well-being."

HOW?

When I first had the idea of founding a research centre I had no idea what to do. I knew I needed administrative, feminist help so invited Joanne R. Silver, HCA, former VGH social worker, and co-founder of the Abortion Counselling Programme at the Surgical Day Care, and former board member of East Vancouver's REACH clinic, to be our part-time executive director. I recall asking a rather more savvy academic dermatology colleague and he said, "Decide on your purpose, make a brochure, and letterhead—just do it!" So we did.

CeMCOR has always been mostly virtual, with my academic office as its physical hub, involving volunteers who may be students, international medical graduates or others in the community. It is in UBC's division of endocrinology on the VGH campus. We quickly added the work of the BC Centre of the Canadian Multicentre Osteoporosis Study, which I also direct. In 2001 we published the first population-based data in menstruating women showing that use of birth control pills (combined hormonal contraception) was associated with lower bone mineral density.[38] In the mid-1990s, as perimenopausal women increasingly sought explanations for and treatment of heavy flow, night sweats, increased premenstrual symptoms, and sleep problems, CeMCOR focused research on these mid-life women's misunderstood issues.[39] Since 2012, CeMCOR has focused research on the experiences and needs of adolescent women.[40]

Recounting the history of CeMCOR has been a welcome opportunity for me to look back. I am now seventy-four years old, working full-time as a professor of endocrinology at UBC. But I am still not able to secure infrastructure support for CeMCOR and continue to struggle for publication of research results that don't fit existing paradigms. Realistically, the future is dim. Between the $50,000 to $75,000 needed for annual infrastructure support and UBC's fiscally driven ban on professor replacement in 2015–2017, CeMCOR will likely be dissolved when I retire despite the diligent efforts of myself and many others. For CeMCOR to survive at all, it is important that women know why and how the centre was founded, what we set out to do, and what has been achieved.

We still need a simple, non-invasive test that today's young women can do that will tell them, cycle by cycle, if they are ovulating normally. We still need randomized controlled trials of cyclic progesterone treatment for menstrual cycle and ovulatory disturbances and for anovulatory androgen excess (also known as polycystic ovary syndrome). We also need to include normal ovulation as well as menstruation in viewing women's ovulatory menstrual cycles as a "vital sign" and essential for women's health. Despite these ongoing challenges, there is reason to persist. CeMCOR is still the first-ever and only women's research and outreach centre focusing on ovulation as well as menstruation and their key influences *beyond fertility* on women's whole health. In saying that I recall the grilling I was given by a local older woman in a participatory research planning meeting at Victoria's James Bay Community Centre in 2004. She plopped into a chair, planting her black-and-white basketball trainers on another, and asked "Is there any other centre in British Columbia like CeMCOR?" I confidently said, "No." "Is there any other centre in Canada like CeMCOR?" "Not that I know," I responded. But still not satisfied, she asked, "Is there any research centre anywhere in the world that is similar to CeMCOR?" Less sure, I said I didn't *think* so. She then declared, "Well, you cheeky bugger!"

BODY BEAUTIFUL/BODY PERFECT: WHERE DO WOMEN WITH DISABILITIES FIT IN?

Francine Odette

This article originally appeared in the National Eating Disorders Information Centre's 1993 Bulletin.

With a body that doesn't "measure up," we learn pretty quickly what our culture wants from women.[41]

When I decided to write about the issue of body image and its impact on women with disabilities, the challenge brought with it a chance to explore the link between fat oppression and the experiences of women with disabilities. Unfortunately, little research has been conducted on this issue as it affects the lives of women with disabilities. This may reflect the belief that the lived experiences of many women with disabilities are not important nor perceived as valid by mainstream researchers.

I do not represent the experiences of all women with disabilities regarding the issues of body image and self perceptions, however, over the years I have listened to the stories of many women who have a range of disabilities. These women's disabilities include being non-verbal, mobility, deaf, hard of hearing, and/or visual impairments. Many of these women spoke of their lives and how they have begun to deal with some of their concerns. While recognizing that the issues for women with disabilities may vary from those of non-disabled women, our lives, experiences, and fears are very similar.

Women are identified socially with our bodies. For women living in western culture, thinness is often equated with health and success. We are taught early to be conscious of our body shape, size, weight, and physical attributes. The current cultural "norm" or ideal is unattainable for most women. Fat women, women with disabilities, women from particular racial or ethnic groups or with non-heterosexual orientation, and other women who do not conform to the prescribed norm of social desirability are often viewed as having experiences and attributes somewhat different from that of other women in this culture and as a result are often isolated.

Women with disabilities living in this society are not exempt from the influence of messages that attempt to dictate what is desirable, and what is not, in a woman. These messages are often internalized, and have an impact on how we see ourselves. The farther we see ourselves from the popular standard of beauty, the more likely our self-image will suffer. We may experience a greater need to gain control over our bodies, either by our own efforts of restrictive eating and exercising, or the intrusive procedures performed by those deemed to be the "experts"—the medical profession.

We form images of ourselves early in infancy and these are confirmed or altered by the responses, or evaluations, made by others in our lives. Based on physical judgements, women with disabilities hear various messages from family, friends, and society at large about our perceived inability to participate in the roles that are usually expected of women. Society believes that lack of physical attractiveness, as defined by the dominant culture, hampers our ability to be intimate. These misperceptions hamper our ability to get beyond our physical differences, perpetuate body-image dissatisfaction, and contribute to eating problems.

Within this culture, having a disability is viewed negatively. This notion is supported by the fact that the lives of women with different disabilities are not reflected in the media. We are invisible. However, when our lives are spoken of, they are distorted through romantic or bizarre portrayals of child-like dependency, monster-like anger, or super-human feats. This increases the discomfort of others when in contact with women with disabilities, which in turn perpetuates the sense of "otherness" that women with disabilities may feel.

As women and individuals with disabilities, the messages that we receive often indicate the lack of role expectations for us. For young girls with disabilities, the invisibility of our lives becomes reinforced by the fact that popular advertising suggests the "normal" body is that which is desirable. Once these messages become internalized and reinforced, young girls and women with disabilities may try to compensate for their disabilities by striving to look as close to the non-disabled "norm" as possible. Similar to many non-disabled women's experiences, some girls and women with different disabilities may try to hide their bodies or change how their bodies look. Comfort and health may be sacrificed as we attempt to move closer to the realm of what the "normal" body appears to be by manipulating our bodies through continuous dieting, plucking, shaving, cutting, and constricting.

MEDICALIZING OUR BODIES

Much feminist theory has been focused on identifying the reality that within western culture, women's bodies are objectified for the purpose of male pleasure and domination. As a result, women's perceptions of themselves and their bodies become distorted. We are taught to mistrust our own experience and judgement about the notion of desirability and acceptance. These qualities are defined as the dominant culture. They are socially and economically defined by those in power—white, able-bodied, heterosexual men. Within this context, the body becomes a commodity with which one may bargain with in order to obtain more desirable opportunities, for example, work or security.[42]

Feminist analysis identifies women's alienation from themselves and their bodies as a result of the objectification of the female body. However, a great deal of feminist analysis may not be reflective of all women's experience. The way in which women's bodies are portrayed as commodities in the media may not be a reality for many women labelled "disabled." In reflecting societal beliefs regarding disability, our bodies become objectified for the purposes of domination, but within a different context.

Traditionally, disability, whether it is visible or invisible, has tended to be viewed as something that is undesirable. Whether we are born with our disability or acquire it later, our bodies become objectified as part of the medical process. Medical examinations are often undertaken by groups of male doctors who despite their aura of "professionalism" are still perceived by the patient as a group of anonymous men. Regular routines such as dressing ourselves or other activities are observed by doctors while on their "rounds," as this is seen as an excellent training for new doctors.

Many of us recount our experiences of having to display our bodies to groups of male doctors in the guise of "medical treatment" without prior knowledge or consent. We may have been asked to strip, walk back and forth in front of complete strangers so that they can get a better view of what the physical "problem" is, or to manually manipulate our limbs to determine flexibility and dexterity. Today, pictures or videos are taken of us and used as educational tools for future doctors, with little thought given to our needs to have control over what happens to our bodies or who sees us. While the medical profession attempts to maintain control over our bodies, some women with disabilities may attempt to regain control through dieting, bingeing, or other methods of body mutilation.

Some disabled women speak of having numerous surgeries conducted with the hope of a "cure," when in reality, the surgeries result in increased pain, discomfort, and altered physical state of one's body. The concept of body image as it impacts young girls and women with disabilities is crucial, especially when one looks at instances where the functioning of certain body parts must change and be altered, resulting in scars, diminished sensation, or radically changing the physical state, for example, amputation, mastectomies. A common theme emerges between intrusive medical intervention and popular methods of cosmetic surgery; the perceived need to change or alter the "imperfect" body. For many women with disabilities the message is clear—the way our bodies are now is neither acceptable nor desirable. To be non-disabled is the "ideal" and along with that comes the additional expectations for the quest of the "perfect body."

Body image, self-image, and esteem are often linked with the perceptions held by society, family, and friends. Disability is often seen as a "deficit" and women with disabilities must address the reality that the "ideal" imposed by the dominant culture regarding women's bodies is neither part of our experience nor within our reach. As women with disabilities, some of us experience difficulty in having others identify us as "female."

Disability and "differentness" results in many of us living our lives from the margins of society. As women with disabilities, we must begin to challenge the perceptions of "body beautiful" along with the perceptions held by some non-disabled feminists who resist the "body beautiful" but ignore or affirm the notion of the "body perfect." Disability challenges all notions of perfection and beauty as defined by popular, dominant culture. We must reclaim what has been traditionally viewed as "negative" and accentuate the reality that "differentness" carries with it exciting and creative opportunities for change. A lot can be learned by the experiences of women with different disabilities as we begin the process of reclaiming and embracing our "differences." This includes both a celebration of our range of sizes and shapes and abilities.

Cheryl Anderson with one-year old Scott on the Medical Bus Tour, Lillooet, BC, August, 1972. To Cheryl's left, Dan the lab technician, Dr. Charles King and the host family. Photograph by Dennis Skinner gifted to Cheryl in 1973

Vancouver Birth Centre staff reunion in Vancouver, 2018. Left to Right: Jill Kelly, Raven Lang, Cheryl Anderson, Camille Bush, Sandy Pollard, Don Forsyth, Anne Mills. Photo by Susan Boyd

VOLUNTEERS needed for RAPE CRISIS CENTRE

WILL RECEIVE TRAINING IN COUNSELLING RAPE AND ASSAULT VICTIMS

ESPECIALLY INTERESTED IN WOMEN WHO HAVE BEEN VICTIMS

Above: Ad from *Equal Times* (1975)
Left: Andrea Knight drawing from *Equal Times* (1975)

SECTION THREE:
FIGHTING FOR SERVICES

It soon became clear that health services were deficient when it came to women and the only real way to fix that was to start our own. What a job. The endless committee meetings, proposals, plans, and advocacy. The energy and commitment. The learning curves! The ability to withstand patronizing and closed systems in order to get a new model funded or an old model changed. All of this was necessary and on a range of services. But second-wave feminists addressed them all.

The health care professions also needed to change. Simkin details the invisibility of lesbians to doctors because of assumptions made about sexuality, heterosexism, and homophobia. Payne describes the alienation involved in childbirth for many women and the struggle to re-establish midwifery in Canada amid the resistance of doctors to giving up control over birth. Anderson and Bush recall the incredible Vancouver Birth Centre established in 1974, where women could go for education on pregnancy and birth, exert choice over their births, and then give birth either inside or outside of hospitals with lay midwives. Women and men worked at this clinic, often practising illegally, at great personal risk. Whynot and Herbert describe the politics of establishing the sexual assault service in Vancouver four decades ago, including their inspiration from Seattle and their astute assessment of the context.

Landsberg, Pepino, and Christilaw address complex and underhanded hospital politics in Toronto and Vancouver that threatened the very existence of women's hospitals. These fights are ongoing as health services get continually rationalized, often at women's expense. Landsberg and Pepino describe two different stages in the fight to keep Toronto's Women's College Hospital alive, which was originally established as a haven for both women doctors and women patients. Christilaw describes the more recent efforts that forged BC Women's Hospital and Health Centre, and the relentless forces eroding this vision. The fixing of services to better serve women involves many hands, lay and professional. Patience, action, and vigilance.

ASK THE RIGHT QUESTIONS: LESBIANS AND THE HEALTH CARE SYSTEM

Ruth Simkin

When I first started practising medicine in the early 1970s, there was no such entity as "women's health." It was assumed that "health care" included everyone—men, women, lesbians, gay men, etc. The only problem was that health care was often based on studies done on men. Women were just thrown into the pot and lesbians were totally invisible. The ludicrousness of this became obvious in a study done many years ago on uterine illness, with studies conducted on men![43]

Luckily, today we are able to recognize that women's health and health care is very different from men's. And that lesbian health care is very different from gay men's health care. Indeed, to assume that lesbians have the same health concerns as gay men is akin to assuming women have the same health concerns as men.

I started writing about lesbian health care when I kept hearing doctors say they had never met a lesbian in their lives. The fact that lesbians constitute a significant minority of the population makes this fairly unbelievable. Doctors usually didn't recognize lesbians because they didn't ask the right questions, or think about the possibilities. I showed doctors how to ask questions that would elicit helpful responses. And once society began to recognize the possibilities, lesbians became much more visible and able to get better health care.

Over the last fifty years, all women have begun to be treated better because of improvements and changes in attitudes and approaches to health and health care. Women's health has become more inclusive of context and takes into account the social, cultural, spiritual, emotional, and physical aspects of well-being. Now, the health care system is starting to address issues like poverty and violence against women and their impact on health care.

The situation is better than it was fifty years ago, but it still is not good enough for many women who suffer because of homophobia, heterosexism, and an establishment that is still blind to the indignities that women suffer on a regular basis. For example, we still have judges telling women to keep their knees closed instead of chastising the rapist, or not recognizing same-sex unions or parents. Unfortunately, although we have come a long way, the journey is far from over and there is still much work that needs to be done, not just for lesbians but for all women to receive equal health care and consideration.

CENTURIES OF STRUGGLE: LEGALIZING MIDWIFERY

Sarah Payne

There has always been midwifery in Canada amongst Indigenous peoples.[44] The first European midwives in Canada came to New France (now Quebec) in the seventeenth century. These midwives were paid by the King of France; they were expected to be available at all times and to meet the needs of the poor. Amongst the European settlers many women served the community as midwives with no formal training.[45] But by just over a century later, birth had been redefined from a process in which women helped each other to give birth to a dangerous, high-risk activity in which women needed medicine and technology to be "delivered."

Beginning in the mid-1800s in Canada, doctors had launched a very successful campaign to denigrate midwives, and nurses joined this campaign in the early 1900s. Anti-midwife ideology equated lay midwifery with ignorance, lack of education, injury, and death.[46] By the 1930s, women were being exhorted by doctors and health officials to ignore traditional sources of information and support and to follow "scientific" child-rearing advice.[47] The clear message was to distrust other women and to trust doctors, even though this "science" often lacked empirical support. So began the socialization of birthing women into dependence and passivity. Doctors consolidated their power base by discrediting competing practitioners and subjecting others in the system to a hierarchical structure based on class and gender.[48]

In the process, women lost the normalcy of their birthing experiences. Shortly, though, by the early 1950s, there was evidence that women and some nurses were alarmed about the cruelty of labour wards. Articles appeared in magazines such as the *National Ladies Home Journal*.[49] Women's traditional trust in their caregivers was breaking down and this influenced the resurgence of independent midwifery. There was a practice of drugging women in labour, tying their hands down to the table, and using a large episiotomy and forceps to "deliver" the baby. This practice was called "twilight sleep" and was touted as the new, painless way to give birth. The practice had started in the 1930s and become common in the 1950s.

On more than one occasion, in the early 1990s, the mothers of women I was caring for in labour broke down in tears because they did not remember the birth. They had been given "twilight sleep" and had no recollection of their birth experience. Watching their daughters choose their birth experience and be supported and empowered by those choices brought back the sadness of the loss. Even in the 1990s, in some hospitals, women were still having their hands tied down and forced to lie flat on their backs to give birth.

In the 1960s and 1970s, feminists and the women's movement provided a forum for women's voices. However, it is interesting that early second-wave feminism offered little or no support for women on issues of childbirth. Feminist theorists such as Shulamith Firestone believed that women's freedom would only be gained by freedom from the tyranny of reproduction. Nonetheless, the Canadian midwifery movement has been very influenced by feminist principles.[50] Ina May Gaskin, an American woman from Tennessee, was extremely influential in the resurgence of midwifery. In 1971 she and other midwives created the Farm Midwifery Center, one of the first out-of-hospital birthing centres in the USA. Her book *Spiritual Midwifery* (1977) presented pregnancy from a natural and normal perspective rather than a clinical one, and she became very respected as a teacher and writer. Feminism values and honours women and believes in dismantling injustices based on gender. Feminism also supports validating aspects of female experience that empower women. It is this tenet that is central to Canadian midwifery and on which woman-centred care is based.

Many women discovered that they were not alone in feeling alienated by their birth experiences. Some wrote about the traumatic birth experiences they had in the hospital and began to look outside the formal health care system for a more "humane" birthing experience. A client of mine in the early 1990's stated:

> "What I fear most is that I will end up in hospital and things will be done to me that I don't give

my wholehearted consent to. That my body will be violated by well meaning professionals and the sacredness of the moment will be destroyed. That I will lose control of the situation, not physically, but that my stated wishes will not be central to the event. That others will abuse me by taking advantage of my vulnerability and manipulating me to do things that are congruent with their beliefs, not with my own."

This woman and her partner had chosen a home birth against the advice of all those around them, mainly due to the fact that home birth with a midwife was not the cultural norm. What she wanted to maintain in her pregnancy and birth was a sense of control, and a sense of herself as an individual experiencing birth her way. She was unconvinced that this was possible within the existing maternity system.

Midwifery was illegal in Canada until 1994 when legislation in various jurisdictions began to change. In order to redefine birth as normal it needed to move back to the community and be reclaimed by women. So women again began to serve women, forming networks to serve the community. In the mid-1970s in BC the Maternal Health Society was formed. They produced a newspaper in which there were articles about birth and breastfeeding. In 1981, as the community of women and midwives evolved, midwives in British Columbia organized politically and formed the Midwifery Association of BC (MABC). Consumers (women and men who believed strongly in birthing choices) organized and formed the Midwifery Task Force (MTF) in 1981, which became a powerful lobby for the legalization of midwifery. They had their first meeting in the house of one of the midwives.

The renegade BC School of Midwifery was started in 1983 in Vancouver. This was an "underground" school and was taught by a midwife from England, an obstetrician, and a physician who supported midwifery. But as there was nowhere in BC or Canada for the students to get official placements, they arranged preceptorship placements in Jamaica, Germany, and Holland. Then they had to sit the Washington State Midwifery exams to obtain accreditation. Despite these obstacles, twelve midwives graduated through this school in two intakes.

In Ontario, there was a very effective consumer organization called the Midwifery Task Force (MTFO) focused on legalization and public funding for the profession of midwifery. The MTFO was very well organized and comprised of mostly, but not all, parents who had chosen midwives and clearly focused on the right of women to choose their caregiver and their place of birth. The midwifery supporters and activists continued to play an important role after legislation as public oversight members of the funding transfer payments and on the regulatory body, the College of Midwives of Ontario, and the professional organization, the Association of Ontario Midwives. Amendments to the *Ontario Health Disciplines Act* were passed in 1983. Professions were invited to submit a brief for the inclusion of their profession into the act. Practising midwives put in their brief, but faced opposing claims. One was from nurses who wanted midwifery to be part of nursing under the supervision of physicians and not to include home birth.

It was 1991 before midwives were successful and were invited to develop independent midwifery. Of the sixty-five midwives practising at that time, at least a third had formal midwifery education from elsewhere. The others had apprenticed with the trained midwives, or with physicians supportive of midwifery. The Task Force on the Implementation of Midwifery was formed in 1985, (separate from the consumer organization the MTFO) and members of the task force travelled around the world looking at different models of midwifery. They concluded that midwifery should be an autonomous profession separate and distinct from nursing.

The Ontario government, in 1991, hired a multidisciplinary committee, headed by Holliday Tyson, to create the first curriculum for a four-year midwifery programme. Holliday Tyson also headed the team to create an integration programme for the existing sixty-five midwives. This was held at the Michener Institute in 1992. Midwives were hired from England, Holland, and New Zealand to run this programme. The four-year direct entry programmes for midwifery education were begun at Laurentian, McMaster, and Ryerson Universities. From the sixty-five midwives practising in the 1980s, there are now 850 registered midwives in Ontario.

In the early 1990s three provinces (Ontario, Alberta, and BC) were on the brink of the legalization process. Midwives practised outside the system with the support of some general practitioners who ordered blood work or an ultrasound if needed and worked with the midwives if a transfer to hospital was needed. Due to the controversy associated with legalization, midwives played a central role in reclaiming the power of women over birth. Indeed it has been called a "social revolution." Birthing women also decided to take action and in partnership with midwives they gained a political voice. Childbearing women and midwives turned their attention to other countries where midwifery was legal and home birth was sanctioned to get examples of more humane approaches to childbirth.

In 1987, the Canadian midwives had lobbied the International Confederation of Midwives (ICM) to hold their congress in Canada. This would give them credence in their fight for legalization. They lobbied the ICM to have their next congress in Vancouver and won by one vote while attending the congress in The Hague in Holland in 1987. Although there were only approximately fourteen members (compared to thousands in others in other countries) the Canadian midwives had been referred to as "small but mighty" and had garnered tremendous respect in their quest for legalization. They booked the Vancouver Trade and Convention Centre and, after years of rejection, Canada was the first country that had no legalized midwifery to hold an ICM Congress. This was 1993, and the then-minister of health, Elizabeth Cull, announced that there was to be legalization of midwifery in BC. However, it would not be until 1998 that this took place. British Columbia implemented legislation in 1998 requiring registration of midwives in British Columbia, with an exemption for Indigenous midwives who were practising in Indigenous communities prior to the legislation coming into force.

Prior to 1998, Lee Saxell, a graduate from the BC School of Midwifery and one of the original midwives who began organizing in BC in the mid 1970s, helped arrange for five midwives to go to England and take their masters of arts in midwifery practice through the University of London and Queen Charlotte's Maternity Hospital. I attended this programme and obtained my MA. This was a strategic move to set ourselves up with enough credentials that we could not only practise midwifery but join the system as change agents.

Initially, there was little understanding between the members of the formal health care system (doctors and nurses) and community midwives. The medical community resisted change and power struggles occurred. Legally, these took the form of criminal prosecutions, charges of practising medicine without a license (although these never ended in a conviction), and coroners' inquests. Community midwives met resistance and contempt from hospital staff when transferring women into hospital who had originally planned a home birth. Over the years however, bridges were built between midwives and the members of the formal health care system through the efforts of individual midwives, supportive doctors, the Midwifery Association of BC, and the Midwifery Task Force. The Grace Hospital Midwifery Programme was started in the 1980s in Vancouver by midwives and two supportive obstetricians, thereby introducing midwifery into the formal health care system.

I worked in this programme between 1990 and 1994 and was also a community midwife attending home births. I observed how women choosing midwifery care faced a dilemma. They wished to be in control and to actively engage with their birthing experience. Yet they feared the hospital and its routines despite the ingrained belief that hospitals were the only "safe" place to give birth. I saw myself and other midwives acting as catalysts and partners with women, supporting them to overcome their belief that childbirth is abnormal to believing that it is normal. It was often hard for women and their partners to make this shift with any confidence. With increasing technology it became normal to accept the constructs of science as definers of reality and to depend on science to monitor and control human reproduction. Kloosterman, a Dutch obstetrician, stated that without the presence and acceptance of the midwife, obstetrics becomes aggressive, technological, and inhuman.

As a midwife in the Grace Hospital Midwifery Programme, I also fought for the right of women to choose who attended their births. At one point the midwives were told that all women in our programme must have medical students attending their births. It was a policy of the hospital that women have the right to choose who attends their birth, with the understanding that it is a teaching hospital and students must learn. However, to mandate this was unethical. I took this issue to the Ethics Committee and it upheld my view that this was unethical, that all women had a right to choose who was in the room with them during birth. As one woman stated of her hospital birth, "...I felt really, really angry about all these people in the room, there was absolutely no need for all those people in the room, none. I felt totally stripped of any power, any control, there was this whole thing about territory.... I'm a territorial beast and I was totally out of my depth in this place...so foreign. I wasn't sick, I was having a baby."

Health ministries were being forced to respond to social movements promoting different forms of care. It was imperative to decrease health care costs, including the attendant costs of medicalized childbirth. Midwifery-based care is one way to do this, and midwives successfully used this argument of cost-saving through community-based care, and the decreased use of technology such as epidural anesthesia and ultrasound. However, the move to denigrate the midwife in Canada that started in the mid-1800s had been very successful. Midwives and consumers faced a huge challenge to recreate a midwifery profession true to autonomy and woman-centred care, with the ability to work collegially with other care professionals.

In Canada, midwifery falls under provincial and territorial jurisdiction, and midwifery was legalized in Ontario and Alberta in 1994, with British Columbia following in 1998. Midwifery is now regulated in most provinces and territories. Although New Brunswick proclaimed its *Midwifery Act* on August 12, 2010, and passed a general regulation, no midwives registered to practise and so, in 2013, the province disbanded its midwifery licensing body to save money.

It is cultural and societal expectations that shape birth experience. Canadian midwives, against a century of medicalization, reclaimed, and then promoted birth as normal and were instrumental in shaping birth experiences. This was possible because they defined themselves separately from the existing culture and worked in partnership with women. Autonomous, independent practice was a vital part of this. However, the power to exercise autonomy required the existence of supportive cultural, institutional, and economical structures. The challenge for Canadian midwives after legalization was not only to gain mainstream acceptance, but to also resist the dangers of co-optation.

I asked midwives who were part of the struggle to legalize and who are still practising today what they like about being part of the system. One mentioned the respect now shown women regarding their birthing choice. For instance, women who had chosen a home birth but had to transfer into hospital and the staff in hospital now showed genuine concern and were very respectful of her wishes and concerns. Another says that is wonderful that women no longer have to pay for her services. Another stated that before legalization nurses were very territorial and would not let her behind the nurses' desk to view her patient's chart. Now, obviously, this is not an issue.

Midwives have stayed true to the concept of woman-centred care and partnership inspired by feminist principles. Feminist approaches were integral for Canadian midwives and women to begin talking about birth and work in partnership against a dominant system. Feminism influenced midwives as they developed woman-centred care and sought out professionalization and legalization. Feminist theory is integrated into the teaching of midwives, so midwives understand the nature of patriarchal society and its effect on birthing women. The reality of professional midwifery practice in Canada is that midwives have carried both the tradition and the science of midwifery with them into the present day and will hopefully do so well into the future.

REFERENCES

S. Fisher, *In the Patient's Best Interest. Women and the Politics of Medical Decisions* (New Brunswick, New Jersey: Rutgers University Press 1986.

"Midwifery in Ontario: A feminist struggle, past, present and future," *Journal of Women and the Law* (Canada, 1994).

THE VANCOUVER BIRTH CENTRE

Cheryl Anderson and Camille Bush

"Toward a better birth—a house on Glen Drive in East Vancouver. It's a happy atmosphere— hopeful, positive, supporting. Women walk in proudly, compare diets, share feelings, eager for the birth." Rhody Lake, 1974

To fully appreciate the progress and challenges of midwifery it is necessary to recall the beginnings of the resurgence of women reclaiming their own birth care in the context of the times. It was 1974, and although such commentary as Rhody Lake's would not be necessary now, with several well-established thriving regulated midwifery practices serving a diverse clientele in Vancouver, such was far from the case in those times.

The North American landscape in the early 1970s reflected a recovery from the turbulent 1960s, more notably seen in the United States but also present in Canada. Out of the protests for social justice seen in civil rights, anti-war, and the development of the women's movement, it was a time to find ways to move forward for those who survived the 1960s with their ideals and vision intact. Other movements that arose included environmentalism, co-operative housing alternatives, and back-to-the-land self-sufficiency. For many young women, the women's movement was a powerful thread that wove through and informed all the other movements. So it was with women's health care, including the demand by women for choice on how to give birth on their own terms, whatever those were.

As women one by one opted out of medicalized birth, other women, one by one, started to attend them. They studied the art and science of midwifery, stepping into the void created by the absence of choice in the medical establishment. Women empowered themselves to do what the system was not doing for them. It was in this climate of social revolution that a small group of women came together in Vancouver in the autumn of 1972 to brainstorm what could be done in British Columbia to provide services that would support women's choice in childbirth. Out of this brainstorming, a collective was formed that became known as the Vancouver Birth Centre. As one of the founding members, Cheryl Anderson, recalls:

> In 1971 when I gave birth to my first child, I wanted to stay home, but the doctor who had agreed to help me backed out. I didn't want to be at home without care, so I gave birth at the hospital, and must credit the nurse who assisted for sparking what became my mission to bring midwifery into the public domain. It wasn't what she did, but what she said: "This is the best birth I've ever seen." I still remember being shocked, for while I had given birth without difficulty, I was in a lithotomy position, my legs were in stirrups, and my hands were tied down for giving birth.
>
> The question that came to mind was, "If this is the best, what else goes on in here?" The answers started to come almost immediately. I wasn't allowed to touch or hold my baby for another twelve hours, was transferred to an open ward with sixteen beds in two adjoining rooms, and my son was put in the nursery and only brought to me every four hours for feeding. Because I was breastfeeding, I at least had the advantage of having him brought to me first before the other mothers got their babies, and taken from me last.
>
> And so started my exploration of the history of medicalization of childbirth. What I discovered inspired my search for a viable alternative. It didn't take long to find the Birth Centre that had sprung up in the Santa Cruz mountains south of San Francisco.

The Vancouver Cool-Aid Clinic, which had opened in the 1960s to provide medical care for youth in transition, organized a medical bus to tour remote areas of British Columbia in the summer of 1972. Along with a physician, lab technician, and the driver, Cheryl was invited to join the bus as a women's health counsellor. The bus twice toured the province from the Kootenays to the far north and many of the rural communities along the way. Cheryl had just completed six months of apprenticeship with

Raven Lang at the Birth Centre in Santa Cruz, and Raven accompanied her on one of the tours. They learned that there were many women opting out of standard medical care for their pregnancies, with no one stepping forward to help them. The exception was in the West Kootenays where Pat Morrison (formerly Armstrong), was helping with home births. In 1970, Pat had moved to the West Kootenays from the Santa Cruz mountains where she had previously been the first midwife to help women have babies at home. Pat reflects on her motivation to help women have choice in childbirth:

> The reason I helped women was because of the birth experience of my first child in the 1950s, where my hands were tied down so I could not contaminate the field. I was motivated to help women so they wouldn't have to go through what I had. Having worked as a maternity nurse at Stanford Hospital, I had lots of experience when I started working as a midwife, helping women in the Santa Cruz mountains to have their babies at home [in the 1960s]. I was happy for the women wanting this choice when Raven started to help them shortly before I moved to Canada in 1970.

Recognizing the need for childbirth preparation and attendance at home birth, Cheryl returned to Vancouver in the fall of 1972 and gathered like-minded women together to address this gap in services. They met in each other's living rooms, and applied for and received a federal government Local Initiative Project (LIP) Grant to open the Free Childbirth Education Centre. The application was supported by Vancouver member of Parliament Margaret Mitchell, and Vancouver medical health officer Dr. Gerry Bonham. The grant funded space and eight staff at $400 per month for eighteen months. The Free Childbirth Education Centre, which became known as the Vancouver Birth Centre, opened its doors at 531 Glen Drive in early 1973. This small group of women was joined by Raven Lang when she accepted an invitation to work with them. She recalls how the Birth Centre opened at "a three-storey house with a sweet character. It didn't take long before the doors were revolving with one pregnancy after another, and within no time at all we had a clinic, childbirth education classes, postpartum support groups, and study groups."

To better meet the needs of women in remote communities, the booklet "Free Delivery" was assembled by Birth Centre staff and was "dedicated towards the demystification of childbirth." The booklet was composed of comprehensive information on pregnancy, birth, and postpartum. And it was affordable, selling for $1 to cover the cost of the printing by Press Gang, a feminist printing press in Vancouver.

The Vancouver Birth Centre functioned as a collective and, as the demand for services quickly grew, the staff soon decided to expand, dividing the eight salaries twelve ways. There were ten women and two men working at the Birth Centre—the latter providing childcare services while the women provided a comprehensive programme in maternity care. All services were provided free of charge. More midwives were trained, learning through self-study and apprenticeship. They learned from each other, from sympathetic physicians, and from their mentor, Raven Lang. She recalls that, most importantly, midwives learned from the births attended: "We learned so much, of course, from the difficult births, which were few and far between. Most were easy, straightforward, blessed with the faith and courage that was a warp thread in the fabric of the era."

Textbooks for the study groups included *A Textbook for Midwives* by Margaret F. Myles; *Williams Obstetrics*; *Emergency Childbirth: A Manual* by Gregory J. White, MD; and *Pregnancy, Childbirth and the Newborn: A Manual for Rural Midwives* by Leo Eleosser, Edith J. Galt, and Isabel Hemingway (3rd English edition, 1973). Other books relevant to the women's health movement were also studied, such as *The Birth Book* by Raven Lang; *Witches, Midwives, and Nurses: A History of Women Healers* by Barbara Ehrenreich and Deirdre English (The Feminist Press, 1973), which described the politics of the self-help movement; and *Our Bodies, Ourselves*, published by the Boston Women's Health Collective.

Camille Bush, one of the apprentice midwives at the Birth Centre, recalls:

> When I arrived at the Birth Centre from the BC Interior in January, 1974, to apprentice in midwifery, I soon learned that, for me, studying midwifery also necessarily involved studying all aspects of women's health. I learned of a similar course of study at the Vancouver Women's Health Collective, also situated in a three-storey character home in Vancouver's eastside.

We studied the recently published *Our Bodies, Ourselves* chapter by chapter; from anatomy to contraception to sexuality to abortion to pelvic and breast health. There was a self-help clinic training programme in which I readily enrolled, soon participating in weekly clinics held at the Seymour Medical Clinic.

For me, birthing rights were always intertwined and inseparable from women's rights. This worked well for my next employment in January 1975 as the women's health worker at the Nelson Women's Centre in the West Kootenays.

Victoria Bitonti-Brown (formerly Morris), a nurse and certified childbirth instructor, recalls her experience as one of the staff of the Birth Centre:

> I taught late pregnancy classes at the Birth Center in 1973. I remember the joy of belonging to a group of women focused on caring for pregnant women. We celebrated home and hospital births by doing what our "mothers-to-be" wanted from backrubs, to different birthing positions, to babies put to breast, to family and friends supporting her....

While the midwives were prepared to help women wherever they chose to give birth, the Birth Centre was not intended as a place to give birth. However, when an out-of-town mother arrived from her doctor's office in labour, progressing rapidly, the midwives, who had birth kits ready to go, quickly set up to help her deliver. It was a highlight for the staff and for the pregnant women in the adjoining room who happened to be attending what turned out to be the ultimate prenatal class. The birthing mother gave her consent for the pregnant women to look in as the baby was being born. Raven recalls:

> About half an hour later I went [back] into their space and wondered how they did with such an experience. I was shocked to see that each of them had wet spots on their clothes from both breasts. It was then I realized that the oxytocin was flowing deeply for those women and that

birth causes the oxytocin to flow for everyone,
not just the birthing mother.

Raven's recollection illustrates so well how midwives gleaned
a lot not only from their studies, but from the best teacher of all,
experience. And the lessons were not only on the physiology and
pathology of birth, but were also on the deepest emotional aspects of childbirth as expressed by Sandy Pollard, a founding staff
member of the Birth Centre:

> I learned to deeply value and honour this work
> women did, birthing babies.... I learned the
> difference in having a baby and giving birth....
> I learned that midwives have been one of the
> strongest guardians of the normal birthing pro-
> cess in the varied ways it might present. I think
> for most it is a sacred calling.... Learning to listen
> deeply, to myself, to the mother, to the father,
> to the deeply emotional as well as the utterly
> physiological; what an astounding interplay of
> history, emotions, muscles, dreams, hopes, fears,
> landmarks, techniques, sexuality, family histo-
> ry—such a complex and richly revealing human
> experience."

The LIP grant for the Free Childbirth Education Centre
funded what became the de facto beginning of organized midwifery as an autonomous profession in British Columbia. While
choice was always important to Birth Centre staff, so was safety.
The early seeds of screening women for risk were planted. The
goal was for the right people to be at home for their births if they
so chose, and when there was an indication of risk, to seek appropriate medical care. As Anne Mills, a founding member of the
Birth Centre who worked as a prenatal instructor and provided
labour support, recalls:

> What I remember most clearly about being a part
> of the Birth Centre is being in the company of a
> number of active, intelligent, forward-thinking
> women who were willing to devote themselves
> to establishing an alternative model for women
> giving birth. It was a particularly satisfying
> and bonding experience being with wonderful

women finding ways to support other women to do what only women can do—birth a baby—and do that safely in a way that honours their hopes and needs.

Hundreds of women sought and received care through the Vancouver Birth Centre, and there were no maternal deaths and no perinatal morbidity or mortality in the hands of Birth Centre staff in the eighteen months it was funded. Supportive doctors were indispensable for this work, from lab tests to backup for complications of pregnancy, including attending women who were transferred intrapartum from home to hospital. The courage of these doctors to help, in the face of the resistance from the College of Physicians and Surgeons of BC, was a testimony to their commitment to providing the best possible care for women choosing midwives and homebirth. Vaginal Birth After Caesarean (VBAC) was not an option at that time, but one of the women who came through the Birth Centre had had a caesarean birth with her first child, and was determined to have a vaginal birth with her second. One of the obstetricians who gave support to the Birth Centre agreed to help. Jill Kelly, founding member on staff at the Birth Centre, attended the birth as a labour guide and recalls: "The birth was successful, without any problems. The obstetrician gave me a ride home after (from Vancouver General Hospital). When I asked him whether there was any point where he thought he might have to call off the labour and do a C-section, he said, 'The entire time!'" Such was the dedication of these doctors to change what had become the standard medical approach to childbirth.

The staff of the Birth Centre showed the same degree of courage and commitment, especially considering the legal ramifications they could face. The risk of legal consequences for midwives was not only in the event of an adverse outcome, but also for the mere act of assisting at a birth. Just the previous year, midwives in Santa Cruz had been set up in a sting operation and arrested for practising medicine without a license. As a single parent, Cheryl worried about what would happen to her son if this were to occur at the Birth Centre, but she found a solution: family law in BC allowed Cheryl to appoint a friend as her son's guardian while preserving her parental rights as the mother. The friend was Don Forsyth, a trusted and beloved childcare worker at the Birth Centre. There never were any legal charges arising from the work of the Birth Centre, but this single act by Cheryl illustrates the kind of personal challenges staff faced in working as midwives and attending women at home births without any legal status to do so.

Birth Centre staff, while respecting the choice of women, also respected the power of birth in all its forms—from straightforward to difficult. Some of the staff had grandmothers or great-grandmothers who had died in childbirth—at home and at hospital. Aspiring to the best standard of care, they knew it was imperative to not go underground and to work with the system, not against it. They were fortunate to have many tried and true models of care to look to. Midwifery was a recognized profession in most western countries that were consistently achieving the best birth outcomes in the world. But it was the Dutch model that most influenced the practice of the midwives at the Birth Centre.

In the Netherlands more than half of all births took place at home in the early 1970s, attended by midwives. The key was to have clear guidelines for when to transfer care from home to hospital, from midwife to obstetrician, and for that transition to be non-judgemental and supportive. The Dutch not only had well developed guidelines and practices, but also a firmly rooted profession of direct-entry midwifery; it stood on its own, a profession distinct from medicine and from nursing. The Netherlands had more home births than any other developed country and was amongst the countries with the best overall track record. The Dutch model of midwifery care was the perfect choice for BC midwives to adopt in the early 1970s and would later inform the evolution of regulated midwifery across Canada.

The women and their partners who came to the Vancouver Birth Centre were from diverse backgrounds. They were single moms as well as couples in conventional relationships and those who lived communally; some were students, some were from the back-to-the-land movement, some had religious affiliations. Most were of European descent, reflecting the dominant demographic of Vancouver's population in the 1970s, but there were also Indigenous, Asian, Hispanic, and Black women. Some were hippies who had dropped out of mainstream society and others were employed in occupations across the spectrum, including some middle-class professionals. Assisted reproductive technologies were not readily available at that time, but this did not preclude lesbians from having babies, and they also chose to attend the Birth Centre. No matter what the background, all were committed to having a different kind of birth experience than what they saw available in standard obstetrical care.

The women who came to the Vancouver Birth Centre were diverse in many ways, but they shared a common thread in their search for choice in childbirth. Elizabeth Shefrin, an artist living on Gabriola Island, describes her experience in making the decision about where to have her baby in 1974:

> Although I'd been going to the Birth Centre for months I was undecided about whether to have a home birth or a hospital one. It was the alienating nature of the hospital tour that decided me against that option. But I knew that the Birth Centre people would support me whichever choice I made. They weren't pushing home births, just making sure we knew it was an option. They were encouraging us to take charge of our own bodies and our own lives, including the birth process.

Nancy Taylor, who later became a childbirth educator and counsellor in the Robson Valley, recalls the influence Birth Centre midwives had on her when the Cool-Aid Medical Bus came to her community of Lumby in the summer of 1972:

> Before I became pregnant with my second child, I was living in a rural BC community when lay midwives were travelling the province teaching women like me about our right to choose the way we birthed. It took me a long time to get pregnant, but when I did, I chose a home birth with a lay midwife. In preparation, I did everything I could [involving] diet, exercise, education, and total body awareness to ensure an ideal outcome.
>
> I developed a trusting relationship with my midwife, connected with other birthing families and secured medical backup. This pregnancy was in stark contrast to my first birth experience where my passivity led to a sense of helplessness and victimization. Consequently, my second child's birth, attended by a midwife, was empowering and deeply fulfilling.

Just as choice in childbirth was critical to the staff of the Birth Centre, so was training those who wanted to be midwives, many motivated by their own birth experience. Diana Johansen (formerly Brownrigg), who attended the Birth Centre for pregnancy care, describes how giving birth at home with the help of a midwife also led to her decision to study midwifery:

> I have thought about those days often.... I remember attending a prenatal class...and learning for the first time that it was possible to have my baby at home. The idea excited me and terrified me at the same time. But I think the idea of having a baby in the hospital in the conditions of the times terrified me even more. And so, as I learned more, I became more confident and convinced that, yes, I could do this. Raven...who assisted me in my labour and delivery, couldn't have been more attentive and really helped me have a most memorable experience. I was so moved...I went on to become a lay midwife. I think it was the most empowering time of my life.

The staff at the Birth Centre also came from occupations across the spectrum, from artists to farmers, teachers, and nurses. They ranged in age from late teens to early thirties. They were self-starters and self-learners, such as Jill Kelly, who did the bookkeeping that launched her career as an accountant and future manager of Vancouver's CCEC Credit Union:

> I clearly remember the first planning meeting that...I attended was the week after I got out of the hospital after Cassia was born, and she was born forty-four years ago today! (October 1, 1972). I was hired to do the bookkeeping, but had never actually learned [this skill]. I learned double-entry bookkeeping from our project officer. I thought it was a fantastic concept!

After the grant for the Birth Centre ended in August 1974, the roads ahead for these 1970s pioneers of BC midwifery took many directions. Some of the staff remained in Vancouver, continuing to attend women in childbirth while keeping the Birth Centre open a little longer through donations. Some, like Diana, went into completely different work initially but later returned to the health field. She recalls:

After a ten-year stint driving a Vancouver city bus and then a Powell River school bus, I went to university and ultimately combined my two loves, nutrition and women's health. I worked as the dietician at the Women and Family HIV Clinic [Oak Tree Clinic at BC Women's Hospital and Health Centre] for sixteen years where I counselled women and children living with HIV.... I am sure my early work as a lay midwife created a lifelong interest in working with women and families in the health arena.

Some moved on to other communities, replicating the apprenticeship model of training. Sandy Pollard moved to Vancouver Island where she continued her work for choice in childbirth as a founding member of Birth Options for Nanaimo District (BOND). Raven Lang, who had moved to Vancouver Island earlier in the year, continued attending births and taught more midwives, including Luba Lyons Richardson. While Raven returned to California a couple of years later, her legacy in Canada is clear: Luba was the first president of the board of the College of Midwives of BC, appointed by the BC government in the process of establishing midwifery as an autonomous profession in BC; the first registrants started January 1, 1998. She was also among the first department heads of midwifery in BC, appointed by the Vancouver Island Health Authority in 1998. Luba has only recently retired from an active practice of midwifery that began under Raven's tutelage more than forty years ago.

Cheryl relocated to Montreal, providing care at home births and teaching midwifery skills at L'Auto-Santé from 1975 to 1976 before entering pre-medical studies in 1977. And Camille moved to the West Kootenays, training more midwives to meet a rapidly increasing demand where, by the late 1970s and early 1980s, close to 10 per cent of births were home births with midwives. Camille later returned to Vancouver and was in the group of the first fourteen General Registrants in BC, catching the first registered midwife (RM)–assisted baby to be born in British Columbia at thirty-two minutes after midnight on January 1, 1998.

Some of the staff went into other health professions, including massage therapy, western medicine, eastern medicine, acupuncture, nursing (often in the field of maternity care or community health), and nutrition. Others went on to explore different ways to positively affect children and families, such as social services, counselling, and teaching, including alternative education models. And some developed careers in other grassroots community-based programmes such as co-op housing and founding a community credit union. "I like saying that my bank manager was my midwife," muses Elizabeth Shefrin, a member of CCEC who was attended by Jill when her son was born in 1974. A few have carried on as practising midwives, staying the course in the evolution of the profession. Two of the staff, Vickie LaVaun Ishee (née Anderson) and Brenda Goldman, have since died.

Cheryl recalls how her sister Vickie was only eighteen years old when the Birth Centre opened in February 1973:

She was the mother of a one-year-old, and lived on the top floor of the Birth Centre for the first six months. She was an enthusiastic learner, attending births as an apprentice midwife, but she decided she needed a "real job" to support herself and her daughter. That fall she left the Centre to begin nursing school at Langara College, graduating in 1975. Maternity care was her focus for several years, initially working in Oakland. I remember how she crocheted booties for every baby whose birth she attended. By 1980 she was settled in New Orleans, enrolled in pre-medicine at Tulane. But her studies were interrupted by other life events, and she returned to nursing, in which she continued to work until the last year of her life when she was too sick to work.

Just as she had been committed to women's choice in childbirth and to the advancement of her own skills as a lay midwife while working at the Birth Centre, Vickie remained committed to social justice movements and was a lifelong learner. She was only a few classes short of a degree in women's studies when she died of AIDS in 1996 at the age of forty-two, infected by a needle-stick injury while working as an ICU nurse eleven years earlier. Her daughter gifted me with a paper Vickie wrote on birth, death, and spiritualism when she was a young nursing student at Langara, in which she writes, "Birth and Death are the two most important, most spiritual, and most respectful acts in our lives."

Even then she understood the parallel processes involved in birth and death.

Brenda Goldman joined the Vancouver Birth Centre in 1973. She was among the first bachelor-degree nurses in Canada, graduating from McGill in the mid-1960s with a bachelor of science degree in nursing, then earning a master of science degree in nursing education from Boston University, where she was also hired as an instructor after completing her master's. Drawing on her experience as a nurse educator, she taught vital skills to the apprenticing midwives at the Birth Centre, honing their knowledge and enhancing what they learned through self-study. Brenda also attended births, where she saw the contrast between the home births attended by midwives from the Birth Centre and what she had seen during her nursing training. When she had her own children several years later, she was very clear in her choice—her first child was born in 1977, an uncomplicated birth at home with a midwife, as was her second child in 1979. In the 1980s Brenda returned to teaching nursing. She was the first coordinator of the graduate nursing English as an additional language programme at Kwantlen University College, established to prepare foreign-trained nurses for registration in Canada. Brenda died in 2005 at the age of sixty-two shortly after her retirement from Kwantlen.

The words of Sandy Pollard further reflect the impact working at the Birth Centre had upon its practitioners regardless of the career paths they later followed:

> Though I went forward to leave midwifery and move into education...I do know the skills I learned with my personal birth work have been the bedrock of my approach to all my work: what is mine to do in this particular situation with this particular set of conditions and challenges, with this particular person and their individual set of gifts and challenges, to support and guide, where I can, using all my skills in service to the work before us.

As with many initiatives of the early to mid-1970s, those who survived the era might look back with fond affection (and admittedly some degree of embarrassment) at the methods chosen to achieve a given goal. In this case the goal was shifting the societal view of childbirth and taking actions accordingly to empower women with knowledge and choice. Hospitals ultimately adapted and changed how they provided care. Many medically unfounded practices were abandoned and new methods adopted to make hospitals more welcoming to a birthing woman and her support. Medical practices have evolved since that time: for instance, "preps" that included enemas and pubic hair shaving are no longer done; partners are no longer excluded from the birth nor required to don gowns and masks to attend when it is a vaginal birth; routine episiotomies are no longer performed; and newborns are no longer held upside down and slapped on the bottom.

Nancy Taylor illustrates this evolution of hospital maternity care as she describes the difference between her first and fourth children's births:

> In contrast to my first experience of giving birth in a large urban hospital in 1968, the birth of my fourth child seventeen years later in a rural BC hospital was wonderful. There was only one doctor serving this rural community and, with the demands on his time, he often relied on the two British-trained midwives who worked as nurses at the hospital as his backup. It was one of these midwives who helped with the birth, and I felt totally safe and supported in her care. I had a quick delivery, slept well afterwards with my baby in the room with me constantly. I was left alone unless I needed help and visitors were by invitation only.

Single-room maternity care in hospitals is now increasingly available and rooming-in has become the norm, as has immediate skin-to-skin contact between the mother and infant, with delayed clamping of the umbilical cord now considered a best practice. Mobility in labour, use of tubs and showers and other non-pharmacological comfort measures are now encouraged, as are different positions for giving birth. Though these practice changes may appear small, cumulatively they reflect the medical community's increasing respect for the birthing woman, sensitivity for the needs of the newborn, and support for the integrity of both. These were the kinds of changes the generation of women in the 1970s was looking for. The evolution of care in childbirth has inevitably led to other challenges and for today's generation, there is the challenge of finding the balance between the use of new technologies, which can be lifesaving, and the overuse of these same technologies, which can generate other problems.

It could be said that the Free Childbirth Education Centre Local Initiative Project marked a crucial turning point for birthing women and families in Vancouver and in the rest of British Columbia. Many steps were yet to be taken in the journey to what British Columbia enjoys now in terms of childbirth choices for women. Registered midwives now attend births at home and have hospital privileges, working as full members of the health care team while continuing to advocate for birthing families' needs, best practices, and innovative solutions to provide care. And hospitals have made great strides to be welcoming and respectful of women's choices.

The Vancouver Birth Centre marks only one place and one point in time in women's struggle to join together and reclaim the birth process as their own, to create choices for themselves and their daughters, but it represents the seminal moment in the birth of organized midwifery in British Columbia.

CONTRIBUTORS TO THIS ARTICLE

Cheryl Anderson, lay midwife (1972–1983); MD (UW 1983); licensed midwife (Washington State, 1987); MHSC (UBC 1994); clinical associate professor (School of Population and Public Health UBC)

Victoria Bitonti-Brown (formerly Vicki Morris), RN (1970); certified childbirth instructor and apprentice midwife at the Birth Centre (1973); prenatal instructor Torrance Family Birth Center and YWCA (1974); obstetrical nurse (1974–1984), social worker and nurse consultant for at risk infants and toddlers (Ukiah, California)

Camille Bush, lay midwife (1974–87); licensed midwife (Washington State, 1987); BScN (UBC, 1994); registered midwife (BC, January 1, 1998); preceptor and clinical assistant professor, School of Midwifery, UBC

Diana Johansen (formerly Brownrigg), lay midwife (1974–75); bus driver (Vancouver and Powell River School District 1975–85); registered dietician (1992– 2010; RD at UBC, 1991); dietician for Oak Tree Clinic (Vancouver Women's Hospital and Health Centre, 1994–2010)

Jill Kelly, prenatal educator, labour guide, apprentice midwife, and bookkeeper for the Birth Centre (1973–74); bookkeeper,

Markara Graphic Arts Design Cooperative (1976–82); co-op housing developer (1984–87); accounting diploma (Langara) and CGA (1988); manager CCEC, a community development credit union (1988–2012)

Raven Lang, BFA (1968); lay midwife (1969 forward); author (including *The Birth Book* 1972); licensed acupuncturist (California, 1984); doctor of oriental medicine specializing in pediatrics and obstetrics (California, 1986)

Anne Mills, RN (1960s); Vancouver Birth Centre labour guide and prenatal instructor (1973–74), co-founder and instructor, West Coast College of Massage Therapy (1981); BA (Antioch, 1970s); registered clinical counsellor (BC, 1970s forward); MA (SFU, 1990s)

Pat Morrison (formerly Armstrong), RN and midwife (1960s, forward); BScN (UBC, 1970s)

Sandy Pollard, childbirth educator, post-partum/newborn support, apprentice midwife (Vancouver Birth Centre, 1973–74); founding member of Birth Options for Nanaimo and District (BOND, 1975); youth care worker/special education teaching assistant (1970s forward)

Elizabeth Shefrin, artist and cultural worker, Gabriola Island, BC

Nancy Taylor, early childhood educator (Langara College, 1972); organic grower (Robson Valley, 1974 forward); childbirth educator (ICEA, 1988); BA (UVic Women's Studies, 2000); MEd Counselling (Acadia U, 2009); certified Canadian counsellor (CCPA, 2009)

THE VANCOUVER SEXUAL ASSAULT SERVICE: A VERY SHORT HISTORY

Elizabeth Whynot and Carol Herbert

"Before practical change is possible, it must be imaginable"[51]

The Vancouver Sexual Assault Assessment Service (SAAS) became a reality in late 1981 with funding from the BC Ministry of Human Resources to provide expert medical examinations for children who had been sexually assaulted. This funding ultimately enabled the concurrent development of a woman-centred emergency service for adults who had been sexually assaulted. The Sexual Assault Service was implemented at Shaughnessy Hospital in 1982 and continues today as a partnership between BC Women's Hospital and Health Centre and Vancouver General Hospital.

ELIZABETH WHYNOT (1972–1980)

I strain to recall exactly where we got the idea that we could develop a different, better medical response for women who had been raped. It seems to me to have emerged gradually from an awareness of the women's health movement of the sixties and seventies, and the critical narrative developing about how women experienced or were treated by the medical system.

I graduated from Queen's University in 1972 and then moved to Vancouver for the trial by fire then known as a rotating internship at St. Paul's Hospital. I was a walking, sleep-deprived danger to patients that year and mostly missed any relevant consciousness-changing, sociological events. Ironically, it was at the annual drunken party, attended by both staff and trainee physicians that a more senior female colleague, Dr. Hedy Fry, approached me to suggest that I might want to join her in volunteering at the Vancouver Women's Health Collective Clinic. They wanted a fourth licensed female MD to attend and would I join her, Dr.

Diane Watson, and Dr. Fran Wilt in that? A month or so later, medical license in hand, I did.

One thing led to another. A collective member who worked at the Pine Street Clinic told me that Pine needed another doctor and that became my first job in BC outside the hospital. I worked there from 1973 to 1977 and volunteered with the Health Collective Clinic for the next several years. The women of the collective provided my education in women's health, engaged me in political action, and provided an identity that I could wear as a self-defined "outsider" in relation to the medical profession. I participated in advocating for access to abortion and worked with other collective members in providing alternative education on women's health matters such as sex education for alternative schools, and that feminist approaches to health and health advocacy for women's groups across the province.

Other members of the Health Collective, specifically Johanna Den Hertog, Janet Torge, and Teresa Moore had already been thinking about how best to support women who had been raped. These activists initiated the discussion, education, and advocacy that led to the first feminist rape crisis responses in Vancouver. They sought training and inspiration from centres in the US such as Boston and Seattle, and developed training sessions for other volunteers to support women who had been sexually assaulted. Janet, Johanna, and Teresa formed Vancouver Rape Relief (VRR) in 1973, and over the next several years applied for and received funding to support the organization, continuing their education and outreach efforts with support from many high-profile women in Vancouver. It was these women and others in the community, feminist health advocates, who made the change we needed in the medical system "imaginable."

As the community at large, including government and other community agencies began to acknowledge the importance of responding differently to women who had been assaulted, various institutional responses began to develop. For example in about 1978, I was invited by the United Way of the Lower Mainland to join a working group called UWLM Social Planning and Research Committee on the Social and Health Aspects of Rape. The United Way had conducted a survey of victims' experiences of hospital services and then convened a multidisciplinary group including community activists, police, and doctors to develop ways to improve services. This committee reviewed the potential of "rape kits" to improve the gathering of forensic evidence from women attending emergency rooms after being assaulted and developed the first edition of the booklet "Information for survivors of sexual assault." [52, 53]

In the late 1970s, many other Vancouver and provincial institutions began to work on improving system responses to both women and children who had experienced sexual assault. Inspired by emerging knowledge and activism (especially in the United States) about child sexual abuse, the BC ministry of human resources, responsible for child protection, sponsored educational forums featuring experts such as Dr. Roland Summit from California and Lucy Berliner from Seattle. The University of British Columbia (UBC) Faculty of Medicine and the BC Medical Association (BCMA) developed continuing medical education modules on the same subject.

I left the Pine Clinic in 1977 and in 1978 took a job as a public health doctor for the Vancouver health department. Thus, when the Vancouver Police Department approached the health department to help find doctors to take over the medical examiner role (their usual medical examiners, a group of pathologists, wanted to discontinue their contract), they found their way to me, or I to them. I left the health department in 1979 to join a family practice being set up by my friend, Dr. Art Hister, who had given me the job at Pine. Shortly after, early in 1980, the Vancouver Police Department called me to ask about whether I could help provide the medical service they needed for rape complainants.

Around this time, I met Dr. Carol Herbert, a physician at the REACH Medical Clinic, who was also interested in improving services. Through contacts outside of the medical system, and at the medical conference[s] addressing child sexual abuse, we had both become aware that the ministry of human resources was looking for medical help in assessing children who may have been sexually abused. Carol and other MDs at the REACH Clinic had previously connected with Vancouver Rape Relief and were already providing medical care on request for some of the women supported by VRR.

CAROL HERBERT (1970–1980)

I graduated from UBC Faculty of Medicine in 1969 and did my internship at St. Paul's Hospital from 1969 to 1970. As a medical student, I had been involved in community health outreach as a volunteer in Vancouver, went to Turkey on a World University Service seminar, and attended a summer school in the North, where I experienced the reality of life and health on reserves. I wanted to "do good" as a doctor but wasn't quite clear how or where I should work. I recall being warned by an attending physician against having anything to do with the "pinko-commie" clinic, the REACH Centre, that was just getting started in the east side of Vancouver in 1970 to provide service to Grandview-Woodland and serve as a teaching site for pediatrics. The clinic was modelled on the Pointe Ste. Charles community health centre in Montreal to provide team-based primary care with easy access.

Sound familiar? These are considered cutting edge ideas forty years later! What was troubling to the establishment was that five family doctors were donating their fee-for-service income from seeing patients one afternoon each week so that the clinic could become operational. Subsequently, the founder and director, Dr. Roger Tonkin, was able to develop alternate funding to hire two full-time physicians. I came on the scene in November 1970 as a part-time locum tenens to develop a practice for the second physician who was coming from Winnipeg the following spring. However, a community health centre practice was such a good fit for me that I didn't leave REACH until I moved to the UBC Department of Family Practice full-time in 1982, subsequently becoming head of the Department of Family Practice in 1988.

The patients who came to REACH were in three categories:

1. Individuals who wanted alternative medical care, including shared decision-making. This group included feminist activists.
2. Individuals and families from the local Italian and Portuguese community
3. Individuals and families who could not or would not get care at usual family practice offices.

Some had mental health or addiction issues; others needed extra time and attention because of multiple medical conditions or special needs. Many were poor, some had been on welfare for more than one generation, and their medical conditions were impacted by poverty and social deprivation.

My consciousness was raised by my patients, particularly the feminist activists. When I saw people with a history of abuse or family violence, what I had learned in medical school was clearly insufficient to meet their needs. I learned from feminist advocates how to be more useful as a physician. This included non-traditional activities like linking to Rape Relief and later Women Against Violence Against Women (WAVAW) to provide care for women who had been assaulted.

When the Vancouver police were searching for an alternative to the police physician, I was happy to work with Liz to develop a team, write protocols for care, and do the political work necessary to getting space and support at Shaughnessy. As I had a clinical appointment at UBC, we became affiliated with UBC from the outset, giving us credibility. When I moved to UBC full-time in 1982, I continued the work I was doing on sexual assault and sexual abuse and began to do research and write about the model. Subsequently, the model was copied in a number of centres, including Toronto, where Mimi Divinsky, who had been a medical student at UBC, organized a roster of women physicians to provide 24/7 care, just as we had done in Vancouver.

Both Liz and I attended a BCMA-sponsored continuing education session where Dr. Shirley Cook Anderson from Seattle spoke about their services for sexually abused children. I clearly recall saying to Liz that something needed to be done in Vancouver— and us both realizing we were the likeliest doctors to take it on. My colleagues at REACH were supportive and I began to see children referred with a history of sexual abuse; soon after Liz and I started (with Dr. Georgia Hunt [Immega]), a sessionally funded clinic at the ministry of human resources offices.

VANCOUVER SEXUAL ASSAULT ASSESSMENT SERVICE

[I became involved with SAS because] I wanted to be a women's doctor. To be a woman's doctor, I decided I wanted to be able to provide complete clinical care.
—Ellen Wiebe, in conversation with Liz Whynot

Working out of emergency departments was fascinating. Dealing with emergency staff was really difficult because the focus of their work was on life and death medical conditions. Classic ER work culture did not include such things as giving someone time to choose, to make decisions...emergency staff had very limited respect for the SAS.
—Anneke Van Vliet in conversation with Liz Whynot

The development and implementation of the Vancouver Sexual Assault Assessment Service was possible in 1981 because of the confluence of several factors: community-based feminist activism, increasing (feminist) awareness among women physicians, and acknowledgement within government and institutions (hospitals, social services, police, e.g.) that the system lacked capacity to provide competent services for both women and children experiencing sexual assault. Context was hugely important then, as it is today.

In fact, the initial funding support for the Vancouver Sexual Assault Assessment Service was provided in September 1981 by the child protection arm of the provincial ministry of human resources (MHR). As stated in the first contract for the services:

> The Ministry wishes to make provision for appropriate medical resources for childhood sexual assault victims, wishes to improve and co-ordinate existing hospital emergency procedures for assisting victims of sexual assault, and wishes to provide back-up consultation to hospital emergency room physicians, surgeons, and nurses regarding sexual assault victims...the resource physicians have indicated a willingness to offer their services to this end....

The proposal was for both non-emergency and emergency services. The emergency service was extended and developed (with the tacit support of MHR) into a twenty-four-hour service for not only children but also adults who had been assaulted.[54] In March 1982, we were able to present a formal "Proposal for Sexual Assault Assessment Service at Shaughnessy Hospital Emergency Room." The proposal suggested that:

> examinations could be carried out in the Cast Room which is more private and less in demand than the OR, particularly at night, when the majority of cases are seen. A proper pelvic table will be essential if the service is continued after the first 6 months. Initially, however we can use the bed in that room and carry out an adequate examination.

We invited all the women GPs we could think of to discuss and ultimately participate in providing these emergency services and ten willing volunteers joined our first roster.[55] Using modified Seattle Harborview Hospital Protocols, we began providing medical examinations on an on-call basis in October 1982. In setting this up, we engaged a number of key partners, including the Women Against Violence Against Women Rape Crisis Centre who provided volunteers to attend the emergency if the patient requested this support.[56] We worked with the newly established Vancouver Police Sexual Offenses Squad, crown counsel, hospital administrators, and emergency room doctors to develop communication and training protocols.

It's not hard to recall the tone of some of those necessary meetings—virtually all with the men in charge: doctors, crown prosecutors, police, and administrators. Attitudes varied, but *defensive, dismissive, patronizing, avuncular*, and *aggressive* are words that quickly come to mind. We each played different roles in response, sometimes cajoling, placating, confrontational, but always with the ultimate aim of establishing a service that made sense. These meetings were not always easy, but in the end we came up with ways of collaborating on behalf of women seeking care and support.

Inspired by our Seattle mentors and feminist health advocates, we committed the SAAS to a woman-centred approach to care. This meant the woman would always have as much control as we could provide (consent at all stages) and high quality medical care would always come first, before forensic requirements. Any formal reports to the police (even when police brought the person to the ER) would only be sent with consent, and a rape crisis support worker would only be called if the patient requested this. If a woman did not want to make a report to the police, we would collect and store evidence for her in case she changed her mind over the next year and WAVAW would record a third-party report of the assault details that could be used at a later date. The only exceptions to the SAAS principles were made in the cases of children and young adolescents whose care was provided in the context of child protection reporting requirements.

In many ways the character of the Sexual Assault Service (SAS)[57] then and now has been defined by the partnership with WAVAW. This collaboration with WAVAW continues to ensure a meaningful connection with community-based feminist advocacy. In the late 1980s, when funding became available for SAS to hire a coordinator, WAVAW member Anneke Van Vliet was recruited for this role. Anneke describes herself eloquently as having been a "radical feminist in an alien environment," i.e. the hospital. When the Shaughnessy Hospital itself was largely closed in 1992, the impact of the feminist-oriented SAS, and our "alien intruder" was profound. SAS became a defining programme of the new Women's Health Centre and ultimately BC Women's Hospital and Health Centre. Anneke notes as well that it was important to have the support of feminist leaders within the hospital: "I did not have enough power in the hospital hierarchy to ensure a woman-centred focus but I knew that I had the support of the women who did have the power." This speaks to the importance of a women's hospital as an environment to nurture and support feminist-informed programmes. In fact, the continued success of SAS was enabled by many partnerships fostering work and communication across many sectors: community, hospital, physicians, nurses, police, and prosecutors.

LOOKING BACK:
REFLECTIONS FROM WHERE WE ARE NOW

In many ways, the Vancouver Women's Health Collective's success at maintaining a political edge while providing a service can be attributed to the fact that, for the Collective, creating and operating a feminist self-help clinic was in itself a political act.[58]

I have no doubt that our woman-centred feminist approach to caring for survivors continues to this day because of Liz, Carol, and WAVAW and even more specifically because our first programme coordinator, Anneke Van Vliet, came from working at WAVAW Rape Crisis Centre. As a result, right from the beginning all of our policies and procedures were developed through a feminist lens. The programme was built on the understanding that sexual assault is a social and political issue and every protocol we have puts the needs of the women first.
—Lianne Ritch, current SAS
Nursing Coordinator

The seeds of the Vancouver Sexual Assault Service were planted over forty years ago, and it has been in continuous operation for more than thirty-five years, weathering changes in hospital organization, service locations, leadership, government priorities, and social context. It continues to feature a unique partnership with a community-based feminist organization, WAVAW, and it continues to offer high quality, woman-centred sexual assault care in the "alien" setting of a busy emergency department. In 1995 the programme implemented the first sexual assault nurse examiner (SANE) training programme in Canada.

Over the decades, the SAS team members (medical directors, coordinators, nurse clinicians) have trained hundreds of health professionals, police, crown counsel, and community-based workers in everything from how to set up an appropriate service in the community to forensic evidence-gathering best practices and provision of testimony in court. SAS protocols and training have been taken up in a large scale in Japan through an unusual and inspiring partnership with advocates and professionals there.[59] The intervening decades have witnessed not only improvement in the BC health system's competence in providing care for victims, but also continued improvement in police response and updates in Canadian criminal law.

Has the work of the Vancouver SAS been a political act? We think the answer is definitely yes. The SAS was born from the political, feminist health critiques of the late seventies and early eighties. Its philosophy of care and service model incorporate woman-centred care principles. It has continued to work with and support community-based women's health and service advocacy organizations. It has changed, positively, how the BC health and legal systems respond to sexual assault victims. The continued existence of this feminist programme within the larger medical system lays out a standard of practice against which health care providers and institutions can measure the quality of their services for women. This is activism from within.

As a programme within the larger health system in BC, SAS is inevitably affected by the philosophies and priorities of the governments of the day. From the early 1980s to the early 2000s, the SAS and BC Women's Hospital and Health Centre were part of an emerging provincial agenda for women's health. In that context, SAS was enabled to provide its expertise provincially, facilitating the development of programmes and training of health practitioners. Unfortunately, after that there was some erosion in the provincial focus on women's health as well as SAS resources oriented to provincial service development. The development of a provincial standard of access for competent, coordinated sexual assault services has not yet been fully realized in BC. SANE or medical examiners are available in many larger centres and coordinated community partnerships have developed in some areas, but there are still many parts of BC, a very large province, where services have not developed. That being said, over thirty-five years after the establishment of the Vancouver SAS, Vancouver Coastal Health (one of five regional health authorities in BC) adopted the first comprehensive Sexual Assault Health Care Policy in BC, mandating all hospitals and urgent care centres in the region to ensure provision of care for sexual assault victims. Section 2.2.4 of this policy states "the current standard is the training provided by BC Women's Hospital Sexual Assault Programme." It remains for us in BC to make the case with the provincial government and all the other health regions for a strategy to mandate access, especially for women in small rural communities and women living on the margins in urban settings.

Have feminist, woman-centred sexual assault services had the societal impact we would have wished? Clearly not. In December 1983, *Maclean's* magazine published a short article on the emergence of co-ordinated responses to sexual assault in several centres across Canada. It quotes Regina Lorek as saying, "with a 2 per cent conviction rate across the country, most women do not think it will do any good (to report sexual assault). They do not want to deal with the police or relive the experience during a one to two-year court battle." We thought when we set up SAS and did all that work with the hospital, police, and crown counsel that we would be able to change our system in such a way that women would no longer hesitate to come forward when they had been assaulted, and ultimately effect a reduction in risk because successful prosecution of offenders would be more likely.

We were very naïve. High-profile cases in recent years in Canada and internationally have underscored our global collective failure in making communities and the legal system safer for women. Woman-centred, feminist-oriented services have had no measurable impact on the risk for women of being assaulted. As noted in a 2009 Canadian national survey, women reported 460,000 incidents of sexual assault in just one year. Only about 10 per cent of all sexual assaults are reported to police. When it comes to sexual assault, women are frequently not believed, blamed for being assaulted, "or subjected to callous or insensitive treatment, when police fail to take evidence, or when their cases are dropped arbitrarily." Only a handful of reported assaults ever result in a conviction: Each year, only about 1,500 sexual assault offenders are actually convicted.[60]

Women are not safe from sexual assault. And as a society we don't seem any closer now than we were in 1981 to making them safe. In fact, now there is a misogynist, self-confessed abuser of women elected as the president of the USA with every expectation that he and his government will attack the already fragile systems of support for women in that country.

In contrast, in Canada there are some recent very positive indications of societal interest in making women safer. In March 2015, under the leadership of Premier Kathleen Wynne, the province of Ontario released "It's never okay, an action plan to stop sexual violence and harassment." In April 2015, the province of British Columbia under the leadership of Premier Christy Clark, released "A vision for a violence-free BC: Addressing violence against women in British Columbia." These are ambitious strategies each with several areas of focus such as raising public awareness (Ontario), changing behaviours through school-based prevention programmes (both), and fostering intersectoral partnerships (BC). If these or other governments can, with our support, identify and implement truly effective strategies then we may finally begin to see some improvement in the numbers we know only too well.

WOMEN'S HOSPITALS

HOW FEMINISM SAVED THE GRAND OLD
LADY OF GRENVILLE STREET

Michele Landsberg

At the corner of Grenville Street and Emily Stowe Way, just blocks away from the venerable teaching hospitals that dominate the medical landscape in Toronto, a gleaming new building rises, crowned by a defiantly rose-pink cube—an entire room sheathed in pink glass. In a time of government austerity at the end of two decades of constant budget cutbacks and hospital closings, this is the only newly built hospital in Toronto. It is Women's College Hospital—"Women's," or WCH—triumphantly risen from the ashes. Not only is it a striking achievement in itself, but it stands as a beacon of hope in dark political times.

The continued existence and new incarnation of this women's medical facility is due entirely to feminist activists with well-honed political acumen. Its history is one of struggle against male domination and frequent hostility; that a relatively small band of feminists were able to prevent its demolition into dust and actually managed to resuscitate a nearly moribund institution, is a story that must be told—especially because chauvinist counter-narratives already proliferate. I'm motivated to tell this story now because, to my surprise, so few people—even those inside the hospital structure—are aware of the remarkable role played by feminist activists.

I cherish the stories of all those women who played vital roles in creating Women's College Hospital—the only public institution in Ontario, to my knowledge, with the word "women" in its name. We own it. It rightly belongs to us. Right back to its founding by the sturdy suffragist Emily Stowe, we owe a century of gratitude to these women. Emily Stowe, Canada's first female doctor, learned her medicine in New York because the Toronto College of Medicine adamantly refused to admit female students. (In a rare and delicious piece of historical justice, Emily's daughter, Augusta Stowe-Gullen, also a suffragist, became the first woman in Canada to earn a medical degree.) Emily returned to Toronto in 1868 to open a small clinic for poor women in downtown Toronto. Before the turn of the twentieth century, women's demand for medical training was so insistent that the clinic morphed into a school (hence its name, to this day) and later into a hospital.

For its first half century, Women's College Hospital was led by female doctors who headed all the departments—including surgery—and guided the research, some of which led to important breakthroughs for women's health. Mid-twentieth century, as the hospital's leading physicians sought accreditation as a teaching hospital, they made a deal with—if not exactly the devil, then at least with men who had less than honourable intentions. In return for the University of Toronto's seal of approval, Women's agreed to admit male medical staff for the first time in its history. Almost at once, men became the heads of at least half the departments, and powerful male medical leaders exerted control over hospital policies...some with near-fatal outcomes, eventually, for a beloved women's institution.

Still, at least some of the men who came on board in the following decades were attracted by, and loyal to, the ethos of Women's: an intensely collegial community hospital with a relatively flat hierarchy, a large and admired family practice serving both women and men, a focus on women's health research, and a busy and trusted maternity department. In the decades immediately after mid-century, Women's was bursting with innovation. In the sixties, renowned ob-gyn Marion Powell founded the Bay Centre for Birth Control in a friendly old house on Bay Street, a no-questions-asked sanctuary for teens (and others) seeking birth control, reproductive advice, and abortions in the still-repressive 1960s. It pioneered the Brief Psychotherapy Centre for Women, a rare self-governed refuge where women could self-refer and receive feminist therapy. The hospital was the first to open an innovative Sexual Assault Care Centre and, later, an unusually effective therapy programme called WRAP—Women Recovering from Abuse—for survivors of childhood sexual abuse. Its family practice was the largest in Ontario and, most unusually, its family practitioners continued to deliver babies—800 a year—long after most GPs had stopped.

This is my account of how some of us members, feminist allies all, banded together in 1989 when a serious threat of extinction faced Women's. We called ourselves Friends of Women's College ("the Friends"). We were determined to keep the hospital alive despite nearly constant threats of takeovers from the large downtown institutions and the powerful University of Toronto medical school. Women's, after all, sat on a prize piece of downtown real estate, valued in the eighties and nineties at $80 million. Coincidentally, the Toronto Hospital Corporation (as Toronto General called itself in the corporate-mad 1990s) calculated that it would need $80 million to build a fancy new maternity wing to accommodate the patients it planned to take over from Women's.

Key to the ongoing survival of this paragon of woman-friendly hospitals was the almost-quaint practice (once widespread in Ontario) of public memberships. For a relatively small fee, around $40, anyone could become a member of the Women's College Hospital corporation and have a vote at the annual general meeting. Later, I myself, as chair of the Women's board of directors, reluctantly and with a bitter sense of irony, dealt the fatal blow to the cherished custom of public memberships. That story comes a little bit farther along in this account. In the meantime, to understand the triumph of saving the hospital, it's important to grasp that this simple, democratic measure underpinned everything.

The first great battle came in 1990, when Toronto General Hospital and the University of Toronto mounted their putsch against Women's College Hospital. It seemed that the hospital was in a death spiral. Dr. Walter Hannah, highly esteemed head of obstetrics and gynecology at Women's (and son-in-law of Lester Pearson) was determined to fold the hospital into Toronto General—or the Toronto Hospital Corporation, as it then called itself—as an obstetrical wing of the male-dominated giant of University Avenue. The members of the WCH board, headed by Susan McCutcheon, daughter of Conservative Senator Wallace McCutcheon, were fully in support of this demolition of Women's. I do not have access to the records of the thinking behind their decision. But, having been in the position of chair myself, I know the powerful, almost overwhelming forces of persuasion exerted by the provincial government, the medical schools, and the supremely confident big boys of University Avenue. I would not blame those women on the board if they had been convinced that the hospital's funding was doomed and there was no way out but to save a scrap of maternity services as a little mutilated stump attached to the Toronto General Hospital.

The Friends of WCH sprang into existence in 1989, a true grassroots uprising of patients and other loyalists who cherished the uniquely non-corporate, patient-embracing culture of Women's. The group had to be re-mobilized several times in the fifteen years it took to regain the WCH independence we know today, and every time a new battle threatened, the core leadership group regrouped. They included Dr. Bev Richardson, a gastroenterologist and fiercely focused feminist on the staff of the hospital; general practitioner Dr. Carolyn Bennett, also a WCH staffer, public health activist, and later a Liberal MP and cabinet minister; Marilou McPhedran, a resolute feminist lawyer who later became a senator and who had played a leading role in the battle for equality rights in the Canadian Charter of Rights; Jocelyn "Joc" Palm, owner and director of a renowned girls' summer camp, acting as the executive director of the Friends of Women's College (along with McPhedran, she was paid with money donated by philanthropist Gail Regan); and Gail Regan herself, a board executive in her family's food empire, Cara. Marilou was the vital activist link who went outside the ranks of the Friends and the inner circle of hospital loyalists to alert the wider world to the threat to Women's, and who knew how to mobilize a public phalanx of support.

Throughout the 1990 merger menace, I played my part by writing furious columns in the *Toronto Star* denouncing the plans, and so did the influential leader Doris Anderson, who by then had retired from editorship of *Chatelaine* magazine and resigned from the chair of the federal Status of Women Council. Many others played a role. Significant among them were social activist Marcia Gilbert and nurse Joan Hill, who was chair of the hospital volunteers and later the chair of the Retired Nurses' Association.

The Friends were an extraordinary collective force of doctors, nurses, security guards, social workers, cleaners, and secretaries working at WCH, joined by patients—men and women—that rose up to protest the destruction of a beloved institution. This dedicated cohort remained responsive to calls for action in defence of WCH for more than a decade. At their peak, during the first campaign against the merger with Toronto Hospital, their numbers (according to Joc Palm, keeper of the membership list) reached 10,000. They were formidable and unbiddable.

Engineering a "reverse takeover," the Friends galvanized voting members to attend the AGM where the merger was to be affirmed by vote. They successfully defeated the board members who supported the merger and killed the deal. Men in government were enraged and the power wielded by the Friends that day plagued establishment memories for years, as I learned when I became chair of the board in another "coup" fifteen years later. But that day, the Friends prevailed. Against the supreme financial power of the government and the medical establishment, the cannibalistic merger was voted into oblivion.

Our jubilation didn't have long to live. The New Democratic Party government of Bob Rae was not particularly friendly to Women's; in the teeth of an economic recession, it pushed for hospital amalgamations, imposing more and more hospital budget cuts. Women's was in a tight economic squeeze. By 1995, with the far-right Conservative government led by Mike Harris newly in power, ominous drums began to beat again. Harris announced that he would close thirteen hospitals in Toronto, and Women's College was almost certainly on the list. To wield the axe, Harris set up a puppet "arm's length" commission for hospital restructuring, the Health Services Restructuring Commission. All the appointees had connections with one or another of the big Toronto hospitals, but this conflict of interest seemed invisible to the public. As a *Toronto Star* columnist at the time, I railed in column after column against the "Hospital Destruction Commission" and the public turned up at hearings to protest the commission's plans, but no one ever officially questioned the motives of the axe-wielders, almost all of them representing big hospitals that would materially benefit from the proposed closings and mergers.

And now the scene was ripe for the next matricide. This time, the public seemed exhausted from years of struggle to save Women's College, and even more strung out by the confusing, hectic barrage of merger proposals emanating from a jumble of conflicting sources. Some of the executives at Women's rejected the idea of being merged (once again) into Toronto Hospital, instead floating a merger with the suburban veterans' hospital, Sunnybrook. Meanwhile, some of the more idealistic Women's doctors fought for a merger with the equally small and community-minded downtown Wellesley Hospital, which would have saved both hospitals and conserved resources. The general public must have been baffled. Competing agendas, conflicting proposals, an overall atmosphere of pending doom...the result, as always, and to the government's satisfaction, was public apathy. This time around, there would not be 10,000 members rallying, no march of Men for Women's (wearing straw boaters) around the venerable and imperilled hospital building. Even so, the Friends did manage to rouse enough members to hold hands in a symbolic circle around the entire hospital building. There was poignancy in the symbol: determined humans, joining in futile defence against a destructive bulldozer of a government.

Desperate, I taxed my readers' patience with yet more columns trying to rally opposition to the closing and to capture the very distinctive culture of Women's College that so endeared it to so many patients. I wrote in the *Star*:

> "I know that my personal feelings about this hospital hardly matter in the larger scheme of things. But it does begin to count for something when thousands of others have the same web of attachment and reassurance, the same depth of history with the place, the same intimacy.
>
> Two of my three children were born there. The emergency department saved my life not once but twice. I stopped to compliment the gardener on his fine show of ranunculas one sunny spring morning on my way in for chemotherapy, and that brief exchange gave me a beam of warmth and normalcy to hold on to that day.
>
> Maria at the out-patient check-in desk whose smile brightened many a fearful morning, the cheerful woman who painlessly took blood samples, the nurses who radiated confidence and commitment that comes of working in a collegial atmosphere—all these are part of a significant human community that extends far beyond the hospital walls.
>
> Women's College Hospital is now supposed to close up shop, dismember itself, and ship a few of its body parts (neonatal, breast care) to Sunnybrook Hospital in the 'burbs, according to the Metropolitan District Health Council "hospital restructuring committee."

Looking back, I understand better that it was my passion as a feminist that made me so committed to Women's survival. If you weren't a feminist, but just someone interested in economics or health care, you might find many rational reasons to close a smaller institution and go gung-ho for the corporate belief in bigness and uniformity—the so-called "economies of scale." But I argued even with the economics of the move.

"To dismantle Women's College, scatter its eighty-six years of expertise to the winds and move its special programmemes to the wilderness of Sunnybrook is emphatically not a cost-cutter," I wrote. "It will cost millions." (Yes. It did. And many brilliant women's programme were lost.)

I couldn't believe that those in power were so dead to the special urgencies of women's health care. The self-important brass in the ministry of health and at Sunnybrook Hospital were outraged at my suggestion that they wouldn't serve women as well as Women's. The CEO at Sunnybrook was especially indignant when I pointed out that there were no female department heads in that entire huge establishment. "Mere head-counting," he snorted in dismissal. Yes, precisely. Others, in turn, angered me by dismissing Women's case as a "special interest."

> We will not stand by and see this dismissed as "special pleading." Women's College is a well-spring of research, innovation, hope and compassion for women everywhere. It's shocking that these functionaries dare write it off with a careless sweep of the pen.
>
> The Prime Minister himself is protesting the order to close Ottawa's Montfort Hospital, the only one offering psychiatric care in French. Who will climb the podium to fight for women? We are half the population and 58 per cent of hospital users.
>
> Only Montfort "speaks French," they say.
> Only Women's College speaks woman.

Luckily, at the time of the 1990s struggle, developer Maxwell Goldhar, a prominent male member of the Friends, had managed to secure 790 Bay St., an office building at the corner of Bay Street and College Street, in the name of Women's Health Research, a corporation dominated by the Friends of WCH and dedicated to passing any rental profits to Women's College Hospital. Because of their ownership of 790 Bay, the Friends were able to raise funds to hire lawyers to resist more takeover attempts.

After years of strong-arm tactics behind the scenes, the doctors and the most illustrious programmes at Women's were moved holus-bolus up to Sunnybrook, but the historic building on Grenville St. was allowed to stand, supposedly as a new ambulatory centre. It had a board of its own and a beloved executive director, Nancy Malcolm, though both answered to the larger board and the executives at Sunnybrook. To those of us who continued to visit our doctors in the old building, it was sad to see Women's so diminished, with the new name "Sunnybrook and Women's" garishly slapped across its modest old entrance and the halls echoing emptily, whole wards silent and shuttered. It was a ghost hospital, haunted by the shadows of women's dreams of equality.

A legal agreement (Bill 51) had been hammered out at the time of the forced marriage between Sunnybrook and Women's. Sunnybrook was to ensure that women's health would be "a priority programme." The building on Grenville Street was to become a centre of excellence for ambulatory care. Although Sunnybrook's budget increased by $100 million above inflation over the next seven years (1996 to 2004), women's health was never made a priority programme, the allocation to Women's decreased by $62 million, and these cuts meant a reduction in ambulatory care, access, services, and education.

The merger proved a spectacular failure. But *mutatis mutandis*...in the fall of 2003 came a provincial election. In the balmy September weather, I joined a crowd of Friends of Women's outside the Grenville Street building—many of us averted our eyes from the loathed Sunnybrook and Women's sign—and waved banners and placards demanding a return to our hospital's independent status. Suddenly, the campaign bus of the provincial Liberals swung into the driveway. The Liberal leader, Dalton McGuinty, climbed down beaming and vowed to answer our demands if he won the election. Beside him was George Smitherman, the local MPP, echoing the pledge. And lo, the election came and the hated Harris government was swept away.

By the spring of 2005, however, the Friends were fighting on all fronts. The board of Women's College Hospital seemed to have developed Stockholm syndrome as they sought to please and placate Sunnybrook's authorities. They moved to abolish the seats on their board reserved for representatives of the Friends, the volunteers, and the medical staff; simultaneously, they wanted to do away with the voting membership. Members of the Friends moved swiftly to head them off by strong interventions with the ministry. Dr. Carolyn Bennett, by then federal minister of public health, quietly used back channels, while Dr. Bev Richardson bombarded the health minister with detailed economic analyses of the harms inflicted on women's health care by the merger.

Later that summer, I was visiting family on the west coast when I received a phone call from Ontario Minister of Health George Smitherman. I was astonished; I had no personal connection with him and, aside from that demonstration in the hospital driveway, I had never met him. Even more astonishing: he was calling to tell me that he was about to announce "good news and bad news." We would get our hospital back, with independent governance and a mandate to excel in women's health as well as ambulatory care. The bad news: no new money. Our entire budget would have to come from negotiating the return of our programmes, with their dollars attached, from Sunnybrook. And what a protracted and anguishing struggle that turned out to be, but that's another story.

Minister Smitherman made his historic public announcement soon after: Women's College would be returned to independent governance, severed from Sunnybrook. He reaffirmed its mandate of developing a centre of excellence for women's health as well as ambulatory care.

Divorce! Just what we had longed for! Just then, the Friends learned that there would be six to eight vacancies on the Women's College board within a few weeks. The chair, Carol Cowan, was stepping down and a number of others were at the end of their terms. The Friends immediately began a quiet campaign to fill those board vacancies with increased diversity and feminist presence.

I had retired from twenty-five years as a feminist columnist at the *Star* just one year earlier, weathered a heart attack, and done my cardio rehab at Women's, which housed the only woman-focused, woman-specific hospital cardio rehab programme in the country. Now, returned to health, I had bought my first pass to the Toronto Film Festival (TIFF) for the coming September, rejoicing in my newfound leisure.

The phone call on behalf of the Friends came from Marilou McPhedran, well known to me as an aggressively successful feminist strategist. The Friends were about to begin intensive meetings to prepare for a battle at the board of the hospital, determined to restore feminism to its rightful prominence. Marilou was calling to ask me to be a leader in steering the new hospital in a meaningful direction for women. The summons was irresistible.

Marilou invited a number of potential new board recruits for a strategy session at 790 Bay Street and, after the first meeting, I resignedly ditched my film passes and settled in: weekly meetings at 790, endless phone calls to rouse up the Friends members, regular Sunday night conference calls. While we met—under a cone of silence, slipping quietly into a vacant room at 790 — the Friends' leaders were trying to establish an agreement with the existing board. Since the Friends had been instrumental in regaining the hospital's independence, it seemed only right that we should have some representatives on the board. But the board members were adamant. Despite the looming vacancies, they refused to allot any of the seats to the Friends.

Gail Regan had agreed, once more, to fund our efforts. Lawyer Lorie Stoltz was hired and she and Bev Richardson, and sometimes Carolyn Bennett, met several times with board chair Carol Cowan and others, but to no avail. Why were they so afraid of us? Naively, I had thought that as Friends who wanted only the success of the hospital, we should be welcomed as allies, not treated as apparent enemies.

To many of us, the planning for the annual general meeting had an exciting whiff of gunpowder; we were reminded of past election campaigns and of our 1990 triumph over an earlier conformist board at Women's. We were further fuelled by the incredible arrogance of statements emanating from Sunnybrook, whose board chair, Virginia McLaughlin, issued a smug edict that "Sunnybrook and Women's" would keep its name (including OUR name!) and logo and even our foundation money, which had been linked to Sunnybrook's in the amalgamation but safeguarded as separate for Women's. Further, because Sunnybrook was such an innovator, she said, "it makes perfect sense that a provincial programme dedicated to women's health would be generated from the hospital." In another obnoxious press release, McLaughlin vowed condescendingly that Sunnybrook "would assist our colleagues at the Women's College Campus to develop a vision for a women's health centre of excellence." In seven years of the occupation, Sunnybrook had done little but diminish and deplete women's health programmes.

We ground our teeth at the sheer effrontery of Sunnybrook, as they pretended that the liberated Women's College Hospital was merely the "Women's College campus" (their dismissive phrase) whose women's health programmes had been created by Sunnybrook. Throughout our struggle to reclaim our programmes and budget from Sunnybrook, that hospital, whose manpower and money dwarfed ours a thousand-fold, well understood the power of our name and our reputation. They fought doggedly to appropriate our name permanently (good for fundraising, I guess) and it took endless hours of negotiation and argument with provincial mediator Elinor Caplan to win the right to keep our historic and rightful title. The indignity of having to fight for our own name and identity lent heated energy to my efforts. A profound part of my motivation in working to save the hospital, and indeed in recording a part of its history here, is that the erasure of women and women's achievements from the recorded past is an injustice that goads me intolerably. I literally cannot bear it.

The actions of those controlling the WCH board gave us extra motivation. They were arbitrarily changing the date of the AGM, stalling on distributing to hospital members the names and profiles of our nominees while promoting their own, and seemed to be putting every possible obstacle in our way. Still, there were moments of amusement to be savoured. We learned, for instance, that the board was unable to gain access to the hospital's membership lists to round up supporters for the AGM—Sunnybrook owned everything and typically refused to share. Sitting on our treasure trove of thousands of Friends' names on Joc's lists, we smirked. We also outclassed the board in organizing power. Joan Hill, with volunteers from the extensive network of the hospital's nurses, tirelessly called and urged them to come out to vote; Joc and Bev Richardson were equally energetic.

Marilou McPhedran had assembled a stellar group of candidates, well qualified and diverse. They were Alia Hogben, a social worker who had led social services for abused women and children, and was founding executive director of the Canadian Council of Muslim Women, which fought the imposition of sharia law in Ontario; Tekla Hendrikson, provincial director of the Ontario Women's Health Network (a coalition of grassroots groups); Nan Hudson, a United Church minister with international aid experience; Hazelle Palmer, then director of Planned Parenthood of Toronto; Wendy Sutton, a lawyer and incoming chair of the Michener Institute (health professions); Patricia O'Connell, with corporate management and community board experience; and me. Among us were two lesbians, a Jew, a Muslim, and two women of colour. Marilou's strategy included additional well-qualified feminist candidates to be ready for any version of the board vote to come.

Behind the scenes, the board of WCH was scrambling to set up defences against the possible encroachment of the Friends. They quietly appointed a negotiator with Sunnybrook and blithely announced that they had chosen a steering committee to oversee the de-amalgamation. These appointments, coming a week before the AGM, seemed illegitimate to us. The illegitimacy became resoundingly clear when, after a board meeting, the executive director Nancy Malcolm let slip, in chatting with Bev Richardson, that the CEO of Sunnybrook was vetoing and approving names for the WCH de-amalgamation team. That's like letting Ford choose the contract negotiators for the auto workers' union—an utterly absurd abuse of power, to which the board was evidently submitting!

Our resolve was only strengthened by these shenanigans and on the evening of the annual general meeting, a suppressed murmur of excitement buzzed through the packed auditorium at the hospital. The board, fearing who knows what disruption, had hired CIBC auditors to supervise the vote count.

When the vote was tallied, all six of us had swept in. The previous board members, who had assumed they would be re-elected, were in various pale and trembling states of shock, tears, and fury. Then, according to custom, the new board (a mix of previous members and new Friends) adjourned to the hospital's boardroom where a new chair was to be elected.

Until that moment, while I had agreed to Marilou's request to stand for election as chair, I certainly hadn't imagined it becoming a reality. But the vote was quick, and my life suddenly took a dramatic turn. I, who had never chaired so much as a meeting, had suddenly to guide a board split down the middle and tackle an immense legal tangle of negotiations—without any infrastructure at all. Women's College had been stripped bare of almost all senior staff and the government resisted our hiring lawyers. (An absurdity: They had to give in when executive director Nancy Malcolm and I were left on our own facing a phalanx of the most high-powered lawyers in Toronto.)

The workload was gigantic. I had to acquire some suits and most mornings I hurried in to my office by 8:00 or 9:00 a.m. to face a full day of hasty meetings and myriad complex demands. Luckily, as a journalist, I was a quick study. And nothing but feminist commitment could have made me immerse myself so deeply in a foreign world of governance, strategic planning, Robert's Rules, and constant meetings with ministry officials. The learning curve was dizzying, but the camaraderie of sister board members, the shared dedication and uproarious debates kept us in high spirits. There is probably nothing more exhilarating in working life than to have a mission and trusted comrades with whom to pursue it.

The power imbalance between WCH and Sunnybrook had its grotesque moments. One dark, wintry morning I arrived at 7:30 a.m. for a meeting with the CEO and board chair of

Sunnybrook, to be held in Nancy Malcolm's office. I arrived before Nancy but, strangely, saw a light on in my office. To my astonishment, there were Leo Stevens, Sunnybrook CEO, and board chair Virginia McLaughlin, sitting behind my desk. They were surprised to see me.

"Oh, we're used to using this office," said Virginia. "Could you wait outside, please?" Dumbfounded by their arrogance, I went back to Nancy's office—she had just arrived—and told her what had happened. I urged Nancy to tell them to vacate my office till our meeting began. Nancy dutifully went down the hall, but found herself unable to confront and challenge the powers to whom she had been answering for many years.

This small incident shows what we were up against at the beginning: a culture of compliance on the part of Women's, and a culture of bullying on the part of Sunnybrook. Another morning, I arrived pre-dawn to be greeted by one of our most loyal security guards. She was in a panic. "Some guys from Sunnybrook just came and took away our best mammogram machine! Unscrewed it right from the floor!" Sunnybrook seemed intent on pillaging whatever was left in our rickety old building. But this time, Nancy Malcolm was up to the challenge; after a stern phone call to Leo Stevens, she informed me that the machine would be returned later that day.

The leadership at Sunnybrook seemed unable to accept that we had any power or agency of our own. They would sail into meetings with high-handed statements: "By the way, we're keeping the Henrietta Banting breast care programme" was typical.

The heady intensity of that first year began to subside as we ran into our first bitter realities. I learned, to my amazement, how hated and feared some of our Friends leaders were; highly ranked civil servants would actually ask me, nervously, if Dr. Richardson was angry about anything. They tried to pry out of me how many members the Friends actually had, and were we planning any public demonstrations. I learned from their anxiety just how powerful a strong, organized citizen group could be. But ultimately, though they feared us, they were the ones with the real power.

Our negotiations with Sunnybrook left us drastically short of the money we needed to offer services to the public. My money-begging trips across the street to meet with George Smitherman were delightfully affable on the surface and fraught underneath. One winter day, heading to a make-or-break session with George, I slipped on the ice outside the ministry building and cracked a finger bone. The pain was sharp, but I was not about to sacrifice the meeting. In the elevator, being introduced to powerful ministry officials, I grinned in agony through firm handshakes and then sat through a tooth-gritting and fruitless session with George. It became clear that we were never going to get the money we needed until...until...we ended the voting membership.

That was their "bottom line." Voting memberships were unstable. The government couldn't and wouldn't give public money to a hospital subject to a public vote. More persuasively, I was reminded that anti-choice fanatics could gain control of the hospital membership if they turned their minds to it, and overturn our most basic principles of equity and access to reproductive choice.

It took me months of quiet consultations and secretive campaigning, courting and convincing the very stalwarts who had been key to our AGM victory that we had to vote to give up one of our most cherished principles. It was painful. Those who held out against me used the very arguments I would have made, but I saw no way out. By the time of the next AGM, I had gathered enough votes to vote our voting mechanism out of existence... and that very night, the ministry announced our capital funding.

Now, the new building is a gleaming monument to our dedication; I put eight years of hard volunteer labour on the board into it, and others did the same. I haven't mentioned here the wonderful doctors, scientists, and researchers who stayed loyal to Women's through all the battles, or the executives who took up the challenge. Theirs is a separate story.

The campaign by the Friends is what I wanted to memorialize because a feminist, citizen-based campaign like ours is very rare in our corporate world, but still possible where the will exists. Every time I drive past the hospital now, and see those giant letters emblazoned across the glass wall—W O M E N' S—I am not only moved, but inspired to think of what victories might still be ours, if we will it.

THE FIGHT TO SAVE WOMEN'S
COLLEGE HOSPITAL (AGAIN)

Jane Pepino

I was part of the lengthy, tumultuous, and sometimes bitter
battle to save Women's College Hospital in downtown Toronto.
There were many ups and downs and "sides" taken in this process which ran between 1995 and 1998. And the need to save the
hospital emerged more than once over the course of almost three
decades. It illustrated the ease with which some in power will persist in remaining oblivious and uncaring about saving women's
hospitals and women's spaces—even those with such a solid and
venerable women's history. It led me to tears and exhaustion, and
indeed to marvel at the convoluted nature of hospital politics in
Toronto and Ontario. But ultimately the story is one of struggle,
strategy, and success.[61]

Women's College Hospital is resolutely urban and had its roots
in a medical college to train women doctors, founded in 1883:

> The roots of Women's College date back to the
> founding of the Women's Medical College by
> a small group of Canadian women physicians
> in 1883. At a time when gender discrimination
> denied women admission to the Faculty of
> Medicine at the University of Toronto, this fa-
> cility provided women in Ontario with their first
> opportunity to study medicine.
>
> Between 1905, when the first women were
> admitted to the Faculty of Medicine at the
> University of Toronto, and 1961 when Women's
> College changed its bylaws to permit the ap-
> pointment of men to its permanent medical

staff, Women's College was run by women for women. With the addition of men to the medical staff, the skills and expertise of physicians of both genders were deployed in the service of women's health. Today at Women's College, women hold more than 50% of the women's medical staff, clinical chiefs of staff, and senior management positions, as compared to other hospitals where few, if any, women hold these positions.[62]

Despite this history, on September 29, 1995, the Metro Toronto District Health Council's final report on hospital restructuring recommended that Women's College Hospital either merge with or relocate to the Sunnybrook Health Science Centre, creating a "women's health presence" at the Sunnybrook site.[63] Thus began another battle to save Women's.

September 29, 1995, was also my first meeting as a board member of Women's College Hospital. Earlier that spring, I had been recruited by Marilou McPhedran, who had been an active and key leader in the Friends of Women's College Hospital. The Friends had formed in 1989 to successfully defeat a move by the then Board of Women's College to consent to a merger with Toronto General Hospital. Marilou worked with a group including Gail Regan, Dr. Carolyn Bennett, Joc Palm, Dr. Beverly Richardson, Nancy Ruth, and many others to successfully organize public protests and a strategic replacement of the board with one that remained committed to the independence of Women's College.

There could not have been a more unlikely suitor for Women's College than Sunnybrook if a love match was the goal. It was clear, however, that those intent on arranging this union thought it could—and should—work. Sunnybrook Health Science Centre had started as a veteran's hospital post-World War II and was located in a suburban area not readily accessible for women without a car. Even as a "general" hospital with a broad range of programmes, it did not have an obstetrical or birthing programme. Acquisition of the Women's College panoply of obstetrical programmes, including its widely acclaimed Level 3 neonatal intensive care unit, was what Sunnybrook needed to become "complete" in its offerings to the public and in its ability to provide full academic training.

The release of the District Health Council report on September 29, 1995, was the opening bell for a spirited defence of Women's College as an independent hospital that had at the core of its mission research into women's health; advocacy for improvement of the delivery of medical care and public policy affecting women's health; and the training and advancement of women medical leaders including doctors, allied health professionals, and hospital executive leadership.

Even though I had not been personally involved in the 1989 struggle to save Women's College, sitting in that September board meeting, listening to the CEO report on yet another external assessment of Women's College as unsustainable, possibly unnecessary, and whose programmes were more likely to succeed nestled into a larger more diverse whole was, simply, déjà vu: it constituted yet another devaluation of a uniquely women-serving institution, and another attack on a women-led institution. We immediately decided it was not to be accepted or tolerated.

The board quickly resolved on a course of action to fight back and to do everything possible to ensure that the Health Council's recommendations for Metro Toronto were not picked up by the newly forming Provincial Health Services Restructuring Commission (HSRC). The HSRC was being created by the Mike Harris Conservative government with the stated goal of "rationalizing" and "streamlining" and thereby "improving" the provincial health care system. We knew that unless Women's College was viewed as valuable, unique, and necessary, it would disappear.

So we quickly created a "Strategic Options Committee." Despite it being my first meeting, I was appointed to chair that committee. We quickly undertook a survey of all medical and allied professional staff, the Friends, board members past and present, community groups, donors, and many others. Frankly, this work was not merely to seek their opinions, but also to alert them to the threat and to gather support for Women's College.

This led to an internal report entitled "Draft Action Plan," dated December 14, 1995, setting out three principles that would underlie any acceptable change to the status quo. We were realistic enough to understand that Women's had to be seen as open to change, but idealistic enough to insist on what any change had to achieve. Those principles were:

1. independent governance;
2. Women's College's focus on academic health should be strengthened and enhanced; and
3. maintenance of a downtown location.

Ironically, the *Metropolitan Toronto Health Council Report* had stated that the "unique focus of Women's College on women's health must be preserved." How this was to be achieved was a mystery since Sunnybrook had never had a women's health focus, nor provided programmes in a woman-centred environment, nor emphasized training and promotion of women leaders. This bureaucratic habit of stating a rational principle and then smothering it in contradictory recommendations was to be consistently frustrating.

However, we seized on this acknowledgement by the District Health Council of the value of maintaining the "unique focus of Women's College on women's health," and it became the theme of our campaign to show why its recommendations did not deliver that goal.

On the issue of independent governance, the *District Health Council Report* only recommended that there be a "significant, if not equivalent, representation from the existing Women's College Board on the Board of the new organization." The problem, however, was that it also recommended a single organization with a single board.

In what ultimately turned out to be the kernel of Women's College salvation, the University of Toronto Faculty of Medicine filed a response to the District Health Council report, dated October 31, 1995. That response stated that in the view of the University of Toronto, *without separate governance,* women's health programmes could be de-emphasized in competition for resources with other clinical programmes. That report then went on to outline the resulting loss of the "educational value of a distinct approach to women's health" as well as the risk that "special academic programmes that are internationally recognized risk being diluted if merged into a large general hospital."

By November 30, 1995, the District Health Council revised its recommendation somewhat, recommending to the minister of health that Women's College should retain separate governance, with the overall model being "linked separate governance." The Council had recognized that separate governance and separate committed leadership were necessary to ensure the continued focus and priority be given to women's health programmes, including care, research, and teaching.

Excellent, we thought. Seemingly, the battle for Women's had already been two-thirds won—of our three principles, it appeared only the fight over maintaining an open downtown location was left. Sadly, however, that was not the result.

1996

While the revised District Health Council recommendations were working their way into the newly forming provincial Health Services Restructuring Commission, our Strategic Options Committee continued discussions with various downtown academic hospitals, and Sunnybrook, to determine if a strategic alliance to achieve Women's College's three principles could be accomplished.

On March 28, 1996, I received a telephone call from Tom Brent, the chair of the board of Sunnybrook. He indicated that he did not believe Sunnybrook could meet the goals of Women's College, and that his board had decided to wait to see what recommendations came down from the HSRC. He was clear that he wanted to "grow Sunnybrook" and that its goal of becoming one of three future academic health centres required it to have obstetrical services on its site, for academic purposes. He also confirmed that he finally understood just how different the cultures our two institutions were; he said his tour of Women's was "like coming from a busy supermarket to a high class boutique." He ended by saying there was nothing to be gained for Sunnybrook in negotiating with Women's College, and that he didn't want the government to be confused or delayed in its decision by thinking that meaningful discussions were underway. A letter arrived the next day to the same effect.

Sunnybrook apparently entirely withdrew from the discussions about a strategic partnership with Women's College. But we were later to learn through correspondence and comments at a later meeting, that it did so with the hope and expectation that the provincial HSRC would order the transfer of Women's College programmes and assets to Sunnybrook on conditions that did not include pesky matters such as independent governance, a singular focus on women's academic research and teaching, or maintenance of a downtown location.

In April 1996, by legislation, the provincial Health Services Restructuring Commission was finally established with broad ranging powers to close hospitals, transfer services, and otherwise "take all necessary steps required for amalgamation." The commission had a mandate for four years, so, building on the support of both the University of Toronto and the District Health Council for independent governance, we set about trying to create positive alternatives to place before the commission. Having met with all academic health science centres over a period of months, Women's College commenced formal negotiations with the board of the

Wellesley Central Hospital. I chaired the negotiating committee appointed by Women's College. Work continued apace, and on July 24, 1996, Women's College and Wellesley jointly presented a proposal to the Commission for an alliance.

> While the Commission reserved its judgment on the proposal, it congratulated Women's College and Wellesley Central on seeking a cooperative local solution....The Commission encouraged the two hospitals to move ahead with the Alliance with Dr. Sinclair expressly stating "go as far and as fast as possible." Women's College and Wellesley Central took this response as a positive sign, stepping up their efforts to make the Alliance a reality.[64]

Over the next few months an implementation committee was struck, along with thirteen task forces. By late November, all task forces had reported to the implementation steering committee, which was meeting at least weekly. When all task force reports were endorsed by the two boards, we thought we were on the path to restructuring, but with self-determination.

1997

In January 1997, the commission issued several documents setting out what it termed a "vision of Ontario's future health services system" and provided guidelines on procedures and expectations for the upcoming process. Without being asked, we provided regular progress reports and continued to update the ministry of health on how far and how fast the two hospitals were moving on the alliance. We provided a vision statement, organizational structure and appointment of senior management staff, single budget process for 1997/1998, plans for clinical integration, etc.

Interestingly enough, a commission representative requested projected capital costs, which we forwarded on January 20, 1997, demonstrating that projected capital costs for the alliance were less than those projected by the Metro Toronto District Health Council report and less than original alliance estimates. On March 3, 1997, after months of work, a copy of the executed final agreement between Women's College and Wellesley Central Hospital was delivered to the commission.

But just three days later, it was clear that all the work of the prior nine months was for naught. On March 6, 1997, the commission released its report, and recommended merging the specialized facility and transforming the programmes of the Orthopaedic and Arthritic Hospital (O & A) also downtown, with Sunnybrook Hospital. With respect to Women's College, the commission supported the prior recommendation to close Women's College's physical facility and to relocate all but one of its programmes (the Sexual Assault Care Centre) to Sunnybrook. The Sexual Assault Care Centre was to be transferred to Toronto Western. The effect of this recommendation was to destroy our governance and to abolish the programmes established to be responsive and sensitive to the needs of women. That same day, the commission issued a notice providing Women's College with thirty days in which to make written submissions on its notice to the commission.

What the commission had not bargained for, however, was that we understood the legal structure of the commission, its guidelines for representations, and its obligations under the *Ministry of Health Act*. The guidelines permitted an application for extension of time in which submissions could be made, so Women's College made the request through its counsel, Tom Lockwood. We also formally requested access to the documentation and information relied on by the commission. The commission responded by holding an "information session on the methodology for estimating costs and savings that have been used the Commission."

This was the first time that the methodology used by the commission was to be made public. Suffice to say that both the briefing and subsequent provision of information did not satisfy us! So we made more written demands for information and documentation. Eventually, we wrote to the HSRC to put on record that Women's College's interests had been prejudiced in that it had been denied the opportunity to know the case it must meet; that the commission had failed to follow its own guidelines; that Women's College had complied with the time limits set out in the guidelines; and that commission had provided no explanation for its failure to respond in accordance with its own guidelines.

On April 2, 1997, our lawyer advised the commission that we were off to court to seek the documents and obtain a further extension. Two days later, we received a whack of documentation, but also a denial for our request for a further time extension. When we reviewed the material, however, it was all historical and consisted of little more than previously prepared material and briefs submitted.

So on April 8, our first legal challenge was launched. We brought an application for a judicial review of the commission's notice, asking that the additional documentation requested be provided; that a meaningful extension be provided to respond; and that oral representation be heard.

While all this was going on, the Women's College Hospital annual general meeting rolled around in June, and I was elected chair of the board. I was prepared to take on this role. It wasn't going to meaningfully change the nature or quantity of time spent in strategizing and executing the hospital's battle with the HSRC and, frankly, the role gave me an accepted platform that the opponents could not question, to lead the battle. We had regular strategy sessions on legal tactics with our lawyer, Tom Lockwood, and Friends' counsel, Mary Eberts. The Friends also continued to push hard in the media and with the public, and were getting media traction and broad public support that we hoped to translate into political support. Moreover, by this time, the hospital had developed an extraordinarily accomplished internal team: Pat Campbell was a very effective CEO and strategic advisor; Sharon Salson was the new director of public affairs, and there continued to be a gritty determination amongst all staff that we would see this through to the end.

That gritty determination was needed: On July 23, 1997, the HSRC ordered Women's College (and the O & A) to amalgamate services with Sunnybrook under a single corporation called the Bayview Corporation. To address worries that women's programmes might be lost in the merger, the commission recommended that women—any women—hold the majority of the seats on the new megacentre's governing board. However, mere gender representation did not meet our principle of a separate and independent hospital board representing and protecting the values of Women's College.

At an announcement to staff the next day, there were many tears and real fear on the faces of the staff and patients who gathered outside the hospital's doors that summer day. But the gritty determination continued and people were cheered by our vow to continue to fight to save the hospital. As I said that day, our fight wasn't a refusal to compromise, it was about "getting it right."

Our next step was another legal challenge, this time to the HSRC's final Directions of July 23. Our press release contained our request for settlement negotiations to the government and the HSRC:

"It is not with enthusiasm that we take this course of action," says hospital chair, Jane Pepino. "We are trying to keep all of our options open and protect our legal rights as we make every attempt to sit down with the Minister of Health to work out a solution that would benefit everyone. If the government or the Commission sees the wisdom in what we are advocating, there would be no need to go further with this."

"Without a governance structure that would protect Women's College's vision, values and unique approach to women's health care, we can be sure all of the progress we've made will be lost and the quality of care for women in Ontario will suffer," says Pepino. "All we want to do is find a way to make sure that won't happen. We hope the government, and particularly the Minister of Health, will listen."

To increase the political pressure we also requested an order to ban the minister from approving any governance plan. It was felt necessary to seek this since the minister had already announced he would follow the commission's direction.

For two years we had made repeated requests to the minister of health to meet with us, but we had either been declined, or worse, ignored by his office. Other cabinet ministers and MPPs met with us and although often personally sympathetic or even just cowed by angry constituents, the refrain was the same. "This is a decision for the premier and the minister." We hoped both the launch of the suit and the relief requested would finally cause the minister of health also to initiate a dialogue. Unless we could get the political directive to the HSRC changed then even the sympathetic members of the ministry's bureaucracy could not assist.

The next two and a half weeks were intense, with many behind the scenes discussions with cabinet ministers and bureaucrats in the ministry of health, and beyond. Eventually, the Health Services Restructuring Commission staff, and particularly Mark Rochon, its CEO, were willing to commence dialogue. It seemed clear they finally had been given either direction, or at a minimum, permission, to do so by the government.

At 2:30 a.m. on the morning of August 29, 1997, I completed a telephone call with Mark Rochon from his home, during which we had agreed on terms to allow the hospital to adjourn its judicial review, scheduled to commence at 10 a.m. that same morning. Although Women's College reserved the right to go back to court if required, we were successful in having the HSRC agree that the governance and organizational models for the amalgamated entity would be arrived at through a facilitated negotiation. This specifically left open the option for continuation of Women's College as a public hospital, and with its own board.

Perhaps the best description of the pressure-laden period is the following quote from the commissioners themselves, in a 2005 publication.[65]

The commission noted that it was "committing itself to use its good offices to broker a mutually satisfactory deal among the parties." That became our next task.

THE NEGOTIATIONS

A short time after the adjournment of the court case, the HSRC had retained two highly experienced mediators to work with the Orthopaedic and Arthritic Hospital, Sunnybrook Health Science Centre, the University of Toronto, and Women's College Hospital to achieve a facilitated settlement. Our first session was scheduled for October 16, but was abruptly adjourned just before commencement. The background was convoluted, but underscored an ongoing problem of promises being made to some parties that were contrary to agreements reached with others. The sessions were cancelled when previously undisclosed commitments by the commission surfaced. It was clear that different parties had been told different things by the commission.

In an attempt to clear the air, the Women's College negotiating committee (Pat Campbell, Dr. Bev Richardson, and I) met with Dr. Sinclair, chair of the HSRC, and Mark Rochon on October 21. At that meeting it was acknowledged that correspondence between the HSRC and Tom Brent, chair of the board at Sunnybrook, should have been provided to Women's College to form part of the public record. At a rescheduled facilitated meeting on October 23, Dr. Sinclair emphasized that funds from the ministry of health were intended to flow by way of one cheque to the amalgamated corporation and that there had to be a "single point of accountability." He went on, however, to state that the commission would consider favourably any plan that contained those two elements as well as "whether the proposal met the Directions, is legal and feasible, and provides confidence that it will work well and provide appropriate protections for specified programmes."

For the first time publicly, and in answer to my question whether one or all of the existing hospitals could continue to exist as public hospitals, Dr. Sinclair agreed that if a legal and feasible structure could be created to accomplish that and achieve a single point of accountability, then in all likelihood, it would be acceptable to the commission.

At this point, Mr. Brent and other representatives of Sunnybrook became quite agitated and indicated that their interpretation of the HSRC Directions *and the assurances they had received* indicated that the three hospitals would cease to exist when the new corporation was formed. Dr. Sinclair replied that this was not necessarily the case, saying repeatedly that neither he nor the commission were going to preordain any particular structure, but rather leave it to the facilitation process. But clearly, the issue of Women's College remaining an independent public hospital, albeit within a larger organization, still was not sitting well with Sunnybrook.

Although our facilitated meetings continued for a number of weeks, we were also dealing with parallel attacks on our determination to maintain independent status. A letter from the ministry of health setting out "the Ministry's views on the legal elements associated with status as a public hospital under the *Public Hospitals Act*" surfaced. Sunnybrook took the position that the letter constituted a legal opinion that would have the effect of prohibiting more than one public hospital within the governance administrative structure intended to result out of the facilitation process.

Again, we formally disagreed with this suggestion, setting out our reasons. That letter, dated November 10, 1997, was copied to all parties at the facilitation, and subsequent events made it clear it was not well received from Sunnybrook. Sunnybrook simply picked up its marbles and refused to play anymore, resulting in another last-minute cancellation of a scheduled facilitation.

In a demonstration that bad behaviour brings its own bad reward, on November 17, 1997, the facilitators wrote directly to Duncan Sinclair and Mark Rochon of the HSRC, pointing out that "one of the parties to our facilitation[66] has taken the position it will not meet or further participate in the facilitation, on the basis that any result of the facilitation must consist only of a single hospital, a single Board, and a single path for funding…for various reasons including the Ministry of Health's October 30th letter."

On November 20, the HSRC responded simply restating the tests it would apply in determining whether the outcome of negotiations were consistent with any Directions of July 23, while also noting that although it had not in the past amended its Directions, it had "however issued additional Directions based on the work of the parties and facilitator." This signalled the kind of flexibility Women's College had sought. Pointedly, the letter closes by stating, "we are pleased that you have scheduled the next meeting with the parties for November 24 and 25, 1997."

As a result, we entered into the continuing facilitations in late November with a clear commitment by the HSRC to recognize independent governance that met its other requirements, if this was the outcome of the facilitated negotiation. Additionally, we were now certain that the facilitators had a clear grasp on the position of the HSRC, and of the motivations and positions of each of the parties going in.

The process was painstaking. The facilitators created a document called a "One Text" in various versions, to attempt to capture suggestions and the state of discussions as they continued. Draft after draft was produced, on the understanding that no draft was final until all parties had signed off as having that draft constitute a complete consensus. We continued on in this process, and on December 17, 1997, a document was issued entitled "One Text–Draft Six".

We quickly turned around our comments, responding on December 22. This draft included our position that the total votes of board members nominated by Women's College,[67] together with those appointed by the Orthopaedic and Arthritic Hospital board, should be at least equal to the number of votes of directors nominated by the Sunnybrook board. We felt that only by ensuring Sunnybrook did not appoint the majority of directors that we would have any confidence that we could maintain the hard-won rights to public hospital status. Having provided that mark-up, everyone went away to take a well-deserved break over the holidays.

THE GRENADE
However, on January 5, 1998, the negotiating committee of Sunnybrook forwarded a letter to the facilitators that lobbed a grenade into the room. The leaders at Sunnybrook suggested that a brand new board be created, with all current board members

resigning at both Sunnybrook and Women's, and that the ratio of board members in a new board be 9:5:3. Consistent with the view that "might makes right," these numbers reflected the respective size of the operating budgets of the hospitals (Sunnybrook, Women's, and O&A).

Attached to this letter was a page of signatures of each board member of Sunnybrook, indicating that if the negotiating teams were not able to reach a consensus for board composition of the new hospital, "the Board members of all three hospitals should step aside in favour of a new unencumbered 'Board' and indicating their preparedness to do so."

The position of Sunnybrook that governance should be considered solely on the basis of budget or "resources contributed by each pre-existing hospital" simply underscored the "control and command" culture of Sunnybrook. Further, it appeared to us to be rooted in the continuing hope and expectation that Sunnybrook would be able to succeed in achieving this goal, based on its political read of the provincial government, the HRSC, and, as well, the University of Toronto. Dean Arnold Aberman, dean of medicine, appeared to be viewed by Sunnybrook (and, with concern by Women's College) as an ally to Sunnybrook given its goal to provide a full academic offering including obstetrical, gynaecological, and other women's health programmes that it presently did not offer.

The university had not regularly participated in the facilitations, or to publically or formally press its original position that Women's College needed separate governance to ensure continuing focus on Women's health programmes. It appeared throughout the facilitation that the university's silence was taken by Sunnybrook as a sign the university no longer supported separate governance and Dean Aberman did not appear to explicitly dispel that belief.

As galling as the Sunnybrook "final position" that "a new Board composition of 9:5:3 will prevent the new hospital's Board from being disfunctional (sic)" was the fact that its creation and dissemination had been part of a thoroughly planned and well-hidden initiative taken over the holiday period. The terms of our negotiations had clearly been breached. The CEO of Sunnybrook, Mr. Closson had been aware of the plot since December 24, but had not mentioned it during the preparations for our meeting in January. Further, news of Sunnybrook's plan had reached the *Toronto Star* before it reached Women's College Hospital.

My response of January 7 to the Sunnybrook negotiating team was clear, but unequivocal. In fact, I was seething. I concluded, "You ask us to trust that Sunnybrook is dealing with us in good faith and yet your recent actions do not support the development of the relationship and the creation of trust."

JANUARY 9, 1998

The CEOs of the three hospitals had already made arrangements to meet on January 9. This meeting was converted to a meeting at which all parties attended, including the University of Toronto. Given the bombshell of the Sunnybrook letter, and its position that the facilitation and negotiations were at a stalemate, it appeared the negotiated outcome we had worked so hard to achieve would be impossible to accomplish. Faced with the intransigency of Sunnybrook, it appeared the facilitation would end and the HSRC Directions of July, 1997 would be confirmed. All that we had been able to accomplish both politically and at the negotiating table could be swept away.

The Women's College negotiating team arrived about half an hour before the meeting was due to start and met in a private anteroom to regroup and determine a position. Quickly reviewing our options, nothing seemed possible. The "One Text–Draft Six" document had been as close to success as we had been able to get and it had been rejected out of hand by Sunnybrook.

Personally I was exhausted, drained by both the anger of the last two days and the fear of the loss of all that we had accomplished. We were facing the elimination of Women's College as an independent entity with the power to drive and protect women's health programmes, as well as crushing the potential to exist in future until it could be reshaped and potentially reconstituted in future under a different political circumstance. Our insistence on continuing to fight for independent governance was underpinned by the belief that "where there is life, there is hope." Maintaining the Women's College identity, brand, and programmes could, we believed, allow a future renaissance. In time, and with continuing gritty determination, this proved to be true.

In the room with me at that pre-meeting was our negotiating team: Carol Cowan Levine, Dr. Bev Richardson, and Pat Campbell. Someone asked if we were going to accept the Sunnybrook position. It was immediately agreed it was unacceptable and that we could not accept their position. And someone, I think Carol, asked me directly, "What are we going to do?" At that point I had no answer. Instead, I simply broke down and wept in frustration, bitter disappointment, and grief. We all had simply run out of answers and it appeared likely that Sunnybrook's line in the sand would defeat our dreams. Nevertheless, I mopped myself up and we all pulled ourselves together and entered the meeting room, with all eyes upon us.

The chair of the meeting asked for our response to the Sunnybrook position and I replied that it was unacceptable and was rejected by Women's College. But at this point, I realized that there was a new individual in the room, beyond the usual faces we had met with so many times before.

In addition to Dean Aberman, Dr. David Naylor was present as part of the University of Toronto delegation. Dr. Naylor was the incoming dean of medicine and vice-provost, relations with health care institutions at the University. In addition he had been a senior advisor to the HSRC since its inception in 1996. However, his presence in that room that day changed everything for Women's College.

Since both Sunnybrook and Women's College were members of the Toronto Area Health Sciences Network (TAHSN), we each had a board member who was a delegate of the president of the University. That meant that, throughout the entire negotiations, it had been assumed the University of Toronto would send two members to the newly constituted board, no matter how config-ured. But Dr. Naylor changed everything that day by advising the meeting that the University of Toronto was going to give one of its seats to ensure that, together, Women's College (and O&A) would hold a total of eight seats on the board of directors, while Sunnybrook would have seven.

There was a very long silence across the room. The O&A and Women's College representatives were digesting the news, mentally checking the arithmetic and almost fainting with relief. Although the Sunnybrook representatives may have previously known of the university position it was clear that they, too, were digesting the impact of Dr. Naylor's statement. Whether or not there had been specific commitments made to Sunnybrook by Dr. Aberman, I don't know. What was clear was that we were being provided a lifeline for continuing independent governance at Women's College. I don't remember much of the rest of the meeting, or of that day.

On February 13, a document entitled "Proposed Amalgamation Plan Principles for Sunnybrook and Women's College Health

Sciences Centre" was agreed to by the parties and submitted to the HSRC and the ministry of health. The parties issued, for the first time, a joint press release. With respect to Women's College, it stated as follows:

> One of the concerns expressed by Women in Ontario has been the potential loss of services for them, should Women's College Hospital disappear. According to Women's College Board Chair, Jane Pepino, "we feel confident that Women's health care will not only be safeguarded in this new organization, but will be developed and enhanced. It has been agreed by all parties that Women's health care will be a priority for the new organization, an objective that has been enshrined in the new mission statement. Women will have access to services both at the Bayview site and at the Women's College Hospital Ambulatory Centre located downtown."

Finally, we seemed to have been able to deliver on the three principles established in December 1996. Although years of hard work and some acrimony remained ahead of us, we were able to keep the spirit and mission of Women's College alive. This spirit was best captured in the tagline used for the next year or so as we continued to work through the transition to the new organization:

WE'RE OPEN...IN MORE WAYS THAN ONE

RESILIENCE UNDER FIRE: MAINTAINING A BEACON FOR WOMEN'S HEALTH IN BRITISH COLUMBIA

Jan Christilaw

I first came to BC Women's Hospital and Health Centre in 1982 while it was still the Grace Hospital, and where I spent many hundreds of hours as an obstetrical resident. I was already passionate about global women's health and reproductive rights by that time and had spent most of my holidays during my residency working in Nicaragua and El Salvador during the war there. By the spring of 1985, I was one of the senior residents in obstetrics-gynecology at Grace Hospital when we had a very special visitor: Dr. George Povey, ob-gyn, who had worked most of his life in Mozambique. He was famous in health circles as a committed internationalist and someone I respected highly. He was back for a few weeks of skills upgrading before again returning to Africa, where he was training obstetricians and midwives to decrease maternal mortality in the area. As senior resident, I was responsible for assuring that he had the experience he needed and we spent many hours in the operating room and delivery suite together. I told him how much I loved global health and how I longed to work in Africa to have the greatest impact in terms of saving women's lives. His response surprised me:

> What the world really needs more than anything is a beacon. They need to know that there are places where women are treated with respect, where maximal care is available and where the cutting-edge innovations and changes are going to come from. In other words, the world needs

to know that this hospital is here, because you need to be a beacon for women's health for the world.

That stayed with me, though in my wildest dreams I never expected to end up as the president of the (later renamed) BC Women's Hospital. But it did make me reflect on the importance of having an enclave, a place where woman-centred care could flourish, where excellence was expected, where maternal mortality—the chance of dying in childbirth—was lower than anywhere else in the world.

How do you do that? How do you create a place where staff and doctors care so much about the care of women, respect for choice, and eroding barriers to care? Sometimes it takes raw determination, striving to protect women's health in a system that does not always understand it, fund it, or support it. It also requires a culture where woman-centred care is the expectation. It certainly requires remembering our history, building on our strengths, and responding to our community.

THE EARLY DAYS
There has been a women's hospital is some shape or form in Vancouver for ninety years. The Grace Hospital first opened its doors in Vancouver in 1927 as a faith-based hospital run by the Salvation Army. In its early days, however, it was all about pregnancy and birth. The concept of women's health in its broader social and political sense did not emerge until the "second-wave" women's movement activated it many decades later. Although great strides occurred in obstetrical and gynecologic care in the first half of the 1900s, this was really the extent of the medical agenda relating to women. Between 1900 and 1980, the maternal mortality rate in Canada had fallen from 100 in 100,000 to less than 20 in 100,000. Although there are other reasons for this, including septic technique, community measures such as sanitation, improved education, etc., some of it is attributable to the pioneers of obstetrical and gynecologic care such as those at the Grace. Significant advances such as screening for gynecologic cancers, improved prenatal care, improved training for providers of care and, of course, the addition of midwifery to our maternity care system have all played a role in saving many women's lives.

With the building of an acute care hospital on Oak Street in Vancouver in 1982, Grace Hospital moved from its location on

33rd Avenue, and the high-risk obstetrical unit at Willow Pavilion of Vancouver General Hospital moved in as well, resulting in both high- and low-risk obstetrics housed together on the same campus. The Women's Health Centre in the Shaughnessy building of the hospital also became part of the women's health campus of care, serving broader women's health and reproductive needs.

Like all other Grace hospitals across the country, Grace Hospital in Vancouver had always been a faith-based hospital operated by the Salvation Army. This brings with it obvious and critical concerns, including support of women's choice, support for a more inclusive definition of women's health, and a generally conservative framework through which to view the world. No one would have accused the Grace Hospital of having what we now call a women's health agenda. So the change to a secular hospital with the establishment of BC Women's Hospital in 1994 was long overdue and welcomed by the public and government alike. This was the birth of BC Women's.

The early leaders of BC Women's included visionary leaders such as Dr. Penny Ballem, who supported a broader women's health approach that helped to ground the formation of the BC Women's Health Centre on the Oak Street campus. The first programmes included those supporting reproductive choice, gynecologic programmes, and a myriad of other clinics.

At the inception of the BC Women's Hospital and Health Centre, there were already several clinics in place to assure access to women's health services. This period was a time of great angst for women and doctors alike in terms of abortion services. In November 1994, there was a dramatic attempted murder of Dr. Gary Romalis, an abortion provider in Vancouver. After this, the decision was made to focus on running a very secure abortion clinic within the hospital and the CARE (Comprehensive Abortion and Reproductive Education) clinic was born. During this time the Sexual Assault Service, founded by Dr. Liz Whynot and Dr. Carol Herbert, was also housed at BC Women's.

In the next few years more clinics came on board, including the Oak Tree clinic for women living with HIV that started in 1996. The clinic took a new approach to care, a team-based approach to the complex care of these women that was immediately successful in improving the lives of women with HIV. This was the result of both great clinical work and a great research team. The fact that there have been no HIV transmission from mothers to their babies (vertical transmission) is a testament to this, and BC

Women's continues to be a world leader because of the work of leaders such as David Burdge, Deborah Money, and Jack Forbes.

But BC Women's was about to embrace the whole women's health agenda by augmenting clinical programmes with research. In 1995–96, Dr. Penny Ballem held a series of province-wide consultations and forged an extensive consortium of women's health activists, researchers, practitioners, policy-makers, and consumer/patient groups across all of British Columbia in order to develop a proposal for federal funding for a Centre of Excellence for Women's Health. This proposal was entitled "Closing the Loop" and focused on linking evidence to practice to policy in women's health, a precursor to the type of effective knowledge translation later espoused and required by funding agencies. Out of over forty applications, five centres were named, and the British Columbia Centre of Excellence for Women's Health (BCCEWH) was established in 1996. It was funded through the Women's Health Contribution Programme of Health Canada from 1996 until 2012 when the Harper government cut funding to all five women's health research centres, the Canadian Women's Health Network, and numerous other woman-centred agencies.

The BC Centre of Excellence for Women's Health was established by Dr. Lorraine Greaves who was recruited from Ontario, where she had founded the Centre for Research on Violence Against Women and Children in London. Under her leadership, the BC Centre was the only centre that was able to survive defunding in the Harper government budget cuts. It achieved this by diversifying its funding streams and continuing to exist as a research-to-practice and policy centre in women's health—and later, in gender and health—becoming well known across Canada and internationally.

At the very same time the leaders at BC Women's successfully negotiated a separation from the Children's and Women's Hospital entity, the corporation that administered both hospitals that shared the same campus. This led to the establishing of a specific foundation for fundraising and development for BC Women's. While there were many years of being a "poor cousin" to Children's Hospital, and lots of tension for some who saw themselves as working for both hospitals, this 1997 separation was good news for re-establishing an independent women's hospital in Vancouver and British Columbia.

GROWING THE DREAM:
EXAMPLES OF OUR SUCCESS

Over the ensuing years many other services have been added and expanded. In 2002, FIR Square, an inpatient unit for pregnant women and new mothers dealing with substance issues was started at BC Women's, in partnership with Sheway, a health care service in the Downtown Eastside where the women received their primary and prenatal care. FIR Square has allowed many, many mothers who would have otherwise lost custody of their babies to keep their families together and get the support they need.

In 2001 the Women's Health Development Initiative was established, led by Lorraine Greaves, that carried out planning and negotiations to lay the groundwork for the Women's Health Research Institute. It brought together a plan and support for an independent women's health research entity to complement both BC Women's and the BC Centre of Excellence for Women's Health. It was established utilizing a one-time grant from the BC ministry of health, then under the deputy ministership of Penny Ballem. This created a crucial nidus for clinical research within BC Women's Hospital, augmenting and complementing existing research, and helped support frontline staff with a variety of research needs. It ultimately became part of the hospital and continues to flourish and grow.

In 2006, the Chronic Pelvic Pain clinic, already existing as a small clinical group, received funding to create a comprehensive team-based clinic for women in the province with severe pelvic pain and endometriosis, a serious condition that affects many thousands of women in BC. It has helped many women improve their quality of life and many of those served remain as advisors and supporters to the clinic. The Indigenous Women's Programme, which started over fifteen years ago, has expanded and consolidated in the last several years. The BC Women's Milk Bank, which for many years has served the needs of women and babies at BC Women's, expanded to serve the whole province with depots in all health authorities.

In 2008, BC Women's became the largest hospital in Canada to be designated through World Health Organization (WHO) as part of the Baby-Friendly Hospital Initiative (BFHI). This is based, in part, on very high rates of breastfeeding and strong support for women in establishing breastfeeding. The Early Pregnancy Assessment Clinic has now served women who are experiencing complications of early pregnancy including miscarriage for more than ten years. This is a very woman-centric service where women come in for assessment including ultrasound, get the results immediately, and are offered options for treatment based on their diagnosis. This replaces the widespread practice of having to go to an emergency department and wait for hours for a consultation and assessment, and perhaps even longer for treatment.

Over the years, BC Women's has been successful in working with the Ministry of Health on women's health issues affecting all BC women. The BCCEWH and BC Women's co-wrote the Women's Health Strategy in 2001 and an update in 2007, and along the way convened the Provincial Women's Health Council, a network of community-based women's services and activists. We have grown many programmes since 1994 and now, each year, we see 78,000 women in our clinics, carry out 4,000 surgeries, and help 7,200 women give birth at BC Women's Hospital. We also provide advice and consultation for women experiencing high-risk pregnancies in the province, with more than 60 per cent of those we served coming from outside Vancouver.

STRUGGLING TO KEEP WOMEN'S HEALTH AS A PRIORITY

This has not been done smoothly, however. Like most provinces in Canada, there have been numerous negotiations and reorganizations of the health care system in BC over the years. In 2001, however, the structure of hospital governance in BC completely changed. The province moved from a system where most hospitals had individual boards and existed within locally controlled regions to one where all hospitals reported to one of six health authorities. Because of the provincial nature of BC Women's mandate, we became part of the Provincial Health Services Authority, which, as the entity responsible for provincial services, also governed services such as BC Cancer, BC Children's, BC Transplant, and BC Mental Health.

This forced BC Women's into an era where accountability to the taxpayers of the province was a high priority and an express understanding that our funding was for acute-care clinical services. Any suggestion that our work included advocacy, gender equality, or even global aspects of women's health quickly became a nonstarter. Our funding was for the delivery of hospital-based clinical services. The other work continued, but was done on the side, whether it was the global fight against maternal mortality or the struggle to address the social determinants of health. The very essence of women's health as the second-wave women's movement defined and understood it, was challenged. The Canadian women's health movement had long made a point of expanding the definition of "health" to take into account a range of social and economic determinants, and put less focus on strictly the absence of illness and disease.

Following this critical shift in perspective there were several rounds of budget cuts that affected BC Women's. This was not unique to us and happened across the health care system in the province. With the aging of the population and increasingly complex technological needs, health care costs in the province were skyrocketing and had to be kept in check. But with each of several rounds of cuts, we were tasked with finding savings while maintaining clinical services, and were cut significantly in terms of administrative and other non-clinical services. Even given our successes, it was not easy. And the struggle to assure that women's health stays on an agenda where it is competing with cardiac health, knee and hip replacements, and many other high-priced items was challenging and intense. As increasing centralization and corporate control became the norm, the autonomy of BC Women's gradually diminished. Maintaining our brand and reputation within the community became another challenge that our foundation had to shoulder, and that had a direct impact on fundraising.

WOMAN-CENTRED CARE: A SHINING EXAMPLE

When I returned to BC Women's in 2000 after many years in practice as an ob-gyn in a community hospital, I decided that I would do one clinic a week in the Oak Tree Clinic serving the gynecologic needs of HIV-positive women. I can only describe the women I see in the clinic as resilient and many of them have lived through things that I am sure would have killed me. I remain in awe of the courage and tenacity that I see every day.

One of my patients, Linda (not her real name) required a minor surgery for a pre-cancer of the cervix that we had diagnosed in the clinic. After a lifetime of challenges, she was not well, with serious HIV and significant substance use issues. Linda, after many negative encounters, had lost faith in the acute care system and refused to come in for the surgery. She agreed, however, to go with me to the surgical daycare area to check it out. We walked down together where we met the staff to talk it through. She was welcomed by all with warmth and compassion, the kind of welcome that is vanishingly rare in most acute care hospitals. She agreed to the treatment, luckily, because the cancer would certainly have grown and killed her. On her admission, she was greeted by one of our nurses who said, "Today, Linda, you are queen for a day and we are here to serve you."

And she was treated like royalty, unlike any other acute care encounter she had ever had. Her surgery was flawless and she recovered quickly. She was grateful to the point of tears, though we assured her that we treated her just like we would anyone else. I was enormously grateful to be part of BC Women's that day, and I have been on many other days. Whatever the political or systems issues, respect and woman-centredness happen in the context of individual encounters. We can never underestimate the importance of growing and nurturing a culture that allows that to happen.

Most of the women we serve report similar experiences. It is more than clinical excellence. It is also more than respectful care. It is a truly holistic approach to understanding each woman in the context of her life and giving her the best possible care. Our website states boldly on the home page "We honour women's voices." It is true. We do, with all our hearts, and to the best of our ability.

While it is obvious that women's health is broader than pregnancy and reproductive issues, it remains true that we need to assure that maternity care is assessed using the same measures as other aspects of women's health. The same effort must be taken to assure that women have access to the highest possible quality of obstetrical care, to respectful and woman-centred care, honouring their voices and respecting their choices.

Historically, this has not always been the case. Obstetrics, as it became an increasingly medicalized culture through the twentieth century, was often ignored or abandoned in frustration by those seeking to improve woman-centredness. An entrenched medical model that had developed over two hundred years in a patriarchal system did not welcome the voices of dissenters, especially in the first half of the century. However, the tide has turned dramatically in recent decades, partly because of a cultural shift and partly because of other changes to the health care system.

For example, the implementation of midwifery in BC through the 1990s and early 2000s changed the balance away from intervention-heavy care back toward a more holistic practice of primary care. In the mid-1990s, with the registration of midwifery in BC, BC Women's Hospital became the first hospital in Canada to employ midwives as part of the obstetrical care team. Now at BC Women's, there are more than seventy midwives on staff, the highest number of any hospital in Canada, and they are central to assuring woman-centredness in care. BC Women's also has the largest family practice group providing primary maternity care in Western Canada.

At BC Women's, we have a great combination of skilled care providers, a culture that values women's lives, and adequate resources to assure that we can provide safe care for women during pregnancy and childbirth. I think we sometimes forget that the care of women during pregnancy and birth is the most frequent reason why women interact with the health care system. With 350,000 births a year in Canada, the clear majority in hospital, there are more admissions in Canadian hospitals for obstetrical care than for any other indication, including cancer care and cardiac care.

But herein lies our great dilemma. We are an acute care hospital funded to provide care during pregnancy and childbirth. Everything else, in terms of women's health, must be fought for and justified. Although there have been many successes in funding programmes and expanding services, there have also been many disappointments and I fear there are more to come as the biggest change in recent years has yet to come to fruition.

In 2016, the leadership of the PHSA made the decision that by 2017 there would be only one leader for both BC Women's and BC Children's hospitals. While the plan is to maintain two separate hospitals with two brands and two foundations, it will be difficult to do this in the real world. The child-health agenda is always easy to raise funds for, is always a source of great sympathy from the public, and will likely predominate at the cost of women's health and fundraising for BC Women's hospital.

Twenty years after the separation of BC Women's Hospital and BC Children's Hospital in 1997, and two decades of growth and expansion, the independence of BC Women's Hospital has been challenged. Despite this, BC Women's is a strong, resilient place where the commitment and passion of our staff is palpable. There is determination and resolve to continue the great work that has been done here for many years, building on the vision of all who have contributed before. Despite the challenges, I remain optimistic that BC Women's will be a strong, vibrant place and a beacon for the rest of the world for many years to come.

POSTSCRIPT

As I write this I am sitting in a work lab at a hospital in Kasulu, remote even by Tanzanian standards. And yet, they know of us. They use guidelines from Canada authored by some of our doctors and they know us by reputation. They think of us as one of the "beacon hospitals" of the world. In this region of Tanzania where the maternal mortality ratio (the number of maternal deaths per 100,000 live births) was recorded as 532 per 100,000 in 2016, there is much to be done. There is much to learn from places like BC Women's where the maternal mortality ratio, with less than one death per 20,000 deliveries, is too low to calculate and is among the lowest in the world. I have come each year for many years to teach not just obstetrical and surgical skills, but a reproductive rights framework for approaching the care of women in places where the burden on them seems overwhelming. The doctors and midwives we teach here are skilled and committed, but they work in a culture where women's lives are still not valued equally to men's, and where women's health is not a priority. From here, BC Women's feels like a very special place.

Promise her anything,
but give her valium.

Top Left: From *Healthsharing* Spring 1984
Top Right: From *Healthsharing* 1988
Bottom: From *Healthsharing* Fall 1986

SECTION FOUR:
CHALLENGING THE MEDICAL MODEL

Creating women's services was not the end of changing the shape of health care. It soon became apparent that there were some women's health issues that the system could not be trusted to deal with. Indeed, the medical model was itself the problem, in some cases producing perpetrators, bad actors, and over-prescribers. In addition, some women's health issues were created by patriarchal systems, such as violence against women, incest, over-prescription to psychoactive drugs, and reliance on substances to cope with oppressions.

What a challenge! McPhedran details her leadership in creating three official reports over twenty-five years addressing the sexual abuse of women patients by doctors in Ontario. Not much changed over this period; women continued to be abused and McPhedran suffered through a lawsuit with high personal costs. Rochon Ford describes the legacy of Ruth Cooperstock, a pioneering sociologist who first highlighted the issue of women receiving far too many psychotropic drugs compared to men. Caplan addresses the issue of diagnosis and the incredible sexism and politics involved in defining mental health conditions. Poole describes her efforts to spread the word about these drugs by travelling around Ontario with a flip chart and film, educating and sharing with women in small groups. Decades later, this issue continues to be unresolved.

In Western Canada, Pacey et al. describe the need to create a feminist counselling association, and detail the topics covered as they both educated themselves and offered feminist counselling to women. Thurston analyzes decades of action on violence against women by detailing her personal journey as an activist and scholar as she moved from east to west and through various sectors.

Depressingly, not much has changed on this issue either. In fact, today, the issues of violence against women remain huge and unresolved. My article in this section details a feminist analysis of smoking that brings to the surface the links to women's oppression and reveals how medical systems, researchers, and industry personnel all contributed to sending problematic messages to women about tobacco that influenced even the women's movement.

Fox discusses the booklet developed to challenge medical responses to abnormal Pap tests and its impact on health literacy and empowerment for women. And finally, Tudiver and Seabrooke describe the incredible success of *Side Effects*, a theatre production that travelled widely, detailing the impact of the global pharmaceutical industry on women's health. This, too, was a new route to health literacy, using a different medium. The medical model, it seemed, needed help—more than that, it needed upending!

REMEMBERING RUTH COOPERSTOCK: WOMEN AND PHARMACEUTICALS TWENTY YEARS LATER

The following are two excerpts from a symposium co-sponsored by the Ruth Cooperstock Memorial Lectureship Committee and Women and Health Protection.[68]

Panel Introduction
Anne Rochon Ford

This event has been titled *Remembering Ruth Cooperstock*. For those of you who did not know Ruth, she was a warm, bright, generous woman who shared freely her knowledge, her passion for social justice, and her wry sense of humour. We lost her far too soon from this world when she died of breast cancer while only in her fifties—twenty years ago this year.

Some of us have no trouble at all remembering Ruth Cooperstock because her work of several decades ago is still frighteningly relevant today. We see it particularly in the work Ruth did around women and prescription drugs—her razor-sharp analysis of medicalizing women's social problems, of the dangers inherent in the pharmaceutical industry's promotion of drugs to doctors, and of the over-prescription of psychotropic drugs to the elderly. These are all precisely the problems today that Ruth envisioned they would be when she was researching and writing about them in the 1970s and 1980s.

As a feminist and a strong advocate for social justice, she came to her work as a sociologist with a conviction that solutions would lie not so often with chemical fixes, but with strong support networks, meaningful work lives, freedom from abuse and violence and economic independence.

Personally, I have not only benefitted in my own work from the legacy of writing that Ruth left behind, but also knew her as a mentor for a too-brief period before she died. It is an honour to be able to remember Ruth this way, with an event taking place at the university she worked in, surrounded by people who knew and loved her, talking about the issues she cared so passionately about.

I am so thrilled to be back in Toronto and so honoured to have been asked to be on this panel, and I want to thank everybody who has helped to organize it. I loved Ruth Cooperstock, and I bring regards from Boston from Jean Baker Miller, who was Ruth's roommate in college.

I want to talk about women and mental health and how that relates to pharmaceuticals. I know some of you are familiar with what has been called the "Bible" of mental health professionals, the *Diagnostic and Statistical Manual of Mental Disorders* (DSM), which weighs three pounds (I weighed it) and which contains 374 categories of what the authors, the American Psychiatric Association, claim are mental illnesses. It's published in the United States, but it is used in Canada all the time. It's used globally, it has been translated into dozens of languages, and it's a multi-million dollar business.

The reason I want to talk about diagnosis is that it is the underpinning of everything that happens in the mental health system. You don't have psychotropic drugs prescribed without a psychiatric diagnosis. You don't get psychotherapy paid for unless you have a psychiatric diagnosis. And except for a few feminist health groups in Canada, who have done wonderful things about concerns about the mental health system, a lot of the time we in Canada have uncharacteristically gone along with what Americans are doing with this horrible book.

By definition, everything in the DSM is a mental disorder and, therefore, implicitly a medical disorder. Just the title, *Diagnostic and Statistical Manual*, helps create this aura of scientific precision, so the vast majority of psychiatric diagnoses made in Canada are based on the DSM. As a result, these days in Canada, although less than in the States, almost the only two things that are ever recommended or studied in well-funded research programmes are psychotherapy and drugs. This is not to say that neither therapy nor drugs can ever be helpful, because they can. But the problem is that sometimes each can be harmful, or just not helpful. And certainly the psychiatric labelling itself results in many women going on antidepressants or other drugs because there's just so much pressure to do so.

There are two criteria that I think should always be met when drugs are recommended, or even when psychotherapy or anything at all (even meditation or exercise) is recommended. One is that all of the known pros and cons of the recommended treatment should be disclosed. And the other is that the whole range of things that have been helpful to at least some people should be mentioned. Sadly, those two criteria are almost never met.

"Mental illness" is a construct. It's like "intelligence" or "love." So, although it's often talked about as though it's scientifically grounded and we know what mental illness is and what it isn't, and we know who has one and who doesn't, the fact is that if something is a construct, there is no such real thing out there. Mental illness is not real like a table. Mental illness is what whoever has the most power to create a definition and then get that definition used says it is.

I served on two of the committees that were charged with putting together the current edition of the DSM, the DSM-IV, before I resigned in horror when I saw what the DSM authors did. I learned that the DSM includes whatever the people at the top of the DSM hierarchy—about a dozen mostly white, mostly male, mostly American, mostly psychiatrists—want to include in the DSM. This manual now includes stuttering, math disability, nicotine dependence, and caffeine-induced sleep disorder as "mental illnesses." Dr. Leonore Tiefer has done amazing work exposing how ridiculous and how dangerous female sexual dysfunction is as a category of mental illness.

One of the labels that I find most frightening is major depressive disorder. This is not to say that people don't get depressed, but major depressive disorder includes this criterion: if you have lost somebody close to you and you're still grieving two months later, you fit the description of major depressive disorder. Why do we have to medicalize everything? Where is upsetting stuff that happens to people when they go through life? Why do we have to say, "Oh, you're still grieving and it's been two months, so you had better get to a therapist"? And what does that do to the nature of friendship in North America? You hear people say, "My friend was still grieving, but I'm not a therapist so I didn't know what to do, so I sent her to a therapist." People think that therapists have some magic knowledge. I don't know about others, but I know I don't have magic knowledge. And I worry about the fact that everything is being psychiatrized and psychologized.

In addition, much of what is really the consequence of violence and/or various kinds of oppression ends up being diagnosed as mental illness. If I said, "We took a bunch of people and we regularly humiliated them and said vile things to them, how do you think they're going to feel?" you'd say, "depressed, anxious...." Do we want to say that that's a mental illness, or do we want to say, "Be careful, because we are covering up, we are drawing attention away from major social and political ills?" Currently, in preparation for the DSM-V that's on the way, a committee has been appointed to discuss whether racism should go in the DSM as a mental illness! They've said that it's a way of showing that racism is bad. But there goes hate crime legislation; there goes seeing that racism is a social evil.

In spite of the fact that mental illness itself is a construct and every category in the DSM is a construct, some more descriptive of what people really experience than others, the fact that they're in the DSM and they're put on OHIP cards means that they become reified. People come to believe that there is such a thing as schizophrenia or there are such things as other categories in there, and we know what they are, and those experts must know how to treat them.

In 1987, when I taught at the University of Toronto and at the Ontario Institute for Studies in Education, I was a member of a committee headed by Janet Stoppard. She had gotten the Canadian Mental Health Association (CMHA) to provide a small amount of funding to the committee to prepare a report on women and mental health in Canada. Jeri Wine was on that committee as well. Instead of looking within the mental health framework, we asked, "What would make women in Canada feel better and function better?" We came up with a huge list of recommendations—some for the CMHA, some for various levels of government, and some for training programmes for therapists. The report went out of print almost immediately and, to my knowledge, the CMHA has still not reissued it. And, to my knowledge, few, if any, of the recommendations have been implemented. They included things like making sure that women have enough income, making sure that women will not be victims of violence.... It was the whole feminist social programme.

Serious kinds of harm can come to people as a result of getting *any* diagnosis that is in the DSM, even one that may sound innocuous, like "adjustment disorder." People have lost custody of their children because they're diagnosed with such labels from the DSM. People have lost jobs (that's supposed to be illegal, but you have to be able to prove that that's why you got fired). People have lost the right to make decisions about their medical and legal affairs. This is very serious.

As I said, I was on two DSM committees. One was about the invented category, which two male psychiatrists are said to have thought up on a fishing trip, called premenstrual dysphoric disorder or PMDD. I want to tell you a little about my experience being on that committee, as a kind of a case study. The PMDD category applied only to women, but similar things are being done with a lot of the categories in the DSM. I was appointed to the PMDD committee. The DSM people said, "Don't worry. We're not going to diagnose every woman who has just ordinary premenstrual syndrome as having a mental disorder." They said that they were talking about a "tiny number" of women who really get mentally ill just before their period. They said that they were not talking about PMS—bloating, breast tenderness, food cravings—but rather, about a mental illness. They then designed a category whose symptoms went like this: you had to have one mood symptom (e.g., depressed or anxious or irritable or emotionally labile or angry), then you had to have four of the symptoms on a list that included bloating, breast tenderness, food cravings—the very characteristics usually considered part of ordinary PMS. And you have to wonder: What are those physical factors doing in a manual of *mental* disorders?

When I was living in Toronto, I was involved in organizing a protest against the existence of this category and against putting it in the DSM-III-R, in 1987. They got so much bad press about it that they didn't end up putting it in the main text of the DSM-III-R. They created an appendix for "categories requiring further study," and they put it in there. It had a list of criteria and looked very scientific. However, they did not say, "Don't use this. It hasn't been proven to exist." That's when I got involved, as they were moving toward creating DSM-IV. That was the PMDD committee. We were supposed to look at the research and decide whether premenstrual dysphoric disorder was a real entity. But I saw that they ignored the science that didn't fit with what they wanted, or they distorted it, or they lied about it (I know there are lawyers here but I've never been sued and I've said this in print). And that is why I resigned from that committee.

Let me tell you what the good scientific research actually showed about PMDD. A study was done that was the perfect study to find out if there was such a thing as a premenstrual mental illness. In this study, they removed breast tenderness in order to keep the terms sex-neutral, and they gave the DSM list of PMDD symptoms to three groups of people and asked them to fill out the checklist every day for two months. The groups consisted of women who were diagnosed with PMDD, women who said they had no premenstrual problems, and men. If there were such a thing as a premenstrual mental illness and its criteria had been correctly identified, then of course the three groups would have answered very differently; but there were virtually no differences. And the DSM people knew that. In spite of that, they kept PMDD in the next edition of the DSM.

There are a lot of problems with that. One of the most alarming is this: The people at the top of the DSM hierarchy and the pharmaceutical companies work hand in glove. And of course the insurance systems, whether government or private, help that along because they want labels and want things simplified. Because we had demonstrated that there was no proof there was such a thing as PMDD, the DSM people held a roundtable discussion after DSM-IV was published. The roundtable was funded by Eli Lilly (the makers of Prozac). They got together the DSM's PMDD Committee (needless to say, I wasn't invited) and they published a paper in which they claimed that new evidence had proven that PMDD was a real entity. Well, I read their paper and saw all they did was cite the old evidence that didn't prove that and new evidence that didn't prove it either.

One of the members of this PMDD Committee went to the Food and Drug Administration (FDA) meeting with Eli Lilly when the FDA had to vote on whether to extend the patent on Prozac, which was about to expire. This expiration would have meant the loss of millions of dollars by Eli Lilly. However, if they could prove that Prozac is helpful for another disorder besides depression, for which it had long been approved, they'd get an extension on the patent, which would be worth millions of dollars. So they went to the FDA together and said Prozac helps PMDD. The FDA did not require them to prove that there was such a thing as PMDD. So the next thing you know it's approved, and what happens? They take Prozac and they start manufacturing it in pink and purple and they rename it Sarafem. I believe it's not being sold under that name in Canada, but some of you may have seen the ads on American TV and in magazines.

In one Sarafem commercial, they showed a woman looking enraged and a sweet-looking man who surely never would have provoked that rage. A voiceover said, "You may think you have PMS, but you really have PMDD." Remember how in the beginning the DSM people had said, "We're not talking about PMS; we're talking about a tiny number of women"? Well, they did the exact opposite of what they said they were going to do. In the first few months after Sarafem went on the market (usually women are not told that it is Prozac), there were about a quarter of a million prescriptions written. If you type in "Sarafem" and "Canada" on the Internet, you get lots of drug company websites that say "See Prozac." So lots of women in Canada are taking Prozac for the nonexistent PMDD.

So let me just wrap up. This is dangerous business. Women are still socialized to not want to be angry, not want to be irritable, not want to be depressed, because then we can't meet other people's needs. So when you see a commercial like that, you think, "Look at her. After she took the pill, she's so sweet. I'd like to be like that and I'm so busy. I don't have time for therapy. Just give me the pill." The pressures on women tend to stream us towards asking for this kind of medication. And what the drug companies say is, "Isn't it wonderful that we are teaching women, that we are educating them so they can take control of their mental health care by knowing to ask for Prozac or Sarafem!"

TRAVELLING ONTARIO WITH MOMMY'S LITTLE HELPER

Nancy Poole

I was working as a part-time relief staff at Nellie's in downtown Toronto in the late 1970s. Nellie's Hostel was one of the first shelters for women in Canada. After a while I noticed that some of the women coming in to the shelter seemed sedated and uncoordinated. Sometimes, they were so woozy that they missed the doorway to the office and ran into the wall beside the doorway. When I asked about what they were taking, they mentioned they had been prescribed a new drug called Valium to help cope with the stresses of violence and homelessness. I had no idea what Valium was, but it did not appear to be good for women, so I decided to find out.

Without computers and Google to look it up, I had to use other means. Indeed, as Nellie's was a radical and underfunded community-based women's service, we did not even have a pharmaceutical reference text. So I phoned Health and Welfare Canada and was referred to the Non-Medical Use of Drugs Directorate. I was referred to the Ontario regional office, where I found some women led by Jessica Hill who were putting together educational material on the overprescription of benzodiazepines to women, including the links to women's experience of violence and alcohol use. They welcomed me, with my experience from the anti-violence field, to join them in reviewing a kit of information on these issues, designed by Judith Wright and entitled with maximum irony "It's Just Your Nerves."

The It's Just Your Nerves kit was built on research by Dr. Ruth Cooperstock, a medical sociologist who worked at the Addiction Research Foundation (now the Centre for Addiction and Mental Health) in Toronto in the 1960s and 1970s.[69] Her research was foundational to sharing credible knowledge about tranquillizers, alcohol, and violence with family physicians and others who could act to promote women's health. I have a typed "in press" copy of an article by Ruth Cooperstock entitled "A review of women's psychotropic drug use" that was published in the *Canadian Journal of Psychiatry* in 1979.[70] In it she revealed how Canadian women received more prescriptions of psychotropic drugs than males, with over two-thirds of these drugs prescribed to women.

In addition, she noted that more than twice the number of females than males received ten or more prescriptions in a year. She described how women not in the labour force, not involved in social activities outside the home, and with negative subjective health ratings reported being higher users of these drugs. In addition, she cites studies illustrating how when women and men accessed help from family physicians for symptoms of being "unhappy, crying, depressed, nervous, and worried, restless, and tense," women were more likely to be prescribed psychotropic medication and men more likely to receive referrals for physical therapies and laboratory tests. These findings were a revelation, not just to me, but to many working in community-based agencies with women experiencing violence, poverty, homelessness, and mental health issues.

In another article also published in 1979 in the *Sociology of Health and Illness* journal, entitled "Some social meanings of tranquilizer use," Cooperstock and her co-author, Henry Lennard, critiqued how tranquillizers were being prescribed to women to alleviate their conflicted feelings with the roles of wife, mother, and houseworker, and noted "the inadequacy of the biomedical model in explaining continued tranquillizer use."[71] Indeed!

Ironically, the "Mothers' Little Helper" song written by Mick Jagger of the Rolling Stones in the late sixties and its lyric: "And though she's not really ill, there's a little yellow pill" was being played out over and over again in doctor's offices across Canada.

The It's Just Your Nerves kit is a classic piece of consciousness-raising in the feminist tradition. It relied on face-to-face meetings, papers and posters, and group discussions about shared experiences. Imagine a time without computers and PowerPoint presentations, and no YouTube videos to convey a message to a broad audience. Without these modern aids, we relied on a twenty-page flip chart with colour posters highlighting key issues for discussion and reflection on needed action. In addition, we had a 140-page guidebook providing supplementary information and discussion questions and a fifteen-minute 16mm film entitled *All In The Same Boat*, made in Australia in 1977. The film presented a portrait of a young married woman with children who uses alcohol and tranquillizers, and a husband "who sees his role as narrowly defined"![72]

The flip-chart posters and the workbook covered facts about gender, tranquillizer use, and alcohol, and invited critical thinking. For example, one of the posters simply stated "to cope with what?" The complexities of the marketing of tranquilizers to physicians, the prescribing of tranquillizers to women for non-medical or social reasons, and the inequities and mental health challenges faced by women in Canadian society were all openly raised and explored.

The kit was to be used by "women's groups, social and health care workers, unions, churches, educators, personnel departments and service club affiliates." It met the basic elements of good feminist practice in that it invited an "exchange of facts and experiences" and as the promotional flyer indicated "encourages group problem solving, puts personal use in its social context, examines personal and social responsibility for overuse and enhances women's sense of control over themselves and their bodies."

Soon I was on the road, travelling across Ontario for months upon end. We reached out by phone to health clinics, addictions services, and women's organizations to generate interest in local workshops. The word quickly spread and soon my car was packed full with a 16mm projector, the film, spare film reel, extension cord, flip chart, and boxes of resource booklets. And me, as the catalyzing animator of the kit! The road trips to communities across Ontario included sessions in libraries, town hall meeting rooms, women's services, and every local venue you could imagine. The material was designed to engage small groups of women in small groups in collective discussion and analysis of the issues. This was easily ignited, followed quickly by incredulity, rage, laughter, and empowerment as women learned of the facts surrounding these drugs and women.

In some locations women would open their purses to reveal multiple pill bottles and join the discussion as worried consumers. In others, participants would challenge the portrayal of the husband in the film, who was a heavy alcohol user, and who displayed blatant sexism and exertion of power and control toward his partner. This prompted conversation about the levels and types of violence against women, especially the gender-based violence affecting women isolated in the home. Women's organizations would immediately jump into discussing how this material could be integrated into their activist work right away.

The audiences I encountered loved the kit with its rich, contextualized background information, the comprehensive guidebook, the arresting flip charts, and the film. Together, it all stimulated lively discussions. It was a ground-breaking tool in knowledge sharing, unabashedly feminist in its message. Kits were left behind in many locations and the National Film Board local offices stocked the film for borrowing. Once the kit was presented, it could be used in turn by participants, so that a network of impassioned educators soon grew and took root.

The 1970s were years of remarkable action by Canadian feminists on a range of issues: violence against women, birth control and abortion access, lesbian visibility, women's music, and women's health. While many may now take for granted the need for community-based services for women, at that time we were collectively defining, designing, and opening doors to hidden knowledge, practices, and each others' secrets. I was delighted to play a part in revealing Mommy's little helper mile by mile, small group by small group, across the back roads of Ontario.

THREE INQUIRIES: LOOKING FOR ACCOUNTABILITY FOR THE SEXUAL ABUSE OF PATIENTS IN ONTARIO

Marilou McPhedran

To refer to what...any man accused of wrong doing against women—has gone through as a "witch hunt," even if it is intense and virulent, ignores the reality of what a witch hunt is, and inverts the broken power structure that allows a witch hunt to take place. While being cast as witch-hunters, the women who come forward with their stories of abuse must endure their own persecution, from losing friends and having their reputations destroyed publicly, to being harassed for trying to speak truth to (and about) power.[73]

Over the years, I have seen many inequalities and inequities forced on women, perpetuated by governments that allow systems of victim blaming and silencing to flourish. In ongoing attempts at holding health professionals to account, I have observed governments make extensive investments in the systems that sustain the privileged classes of health professionals to whom we give our highest level of trust—such as medical doctors, dentists, psychologists, and nurses. Governments have refused to use public funds to invest in effective accountability mechanisms by providing equivalent resources to patients and their advocates. Indeed, governments off-load the responsibility to media and to victimized patients to hold predatory professionals and their regulatory health bodies accountable for the harm done to patients, their families, and our society as a whole.

Getting sued for libel by the Ontario Medical Association (OMA) in 2001 thrust me into a tense and dark world for five long years. In 2001, after chairing (for the second time in ten years) an independent inquiry into the sexual abuse of patients commissioned by the government of Ontario, I had written a summary of our final report that was checked and published by *The Globe and Mail* entitled "Do No Harm." It challenged how the OMA was allocating its resources in a doctor's appeal against revocation of his "right" to practice because he was found by the self-regulating body for doctors to have sexually abused a patient.[74] As a result, the OMA utilized "libel chill" through what is known as a strategic lawsuit against public participation (SLAPP) suit by suing only me (a single mother with financial challenges), and not the publisher.[75]

The libel suit of "OMA versus McPhedran" was launched in September 2001 and lasted until late 2006—five years during which the OMA sent me the wording of an apology to be published in *The Globe and Mail* to end it, but for me that apology would have been a lie. Nevertheless, this tactic silenced me as a critic on this issue for five years, while I waited for the trial to regain my voice and for the OMA to become visible to the media. Court-ordered settlement negotiations began right before the trial date and it was then that the parties reached an agreement to walk away. There was no trial, there was no apology from me, and the OMA dropped the suit.

My case—and several others using libel chill tactics against public interest advocates—became the basis for reforming the law in Ontario. As a result, I believe that plaintiffs such as the OMA would have a much harder time now to use the law as their silencing tool. Some risk remains, however, with advocates still getting "cease and desist" notices from lawyers representing rich and powerful people and corporations, threatening to take legal action.

The results of this experience were life-changing. I was thrust farther into debt and some of my legal costs are still in the mortgage on my house. I had to separate the wheat from the chaff among my "friends," accept donations from many supporters, and, as a widely quoted advocate for the right of patients not to be sexually exploited, I was silenced and shunned professionally by many. My children suffered significant protracted anxiety that we would lose our home if I lost the libel suit. It could have ended my activism, but it didn't. However, without the SLAPP suit silencing (and also being fired without cause by a feminist research organization that generated a fair settlement), I would never have had the time needed to finish writing the first Canadian textbook on the sexual abuse of patients.[76]

While we often use the generic term "patients' rights" the fact is that the vast majority of patients sexually exploited by regulated health professionals are women. Early in 1991, as the wave of backlash against the first task force on sexual abuse of patients emerged, my friend and "femtor," Michele Landsberg, reminded me that the struggle for human rights is played out most obviously on the bodies, hearts, and minds of women and girls across the globe. And to support the second task force report in 2000, the courageous Dr. Judith Herman, who herself survived massive backlash against her work with sexual abuse victims, gave me permission to reprint an entire chapter of her book *Trauma and Recovery*:

> Though frightening, these attacks are an implicit tribute to the power of the healing relationship. They remind us that creating a protected space where survivors can speak their truth is an act of liberation. They remind us that bearing witness, even within the confines of that sanctuary, is an act of solidarity. They remind us also that moral neutrality in the conflict between victim and perpetrator is not an option. Like all other bystanders, therapists are sometimes forced to take sides. Those who stand with the victim will inevitably have to face the perpetrator's unmasked fury. For many of us, there can be no greater honor.[77]

Is there a "feminist" side to advocating for the identification and disciplining of doctors who abuse their patients? How many "sides" can there possibly be on such an issue? In 1990, the sexual abuse of patients was first named and exposed, leading to articulation of the standard of zero tolerance of sexual abuse and new laws in Ontario still considered to be among the most comprehensive of governmental responses in the world. Nevertheless, over twenty-five years I was called to lead three inquiries in the province of Ontario (1990–91, 2000–01, and 2015–16) and in each case, donating my time and expertise became necessary in order to complete the hard-hitting reports. While the first inquiry report led to the tough new law on sexual abuse of patients and some distinct improvements, there has been minimal success in implementing and sustaining the protections.

If you detect anger and frustration in my tone years later, you would be correct. The lack of significant progress in patient safety is a question that frequently plagued me in my private hours before the call came for the third task force. I said yes to that call because a feminist premier had asked for me and because I couldn't pass up the chance to see inside the question of why so little had changed.

But it helps to go back to the decade before the very first inquiry. In 1984, I was one of the founders of the Metro Toronto Action Committee on Violence Against Women and Children (METRAC). This was in an era of feminist activism on sexual abuse and other forms of violence focused on creating new services and new coalitions, but under a feminist umbrella. METRAC was among the first feminist organizations in Canada to focus on systemic changes with founders who were all leaders in their fields, such as Jane Pepino (the founding chair), Patricia Marshall, Dr. Gail Robinson, Mary Eberts, Dr. Marion Powell, and Mary Jane Mossman. Upon hearing about boundary violations against patients by physicians, METRAC realized that advocacy on these issues was required, beyond one-on-one counselling, in order to make deep and sustainable change.

As a medical doctor, METRAC board member Dr. Gail Robinson was a member of the regulatory body for doctors, the College of Physicians and Surgeons of Ontario (CPSO), so initially the METRAC concerns about sexual abuse of patients were conveyed internally at College council meetings. Paul Taylor, a young reporter at *The Globe and Mail* at the time began a comprehensive, case-heavy exposé on how patients reporting sexual exploitation were treated when their alleged abusers were "disciplined" by the CPSO. This exposé revealed how "therapy" was misused as a treatment, along with sordid details of the behaviours, abuses, and assaults, and the lacklustre response from the CPSO. Voluble public criticism of the CPSO ensued.

Luckily, in 1991, Ontario had just elected a New Democratic Party (NDP) government with a feminist health minister, Frances Lankin, a smart, progressive deputy health minister, Michael Decter, and a deputy attorney general who was a social justice advocate, Mary Hogan. Hogan had also been my supervisor when I was a law student at the poverty law clinic in Parkdale (Toronto). Lankin questioned whether the self-regulatory system was serving the public interest and the CPSO reacted by announcing it would initiate an independent task force to investigate sexual abuse of patients.

When I was approached about chairing the inquiry, CPSO said it had been advised that they had to name a chair seen by the media as credible and truly independent. I accepted. Neither the CPSO nor I could have known at the start just how much an independent task force would strain that male-dominated organization.[78] I involved METRAC colleagues, particularly Patricia Marshall and Dr. Gail Robinson, in the inquiry; we felt that METRAC's overarching goals to do strategic advocacy for systemic change could be advanced. And when we faced attempts to compromise the confidentiality of reports to the task force, we turned to Jane Pepino for her strength and legal acumen—with success.

The facts belied the common refrain that only a tiny number of patients experience sexual abuse. *Between 1987 and 1990 alone*, the CPSO received about 150 reports of sexual abuse of patients, unnoticed until Paul Taylor started writing about them in *The Globe and Mail*. But in six months in 1991, during which the task force accepted reports, there were 303 reports (203 by phone, 61 in public or private hearings, 39 by letter). Some of these were alerting us to serial abuse by the same doctor, or a group of doctors "sharing" sexual access to their patients. Five recurring themes emerged. For example:

Theme 1: Personal Experiences
"This experience damaged me badly; I have never been able to trust anyone since. I trusted my doctor. He had been the family's doctor for many years."

Theme 2: Third Party Reporting
"Since that experience, she has changed. She locks herself away and does not eat. She quit school. I'm reporting because someone has to do it; someone has to stop these people."

Theme 3: Requests to Testify to the Independent Task Force
"I am doing this so that people will know and, hopefully, stop him and others like him, from damaging women."

Theme 4: Initiatives to Begin Formal Complaints
"This is a difficult process and I am ready to go through it so that his behaviour will stop."

Theme 5: Concerns about Sustainable Change
"I wonder what will happen when the task force is dismantled?"
"It's not just doctors abusing; it's in all the people with power and privilege."

During 1991, numerous attempts were made to undermine the independence of the task force procedures, staffing, and public reporting. First the budget was shrunk, then funding was cut off before the report could be finished, and then the task force office was padlocked by the CPSO. I got a panicked call from our assistant that task force member Roz Roach, a prominent leader in the Black community of Toronto, was escorted out of CPSO headquarters by security, and that our task force secretary had to grab the confidential files and was clutching them sitting on a chair in the middle of the CPSO main office. After a standoff involving my finger on my cell phone button to send calls to media, the office was re-opened and I decided to donate my expertise to finish the public report, with other task force members helping when they could.

In retrospect, it was the looming presence of a strong feminist health minister and an attentive media that enabled the 1991 task force to become the pivotal force in changing the law for Ontario's patients. This law, the *Regulated Health Professions Act, 1991* (RHPA) named sexual abuse of patients for the first time and introduced accountability mechanisms geared to implementing "zero tolerance of sexual abuse of patients." When we released our interim report in May 1991, the task force asked that the zero tolerance standard be the first task force recommendation adopted by the CPSO and affirmed in the legislature by Minister Lankin, which was done. We wanted the zero tolerance commitment to guide the accountability mechanisms put in place through the new RHPA Procedural Code, which all Ontario health regulatory bodies were to be required to apply in complaints of sexual abuse against their members.[79]

Another task force recommendation was to require a five-year review of the RHPA. The NDP lost the next election, so Elizabeth Witmer, a Conservative minister of health, became responsible for this review. On the ground, METRAC was hearing many of the same stories from patients and advocates about systemic avoidance of sexual abuse complaints by health regulatory colleges and government. I invited the original task force members to dinner and we decided to visit Minister Witmer. We learned that Price Waterhouse Coopers (PWC) had been contracted to do the five-year review but the terms of reference seemed to be missing a section on sexual abuse of patients! Not long after our meeting, I was asked to reassemble the task force to do a five-year review alongside the PWC process. In the minister's letter of appointment, it was promised that the task force review would be released to the public as an independent report.

After a few months, Premier Mike Harris shuffled his cabinet and the new health minister had little to say about sexual abuse of patients. Soon this second task force was also starved of budget and we were forced to shrink our scope, staffing, and efforts. And for the second time, I wrote most of the report *pro bono,* finishing in late 2000 with some financial assistance from concerned non-governmental sources. Well into 2001, the health ministry was still saying it could not afford to print the report or make it widely available to the public, so I called a media conference in the legislature building and released the report online, to some considerable consternation. By June 2001, the report was finally printed, but only because of the support of the Women's Health Advisory Council of Ontario, then being chaired by Jane Pepino. Her introduction in the report situated the sexual abuse of patients as a major issue in women's health.[80] In order to raise public awareness in the face of ongoing governmental silence I responded to all media requests and wrote guest opinion articles. But then, one warm September morning in 2001 as I was meeting with a colleague in my garden, a man walked up and served me with notice that the OMA was suing me—and only me—for libel. I was deeply shocked and frightened by this personal introduction to "libel chill."

Of the sixty recommendations made by the first task force, many were made into law, in whole or in part. However, its five-year review revealed the ways that the regulatory health bodies were circumventing the implementation of the "zero tolerance of sexual abuse" standard. So the second task force recommended in 2000 deeper systemic changes in the health professional self-regulatory regime that would bring the needs and rights of patients into the centre of the processes dominated and so skilfully blocked by well-resourced professional organizations.

To actually achieve such major changes in order to implement zero tolerance, government had to make significant investments in patients and their advocates, such as improving research, education of health professions, and patient-centred safety measures to bring accountability and transparency to the regulatory process. But almost nothing was done by anyone in government. Particularly damaging, there was no significant investment in civil society capacity to contribute to preventing and exposing the sexual abuse of patients, and sexual abuse of patients all but disappeared as a rights issue in Ontario. Given that Ontario had been a world leader on this issue, the silence in Ontario had national and international impact as it compounded inattention and inaction. That is until *Toronto Star* reporters, briefly in 2011, and then with more intensity in 2014, shone a steady spotlight on how the CPSO was making pretty much the same weak discipline decisions that had prompted the first task force twenty years before.

Soon after, in 2015, the third inquiry started—twenty-five years since METRAC had first raised these issues. The third inquiry—the independent Minister's Task Force on Preventing Sexual Abuse of Patients—was funded by the ministry of health and long-term care under a Liberal government, except that to get the report finished, I worked *pro bono* for eight of the fifteen months it took to deliver a full and final report. This inquiry led to a public report in 2016, and is the basis of Bill 87 (the *Protecting Patients Act*, 2017).

After three inquiries on this important issue, I would have to say that the medical model and regulated health professions have triumphed. The doctors in Ontario still dominate in the number of complaints but also in action and policy on the issue of sexual abuse of patients. The immense power of the OMA and the Canadian Medical Protective Association (CMPA)—the billion plus legal defence fund for doctors—still resonates. The lawsuit against me intimidated many groups and individuals. Some of those groups have disappeared and some remain silent to this day. Without a doubt, it delayed collective activism on sexual abuse by doctors. It has fed inaction and ongoing, long delays in bringing justice and safety to patients in Ontario. Where are we now? Was it all worth it? Are patients protected or any better off? Am I angry about the lack of implementation of zero tolerance of sexual abuse of patients? Indeed I am. And as Clementine Ford reminds us, "The truth is, women's anger is pathologised as dangerous because it represents a threat to the stability of the gender inequality that relies on its absence."[81]

Feminists, women, and rights-based organizations will have to continue to be the primary leaders on combatting sexual abuse of patients. And women's primary leadership need not discount or diminish the impact on patients of other genders who experience sexual exploitation. The truth is, regardless of gender, race, culture, age, or ability, most patients' voices are not heard and patients are still not anywhere close to the centre of what health ministry officials do in their day-to-day jobs, in spite of the rhetoric and the patient-centric titles given to reports or legislative bills. Investment has not been made in effective accountability mechanisms. Incentives are not in place for officials to uphold a zero tolerance standard, or to ever make protecting patients from sexual abuse an active priority.

And it is perhaps unlikely that sexist and misogynistic attitudes are only the domain of older men, ready to disappear like dinosaurs. In December 2014, it became public that some of the fourth-year dentistry students at Dalhousie University had a private Facebook group to which they had been posting misogynist, racist, homophobic, and sexually violent remarks and images. Ultimately, more than fifty postings were leaked, prompting reactions of disgust, shock, and speculation, and dominating the news in Canada and beyond for weeks. An independent task force was established, chaired by Professor Constance Backhouse, that noted in its final report that the inquiry had been cast by some as a witch hunt:

> A male dental student described the atmosphere around the school as "absolutely a circus" where "certain people are offended about everything that is said." Letters to the editor of *The Chronicle Herald* [newspaper] compared calls to expel the male students with a "witch hunt from the Middle Ages."[82]

And in April 2017, a medical doctor presenting to the standing committee of the Ontario Legislature reviewing proposed amendments, derived from the third task force recommendations on preventing sexual abuse of patients, had this to say:

> ...this draconian bill has the potential to forever compromise the quality and timeliness of patient care.... Short of chasing us out of town *with broomsticks literally out of the province....* [emphasis added][83]

These ongoing examples of sexism continue to affect me as well. In January 2015 one of the civil servants assigned to support me and the (3rd) Task Force on Preventing Sexual Abuse of Patients asked to speak to me privately. She was very upset by what she was hearing in the halls of the health ministry, including one senior official who remarked, "The bitch is back," to the appreciative chuckles of his colleagues. I thanked her for alerting me. It seemed to me it was a good sign that he knew that the inaction and cozy relations with powerful institutions, instead of "zero tolerance of sexual abuse" were going to be exposed. I did assure her, however, that I would have preferred that he had been more accurate in his observation, saying, "The *feminist* bitch is back."

FILLING A GAP: THE WESTERN CANADIAN FEMINIST COUNSELLING ASSOCIATION (1979–1992)

Ingrid Pacey, Marsha Ablowitz, Sandra Friedman,
and Wendy Barrett

INGRID

Since 1992, the Feminist Counselling Association (FCA), later to become the Western Canadian Feminist Counselling Association (WCFCA), was a box of old newsletters, conference flyers, and correspondence in my basement that got moved around with each sorting of old papers, tax returns, etc., and that somehow I could never throw out. I felt that the FCA deserved to be remembered as a part of Vancouver feminist history and that one day such an opportunity would arrive. The box is a bit musty now, but I was amazed at how much we had done and how active we had been. The FCA was active from about 1978 till 1992.

It had started as a lunchtime meeting of feminist therapists using a room at Family Services of Greater Vancouver. The group chose the name for the association. I remember that I had given a talk on "The issue of fusion in lesbian couples" in 1980. After that, I became more involved, as it seemed clear that there was a need for feminist therapy to be talked about in Vancouver and that the many issues—cultural, psychological, therapeutic, and sociological—that feminism was addressing needed a platform.

I am a psychiatrist who has worked in Vancouver in private practice since 1972. I am a feminist. I quickly realized that my psychiatric training (1968–1972) in Vancouver was all from a patriarchal perspective and there was no analysis of women's issues from a feminist perspective in medicine or psychiatry. Nor was it present in the training in any other field of mental health or education or medicine.

So I suggested we start evening meetings that more women could attend, invite all the feminist therapists that we knew, organize speakers from our local feminist therapists and activists, and begin putting out a newsletter of activities. With the help of Dr. Marsha Trew, who was head of the Women's Resource Centre at Capilano College, we began organizing. I became chairperson and we began putting together the next incarnation of the FCA.

Our first big event was our conference in February 1981 called "Feminist Therapy Now" held at a downtown hotel. It felt radical and courageous to be putting ourselves forward as feminists and activists in the centre of downtown Vancouver, challenging current views on women's mental health and therapy.

Our main speakers were Rosemary Brown and Helen Levine. Rosemary Brown was a NDP MLA in the BC legislature and a strong spokeswoman for women's issues. Her speech was titled "Overview: Women, mental health, and social/political action." Helen Levine, on the faculty at Carlton University's School of Social Work in Ottawa, was responsible for bringing feminism to the school and campaigning against sexism. Her topic was "Feminist counselling: Conceptual framework."

I chaired the conference and was thrilled to be doing so. We had small groups in the afternoon on topics such as battered women; re-entry women; issues with lesbian clients; low-income women; and sexual abuse of clients by therapists. All were led by Vancouver feminists. We did not shy away from dealing with difficult topics head-on. It was wonderful to see what resources we had in our community and wonderful to be addressing solutions.

There were approximately one hundred participants, and the fee was $35, including lunch. There was so much enthusiasm and excitement to be finally coming together at a feminist event with relevant and important topics for therapists discussed from a feminist perspective. The final address was by Helen Levine on "Feminist counselling: Political responsibility and social action" or "Beyond patchwork and Band-Aids." We were on a mission!

I remember that a male colleague in my office sent me a bunch of flowers to mark the event and it reminded me of how important and groundbreaking our conference was. It was amazing how quickly our numbers grew; the hunger for new knowledge and community around feminist issues was evident. We formed a co-ordinating committee that year and started a membership list. We decided to be a women-only organization, for the most part.

In May 1981 we held the second conference on "Women's Mental Health and Sexual Orientation" at stately Hycroft House in Shaughnessy, the location of the UBC University Women's Club. They opened their doors to a feminist organization. There was a huge turnout—women who were proud to be feminists and lesbians who could openly talk about themselves and their lives. Marsha Ablowitz spoke about "Myths, definitions, and lifestyles" in the lesbian community.

I spoke about aspects of therapy with lesbian couples. Others spoke about lesbian mothers; counselling adolescents; substance abuse. Again it was a very positive event and we learned a lot. We had good discussions, networked, and had fun. In 1982 we began to organize more events and send out newsletters.

Our conference in April of that year was "Intervention in sexual abuse: A feminist perspective," organized with the Justice Institute of BC and held in their meeting hall; again there was a combination of talks to the whole conference and small group workshops. We had to turn women away because of lack of space.

We even had a positive bank balance by now and started being able to give donations to feminist organizations in the community, and at some point started paying speakers. Marsha remembers that periodically, since I kept track of finances, I would announce at a committee meeting that we had "lots" in the bank and it was time to give some away. How wonderful to be able to support women's organizations that way, too.

Other topics that year in evening seminars were grief, pornography, psychiatric medication, women's health issues, and eating disorders. The presenters were all women from the Vancouver women's community who had been working in their areas of expertise as feminists—often in isolation—and now could spread their knowledge and share their experiences with therapists eager to learn.

In 1983 the organization of the association and newsletters moved to my office in Vancouver from Capilano College and remained there for the rest of its existence. Marsha Ablowitz became the second chairperson. We began collecting names for a directory of feminist therapists and services. It went through three editions up to 1990 and was widely used.

Ultimately, we began the process of drafting a constitution and incorporating as a society under the *BC Societies Act*. This was completed in 1985. The official name became the Western Canadian Feminist Counselling Association. We had a board of directors and started to have annual general meetings. We were growing up. Our conference in March 1983 was another huge success, held at the Unitarian Centre. It was called "Women—Visions of the Future." In her powerful introduction, Marsha said the following:

My name is Marsha Ablowitz and I'm the chair-person of the Feminist Counselling Association. I'm very glad that people came. When we had this conference we got quite a slow turnout of registrants at first and we thought, oops, it's not a topic that appeals to therapists. And the FCA in the past has run conferences on therapy issues, battered women, incest, counselling gay women...we were feeling a little burnt out and thought it would be nice to just talk about something a little different, and we thought that the issue of power for women was important to all of us and, in fact, in therapy, that's what we're doing, trying to empower women. And then, thinking about power, we started thinking, well, once we get power, "what are we going to do with the power?" and Ann Mills came up with the idea of our vision for the future, what we would like to see happen in the future.

This is quite different than anything we've discussed before and I must say that those of us on the committee learned a lot just thinking about what our visions of the future were going to be. And what we thought was that there is a vision in all of us, and that sort of is what keeps us going. If we look at the reality of the situation, women being beaten, raped, starving to death, not making much money...the reality of the situation doesn't really keep us going. What keeps us going is that we have some kind of vision that things are going to be different and that we are somehow going to achieve that. In some way we're moving in that direction.

I wanted to tell you a little bit about the Feminist Counselling Association. This is the third group of feminist counsellors who have gotten together in Vancouver. The other two groups disintegrated after less than a year and the wonderful success of our organization which has now been going, I think, for five years...do you want to know our secret? We very carefully avoided defining what is a feminist counsellor. We decided that we just would not get into that.

So consequently we didn't have to kick anybody out, nobody had to leave in protest, and we're all around together.

Our first presenter was Margaret Mitchell, a strong social activist since the sixties and long-time worker on behalf of women. She ran as an NDP candidate in Vancouver East and was elected to Parliament in 1979, where she championed women's issues. In fact, Margaret Mitchell became known across the country in 1982 after she rose in the house and called for government to take action to stop violence against women. When she cited statistics showing that 10 per cent of husbands beat their wives, the reaction of many male MPs was to laugh out loud. That incident put the issue of domestic violence into greater public awareness.

The next speakers were seven remarkable women: Alice Ages, Margaret Benston, Kirsten Emmott, Meredith Kimball, Darlene Marzari, Catherine Wedge, and Sue Wendall. These women were very different: a counsellor; a PhD chemist; a poet and physician; an alderwoman; a businesswoman; a lawyer; and a philosopher. All feminists with inspiring points of view. It was a powerful event with a focus on the future.

Over the next decade we had many more conferences. In 1983 we held one on feminist family therapy; and in 1984, Dr. Pepper Schwartz, who co-wrote *American Couples: Money, Work and Sex*, spoke about changes in couple issues for heterosexual and homosexual couples. In 1985 we had a conference on "Therapeutic Touch." Evening seminars included self-defence for women; women and aging; childhood development for girls; how to prevent victimization; women and addiction; and women and money.

MARSHA
I joined the WCFCA soon after it started. I was active in the New Left and the women's liberation movements and the WCFCA was a good fit for me. I am an MSW social worker and had been teaching women's self-defense and running women's consciousness-raising groups, so I had heard a lot about abuse.

The WCFCA was the first therapist organization in Western Canada to spearhead the extensive study and education around the issue of physical, psychological, and sexual abuse. At the time the WCFCA began addressing this issue in meetings, conferences, and with political action, sexism and denial reigned supreme. I clearly remember a woman patient where I worked at UBC Health Sciences Psychiatric Hospital. The woman was admitted for depression and anxiety. However she told nursing staff that she was worried her husband was planning to kill her. She said he had threatened her. This topic was discussed extensively in rounds. The head psychiatrist agreed to interview the husband. After this interview the psychiatrist reported that the husband was a well-dressed, polite, educated, professional man who had assured the psychiatrist he was no threat to his wife. The wife was sent home soon after this meeting. Her husband killed her.

As a social worker and therapist in family services and hospital settings, I had often been treated as a sex object on and off the job by male colleagues and associates. I listened to my woman social-work clients speak of being horribly abused. I was also teaching women's self defense so I heard many stories of rape and abuse there. However I was totally unaware of the extent and severity of this issue because I didn't ever ask the relevant questions. Thanks to my education in our organization I was able to improve my practice and start to uncover the hidden traumas.

The WCFCA had several presentations and conferences on abuse including one, in 1987, by Joanne Ransom, a lawyer who spoke on "Custody and access when one parent has been abusive." In 1988, Linda Hutchinson, MSW, spoke on "Women and anger, working with abuse survivors around issues of anger and self-esteem." In April 1989, we had the amazing Shirley Turcotte speak on the NFB film *To a Safer Place* by Beverly Shaffer. There was also a presentation on "Partners in healing" sexuality for incest survivors. In November 1989, Trish Miller, MSW, with Sandy Siegel, PhD spoke about "Working with survivors and their partners and with Jewish/Christian couples — parallel dynamics, healing." In October 1990, Daniela Coats addressed us on "Ritual abuse awareness." In 1991, Myrna Driol spoke on "Working with women sexual abuse survivors who are also substance addicted," and in April 1991 Sue Higgins gave a talk on "Wife assault, the Duluth Model." Bonnie Agnew addressed us in November 1992 on "Feminist counselling as adopted by Rape Relief," and in 1992, Sue Penfold spoke about "Sexual abuse of patients by therapists."

We also had WCFCA conferences on abuse including "Abuse and protection: A feminist issue" in 1987. Topics included abuse of elderly, wife abuse, sexual assault, child abuse, self-defense in the schools, and the documentary *Breaking the Silence*. The same year, in October 1987, WCFCA partnered with the Justice Institute and

Family Services of Greater Vancouver to hold a conference titled "Therapist exchange on sexual abuse."

In April 1988 WCFCA, the Justice Institute, BC Teacher's Federation, and the BC ministry of education held a conference on "Systems issues: Therapeutic, legal, education with regard to child sexual abuse. Current dilemmas, future concerns." We continued to partner with the Justice Institute and held two more conferences, on "Ritual Abuse and Multiple Personality Disorders" and "Body-Mind Approaches in Treatment of Incest Survivors."

The WCFCA also addressed women's addictions and healing. As mental health therapists trained before the awareness of dual diagnosis issues, many WCFCA members tended to compartmentalize mental health disorders separately from alcohol and drug issues. It did not help that in British Columbia, mental health services were organized and funded separately from alcohol and drug services and each agency jealously guarded their turf. Some alcohol and drug professionals were involved with WCFCA, but they were outnumbered by those of us from other agencies and practices. Consequently one of the few places mental health and alcohol and drug treatment professionals met was at conferences. We had common interest in feminist therapeutic issues.

We had several meetings and conferences on addictions such as one conference in 1989 with the Justice Institute on "Women, Addictions, and Healing" with topics that included "Helping the helpers, Native women, and the medicine wheel"; a discussion in 1990 on "Women and addictions: A feminist perspective" with Daphne McKeen; and another with Susan Boyd on "Substance abuse and treatment models" in 1991.

The WCFCA also addressed other issues connected to Native Women. When I started working in the 1970s, Black Power was starting in the USA, but "Red Power" was almost invisible in BC. I knew very few Native people. At the time, the term used for Aboriginal/Indigenous women was Indians. When I had concerns about a specific Native woman I would consult with Gloria, who was a wise Native woman staff member at the Indian Centre. The terms First Nations, Aboriginal, or Indigenous were not used. Racism and systemic abuse of First Nations children was not widely discussed outside Native communities, even in the 1970s and 1980s. Awareness of genocidal persecution and resulting intergenerational trauma in our Native women's population was minimal in the non-Native therapeutic community. On one occasion, a colleague returned from a social planning meeting in Prince George. He said that at night some locals took him out to see the town. There were drunken Native people falling down on the street. He asked a local social planner what was being done about alcohol abuse. The local man replied, "Alcohol abuse? We don't have that problem here."

There were few Native members in WCFCA. I once led an incest survivors support group with a bright young co-leader who was Native. She didn't mention her heritage in the group but wore a silver bracelet and a silver medallion. As the group progressed women began "coming out" as Native. "My mother was part native, but we never spoke about it." "Yes we had a grandmother who was Native, but we never saw her." This was an eye-opener for me as I realized that I would never have learned that half the women in the group were of Native heritage if I had not been lucky enough to have a Native co-leader. Along the way, the WCFCA had several meetings and conferences on the issues of importance to Native women, including Helen Walter, who spoke in 1989 on "Unlearning racism: Working with the Nishga'a people of the Nass Valley" and Ruth Taylor from the Native Education Centre who talked about "The backlash against women in the court system" in 1992. The courts saw many Native women then and now.

In March 1990 our conference was jointly sponsored with the Justice Institute of BC and the Native Women's Professional Association, and addressed "Native Women Counselling and Healing." Some of the topics included "Wings of freedom," dancing and drumming, Medicine Wheel, healing racism and sexism, cultural self-hatred, and child protection. Most of the presenters at this conference were Native women. The conference was very well attended and the feedback was enthusiastic and extremely positive.

The WCFCA didn't focus directly on women and poverty although we worked with many women struggling economically and knew poverty and economic pressures were a major issue facing women in our society. WCFCA donated money to the Downtown Eastside Women's Centre (DEWC) and some of our members worked directly with their members and staff. We did have one meeting though, when in May 1987, Laurel from the DEWC presented a talk on issues facing women living in Vancouver's Downtown Eastside.

We also focused on sexual orientation and gay and lesbian issues. Our members were increasingly open to talking about LGBT issues, including writing letters to the editor of local newspapers supporting gay and lesbian rights. Our organization also lobbied the provincial and federal governments with regard to including sexual orientation protection in the human rights code. Along the way, we had two meetings on this topic, including one by Dr. Ingrid Pacey, speaking on "Sexual orientation" in 1981, and another by Bonnelle Strickling from Vancouver Community College.

We also considered the issues of professional ethics and abuse by therapists, teachers, doctors, and ministers. WCFCA members were acutely aware of abuse by therapists and others in positions of authority. Indeed some members were themselves survivors of this type of abuse. The head of psychiatry at the University of British Columbia was charged with chaining, beating, and abusing his women patients. He and other psychiatric instructors abused female medical students and residents. There were news items and academic articles on the topic, but it was almost taboo to bring complaints forward before the end of the 1970s. When complaints were brought forward in those days, they were often swept under the rug. The WCFCA put a lot of energy into discussion, education, and social action around this issue. WCFAC members also offered support, in services and a referral list of safe feminist therapists to community groups all over British Columbia and even offered support to groups in other parts of Canada. We held several meetings and conferences on this topic. Again Bonnelle Strickling, PhD spoke, this time on "Transference and Counter Transference between women clients and women therapists." In 1992, Dr. Sue Penfold also spoke to our group on "The sexual abuse of patients by therapists." We partnered with the Justice Institute again in 1991 and 1992, and had Laurel S. Brown speak first on "Ethical issues in feminist therapy" and then, the following year, on "Boundaries and boundary violation."

From the outset the WCFCA was very engaged in social action. There were many spinoffs from our meetings involving lobbying governmental and professional organizations to enhance women's rights. For example, in 1981 a telegram was sent to the Honourable Warren Allmand MP regarding the ensuring of women's rights in the Canadian constitution. We also wrote to the Honourable Francis Fox encouraging funding of the Lesbian Resources Project. Over the years we wrote to many others, including *Chatelaine* magazine, the secretary of state for Canada, BC members of the legislature, and the editor of the *Vancouver Sun*. Several times each year we wrote and spoke to the public and to politicians explaining and promoting feminist issues in women's health and safety. We asked for funding and that women's rights be included as prohibited grounds for discrimination. Later we lobbied for sexual orientation to be included as a prohibited ground of discrimination.

We were also involved in writing letters of support for Media Watch in regard to misogynist statements on radio, and to *Chatelaine* magazine about the inappropriate use of anorexic-looking young models in advertising. We wrote to the BC government regarding funding of women's programmes in 1987 and to the *Vancouver Sun* in 1988 protesting the government plan to withdraw funding from abortion. In 1991, we wrote to BC MLAs and to Kim Campbell's office about expanding human rights legislation to include sexual orientation.

But, ultimately, the organization came to an end. I remember our last meeting and farewell party at my house. About twenty-five to thirty women came—previous chairwomen, members of various committees, and some of the general members from over the years. We all spoke that evening of our memories, challenges, and successes. It was moving and powerful to look around the group and feel what we had accomplished as a feminist group in Vancouver through the 1980s and as part of the second wave of feminism in the western world. By now, sexual abuse, childhood trauma, rape, family violence, misogyny, sexual stereotyping, gay and lesbian issues, and gender bias in mental health and psychiatric treatment were out in the open and becoming part of psychiatric and therapeutic language.

SANDRA

In 1976 I left my conservative life as a teacher in Montreal and, when I moved to Vancouver, discovered and embraced feminism. Thus began a transition that brought me not only a new career, but a whole new way of interacting with and being in the world. During my first two years in Vancouver I worked as a peer coun-sellor at the Women's Resource Centre that was part of UBC and then housed in the old Vancouver Public Library. It was my first experience of working with adult women and learning about their issues—many of which were similar to mine. In 1978 I began an MA programme in humanistic psychology. One day I was given a copy of Susie Orbach's book *Fat Is a Feminist Issue*, which turned my life around. After so many years of going up and down the scale, I not only didn't have to diet anymore, but now I also un-derstood why.

When I graduated in 1980, I went into private practice with Doris Maranda, a colleague who shared my philosophy. Our goal was to get women off diets and work with body image issues and weight obsession. We developed a group programme initially called "Facing Your Fat" and later changed to "Learning to Love Yourself." One day a woman in the group shared that she threw up after eating. And then more women disclosed. This was the early 1980s when bulimia was just coming out of the closet. Doris and I moved from being fat therapists to eating disorder specialists.

Being in private practice is isolating. When Doris and I learned about the Feminist Counselling Association we jumped at the chance to join. Being a member of the FCA was an empowering, exciting, and stimulating experience for me and I thank Ingrid Pacey and the founders for running the association and keeping it together for as long as they did. The FCA gave us colleagues and support. The different professions and orientations of the members provided us with a range of new ideas and ways of working with people. It provided us with the opportunity to question and challenge our own assumptions. I had come out of a master's programme that placed a heavy emphasis on psychological origins and causes of the various issues our clients dealt with. We believed, for example, that we could "resolve" depression by working it through without ever taking or prescribing anti-depressants. Through my ongoing dialogue with Liz Whynot, a physician in the group, I was able to see more closely the benefits of combining medication and counselling.

After months of meetings, the FCA decided to organize and host a conference on families. We paid to bring in a speaker from Boston. Not only was she expensive, but she turned out to be boring. During her presentation I sat next to Ingrid and we both suffered silently. Then Ruth Siegal, the executive director of the Women's Resource Centre, stood up and left the room and I was very surprised. As we were all women and Canadian and excessively polite, such behaviour was unheard of. But the FCA gave me some of the best learning ever. The FCA played its part in Vancouver in bringing forward the woman's perspective and feminist analysis into public awareness, but also into the world of psychiatry, therapy, and psychological theory.

WENDY
I started to attend conferences and meetings of the FCA in the early eighties. As a lesbian therapist who had been involved in the experimental expansion of the Human Potential Movement in

the 1970s, I was hungry for more feminist education. I remember the joy of excellent speakers with real information being so willing to give us the education in feminist theory and application I had so deeply desired. It felt exciting to be with these progressive thinkers and become emboldened by their inspiration to think differently about my own work with clients. My perspective as a woman and especially as a lesbian who had many years of homophobic damage to put to rest was helped by the education I received through the FCA.

The first conference I attended at Hycroft House in 1981 on women's mental health and sexual orientation was a lifesaver for me. At that time there were so few places I could go to attain real information about how to understand my own experiences as a lesbian woman seeking to live a full family-oriented life with grace and dignity. I had read books, of course, but to be at the conference, mixing with women who were both respected, professional, and lesbian was for me a profound relief and joy.

I felt encouraged, empowered, and excited by the speakers. It was like having lived in a desert and finding not only an oasis but a whole community of perspectives to nourish my insular lesbian being. For me, the FCA provided soul food. I am grateful that it existed when it did and to all the people who made it happen over the years.

INGRID AGAIN

By 1991 and 1992, though our conferences had good attendance, our evening meetings became less frequent and with smaller attendance. Those of us who had been organizers over the previous years were moving into doing other work and were no longer available. We had to come to the sad decision that the time to end the FCA had come. At the end, we were able to donate financially to the women's community. We had over $2,000 in the bank and gave some to a Downtown Vancouver women's organization, and some to a feminist video company. We had created a vibrant organization and had had a very productive run.

Indeed, we were the longest running feminist therapist association in Canada and were much missed after the FCA was no more. I would get calls and requests for some time after, for names of feminist therapists and for information on feminist resources and literature. Some of the women's issues we had addressed have become part of regular training and education at colleges, universities, and medical schools and are recognized in society generally.

But it was not so thirty years ago. However, there is still no room for complacency, even though so many more women are out in the world, in the workplace, and in professions. The word "feminist" is as important as ever and needs to be spoken boldly. The need for a feminist perspective and analysis continues in all fields as it does in the world of mental health and therapy.

The FCA played its part in the 1980s in Vancouver in bringing forward the woman's perspective and experience into the practice of medicine, psychiatry, psychology, and social work, and into public awareness. I am reminded of how grateful we all were to have been able to be part of creating and nurturing this group. We are grateful for this opportunity to be reminded of what a group of dedicated women can do.

RESPONDING TO VIOLENCE AGAINST WOMEN: NOT MUCH HAS CHANGED

Wilfreda E. Thurston

The evolution of services to female victims of violence from the early 1960s has been multi-faceted and intense. I have been an activist, service developer, researcher, and academic in this period. I have seen the beginning of anti-violence services in the women's movement from the 1960s to the 1980s, the development of a rape crisis sector, the battered women's movement, and a shelter sector.

I sometimes feel that my identity changes with the context in which I find myself, that is, I have learned to fit in, to survive, even prosper, in spaces that challenged my identity while still holding on to my authenticity. I grew up one of six children, the fifth daughter, in a small fishing village in Nova Scotia. My father was working class and my mother was never employed outside the home. We sometimes did not have enough money to pay the monthly costs of living, but whether we saw ourselves or were seen as poor is debatable. I was the first of the siblings to attend university, although all of us were encouraged to value education and to finish high school. I attended the first interdisciplinary women's studies class at Acadia University in 1973, "Women in the Modern World," where I adopted the worldview of feminist criticism.[84]

In about 1976 I became an activist in the women's movement, working on issues such as the need for a sexual assault centre and the problem of women and addictions. I moved to St. John's, Newfoundland in 1979 where I became involved in the women's centre, women's health movement, and the establishing of a shelter for abused women. I became the shelter's executive director when it opened in 1981. I decided to go to graduate school when I had attended a conference on violence against women and realized that the white male PhD keynote speaker had never actually listened to a woman who had experienced violence. I did my master's degree in community medicine while serving as the shelter's executive director and my thesis research was a review of the data collected on the women who used the shelter over three years. I chose community medicine on the recommendation of a feminist friend, Wendy Williams, who knew the programme would talk about community and policy rather than individuals, an approach more in keeping with the feminist principle of "the personal is the political."

Towards the end of my master's degree things started to change on the board of the shelter and I was presented with the decision that a clinical director was needed as a co-director. I argued against the movement from grassroots to professionalization, but I lost and subsequently resigned. It was an emotional time; reflecting how seriously the women's movement looked upon ending violence against girls and women as well as uncertainty about my future, and that of the women's movement. I was accepted into community health sciences (CHS) at the University of Calgary in September 1986. At the admissions interview I said I wanted to get a PhD to enable me to continue my activism at a different level and I was asked why I didn't go into law. In retrospect, I could have seen that question for the warning it was rather than a challenge, but I did not foresee the global drive to push the women's movement underground. I entered academia with a critical lens, but did not appreciate how strong institutional structures were in maintaining the status quo.

I joined the Women's Health Collective shortly after moving to Calgary. Ultimately, I attained a faculty position in CHS, advanced from assistant to full professor, and, upon retirement, to emerita professor. I did research on many topics but VAGW remained a focus and in later years that included Indigenous women. Among other kind words, I was very moved to be honoured at my retirement celebration by a colleague and community members (all men) for my work with Indigenous peoples.

LESSONS I HAVE LEARNED

Both my personal experiences and my reading of the health literature indicate that socioeconomic status is a determinant of the health of individuals and populations. The intersections of education and income are difficult to untangle as these are so correlated; however, poverty is still gendered and is different for women. Academia is a space for the privileged, for instance, and schools of medicine exemplify this where undergraduate medical students "with an average family income of over $100,000 were significantly overrepresented."[85] My working-class roots, my sex, being a non-physician, and acting as a feminist made me an outsider many times, but my determination to succeed was insider behaviour and required chameleon-like skills—I could be a "lady" at times.

Despite advances, women's health has remained "boobs and tubes" in medicine, and violence is still an issue deemed best left to social work and/or the police. While stories from those who have experienced violence are considered important teaching and research tools, the dominant identity is that of the "helpless, needy victim" that is easily attributed by clinicians and aided by other "helping" professions. It remains an identity I will not risk and an ongoing source of struggle.

Indigenous peoples' experiences in the struggles for equality and rights are much like those of women in the 1960s and 1970s, even though the second wave of the woman's movement fell short on race and class analysis. Indigenous world views have the potential to improve practice and research. One experience of Indigenous peoples is "lateral violence," in which people act to diminish the resources of others who are on the same side of a problem. It seems to me that feminists have minimized this by characterizing it as philosophical difference. This deters finding solutions that work. The next generation of feminists will have a chance to develop a movement for change that is informed by an analysis of colonization as well as patriarchy.

The violence that occurs over the life of a woman has defied easy definition or categorization, hence, umbrella terms such as violence against women (VAW) or violence against girls and women (VAGW) are often used. The adjectives to categorize VAGW can vary by a number of characteristics: the relationships involved (e.g., stranger, intimate, family, dating, marital, common law, parental); the type of violence (e.g., sexual abuse, sexual assault, rape, emotional abuse, physical abuse, spiritual abuse, economic abuse, battery); the age of the victim (e.g., child abuse, elder abuse); the degree of social separation of victim and perpetrator (e.g., interpersonal, systemic, conflict zone); the underlying source of the violence (e.g., gendered, patriarchal, state-sanctioned); the time period covered (e.g., chronic, acute, long-term); the degree of force involved (e.g., mild, moderate, severe); and the impact on the victim (e.g., debilitating, normative).

THE SHELTER SECTOR

The roots of services to victims of VAW are in the women's movement and the development of women's centres and sexual assault services. The second wave women's movement largely, but not exclusively, got organized in urban centres.[86] The movement originally focused considerable effort on VAGW, particularly rape of women and the development of non-governmental organizations (NGOs) that offered rape crisis services. In Ontario, for instance, the first rape crisis centre was opened in 1974 and by 1977 the Ontario Coalition of Rape Crisis Centres was established.[87] Rape crisis services were often affiliated with other NGOs that identified as feminist and services were sometimes located within women's centres. Those centres advocated for broad social change to create safety and equal opportunity. Safety and equal opportunity were viewed as integrated outcomes with assurances of physical well-being as well as the ability to participate in society and to make choices on an equal footing with men without fear of harassment of any kind. Those working in women's centres and sexual assault services were joined by academics, professionals in social, health, and legal services, and government bureaucrats to form a policy community that agreed that rape was wrong, a social problem that had to be remedied, although they did not always agree on definitions or solutions.

During the period that members of the women's movement and other participants in the VAGW policy community were addressing marital rape, another related policy community was evolving, that is, those concerned about VAW by partners and spouses. Women who were being abused in their relationships were going to rape crisis centres and other services offered by women's groups because they wanted help and trusted women-focused services to provide a sympathetic response. Sympathetic women in mainstream services also bent the rules to provide temporary respite and protection to women; for instance, some nurses in children's hospitals would ignore policy and allow women to sleep in hospital with their child.

The first shelters for women fleeing abusive relationships were opened in Canada in the early 1970s after the emergence of shelters in the US. Battered women's movements were developing in Canada and the US and subsequently overlapped through use of statistics, research, and experience gathered through media, special meetings, conferences, and personal contact. Since the process of setting up a shelter was localized, however, it took some time before a shelter movement or battered women's movement evolved.[88] As Tutty says,[89]

> The first formal transition houses in Canada developed in the early 1970s and included Vancouver's Transition House, Ishtar in Langley, B.C. and Oasis House (now Calgary Women's Emergency Shelter) in Alberta, Interval House in Toronto and Saskatoon's Interval House all of which opened in 1973 (Hebert & Foley, 1996; F. MacLeod, 1989). Interestingly, as Walker (1990) noted, "houses were being set up in Toronto, in the United States and in Europe during the early 1970s, but, in fact, we knew little about each other's activities at the time" (22).

Despite the shelters and a growing movement, the existence of "battered wives" was a hidden part of society up to the 1980s; wife or girlfriend abuse was not considered a social problem. Gradually, stories and statistics were gathered so that the scope of the problem of VAW in close relationships was being document-ed across the country. When NDP MP Margaret Mitchell rose in 1982 in the House of Commons to question the government concerning action on wife abuse, she gave the statistic that one in ten women were abused by their husbands, only to be met with laughter and shouting. A public outcry resulted and the critique of the response and resulting publicity led to creation of the *Standing Committee on Health, Welfare and Social Affairs Report on Violence in the Family: Wife Battering*, which contained a section entitled "Funding for Shelters" that recommended federal monies be used to create and sustain both emergency and second stage shelters and the staffing thereof.[90] It also recommended that "wife battering should be treated as a crime."[91] Eventually a programme of federal support did stimulate a growth in the number of shelters. Mitchell later warned activists, however, not to make assumptions about the degree of change that had occurred in the halls of power; she reported in an interview that by 1993, "Men were more conscious of the taboos. More careful. But basically the attitudes [of a male dominated culture of Parliament] hadn't changed much."[92]

Conflict arose early between the equality goals and analyses of the women's movement and the goals of the battered wom-en's movement to provide accommodation to all women fleeing violence. Tierney reported, shelter NGOs soon learned that adaptation to the mainstream was essential to survival:

> The data indicate that the organization whose resource mobilization attempts were most efficacious was the only one which combined the attributes of ideological compatibility, goal specificity, domain clarity, linkage breadth and strength, and extra-organizational incentives. Other [social movement organizations] SMOs, which were handicapped along one or more dimensions, did not achieve a comparable degree of success; indeed, organizations which rated low on most dimensions either went out of existence or experienced a marked decline in support.[93]

As feminism once again became an F-word in society in the late 1990s, the requirement of allegiance to equality work was no longer widespread shelter policy. A process of professionalization of staff had occurred and was often labelled co-optation. In the early days of shelters, having been a survivor of woman abuse was considered the only essential qualification for a staff person. When shelters were mainly refuges that provided peer support and advocacy to mainstream services, that policy was generally accepted, but as shelters claimed to be offering counselling on a variety of issues, as well as providing services to children, the professions of social work and psychology, represented on shelter boards and committees, took exception to the "lack of qualifications" of shelter staff.

Both professionalization and co-optation were predicted early as normative outcomes of a growing social movement.[94] The issue of co-optation was debated among shelters and, in the early days, organizational structure defined feminist shelters with collectives being the most feminist. Boards might debate how to test the feminist conviction of potential or existing staff, and ironic conversations about the most progressive "half of the collective" were not impossible outcomes. Gradually, professionalization led to the adaptation of mainstream management models. Along with professionalization comes bureaucratization with clear lines of authority[95] and rules for staff as well as residents.

Shelters often had female-only policies to protect women and staff, but also in keeping with being part of the women's movement: banning men other than abusers from admission except under special circumstances (e.g., plumbers); keeping locations as secret as possible; having intercoms and other devices at entrances; and limiting the age of male children that could be admitted with the mother. In early shelters, the staff often operated in a culture of heightened fear of attack, but the majority of residents were less concerned about physical safety. Staff were all female and other organizational structures (e.g., boards, committees) were often female-only. The accusation of "man hating" was therefore one that shelters had to counter to maintain political and service relationships.

There was originally doubt within the battered women's movement as to whether there should be collaboration with male organizations or treatment programmes for men. Apart from the question of whether these male organizations followed feminist principles was the issue of their competition for limited funds. The White Ribbon campaign, perhaps the best-known advocacy group for improved gender relations, began in Canada in 1991.[96] White Ribbon thus originated during a time when shelters were just gaining prominence and organizing in coalitions. White Ribbon has since grown to an international movement.

THE WOMEN'S SHELTER SECTOR

About the time that NGOs that provided shelter were becoming viewed and socially constructed as a sector unto themselves, the women's movement and the battered women's movement were either pushed underground or disappeared through funding cuts. In this period, women's shelters had been constructed by NGOs as well as government spokespeople as the only *essential* community service to respond to VAW. Shelter directors and boards collaborated widely with different government ministries and services to extend the range of services accessible to women who used shelters, and lobbied for public policies that would protect women. Shelter staff remain the identified experts on spousal violence.

An outcome of the allocation of VAW services to shelters was the move in mainstream responses from a "victim-centred to a perpetrator-centred treatment focus, with the aims of preventing reoffending."[97] Criminal justice responses and men's treatment programmes grew in number. Thus, in Canada, both federal and provincial governments put more money into justice policies and programmes than victim services, although some of the latter are offered in the justice sector as add-ons. Violence once again became a personal issue that was "de-gendered" along with the systems of power in operation.[98]

Although the shelter sector often lobbied the health sector for support, the health sector never embraced a role in preventing or treating VAGW (notwithstanding the requirement of children's services to report suspected child abuse). While numerous attempts by advocates to involve nurses and/or doctors were tried, the health sector remained peripheral. The impact of the health sector on the shelter sector is through the promotion of the medical model of health and illness and the need for expert diagnosis and treatment and its role in reporting of child abuse. With increased claims (and some evidence) that witnessing violence is a threat to children's health, for instance, and legislation in some jurisdictions making this an offence that must be reported, the blaming of mothers and labelling of mothers as "bad" parents continued, especially in the helping professions.[99] Shelters have used the position that children are harmed in order to advocate for funding, but the unintended consequences of this position are yet to be fully addressed.

Most women who left their husbands because of abuse did not go to a shelter because "better alternatives" existed for them, especially if they had means. Tutty reports that shelters were not serving immigrant, older, Indigenous, rural, physically challenged, or lesbian women; a concern that continues to be raised today. VAW could still be seen largely as a problem of individual demographics (low socio-economic status, including income and education, single parenthood) and the resulting individual health and social problems (mental illness, stress, addictions, childhood trauma, including having witnessed VAW). Women who go to shelters are now under surveillance for these and other social and health problems, as are their children. This both serves to perpetuate and is based upon the view that only those women who are "helpless victims" warrant public intervention.[100]

Becoming a sector necessitates maintaining a separate identity so collaboration must be done carefully. A newer and related sector that emerged in the 2000s is the homelessness sector, and women's shelters have largely stayed away from this political movement and policy community, possibly because of the potential loss of identity and because of competition for funding. Regardless, VAGW is seen as a key cause of female homelessness. The number of primary emergency shelters has increased over the ensuing years; however, the battered women's sector was less successful in creating the second stage housing mentioned in the 1982 House of Commons report. The shelter sector is now lobbying more extensively for the creation of second-stage shelters, in part because the lack of affordable housing makes it difficult for low-income women to re-establish independent homes. Part of the justification for having second-stage shelters is that women need ongoing, long-term support from shelter staff.

The creation of five research centres in 1992 by Health and Welfare Canada and the Social Sciences and Humanities Research Council of Canada (in Fredericton, Montreal, London, Vancouver, and one jointly shared by Calgary, Saskatoon, and Winnipeg) was a boost for academic interest and research in violence issues. Even universities that were not funded in this programme created centres and research chairs. Shelters offered sites for recruitment of research participants and the number of academic articles on VAW that allow women to speak personally has increased exponentially over the years. Other places to identify victims (e.g., police, courts, health services) often have rules around access that make research recruitment difficult, so anonymous administrative data is accessed. All data have limitations, but we have to ask what we know today about the causes of VAWG that we did not know in the 1960s, how to effectively prevent it at a population level from occurring in the first place, what role integration of men into the movement does or could play, and the relationships among sexual assault and other VAGW. More recently, I have been part of the move toward understanding the role of structural and systemic violence in gender discrimination and the deep roots of VAGW. We need to understand more about how structural inequality affects women's bargaining positions in relationships, and how services support and strengthen their bargaining positions.

WHERE TO FROM HERE?
The dominance of the shelter sector in shaping the discourse around VAGW offered huge benefits and substantive challenges. Without a doubt, public knowledge of and support for women using shelters has increased exponentially because of the work of shelters and the provincial coalitions. Annual fundraising galas and Christmas campaigns are not only essential to sustaining services, but they do ongoing public education. The demographics of the population of women who use shelters, however, has not changed substantially over three decades; we know much less about the majority—the 75 per cent of women who are abused who do not use shelters.

The intersection of poverty with VAW is obscured when the violence is foregrounded and the multiple needs of the women are highlighted in the discourses. In addition, the advocacy for alternative models of service is muted by loyalty to the shelters that "save lives every day." Increasing the numbers and scope of services in shelters is therefore offered as the necessary policy response even in the face of knowledge that social and economic marginalization are what limit the choices of women. Anti-violence policy is essentially the same as it was five decades ago. Could we do better work with the money allocated to shelters? While this a difficult question to ask, it is time to discuss this as the rates of VAW do not seem to be declining. Is the protection focus of policy and programmes serving women well? Rereading the House of Commons report now raises serious questions about how much more we know today about the issues and how to eradicate VAGW.[101]

POSTSCRIPT

The National Inquiry into Missing and Murdered Indigenous Women and Girls has the potential to shed new light on the overall social problem of VAGW.[102] Asking how Indigenous women access mainstream services, whether they feel culturally safe, and how Indigenous world views inform theories of VAWG are just some of the questions that could stimulate new ideas and critical thinking about our past successes and the way forward. The impacts of colonization on VAGW may be especially informative for all women as we re-examine the roles of patriarchy and misogyny. The way that women were spoken about in 2016, especially during the US presidential campaign, and how that gave permission to some men to assault women in public has also been eye-opening for those who were not feminists in the 1970s and 1980s, when public harassment was sanctioned, formally and informally, by male leaders such as police, clergy, and politicians. For those of us who lived, worked, and organized during that time, it was déjà vu and depressingly familiar.

SUCKING BACK ANGER: WOMEN AND SMOKING

Lorraine Greaves

In the 1950s the very first warnings that smoking was bad for health began to emerge. Smoking was being linked to heart disease and lung cancer. At that point more men than women were smokers in Canada, but women were quickly adopting cigarettes. Higher male smoking rates had a lot to do with heart disease being considered "a man's disease" in the following decades, a misconception that has taken us decades to rectify. Prior to this, however, tobacco advertisers had begun to do a job on women by aiming advertisements directly at them, and linking smoking to women's liberation, independence, and some other less liberating features such as heterosexual attractiveness and sexiness. But somehow, these campaigns did their job on all of us. "You've Come a Long Way, Baby" was a Philip Morris advertising tagline that underpinned a campaign launched in 1968 and co-opted the aspirations of the real-life feminist movement. It implied that smoking was a freedom long overdue to women and was critically entwined with emancipation. It proved to be an extremely lucrative and influential tobacco campaign.

In the mid-1980s I was vice president of the National Action Committee on the Status of Women (NAC) and chair of NAC's health committee. Our job was to examine federal legislation as it emerged, looking at its impact on women. One day in 1987, the *Tobacco Products Control Act* came across our radar, but there was little interest at the NAC executive in its content. It was dismissed, rejected as a focus of activism or action in favour of spending more of our energies on pension reform, pay equity, daycare, or law reform.

This was in spite of the fact that Lynn McDonald, an NDP

MP from Hamilton and a former president of NAC, had tabled a private member's bill in October 1986 called the *Non-Smokers' Health Act*. This was a superb strategy, as it forced the hand of the Progressive Conservative government and the PC health minister, Jake Epp, giving him the motivation to table a government bill and withstand the opposition to any regulation of tobacco from within his own caucus.

But with this exception, the impulse to ignore tobacco use among feminists was widespread. Indeed, the women's movement, despite a deep interest in women's bodies and women's health, had no apparent interest in, or consciousness about, tobacco. At the time, the same was true across the US, Canada, and many other countries. Smoking was common among women in Canada in the 1980s, but was still seen as irrelevant to the women's movement and not at all a women's issue.

I had my doubts. I knew enough about the tactics of the tobacco industry to see that much of their marketing and promotion was being aimed at women. The more I looked into the industry's new strategies, I realized that they were creating and testing female (and girl) specific tobacco products that would be tolerated by young, female bodies, and "light," "slim" cigarettes (with filters) to attract women smokers. I knew this was a powerful and rich industry targeting women and we needed to pay attention to what they were doing.

I also knew that despite growing health promotion and cessation programming, women's rates of smoking in Canada were not declining as fast as men's were. That puzzled me. My initial forays into what was known as the Canadian "tobacco control movement"—a collection of health charities, advocates, and activists trying to lobby governments to clamp down on the tobacco industry—revealed it to be a male-dominated, medical-model, policy-driven group that was formed around battle metaphors and led, mostly, by men. I was simultaneously angered and intrigued. By wanting to cast a feminist gaze on this issue, I felt that I was on the margins of both the women's movement and the "tobacco control" movement.

I tried again to get the issue on the NAC agenda, but many women smoked, both inside and outside NAC, and were dismissive and defensive. I had been one of them until the early 1980s, so I understood the pain of being challenged on addiction to nicotine. There were many other issues of key importance to the women's movement, I was told, that were much more compelling and interesting, and much more inequitable and pressing.

Frustrated, I turned to the few women in the tobacco control movement and eventually found a handful of allies within the leading national health charities in Canada—especially those concerned with cancer, heart disease, and non-smoker's rights—who were interested in women's health. These few women, such as Elinor Wilson with the Heart and Stroke Foundation and later the Canadian Public Health Association, and Cheryl Moyer, with the Canadian Cancer Society, were indispensable in giving me a voice and helping to create a bridge between the women's movement and the tobacco control movement. After all, these women (and a few men) were on the front lines and could see the effects on women, either as smokers or what were then called "passive" smokers.

Unfortunately, the wider tobacco control movement, when pressed about women and tobacco, usually focused only on pregnancy. And the pregnancy focus was not even on women's health, but on fetal health. And it was only ever based on a medical model. It was a sad, sexist state of affairs. The only interest that the tobacco control movement seemed to have in women, especially the medical personnel, was as "receptacles" for reproduction. And the only bit of interest the women's movement had in tobacco was in, well, protesting the pseudo-feminist taglines of a few tobacco companies…maybe.

I didn't know it then, but these challenges would become central preoccupations for me as I moved on in my career, working first on violence against women issues and second on women's health. I have spent the decades since 1985 deriding and challenging the medical model, fighting for a focus on women's health in its own right, shifting the emphasis off women as "vessels," linking substance use to women's experiences of violence and trauma, and working for a social justice approach to tobacco use and other substance use.

In 1988 I spoke at a tobacco conference in Montreal run by the Canadian Council on Smoking and Health, alongside Bobbie Jacobson. She is a feisty physician from the UK who had written *The Ladykillers: Why Smoking is a Feminist Issue*, the first book that applied a feminist analysis to women's smoking. I immediately knew I would like her when I noticed her socks—they had small pink pigs all over them. I stared at those socks as she spoke about her book and waited for my turn to speak to the assembly. I realized that, finally, I had met a kindred spirit.

That inspiring meeting became a lifelong friendship. She had seen the toll of tobacco use on women in public health, but had also taken the time to interview women who smoked.

She had travelled globally in preparing her book, and she was able to use her medical background as a way to influence key figures in the tobacco control movement. She had more patience than I had and tolerated male doctors somewhat better. I learned a lot from her, especially from watching her respond, calmly, to many critics. What was her response to the perpetual medical focus on pregnancy when women and tobacco came up? "Well, the thing is…" she'd say, that kind of campaign "ignores most women most of the time." I still use that line with health officials.

I went on to do a PhD in Australia on women's smoking and ultimately wrote a book in 1996 called *Smoke Screen: Women's Smoking and Social Control*. The book developed an understanding of what smoking means to various women across the social spectrum and firmly brought women's lived experiences into the analysis of tobacco policy. To my surprise, the Canadian Research Institute for the Advancement of Women (CRIAW) awarded it the Laura Jamieson Prize the following year. Finally, there was a critical, feminist appreciation for this issue.

In the meantime, the women (and a few men) with whom I worked in the tobacco control movement had started to beg for a bridge to the women's movement, going so far as to fund projects to develop one and asking me to take on this work. And on the women's health side, the fabulous progressive collective in Boston, Our Bodies Ourselves, publisher of the ground-breaking book by the same name, as well as a few other US feminist groups, were hungry for a feminist analysis of smoking. Ultimately, these pressures came together and by the 1990s, Canada and many other countries slowly became ripe for a more critical analysis of tobacco use, and tobacco policy, prevention, and treatment approaches.

Globally, there was action. In 1990 I had journeyed to Perth, Australia for the 7th World Conference on Tobacco or Health, where I found fifty or so other women from all over the world with similar interests. We held a spontaneous meeting in a hotel room after the conference ended for the day, airing our concerns with the underrepresentation of women speakers and women's issues. In that conference, only 5 per cent of the plenary speakers were women. All the talk on women and tobacco featured pregnancy-related content. That night, in a sweltering, standing-room-only hotel room in Perth, women from all over found common cause. We co-founded the International Network of Women Against Tobacco (INWAT), a global advocacy group that persists to this day. Over the years, it has shifted its focus from high-income countries to include many low and middle income countries that are now dealing with increasing tobacco use by women and girls, along with increasing tobacco growing and industry exploitation.

In 1997, I was recruited by Dr. Penny Ballem at BC Women's Hospital in Vancouver to establish the newly funded British Columbia Centre of Excellence for Women's Health (now the Centre of Excellence for Women's Health). One of the first actions I took was to establish the first (and only) research centre on women, girls, and tobacco, now in its twentieth year. It became a focal point for applying a feminist and a social equity gaze to the issue of tobacco use, especially the responses to tobacco use from government, health charities, and anti-tobacco advocates. Along with keeping an eye on tobacco industry tactics, we had our hands full in fixing, repositioning, challenging, replacing, or critiquing a mainstream response to tobacco use in Canada that was gender-blind, sexist, and ignored women's health, women's agency, equity, and women's lived experiences. In Canada, as the overall smoking rates declined, our centre turned our attention to the many groups that have incredibly high rates: Indigenous girls; young, lone mothers; and those with mental health and other substance use issues.

I had casually observed in my days working on violence against women issues and visiting many women's shelters, that they were often full of smoke. Many women in shelters (and staff) were smoking cigarettes and I wondered what that connection was about. In the end, my research on the meanings of smoking to various women was done with women in shelters who had experienced abuse and among self-described feminists (not mutually exclusive groups) in both Australia and Canada. Indigenous women and women of all social classes participated. The results were strikingly similar, however, and allowed me to figure out the deeper meanings and uses of smoking to women. It turned out that smoking was functioning a lot like benzodiazepenes do—by serving as a buffer between women and their lived realities and injustices. Smoking mediated those ongoing pressures, dangers, traumas, and anxieties for women, no matter what their social locations. Smoking didn't inebriate or render women "difficult" like the overuse of alcohol or drugs, but rather made women compliant.

These findings made me starkly conclude that society had a lot to gain from women's smoking. As long as women were "sucking back their anger," as one of my informants put it, the broader society didn't have to deal with that anger. As long as women were, as described to me, using cigarettes to deflect anger and violence, sometimes as a physical barrier, we were failing to keep women safe. As long as women and girls were carving out their identities using cigarettes as a prop, we were failing to provide adequate alternatives to self-awareness.

It became apparent to me that the tactics of the tobacco industry, by generating links between cigarettes and women's freedom, had simply distracted all of us. The real questions we should have been asking were: Why did women need to smoke? What did we all get out of it? How did this relate to the ongoing gender inequities in life? How did continuing to smoke distract us all from the real issues of gender inequity, sexism, and violence? All these questions were befuddling, but it was little mystery that, in 1987, NAC, the largest national women's group in Canada, when faced with the *Tobacco Products Control Act*, was mostly indifferent. There was, and still is, a lot to unpack with regard to women and smoking.

A FEMINIST APPROACH TO PAP TESTS

Rebecca Fox

In 1983, Robin Barnett and I produced a supplement in the (Vancouver) Status of Women's local newspaper, *Kinesis*, that was later made into a forty-one-page booklet by Press Gang called *A Feminist Approach to Pap Tests*. It contained a description of the pathophysiology of cervical cells, an explanation of the staging of test results, and the potential role of Human Papilloma Virus (HPV). The many, many women who worked, volunteered, were friends of friends, came in to use the resource centre, or called the health collective, contributed to the booklet. We shared our personal stories of healing, provided graphics, and helped with the editing, and worked with several health professionals who acted as valuable resources. As word got around, other health collectives and women's centres ordered copies for fifty cents each (postage included).

It's difficult now to imagine or recall the era when we couldn't access information, good or bad, at our fingertips. However, not that long ago, in the early years of the women's health movement in Canada it wasn't easy to find out more about your health. It was difficult when women received abnormal test results from Pap smears and wanted to investigate, especially when grappling with medical terminology. Questioning medical advice risked challenging authority, medical libraries were not typically open to the public, and available health information rarely included alternatives to "Western" treatments.

Even though British Columbia prided itself on having an early provincially based Pap test database, many women approached the Vancouver Women's Health Collective about their abnormal Pap test results. As with many other screening programmes and particularly when the underlying disease detected has no easily identified symptoms, these abnormal tests elicited shock, confusion, and fear. Our first advice, other than offering reassurance, was always to "go get a copy of your result."

The results were based on three classes of cervical dysplasia (abnormal cells). Often the descriptive information from the laboratory was more useful than just the reported Class I, II, or III. In addition to the interpretation of the test, women would also want to talk to us about the treatment recommended to them such as cervical cryosurgery (freezing) and invasive cone biopsy (cutting out the abnormal section of the cervix). They wanted to know about whether there were other options and how to gauge the urgency for treatment. Many had worries about damage to their future ability to carry a pregnancy and the ongoing threat of cancer. At the same time, a number of women around the collective were investigating "alternative" methods of reversing abnormal Pap test results or, at least, not rushing into standard gynecological treatments of a disease process that was historically detected in older women and known to be one of slow progression.

What strikes me now looking over an old copy of the booklet is how it added to the volumes of cheaply produced and easily available "lay" literature that the women's health movement produced in Canada. We owed our confidence to *Our Bodies, Ourselves* from the Boston Women's Health Collective for our research skills and the ability to form our own opinions. Later, they helped to distribute the booklet worldwide, making our supplement an important Canadian contribution. Women were challenging the professional patriarchy and the lack of control over our bodies. We were driven by a thirst for knowledge and a desire to avoid all the unnecessary hysterectomies that our grandmothers, mothers, and aunts had suffered. We wanted to not blindly trust a system that frequently dismissed our concerns and balked when we hesitated to follow standard advice. I know that in many small ways, we contributed to a new paradigm of access to health information, approaches to women's health, and informed decisions about our bodies.

SIDE EFFECTS:
PUTTING WOMEN'S HEALTH
CENTRE STAGE

Sari Tudiver and Karen Seabrooke

It's hard to separate what I learned from *Side Effects* and what I learned from life. It's how a single initiative is connected to so much else— its antecedents and where it goes next. It just reinforced the links between theory and practice, community activism and national policy work and coalitions and connections, building networks.[103]

Side Effects, a play about women and pharmaceuticals, was conceived and carried out in the early to mid-1980s by Canadian activists from the women's health, international development, and social justice communities in collaboration with the Great Canadian Theatre Company (GCTC) in Ottawa. Based on documented experiences of women in Canada and Bangladesh, the play sought to raise awareness about women's oppression—specifically, their lack of power to make decisions about their health and the pervasive influence of the global pharmaceutical industry in women's lives. Using drama, humour, and song, the play skilfully mocked the aggressive and sexist marketing practices of the industry that designed "a pill for every ill," while ignoring the context of women's emotional distress and physical pain in the stressors of caring for children and other family members, in the pressures to "make ends meet," and in harassment, abuse, and family violence.

Side Effects tackled a wide range of issues, including addictions due to over-prescribing of antidepressants and painkillers; cancers and other illnesses associated with inappropriate prescribing of hormones; and coercive practices of population control programmes. It also showed women's resilience. At the end of the ninety-minute production, audiences saw women "no longer patient," finding their voices and beginning to take charge of their bodies, their health, and their lives.

By all accounts, *Side Effects* was a success. In 1985, the play toured eight provinces in English Canada, performing forty-five shows in thirty-seven communities from Corner Brook, Newfoundland to Terrace, British Columbia. A separate tour of seven communities in Ontario followed. In 1986, the play was translated into French as *Maux Cachés* and a francophone theatre group, Le Théâtre des Filles du Roy, toured six communities in Quebec. In all, more than 10,000 people attended performances in theatres, school auditoriums, community halls, Native Friendship Centres, church basements, and in Kingston, the Prison for Women. Hundreds of women and men engaged in talkback sessions that followed the performances and offered consistently positive and thoughtful reviews. Thousands more read or heard about the play through print, radio, and television coverage. For several years after the tours, organizers received requests from groups in Canada, the US, Europe, India, Sri Lanka, and Australia to use the script for their own productions.

Thirty years later, we reflect on the key elements that captured the imagination and commitment of the organizers and the enthusiasm of *Side Effects'* audiences. We ask: What were some of the major impacts of the project? What is its legacy? Are there lessons to be drawn that can help in struggles for women's rights and social justice?

THE GENESIS OF *SIDE EFFECTS*

Side Effects was created in a time of feminist activism and an emerging women's health movement in Canada and internationally. It was also a period of state support for women's activism. The United Nation's Decade for Women (1975–85) not only reinforced the commitments of UN member states to conventions and frameworks on women's equality, but also stimulated new opportunities for national governments to fund many smaller organizations working on a broad range of issues, including women's health. Many of us were able to travel to international conferences on women and health to share experiences and strategies with activists from Europe, the US, and the global South. In a pre-Internet era, these face-to-face meetings offered unique opportunities to learn, for example, about the Nestlé boycott and the emerging International Baby Food Action Network or hear women's concerns about the safety of contraceptives used in population control programmes in India, Bangladesh, and Latin America.

The origins of the *Side Effects* initiative can be found in the philosophy, values, and commitment of Inter Pares, a Canadian civil society organization supporting community development and social justice initiatives internationally and in Canada. From its inception in 1975, Inter Pares was based on principles and practices of working "among equals" to create mutually-beneficial relationships with organizations in the global South and in Canada. This approach challenged the traditional "top down" and project-focused model of aid between donor and recipient countries by supporting counterparts to strengthen local institutions and by helping to build coalitions of "common cause" among activists working to address the root causes of poverty and inequality.

By the early 1980s, Inter Pares had established strong relationships with a number of progressive organizations in countries of the South. One such organization was the People's Health Centre in Bangladesh that provided primary health care and manufactured basic generic drugs as a way to reduce the country's dependence on the costly, patented medicines of multinational drug companies. Inter Pares was also part of a growing network across Canada of community groups, women's organizations, popular education-based learning centres, progressive church organizations, unions, and non-governmental organizations (NGOs) involved in international development work. Taking advantage of opportunities available through the UN Decade for Women, NGOs sought creative ways to engage Canadians on issues of women's equality, development, and social justice.

Popular theatre and popular education were effective forms of communication and engagement. Based on pedagogy articulated by Paolo Friere of starting from people's own experiences as a way to reach them most profoundly, popular theatre is a methodology for community organizing and literacy used in many parts of the world.[104] In the late 1970s, Inter Pares helped bring SISTREN, an innovative Jamaican women's theatre collective organized by women street cleaners, on a tour to Canada. Buoyed by positive audience response, and building on solidarity work with counterparts in Central America, Inter Pares approached the Great Canadian Theatre Company in Ottawa to develop a play about the Nicaraguan revolution. GCTC agreed and *Sandinista!* written by Canadian playwright Arthur Milner and the GCTC collective, was produced in 1982.

Inter Pares also recognized the value of exchanges among and between organizations in countries of the North and South. Exchanges created spaces for dialogue, encouraged synergies among participants to identify common issues and build agendas for cooperation and action. One key women's exchange proved to be the critical precursor to *Side Effects*. In 1982, Inter Pares invited two social activists from Bangladesh, Shireen Huq and Khushi Kabir, on a tour across Canada to meet with women in their home communities. Whether talking over tea at kitchen tables or at major conferences, the women found opportunities for mutual learning about the challenges they faced. The central theme that emerged from the tour was women and health. As the Inter Pares tour coordinator described in a report:

> [The Bangladeshi women] were shocked to learn that Canadian women didn't always have access to birth control or safe and effective forms of birth control or even adequate health care in rural and Native communities.... They were surprised to learn that women were also critical of some of the drugs being used here, including tranquillizers, for what were clearly social and economic stresses and problems faced by women. They were surprised at the situation for women in Canada, the poverty that they saw, the violence against women that they learned about. They were surprised by the lack of cohesive, sustainable, agricultural policies. There were some parallels that they could see, particularly around women's health and also around pharmaceuticals, as they were actively involved in a campaign in Bangladesh to promote the adoption of a generic drug policy and locally produced drugs. Inter Pares and other Canadian organizations were criticizing the Canadian government for proposing changes to drug patent protection legislation in ways that would assist the multinational pharmaceutical industry to the detriment of Canada's generic drug industry.[105]

The Bangladeshi and Canadian women expressed a desire to collaborate on common issues and follow-up to the tour was planned. In June 1983, Inter Pares organized a workshop on "Women and Pharmaceuticals" in Aylmer, Quebec and invited thirty-five activists, many of whom had met Shireen and Khushi a year earlier. Workshop participants included women and men—doctors, nurses, development educators, patient/consumer advocates, health researchers, policy advisors, union activists, and a member of the GCTC. In preparation for the workshop, Inter Pares staff put together background documents, including primers on advertising and overpricing in the pharmaceutical industry in Canada and globally, on Canada's drug regulations; and examples of the harmful effects of drugs such as the estrogen diethylstilbestrol (DES) prescribed during pregnancy, the injectable contraceptive Depo Provera, and antidepressants. Focusing on realistic solutions, this kit also contained information about preventative health care and consumer campaigns directed to the World Health Organization and other international bodies to curb drug marketing malpractices. Much of these data were drawn from a substantial body of evidence by Canadian, British, Dutch, Malaysian, and other researchers.[106]

The workshop was an interactive and energizing meeting that "solidified a common desire to connect those working on women's rights and health."[107] There was agreement on the goal to build a strong women's health network that would link groups across Canada working on related issues. A suggestion to use popular theatre as a vehicle to help build this movement was enthusiastically received and the GCTC became a partner in this collaboration. A group of participants agreed to form a separate sister organization, Women's Health Interaction (WHI), to lead the planning and coordination of the project, with Inter Pares providing infrastructure, fundraising, and other support to the volunteers. *Side Effects* was launched.

DEVELOPING THE SCRIPT
AND PREPARING FOR THE TOUR

The script for the play was to be based on actual stories of women from Canada and Bangladesh. Organizers explored ways to ensure it would reflect a feminist, participatory, and "among equals" approach. With remaining money from the Bangladeshi women's tour to Canada, Inter Pares funded a return exchange to Bangladesh of two Canadian women—an Inter Pares board member and a member of WHI—to do further research on the subject of women and pharmaceuticals. They heard directly from Bangladeshi women about coercive population control practices and the denial of women's reproductive rights.

> ...when we were in the field, we got a lot of stories on forced sterilization...and the quota system, where they were paying doctors to sterilize a certain number of women a day.... Our counterparts had described the population control measures in Bangladesh, but during this trip we were able to talk to women and document their stories in a more systematic way. Some women had been given high-risk contraceptive drugs with no follow-up care. Intra-uterine devices that were taken off the market and drugs that were restricted for use in Canada were still being promoted in Bangladesh by multinational corporations and through Northern aid programmes, including Canada's.... There was trust from the women to tell their stories.[108]

The information gathered from this tour put population control and women's reproductive rights more clearly on the policy agenda of Inter Pares. These issues would be addressed in the play and later through additional research, policy briefs, and in meetings with government officials and parliamentarians.

The process of developing and work-shopping the *Side Effects* script was collaborative and complex. As GCTC staff described the experience:

> After a winter of meeting with Women's Health Interaction, nurses, doctors, drug detail men, women who had been addicted to prescription drugs, self-help groups, women from Bangladesh, (and) development workers, we began our first script workshop with information overload. We were given the responsibility of portraying dramatically the full impact of the pharmaceutical industry on women world-wide.... We emerged three weeks later with two and half hours of original material, and a commitment to the issues

that has remained with the actors throughout the workshops.... Throughout the process we met with Women's Health Interaction for feedback on the material. Were we covering the issues adequately? Were they presented in a clear fashion? Were the women credible? The "playgroup," as they were often called, gave us detailed and honest direction as to how to proceed, and invaluable support. We thank them for this opportunity to work in popular theatre. *Side Effects* is their statement.[109]

Inter Pares secured funds for a cross-Canada tour of *Side Effects* from Health and Welfare Canada, Secretary of State Women's Programme, foundations, the Ontario Nurses' Association union, and several international development agencies. They produced a "tool kit" for local organizers that included logistical information, media packages, posters, and postcards to send to local, provincial, and federal government officials, background information on the issues, discussion questions, and fundraising tips. Host organizations were encouraged to identify goals and work together on necessary tasks such as securing venues and accommodations.

New collaborations formed. For example, in Winnipeg, representatives from the Alcoholism Foundation of Manitoba, the Women's Health Clinic, the Manitoba Council for International Cooperation, the Manitoba Museum of Man (sic) and Nature, the Immigrant and Refugee Women's Association, the Disabled Women's Network (DAWN), and the Popular Theatre Alliance of Manitoba joined together as the Manitoba *Side Effects* Tour Committee. They secured a small grant from the provincial government and the play toured beyond Winnipeg to five rural and northern communities. Organizing efforts took different forms in other parts of the country, strengthening existing relationships and creating new linkages among groups.[110]

THE ELEMENTS OF SUCCESS

More than 10,000 people came to performances of the play. Comments shared during more than fifty talkback sessions, in workshops held after the play and on evaluation forms, were overwhelmingly positive. The return rate for post-performance evaluation forms was over 70 per cent, an indication of high audience engagement and interest. People wrote detailed personal comments and identified gaps in health services in their communities.

Based on these comments, we attribute the play's success with audiences to several factors.

Side Effects was perceived as authentic and pertinent to everyone. It identified problems with the health care system from the standpoint of women and drew attention to the broader social, political, and economic context that shaped experiences, such as addictions. For some women, it was the first time they saw what they considered their "personal" struggles validated and presented with empathy. As one woman said, "I'm not the only one, I'm not crazy...you put my life on stage." Some men also commented that the play helped them gain greater insight into the struggles of their sisters, wives, and mothers. Health touches everyone.

Side Effects engaged audiences from the start. As people filed into halls and theatres, they were greeted by actors dressed in white medical coats holding small cups of sugar pills and were firmly urged to "take your pills." This playful but disarming moment created an immediate link with the audience and made them curious about what was to follow—a quick-paced quality production with fine actors, memorable songs, and smart dialogue that ranged from deeply sad, to ironic, to angry, to very funny. As an audience member noted, "You got drawn in. When the lights went down, it was real." Perhaps, too, audiences were intrigued to experience a production written, directed, acted, stage-managed, with lighting and sound, entirely by women.

Many people appreciated the careful attention paid by organizers to meet the needs of local organizations, the high quality of the tool kit and resources for action and advocacy. Audiences in rural and more remote communities acknowledged the effort made to bring *Side Effects* to them. They saw hosting the play as an opportunity to collaborate with others in their community in new ways. For example, addictions counsellors and other social service providers who participated in a day-long workshop in The Pas, Manitoba following the play, emerged with an action plan that included an audit of tranquillizer use in their community.[III]

The overall success of the *Side Effects* project rested on several firm pillars. Inter Pares provided institutional support to Women's Health Interaction in the form of office space and equipment (phone, typewriters, photocopiers, and fax machines), help with preparing grant proposals, financial accounting, and updating contact lists and mailings, which was critical to communicating in a pre-computer, pre-Internet era. World Interaction-Mondiale (WI-M), Carleton University's Ontario Public Interest Research Group (OPIRG), and several others gathered research materials and helped prepare the educational resources distributed nationally to host organizations. The *Side Effects* budget covered the time and other resources necessary for these contributions, as well as costs of original artwork, printing, and other essential aspects of the project.

As *Side Effects* gained steam, Inter Pares seconded a staff member to work on the project with the WHI team, the majority of whom were volunteers juggling other work and family responsibilities. Several other Inter Pares staff contributed time, when necessary, throughout the process. Once funding was secured, Inter Pares hired a national tour coordinator who worked from their office in collaboration with the staff coordinator.

The project also depended on the "effort and toil" of the local organizing groups across Canada and the strong commitment of the actors to go above and beyond what might have been expected of them. As some of the WHI team described it:

> We were able to go to so many places because the people in those communities rolled up their sleeves and brought people out.... [There was] a lot of sweat labour from the volunteers. I think they paid $1500 to get the play.... We billeted almost everywhere. Having a hotel night was like, "Yahoo!" Local groups fed us, they put us up. It really was "a whim and a prayer." There were a lot of in-kind contributions.
>
> The commitment from actors—we often don't talk about the actors... they came together, and they also, I think, became radicalized and sensitized to the process. They worked so hard because we would drive from one community to the next. You think of show business being glamorous but it was the actors who set up the stage, did the play, and then we often had to strike the stage, and take it apart and load it up into the truck that night. And we were making $225 a week. It wasn't much money even in those days. But those actors, tired as they were, they'd also have to go and be staying with someone, maybe sleeping on a couch, maybe a bed—we tried to get beds for them. But also then they were with these people who were just so excited! They had seen the play, they wanted to talk, and [the actors] were exhausted.[112]

IMPACTS

As two of the women intimately involved in this project over three decades ago, we have tried to avoid romanticizing its impacts and legacy. But here are some of the impacts; many others can be mined from the *Side Effects* project archives.[113]

In addition to nurturing the development of *Side Effects*, the 1982–83 exchanges between Bangladeshi and Canadian women helped strengthen civil society organizations in Bangladesh. Following their Canadian tour, Shireen Huq and Khushi Kabir joined with others to form Naripokkho (Pro Women). This activist organization, based in Dhaka, continues to work for women's equality and political empowerment, addressing violence against women, health, and reproductive rights.[114] Since the early 1980s, Inter Pares has continued to collaborate with Khushi Kabir through her work with Nijera Kori, an Inter Pares' counterpart that supports the rights of marginalized, landless women and men in Bangladesh.[115]

Second, the Aylmer workshop on women and pharmaceuticals raised many issues relevant to consumer safety and health protection in Canada, including concerns about the testing and approval of drugs and medical devices, particularly those prescribed to healthy women; securing informed consent from clinical trial subjects and patients; consumer access to information about adverse drug reactions; the need for doctors and patients to have credible sources of information about drugs independent of pharmaceutical industry funding; the impacts of patent laws on drug pricing; and the need for woman-centred models of care.

The workshop and the play were remembered decades later by some of the participants as a "transformative moment" that shaped their future careers and personal commitments. Over three decades, many of the thirty-five participants have helped to influence health policy discourse in Canada and internationally on these issues through collaborative research, writing, and teaching; presentations of policy briefs to Canadian parliamentary committees; input to government consultations and international fora.[116]

Third, evidence gathered for *Side Effects* on the harmful impacts of population control programmes was used in efforts to influence government population policies and practices in Canada, including Canadian-funded programmes in Bangladesh. In 1991, Women's Health Interaction, with Inter Pares' assistance and support, convened and coordinated the Canadian Women's Committee on Reproduction, Population, and Development. The objective was to broaden support for an alternative analysis of population control, based on women's reproductive rights, and one that promoted access to primary health care, education, and other resources for women's empowerment. The Women's Committee produced a Canadian Women's Bill of Rights on Reproductive Health and a policy brief to the federal government's inter-agency committee preparing Canada's official position for the 1994 International Conference on Population and Development, held in Cairo.[117] This brief was endorsed by the National Action Committee on the Status of Women and distributed at the Cairo conference. For three decades, the outcomes of engagement and dialogue with government officials at the (then) Canadian International Development Agency (CIDA) varied, depending on the governments in power, but did result in some positive policy changes over time.[118] (Inter Pares, 2011, 35–37.) Current Canadian government policy discourse is well aligned with a sexual and reproductive health and rights framework promoted by Inter Pares and its partners.[119]

Fourth, the goal of building a vibrant women's health network in Canada was articulated and endorsed at the Aylmer workshop. Many of us were inspired by the Latin American and Caribbean Women's Health Network and similar initiatives in other areas of the global South. Through a network, women could seek and exchange information, develop strategies, and advocate with a strong voice for transforming the health care system to be more sensitive to women's needs. The *Side Effects* tour provided a social and geographic mapping of organizations and individuals concerned about women's health in Canada that was used in subsequent planning. Almost eight years after the *Side Effects* tour, at a meeting in Winnipeg in 1993, representatives of more than seventy women's groups and organizations from all provinces and territories came to consensus on a mission statement and outlined common goals. The meeting was hosted by Women's Health Interaction Manitoba (the former *Side Effects* Tour Committee), with the support of Ottawa sisters at WHI and Inter Pares. This was the genesis of the Canadian Women's Health Network.[120]

Fifth, the *Side Effects* process and WHI's strong feminist underpinnings contributed to the development of a democratic, egalitarian, "co-management" structure where all staff at Inter Pares shared in the management and responsibilities of the organization, took important decisions by consensus, and earned the same base salary and benefits. The staff was committed to developing an internal organizational structure that reflected Inter Pares' philosophy of working "among equals" with counterparts and that was consistent with the purpose of the organization. Inter Pares and Women's Health Interaction (WHI) developed a close working relationship during the *Side Effects* project. The feminist analysis and processes of WHI enriched the transformations at Inter Pares. WHI practiced and refined a collaborative way of working, where everyone's voice was heard and valued. The two organizations continued to work both independently and collaboratively, deepening each organization's theory and praxis, until the early 2000s, when the WHI group decided to disband. Inter Pares remains a self-reflective, explicitly feminist organization of women and men, bringing analyses of gender and power relations to all its work, including health and reproductive rights.[121]

LOWERING THE CURTAIN:
THE LEGACY OF *SIDE EFFECTS*

> Anything can happen, so you can dream big because you've got women at your back. There's a wall there supporting you, you can go forward with that belief. And what I'd do differently? I cannot think of anything that I would do differently given the context. We were lucky to be at that time in history when a lot of activism was happening and women were just discovering who they were and feeling the power from themselves or from each other. But it goes back to social activism, doesn't it? That was the point of the play, in a way...we always intended the play to be a vehicle for social activism.[122]

Over the past three decades, there have been advancements towards improving women's health and towards gender equity and women's equality in Canada and in other parts of the world. However, these steps forward are not without barriers and contradictions. Increasing concentration and power of the pharmaceutical industry, the common assumption that "overpopulation," rather than injustice and inequality, is at the root of global social and environmental problems, and the failure of nation states to address poverty, misogyny, violence against women and children, and other social determinants of ill health remain systemic and acute.[123] These dynamics of patriarchy and political economy were an implicit backdrop to the personal stories told in the play. At that time however, we didn't imagine these dynamics would become more pervasive and entrenched.

With hindsight, we have learned that past advancements in women's equality, reproductive rights, and health are fragile and must be renewed and renegotiated by subsequent generations to address the present historical moment. Hopefully, the legacy of *Side Effects* will endure in the strength, tenacity, and power of its feminist analysis and process; in the spirit of joy and positive transformation it generated; and in the collaborative, "among equals" relationships nurtured and sustained by those involved in, and beyond, this play.

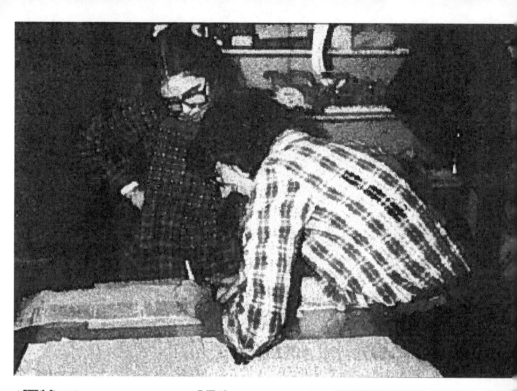

Top: From *Healthsharing* 1980
Bottom: From *Healthsharing* Fall 1991

SECTION FIVE:
SHIFTING SYSTEMS

The big systems were, and still are, a problem for women's health. How does health research get done? What constitutes a women's health issue and how do major diseases affect women? How does the environment and how do new drugs affect women's bodies? What impact does migration have on us? How do the major institutions such as law, child welfare, and medicine collude and collide to undermine us? How can nurses get more attention and respect?

Understanding what we didn't know about women's health meant that we had to take a closer look at medical research. My contribution on research into women's health discusses the difficult birth of the Institute of Gender and Health in Canada and why it remains necessary. Both sex and gender matter in understanding our bodies and ourselves. Messing describes the complex challenges in getting women's work and women's injuries on the agenda of researchers, governments, and unions. Workplace injuries for women are much different than those usually getting the attention—those experienced by men. Visandjée takes us through four countries on her personal migration path and asks why we don't spend more time thinking about women's health and migration. Scaia introduces us, again, to the power of nursing and nurses, and makes the connection between nurses' ongoing struggle for professional recognition and fair wages and a culture that consistently undervalues women's paid and unpaid work. Lucyk takes us back in time to highlight the important role that the Canadian Public Health Association played in championing equitable access to family planning services during the 1960s to 1970s.

Clement describes *Healthsharing*, a major women's health magazine of the second wave. In this personal essay, she recounts the bonding, the sisterhood, the mission, and the impact of creating this vehicle for education and organizing. Nancy Poole and I document the victimizing and stigmatizing of women who use substances, particularly when they are pregnant or mothering. This social and legal barrier offers no actual health care, keeps women powerless and addicted, their children bereft, and mothers re-traumatized. Gahagan looks at the exclusion of women from our understanding HIV and how it continues to have an impact on women's diagnosis and treatment. This display of sexism is resoundingly apparent in many other diseases that affect both women and men. And finally, Simard reveals her bravery as she turns her DES cancer diagnosis into action, something that is emblematic of the courage of the second-wave women's movement.

All of these contributions reveal what we didn't know until we asked new questions. The second-wave women's health movement produced a sea change in women's health in Canada and its impact reverberates still as the work carries on. Onward!

WE DON'T KNOW WHAT WE DON'T KNOW: ADVOCATING FOR WOMEN'S HEALTH RESEARCH

Lorraine Greaves

The early years of the second-stage women's health movement were characterized by reactions to the way medicine was practiced, and the way laws governed our bodily autonomy. It was a time to push back. As consciousness was raised and stories shared, women became angry about their treatment, lack of information, paternalistic attitudes, and lack of control over their own reproduction and other processes. As time went by, we adopted a more proactive stance. We took control of producing health information for ourselves, defining how we would like to be treated, and influencing government programmes and policies to better meet our needs. Ultimately, improving women's health became a matter of gender equity that required legal and social reforms. The women's health movement became embroiled in discussions of gender and health, and gender was recognized as one of the social determinants of health.

Inclusion and consent were emerging as key health issues. What drugs or treatments were being used on women, and why? Were they used because they were necessary or because sexist attitudes influenced medical decisions? Had they even been tested on women? For many years when it came to disease or treatment, women were considered to be just "small men;" medical practitioners lowered dosages of drugs or modified treatments for smaller size bodies. But women were not always—or even often—included in clinical trials, and pregnant women were excluded, leading to high risks for women. What if treatments tested on men didn't work, or worse, harmed women? We realized that we didn't know what we didn't know.

Other than noting (and controlling) reproductive capacities and monthly cycles, women's bodies (and minds) did not get a lot of direct attention in health research. But by the late 1970s and early 1980s women's health activists were getting closer to understanding how central research was to our collective liberation. Centuries of sexism and patriarchal control of medicine had rendered women's wisdom, women's professions, and women's bodies marginal, if not invisible.

But compared to where we were fifty years ago, the women's health research scene in Canada has much improved. Canada now has the only research institute in the world that is focused on gender and health. Awareness has slowly been raised about the difference between, and the importance of, both sex and gender. Decades later, we are slowly moving past the notion that only sex "differences" matter; that our sex and gender are important only if and when we are different from men (the norm). There was, from the medical perspective, no need to understand women's health and women's bodies for their own sake. It is no surprise that the geography of the clitoris was only mapped in 1999.

Other factors have changed too, not the least of which are commitments to sex- and gender-based analysis in research and policy-making. But the story of these changes is complex. You might think health research is about science, but it's actually about politics. Generating evidence is not a linear or necessarily logical path, and getting policy-makers and practitioners to use evidence is not all that easy. Women's health activists have had a lot to do with changing this landscape in Canada.

When the first glimmers of women's health activism emerged, much energy was focused on the fight against sexist attitudes in medicine and the right to control our own bodies. But it quickly became apparent that an underlying problem was the quality, design, and scope of medical research. Several things had to change, such as the lack of inclusion of women in research, especially clinical trials. How could treatments be proved effective for all if they had only been tested on men? How could we be sure a drug tested on men would be safe for women? How could health practices change if women were not participating in research? Even the lab rats and mice were (and often still are) male. Not only did the drug trials exclude women, they ignored reproductive cycles, and the practice and programme initiatives never consulted women in their development. There was a lot of exclusion in health research. In fact, it was the status quo.

There had been some attempts to change this in Canada. In the

1990s, a group of women scientists had reported to the Medical Research Council on the need for including women in research, and federal authorities had examined clinical trial inclusion guidelines. In 1995 the federal government sponsored a bilateral USA/Canada women's health conference to bring ideas on women's health together. In 1996, the Women's Health Contribution Programme was launched by Health Canada to generate more research and to address the policy implications of women's health research. The programme funded the Canadian Women's Health Network and five women's health research centres across Canada (in Atlantic Canada, Montreal, Toronto, the Prairies, and British Columbia, where I was recruited in 1996 to be the founding executive director). Building on this momentum, the proposal to replace the Medical Research Council with the Canadian Institutes of Health Research (CIHR) in 1999 was a golden and important opportunity to change women's health research in a more substantive and structural way, and for the better.

When you think of scientists, you may visualize smart, logical people in lab coats turning over every leaf, going down every logical path, examining and re-examining every variable, testing and checking results five or ten times, and then replicating all of that, just to make sure of their results. You would be right, except for the "examining every variable" part. It's fair to say most health research from the past was sex and gender blind. The full range of sex-related factors that are our biological characteristics were ignored while male bodies, cell lines, and mice were the default. And gender was even further from the health research front. Medical researchers didn't really understand gender, a social science concept that was seen as irrelevant to medical research, but a concept that has a lot to say about health by understanding power, roles, stereotypes, and norms.

In this context in early 1999 I was invited by Allan Rock, the minister of health, to sit on the Interim Governing Council (IGC) of the new Canadian Institutes for Health Research (CIHR). I quickly agreed to this appointment in order to advance women's health research in the design of an all-new health research funding organization. I had been nominated by Chaviva Hošek, the director of policy and research in the prime minister's office (PMO). She had been the president of NAC when I was elected to the NAC executive in the mid-1980s, and I had a great deal of respect for her. She had gone on to become an MPP and cabinet minister in Ontario's Liberal government and then to influential staff positions in the Liberal Party of Canada, drafting election platforms and campaign policies.

This was a big opportunity to argue for an institute on women's health research in Canada, something that colleagues and I had been formulating for a while. We had prepared by convening eighty women's health researchers from across the country to assist in designing new collaborative, interdisciplinary research processes, and smaller working groups had met to design an institute and to formulate the arguments for a women's health focus. We had looked across the world for model solutions, but in the end we opted for a standalone institute to go alongside other predictable suggestions such as a cancer institute, a heart institute, a mental health and addiction institute, a health policy institute, etc. The working groups prepared background documents to identify the key arguments and models for shifting Canadian research structures that would include a keener look at women's health, and regard sex and gender as key health research variables.

I approached the task with enthusiasm, while at the same time feeling daunted. I knew that there was formidable opposition to women's health even as a category, and certainly to women's health research as an activity. There was a dismissal of people like me who were proponents of women's health, equating it with a political, not a scientific stance. The irony was, and is, that all science is political; deciding what we need to know and what we don't know and what we need to figure out is not based on scientific principles, but on political principles. Who is funding what? Who is deciding who is funding what? Who is sorting out what we do not know, and naming it, and pursuing it? Who is in charge of research labs and who is teaching the next generation of health researchers? In 1999, it wasn't women's health activists.

Getting women's health recognized and possibly formally acknowledged as part of the new CIHR agenda was going to take some artful work. I also knew that among women's health researchers across the country there were many activists who were demanding and pressing for change. I felt the pressure. I began to be lobbied almost immediately.

I was right to be daunted. What followed was eighteen months of difficult, draining, marginalizing board meetings in Ottawa. Every three or four weeks I travelled from Vancouver to Ottawa, dreading the lack of support at the table and feeling responsible for making some big, unwelcome arguments. At 5:00 a.m. Pacific time, I would be sitting in a dark meeting room in some Ottawa hotel, called upon to think clearly enough to respond to a bevy of self-satisfied folks who were either all established and well-funded researchers or leaders in health charities. We opened each meeting with a round of "what we were hearing" comments.

The others appeared to be part of a big establishment that didn't recognize "women's health" as an entity. And I was leading a women's health research centre! It was very easy to feel dismissed. There were thirty appointed members but only nine women on the Interim Governing Council, and the women who were there didn't overtly identify as feminists or show any solidarity with me. Indeed, well into the process I was accidently sent an e-mail exchange between five of the women in which its subject was me! It was dismissive and critical of me and my agenda. The embarrassing blooper was followed by an apology, but the lack of solidarity I felt among the appointed women was confirmed.

My best allies were not on the IGC. They turned out to be the political staff of the minister's office, the PMO, and several other high-level bureaucrats and deputy ministers who were non-voting members of, or assigned to attend, the IGC. These folks made a big difference. These people could see what was at stake in defining the CIHR, eliminating the MRC, and modernizing health research in Canada. They had deep concerns about population health, social determinants of health, Indigenous health, and gender and health. They worried about financing health care and health reform. They worried about the pressures on the health care system and Medicare. They had their fingers on the data and trends and were well informed about health research.

It was an era of burgeoning health care budgets and everyone needed to figure out how to arrest the expansion. One way might be through health research that was more sensitive, more multidisciplinary, and more readily turned into prevention and policy advice. They did their best to inform the IGC about these issues, and how they affected the health of Canadians and the health care system and attempted to press the IGC into expanding a view of health research away from medicine, to health.

Over eighteen months, we were slowly inching toward making a set of recommendations about institute selection and, at the same time, drafting and finalizing the *CIHR Act*. In one of my final desperate attempts to make any difference at all for women, I had argued that we should not automatically use the phrase "Canadians" in the *CIHR Act*, but to say "women and men." Even I felt slightly perverse while making this suggestion. But it passed and this change was made. Much later on, one of the justice department lawyers told me it was the first act in Canada to use the phrase "women and men," and remarked that it was an achievement of which I should be proud. But to me it felt like a very minor detail, like window dressing, compared to my main agenda: getting an institute of women's health.

In March 2000, the deadline for the report to the health minister was looming. In my view, I was no closer to the goal: acknowledging women's health concerns. But in that month, Henry Friesen, an esteemed medical researcher who was the chair of the IGC and part of the MRC legacy, ended a particularly contentious, conflict-ridden meeting by declaring that he felt "convergence" emerging. I was flabbergasted. I didn't sense any consensus. The IGC was on the verge of suggesting a slate of institutes and finalizing the act in ways that we had not all agreed upon. At least not in the room where the meetings were held. The option of writing a minority report was not on offer, and I had no co-authors anyway. But consensus? In feminist circles, this would be anything but consensus.

I was out of cards. I had made presentations, brought reams of evidence about sex and gender forward, distributed our reports, placed information on the seats of each IGC member, used case studies, lobbied the other IGC members, met with advisors in Health Canada, tried to make offers and deals, and tried to fully represent the constituency asking for a women's health research institute. Outside of the IGC, key women's health activists and researchers were doing parallel work: lobbying their circles within universities, hospitals, and constituency offices across Canada.

By the end of this period, though, I was reduced to simply arguing for more attention to social determinants of health in research and taking a more social model of health into account. I confronted arguments that said "epidemiology had it all covered," or "women's health would be integrated in all other Institutes," or there was no scientific basis for what I was arguing. I was even the object of a hearty laugh when one of the IGC council members mistakenly referred to me as a "bio terrorist." I was desperate. Time was short, allies were few, and I didn't agree with the forthcoming report.

It went ahead anyway. I was depressed that March, as eleven institutes were recommended and women's health and aboriginal health institutes were not included. This was after last ditch efforts that saw senior advisors such as Bob McMurtry from Health Canada coming to argue for aboriginal health, making lengthy presentations about glaring aboriginal health inequities and looming demographic and financial projections. None of it had worked. I was defeated along with those arguing for aboriginal health. I made a few last phone calls and visits to allies outside the IGC to try to make some final arguments. I was exhausted. My energy was flagging and I felt as if I had disappointed many. Between March and June, I consoled myself by making final visits and calls to my non-Council allies: political staff and various bureaucrats in influential positions.

The eighty women's health activists and researchers who were watching were also being ignored. Our collective arguments were dismissed, and indeed mocked, by a roomful of mostly male scientists who were mostly biomedical or clinical scientists, and who seemed collectively grumpy about losing the Medical Research Council and spreading health research funding across a wider set of issues and disciplines. The few women in the room were trying to fit in, or be apologists.

So you can imagine my surprise when, on July 2, 2000, the CIHR was formally launched and a permanent governing council was named. The announcement named not eleven, but thirteen institutes, including an Institute of Gender and Health and an Institute of Aboriginal Peoples' Health. Between March 2000 and July 2000, the minister had received the report, then joined the fray behind the scenes. He had apparently invited Henry Friesen to amend his report. He, I was told much later on, uniquely and defiantly refused. Forging ahead anyway, Allan Rock announced thirteen institutes in July 2000.

There was a hitch, though. We didn't get our coveted women's health institute, as a compromise was made by the minister with the new Governing Council and president: an Institute of Gender and Health (IGH). But the IGH has become a welcome addition to the research landscape across the world. It is the first, and only, such institute. And women's health research is a big part of its agenda. Over the years, we have, as women's health researchers, emerged as leaders in advancing sex- and gender-based science, which has turned out to be a very complex and constantly evolving field, and one offering many challenges to traditional approaches to health research. We have, under the IGH, facilitated the emergence of the science of gender and health and its many complexities have become respected. We have made it possible for sex and gender to become measures for peer reviewers to look for in awarding research funds. We have made it possible for journals to start demanding reports on sex and gender in research results before publishing. We have made it possible to ask for female mice to be included in lab studies and women to be consulted in health care research. It took a lot of pressure, lobbying, study, and politicking to get this result, but clearly, in creating better health research, especially women's health research, the key variable is politics, not science. The women's health movement in Canada has played a large role in those politics, and now plays a much larger role in that science.

SEATS FOR BANK TELLERS, RESPECT FOR CLEANERS: FIGHTING FOR THE VISIBILITY OF WOMEN IN THE WORKPLACE

Karen Messing

In the 1960s and 1970s, when union movements in North America were pushing to create prevention programmes in occupational health, women were less than a third of the Canadian workforce. The best-identified workplace health problems were industrial accidents and injuries, characteristic of jobs men did in construction, mines, and agriculture, so it was not surprising that most of the research and intervention in occupational health focused on men's jobs. This created a vicious cycle that a number of workers, union activists, women's health specialists, and feminist researchers have worked to break over the past thirty years. After a long struggle, we were able to introduce more prevention activities in women's jobs, and had some notable successes in highlighting women's occupational health.

As recently as 1991, in the Quebec occupational health and safety commission's division of the economy into six sectors according to their priority for intervention, the top three sectors employed 40 per cent of all male workers, but only 15 percent of female workers. These priorities have not changed. Hospital workers, for example, are still in the sector with the very lowest priority. This came about because women are often excluded from jobs where there is visible, dramatic danger. Women comprise only 5 per cent of workers killed on the job and one third of those who claim compensation for injuries.[124] Jobs involving exposure to explosives, poisonous chemicals, working at heights, lifting extremely heavy weights, and exposure to people identified as violent such as male prisoners or military enemies, are more often done by men. So it has taken considerable attention to identify the less discernible problems associated with women's jobs and to reverse the traditional exclusion of women from studies in occupational health in Canada and internationally.[125] As long as women's occupational illnesses and problems were not identified, their health issues tended to be attributed to women's weakness or propensity to complain, reconfirming the invisibility of workplace causes. Indeed, women workers were often forced to deny their work-related health problems if they wanted to continue working.

It has taken, and continues to take, a concerted effort to change all this. In the early 1980s, the impetus for a reconsideration of what women actually do at work came from militant feminist researchers such as Pat and Hugh Armstrong in Canada and Danièle Kergoat in France, who carefully described the sexual division of labour in influential books.[126] At around the same time, Maria De Koninck in Quebec[127] and Jeanne Stellman in the United States[128] were beginning to describe some of the risks women were exposed to at their workplaces.

Freda Paltiel, director of the Women's Health Bureau of Health Canada, played a key role in stimulating interest among researchers and activists. She first collaborated with Labour Canada to commission and publish a 1991 report on women and occupational health, then sponsored a series of conferences on women's occupational and environmental health, held at the Université du Québec à Montréal (UQAM) in the 1990s and early 2000s, attended by biologists, economists, ergonomists, epidemiologists, lawyers, nurses, occupational health practitioners, and sociologists. The conferences led to the publication of a book with 23 chapters written by authors across the country, from Newfoundland to BC,[129] as well as a collection of papers in a scientific journal. These publications were critical to encouraging research and practice on women's occupational health.

Many of the researchers and activists involved in these conferences, as well as their students, later became pioneers in Canadian occupational and environmental health. Barbara Neis founded a group of very active researchers in Newfoundland; Pat Armstrong and others did the same in Ontario; as did Susan Kennedy, Mieke Koehoorn, and Ellen Balka in BC; Dorothy Wigmore in Manitoba; and others across Canada. They all brought a feminist perspective to their work. Similarly, feminist perspectives were picked up and expanded by practitioners at clinics like the Manitoba Federation of Labour and the Occupational Health Clinics for Ontario Workers.

Key to this was the *joint* involvement of activists and researchers, which enabled all involved to focus on our duty to think about protecting workplace equity while working for occupational health, and vice versa. As a researcher, it was so easy to lose touch with the situation of working women! When I started thinking about women and occupational health in the late 1970s, Quebec had just passed its occupational health and safety law that included a provision for "precautionary" reassignment or leave as necessary for pregnant and nursing women exposed to dangerous conditions. I am embarrassed to say that I opposed this because my expertise in genetics told me that risks to pregnant women were not specific to these women. After all, radiations, solvents, prolonged standing, and night work posed a risk for all workers. While I was not wrong about these risks, I changed my mind on the legislation the first time I actually talked about it with the women involved.

When the law passed, Quebec unions rushed into educational sessions to let working women know which conditions would justify reassignment. UQAM has an agreement with community groups to provide them with free access to professors for research and training purposes.[130] I was the only professor with expertise on reproduction, so I read up on the relevant dangers and met with several hundred women workers in union educational sessions on reproductive hazards. I summarized the effects of chemicals on fetuses, explaining that leave or reassignment usually started too late to prevent most damage, and that the chemicals that are harmful to fetuses usually also damaged sperm. Thus, I suggested, cleaning up the workplace should take priority over getting leave.

At my first session, the workers explained their situations carefully so I would understand better. One group had called the inspectors many times to report unlawful levels of solvents, which are very dangerous to pregnant (and non-pregnant) workers. The employer shrugged and paid the tiny fine every time. In the short term, workers saw no way to prevent exposure to chemicals without leaving the workplace. The same was true for pregnant bank clerks exposed to prolonged standing, hospital workers exposed to night shifts, and slaughterhouse workers exposed to frigid temperatures. Only the most hardened theoretician could want pregnant women to wait until similar protection was available for all in their workplaces. At the same time, employers were extremely scared of being accused of callousness to pregnant women or fetuses. Many women were able to avail themselves of precautionary leave without too much opposition; now, about 40 per cent of pregnant women are reassigned or given leave during pregnancy.[131] Although employers have tried several times to get rid of it, precautionary leave is still available forty years later. And one of the best aspects of the legislation turned out to be that it became a tool for identifying dangerous conditions in women's work, leading to heightened awareness. When pregnant bank tellers got seats, they didn't want to give them up at the end of their pregnancy, so the whole bank branch got seats!

Contacts with women workers taught me the importance of exchanging knowledge. Feminist researchers in other countries learned the same lesson, and we organized a series of joint researcher/activist occupational health meetings, such as the Women, Work and Health meetings initiated by Carme Valls-Llobet in Catalonia with the support and advice of local unions and the European Trades Union Congress (ETUC). There was an atmosphere of joyful collaboration and mutual support at these meetings. The 1999 Women, Work and Health conference in Rio de Janeiro inspired research and action in several Latin American countries, including Brazil, Chile, and Venezuela. In 2006, Canadian and French members of the International Ergonomics Association established a Gender and Work Technical Committee, with researchers and practitioners holding regular research and dissemination activities in Europe, Canada, and Asia. This activity was made visible in three special issues of academic journals. In 2006, Canadians were among those who induced the International Congress of Occupational Health to establish its Women, Work and Health Scientific Committee, which has also held symposia in various venues.

These efforts were very successful on a global level. Researchers at the US National Institutes of Health have shown increased inclusion of women in studies of occupational cancer.[132] Also, the World Health Organization has become interested in women's occupational health and commissioned a position paper on the subject.[133] The International Labour Organization has also been persuaded to apply a gender lens to some of their programmes.[134]

Canada has become a recognized source of important research and interventions in women's occupational health. Beginning in the 1990s, the Canadian Women's Health Network and some of the Centres of Excellence for Women's Health were providing information and assistance directly to women workers. The campaign to prevent chemical exposures among nail salon workers is a recent example of collaboration between scientists and feminist activists. In Ontario, Jim Brophy, Margaret Keith, and their collaborators have successfully combined academic and practitioner skills to combat occupational breast cancers, workplace violence, and occupational stresses of women. Occupational health researchers were involved and represented in the struggle leading to the formation of the Institute of Gender and Health (IGH), now part of the Canadian Institutes of Health Research. More recently, in 2013, IGH created nine five-year chairs in gender, work, and health to stimulate research and practice in this area; they have led to an unprecedented volume of activity. Three of the nine chair holders had been students of the workshop presenters in the 1993–2003 conferences on women's occupational and environmental health held in Montreal.

I was directly involved in the struggle in Quebec.[135] In 1980, the women's committee of the union Confédération des syndicats nationaux (CSN) published a brochure on women's occupational health dealing with musculoskeletal problems, risks for pregnancy, and stress at work, among other subjects. To deepen our understanding, the committee organized a 1983 international conference on women's occupational health, where presentations were jointly given by researchers and union representatives. The unions described the problems that were giving rise to the studies and the practical application of the study results, while the researchers described the processes, methods, and outcomes of the studies.[136] Five continents were represented and the conference inspired many union members and activists.

In particular, Lucie Dagenais and others at the CSN education service then involved researchers in a series of educational sessions on health and safety among health care workers. The result was a number of collaborative research projects facilitated by the existing agreements on training and research linking UQAM with the three major labour unions.

However, we couldn't get funding for projects on women's occupational health from the usual occupational health and safety funder. Quebec's Institut de recherche en santé et en sécurité du travail (IRSST) funded research on sectors employing very few women and specifically refused any project specifically directed at women. When a PhD student phoned IRSST in 2000 asking about access to scholarships for studying occupational health among immigrants, the programme officer replied that no aid was available. "It's like research on women's occupational health," she said. "We don't support research on groups." In a letter confirming IRSST's refusal to examine the scholarship application, she said that "in [the Institute's] research priorities there is no policy on specific populations," and suggested that the student focus instead on "accidents, noise and vibrations, protective equipment, tool safety, industrial methods, chemical and biological agents, and musculoskeletal disorders." Only the last of these exposures is found with any frequency in women's jobs, which may explain why women were fewer than 15 per cent of those covered by Institute-supported projects in 1999.

Meanwhile, the unions were becoming increasingly interested in women's occupational health. The European Trade Union Institute published our *Integrating Gender in Ergonomic Analysis* in 1999, and it was immediately translated into six languages. In 1993, the three largest Quebec union confederations, the CSN, the Centrale des enseignants du Quebec (CEQ, now CSQ), and the Fédération des travailleurs et travailleuses du Quebec (FTQ) joined together in a research programme supported by the Ministry of Health and Social Services that was to last fifteen years. It resulted in over thirty studies, covering the recognition of risks in women's jobs in prevention and compensation programmes; the health risks for women entering traditionally male jobs; the health risks associated with the precariousness of women's work; and the legal, policy, and health concerns in work-family balancing.

In 1995, using data from the first studies, the FTQ held a press conference to denounce the low priority given to prevention in women's jobs. The *Montreal Gazette* gave it front-page coverage, forcing the health and safety authorities to reply and then to change some of their orientations and practices. The existence of this body of work also influenced several researchers hired by IRSST, who began to analyze their health and safety data with a gender lens; eventually this became standard practice.[137] By 2013, when IGH announced its nine chairs in gender, work, and health, IRSST had become a co-sponsor of the programme and even held a full-day seminar on gender and occupational health. They also started examining the health of immigrant workers.

At the request of IGH, Quebec researchers are systematically examining the effects of our research on the health of women workers, but we can already point to some improvements in health and equality in Quebec workplaces: seats for bank tellers, a diminished workload for hotel cleaners, the desegregation of hospital cleaning, some protections against work overload for teachers, and some transformations of precarious into full-time jobs.[138] Most importantly, the unions have told us that the programme opened permanent communication between the women's committees and health and safety committees, with the result that employment equity has become part of health and safety concerns.

But all is not fixed yet. While there is somewhat more consciousness of women's occupational health and safety problems, women's jobs in Canada are still not very safe. Factory and service sector jobs still involve awkward postures and high levels of repetition, women's jobs in the public sector are constantly subjected to cuts and consequent overload, and food servers are still sexually harassed. Several areas of research and practice are still neglected, especially among low-paid and immigrant workers subject to discrimination and in workplaces where women's minds and bodies are not respected. For example, after some early documentation of the effects of cold environments, solvent exposures, and physical exertion at work on the menstrual cycle, neither research nor prevention has progressed because menstruation is still a taboo subject. Similarly, there has still been no biomechanics research on the effects of breast size on lifting techniques associated with back pain despite the fact that, in the 1990s, the engineer Angela Tate of Memorial University alerted scientists interested in gender and occupational health to bias in biomechanical studies that is attributable to the use of male cadavers in developing the biomechanical models.

Women's reports of work-related musculoskeletal pain are still treated with skepticism or ascribed to menopause despite accumulating reports that pain systems function differently among women and men.[139] Researchers have only recently noticed that almost all studies of the mechanisms that process pain have involved only male mice. Many were therefore very unhappy when they realized that male and female mice differ enormously in their reactions to pain.

Researchers are only now beginning to examine the ways in which workplace exposures affect the interface between work and family. For example, variable and unpredictable work schedules and work-induced exhaustion not only pose problems for childcare, they prevent workers from fully participating in aspects of family life such as supervising children's homework and involving themselves in school and community activities.

Finally, violence, sexism, and sexual harassment at work are still very common. Despite attention to sexual violence against workers in health, education, and the arts, power imbalances still facilitate abuse in many workplaces, especially where workers are low-paid, low-prestige, or immigrant women.

INTERLOCKING BAOBABS AND MAPLE TREES: GENDER, HEALTH, AND MIGRATION

Bilkis Vissandjée

Migration is not a gender-neutral phenomenon even though it is often discussed in a gender-neutral manner. Gendered differences in immigration class have different effects on rights and health risks, and the interdependent nature of the world means that migration challenges are not limited by geographical boundaries. Indeed, migration is a key health transition that is differentially experienced by women, men, and other gendered identities; it is an intersecting interplay of social determinants of heath and gender.

This reflection on my own journey is a soft-focus dream sequence that originates in India shaped by Malagasy baobabs, wends its way through the French tri-coloured landscape of solidarity, equality, and freedom, and culminates amongst the ever-changing tones of Canadian maple leaves. As I look back on my convoluted, non-linear course of migration through four societies—namely, India, Madagascar, France, and Quebec, Canada—and see myself at the intersections of these dynamic pathways, I am aware of the strong influences of globalization. I find myself led to reflect on some of the significant periods of these countries' histories, fashioned by unique women's visions, hopes, and expectations, and makes comparisons between baobabs and maple trees.

When gender intersects with migration, we need to acknowledge that being an immigrant "does not simply refer to a legal status but encompasses a set of complex realities and differential experience."[140] Yet there are still significant gaps in two of the identified areas for migration and health research: the first is an accumulation of evidence for considering the immigration experience itself as a health determinant; and the second is systematic sex and gender analyses in immigration and health.

RETRACING MY PATHWAY

My origins are in India. I was born and grew up in Madagascar, and bloomed into adolescence and young adulthood in France, prior to settling in Quebec, Canada. I grew up surrounded by a large number of brothers and "cousin brothers" who gave me an appreciation for a social and collective conscience as the bedrock of a prosperous and potentially peaceful society. At the same time, I grew and evolved in gendered environments, obvious in my inner and outer circles, where there are more women of three generations around me now than ever before. A spectrum of pluralism, tolerance, and patience shaped my journeys and coloured my heart and mind.

It is the British government that allowed women in India to vote through the *Government of India Act*, 1919, though the reforms only began being implemented in 1921. Women's participation was still limited by social norms, with most opportunities going to men. From 1921 on, provincial legislatures started giving women voting rights, beginning with Madras. By 1935, women had the same voting status as men in the British Raj. Today, due to the strength and determination of women's movements across India, as well as government-regulated quotas, women's presence in the political arena is increasing through voting and decision-making power, as well as in access to positions in public office (Vissandjée et al., 2005). Nonetheless, gender norms remain highly relevant to women's political participation in India, particularly in rural areas.[141]

Even though India is very slowly moving away from the male-dominated culture, discrimination is still highly visible in rural as well as in urban areas, throughout all social strata. While women are guaranteed equality under the constitution, legal protection has a limited effect, as patriarchal traditions prevail.

The ethnic makeup of Madagascar's population, known collectively as the Malagasy, is as much Indonesian as African. The Malagasy language falls within an Indonesian group, though it also contains many words of African and colonial origin (Bantu, Swahili, and Arabic from the first group, English and French from the second).[142] The island became known to Europeans after being sighted in 1500 by a Portuguese ship on the new route to India, but it is not until a century later that much outside attention was paid to the place. In the seventeenth century, Portuguese missionaries tried to bring to the Malagasy the news of Christianity, and both Britain and France attempted to establish settlements.[143, 144, 145]

By the late 1960s the population was suffering from economic stagnation, a decline in living standards, and the failure to meet modest development goals. Students, mostly male, as women were not involved in creating an opposition, joined forces with the disaffected populations. A turning point occurred on May 13, 1972, when the Republican Security Force (Force Républicaine de Sécurité [FRS]) and protesters set fire to the town hall and to the offices of a French-language newspaper in the capital. The president declared a state of national emergency and on May 18 dissolved his government ending the First Republic (1960–1972). He turned over full power to the National Army which had maintained political neutrality in the crisis.

A number of individuals and families—my family among them—who were seeking social and economic stability were compelled to leave Madagascar. Most went to France, Belgium, and England. Compounding its economic and political challenges, Madagascar is now one of the countries most negatively affected by climate change, evidenced by the increasing severity and unpredictability of natural disasters, such as cyclones, flooding, and drought (International Organization for Migration [IOM], 2016). As one of the poorest countries in the world, the World Bank estimates that 90 per cent of Madagascar's population lives below the poverty line. Yet Madagascar is showing a progressively different social and economic outlook despite selected regional and lingual differences. It is turning out to be the best social experiment where women, men, boys, and girls from diverse groups can experience pluralism and acceptance, tolerance, and patience.

A number of international organizations are active with women in Madagascar, where 24 per cent of women are exposed to violence and many excluded from the social, economic, and political spheres. Most actions are anchored within the recommendations of the Sustainable Development Goals (SDG 5) targeting sixteen to thirty-year-olds, building capacity about women's rights through partnering with teachers to train women on their rights and to sensitize women on gender issues, prevention of violence, and their role in politics.[146]

MOVING ON TO FRANCE: FROM LA DÉCLARATION DES DROITS DE LA FEMME ET DE LA CITOYENNE TO THE "DEUXIÉME SEXE"

The Declaration of the Rights of Woman and the Female Citizen (Déclaration des droits de la femme et de la citoyenne), also known as the Declaration of the Rights of Woman, was written on September 5, 1791, by French activist, feminist, and playwright Olympe de Gouges in response to the Declaration of the Rights of Man and of the Citizen.[147,148] De Gouges hoped to expose the failures of the French Revolution in the recognition of sexual equality, but failed to create any lasting impact on the direction of the Revolution.

As a result she was accused, tried, and convicted of treason, resulting in her immediate execution. She was one of only three women beheaded during the Reign of Terror and the only one executed for her political writings.[149] The Declaration of the Rights of Woman is significant because it brought attention to a set of feminist concerns that collectively reflected and influenced the aims of many French Revolution activists.

Following the French student and worker revolt of May 1968, the Mouvement de Libération des Femmes (MLF) erupted in Paris, France. As in the US, the MLF contained a variety of groups and ideological perspectives.[150] At the end of the 1970s and in the early 1980s, while I was an adolescent in France, I had the good fortune to be exposed to Simone de Beauvoir's writings as a feminist theorist. Controversial from the beginning, *The Second Sex*'s critique of patriarchy continues to challenge social, political, and religious categories used to justify women's inferior status.

Readers of the English translation of *The Second Sex* never had trouble understanding the feminist significance of its analysis of patriarchy. Its philosophical importance was more accessible through the abridged version of *The Second Sex* that was questionably translated by a zoologist, deaf to the philosophical meanings and nuances of Beauvoir's French terms.[151] The 2010 translation of *The Second Sex* changed that. This translation's sensitivity to the philosophical valence of Beauvoir's writing makes it possible for her English readers to understand the existential-phenomenological grounds of her feminist analysis of the forces that subordinate women to men and designate her as the Other.[152,153]

BAOBABS AND MAPLE TREES

In my journey, I learned that both matter equally. The beauty lies in respective and unique strengths and resilience, just like experiences of migration when it intersects with the protective social determinants of health. In the past twenty-five years, human mobility has increased and has produced high levels of immigration in the Western world. Along with native-born populations and other immigrant groups, immigrants contribute to ever-increasing cultural diversity. In addition to historically significant immigration in Canada, the last three decades have witnessed significant changes in Canadian migration trends. Historically, immigrants hailed largely from the United Kingdom, the United States, western and other parts of Europe, and were largely involved in farming, mining, manufacturing, or domestic service. They assisted in the expansion and strengthening of the Canadian labour force after World War II.

According to global experts, policies that promote gender equality, safeguard against violence and exploitation, and provide access to health care make Canada the best place to be a woman among the world's largest economies.[154] The same poll concluded, however, that infanticide, child marriage, and slavery make India the worst. Germany, Britain, Australia, and France rounded out the top five countries out of the Group of 20 according to 370 gender specialists.[155]

Like the beauty of flowers, plants, and trees that exhibit diverse and subtle shades of colour, there are ways in which baobab and maple trees are similar. You can think of an African baobab tree (Adansonia digitata) as a self-indulgent plant, with flowering patterns that suit itself, but not the desires of people. The baobab has showy fruit and the sugar maple has showy leaves. The baobab flowers; the sugar maple does not. The branches are short, thick and twisted. African folklore holds that the unusual branch structure is the result of the tree's constant complaining that it did not have many of the attractive features of other trees.[156] Despite the fact that the flower colour, the leaf colour, and the fruit colour differ, there is, for me, an important feature that these two trees have in common. The baobab does not have thorns, nor does the sugar maple. Nonetheless, they are both strong and can stand and survive. Yet, baobabs will not survive next to a maple tree.

My journey of migration has taken me from chaos in Madagascar to stability in Canada, with a stopover in France, and all of it informed by my ancestry in India. The intersections of gender, migration, and health along this complex pathway have brought me to recognize and work to protect against continued violations and denials of rights. These will always tend to destabilize a society—whether in a developed nation or developing countries. Human rights and women's rights violations are becoming one of the biggest threats to humanity.

Growing a maple tree or a baobab at home in a pot present very different challenges. Baobabs are native to the African Savannah and best suited to warm climates,[157] while maple trees are naturally adapted to the local climate, site conditions, and indigenous species, resistant to severe weather events as demonstrated during the January 1998 ice storm in Montreal. Maple trees evolve with local insects and disease pathogens; they perpetuate local ecosystem functions; they provide evident aesthetic beauty and urban shading. Growing a baobab tree in a pot at home in Canada may be more complex. For one thing, baobab flowers are stinky. And since baobab flowers tend to open only at night, they are difficult for humans to enjoy.[158]

Being patient is very helpful for a "baobab" project. Sometimes it may take weeks and months for the seeds to germinate, inevitably on a schedule of their own. Similarly, accounting for intersecting social determinants of health when it comes to migrant women's health, contribution and recognition to society is *baobably* a complex venture, but it is a tree for life venture. Addressing migration with gender sensitivity is a huge human rights issue and a women's health issue. It needs to be recognized now.

DOUBLE DUTY:
NURSES IN THE SECOND WAVE

Margaret Scaia

Nurses, as women and professional caregivers, were both participants in and subjects of systems of gender, race, and class oppression critiqued by the second-wave women's movement in Canada. Nurses contributed in unique and as yet unrecognized ways to furthering the aims of both labour and liberal feminism and as valuable allies within the women's health movement. Indeed, nurses skilfully and successfully positioned themselves as workers (as labour feminists), leaders (as liberal feminists), and change agents within the dominant male-led health care system.

There were links between the movements and over time. The first- and second-wave feminist movements in Canada were not unconnected nor were they a period of feminist inactivity.[158] Labour women had an impact on the growth of women's workplace rights within the union movements of the 1940s and 1950s, linking the first- and second-wave movements. Indeed, Cobble identifies the labour feminist movement of these decades as being influential in promoting accommodation at work for women's primary role as caregivers, and later, in tandem with other second-wave streams, the inclusion of the health concerns of all women in the paid labour force.[159] In addition to the aims and accomplishments of labour feminists, liberal feminists, who were concerned primarily with gender equality, were starting to bring attention to a broad range of women's issues in the political, economic, and social arena. Unlike the US women's movement, the Canadian women's movement accepted a role for state funding—among them, the organizations that became part of the women's health movement.[160]

Women who came of age in the 1960s are the majority of nurses and nurse leaders in Canada today. Many will retire in the next ten years and be among the first cohort of professional women to reap the benefits of paid employment in their retirement years. Many will have spent their entire working career and adult life doing double duty: both paid and unpaid caregiving. Stories of these women show that nurses were politically astute in harnessing the rhetoric of unionism, feminism, professionalism, and the media in order to achieve their multiple demands. They were certainly not passive bystanders in the women's movements that swept the social landscape of Canada in the 1960s. The strategies they employed to gain fair working conditions and professional recognition for the value of paid caregiving reverberate today. Nursing was anything but a gendered ghetto of female subservience and instead a source of power for women, workers, and feminism.

I interviewed thirty-seven women who became nurses between 1957 and 1976. This period represents the introduction in 1957 of the *Hospital Insurance and Diagnostic Services Act*, which outlined the five pillars of the current *Canada Health Act* (1984), and the closing of the last residential school of nursing in western Canada in Calgary in 1976. A career in nursing in this postwar period in Canada offered young women unusual opportunities for advanced education and guaranteed employment that were not widely available to other young working and middle-class white Canadian women.

For these nurses, the quality of their lives, both at work and at home, was constructed in relation to gendered notions of paid and unpaid caregiving. Indeed, women continue to dominate the profession of nursing, meaning they are still the public face of paid caregiving in the country, while simultaneously, women continue to provide the majority of unpaid caring to others.[161] As the largest group of professional women in Canada, the stories told by nurses provide important insights into women's struggles for equality in the workplace and at home.

Annis May Timpson suggested that "It was in the 1960s, once the second-wave of feminism took root in Canada, that women began to develop a sustained critique of the employment in- equalities they experienced and [to] pressure their governments to address the problem through policy innovation and change."[162] However, the second-wave movement, she clarifies, was not one ideological movement, but rather a term describing a number of overlapping and divergent ideologies, including labour and liberal feminism.[163] Dorothy Sue Cobble, describing the nuances within the second-wave movement, describes the debate between labour feminism and liberal second-wave feminism as one expressing differing priorities in relation to women's equality. For Cobble, working-class women were more likely to promote accommodation for women's domestic responsibilities in the workplace, while middle-class women tended to prioritize gender equality and equal access to male-dominated systems of power.[164] Thus, she explains, labour feminists were concerned mainly with the needs of working-class women, while liberal feminists focused on equal opportunities for education and income.[165] While working-class women may not have identified themselves as feminists, Cobble claims that feminist ideals were expressed in the leadership that drove the increasing involvement of women in unions. Liberal feminists, they argue, focused on promoting opportunities for individual women, often at the expense of social issues and the compounding impact of race and culture as marginalizing forces in working-class women's lives.[166]

Despite these differences, Cobble claims that labour feminists and liberal second-wave feminists had a common goal—the recognition of women's real lived experiences—in ways that addressed fundamental inequalities based on gender, class, and culture.[167] In nursing, the priorities of both labour and liberal feminism took root and bore fruit. For front-line nurses, labour organizing was a tool to address workplace issues; for nurses in supervisory positions, professional status and parity with men in comparable positions took priority. For both groups within nursing, monetary compensation and professional status went against the grain of the assumption that it was a woman's natural ability, and duty, to care.

Nurses, whether front-line staff nurses or supervisors, faced a double bind. Paid caregiving meant less time to maintain the quality of family care that was expected of married women with children. As Susan Reverby has argued, because caring has been associated with women's "intuitive" way of being, it was not valued as a unique set of skills or a particular knowledge held by women or nurses. Nurses, both front-line and supervisory, faced the reality that women's caring labour, both at home and in the workplace, was expected, but not valued. Rona's experience in 1965 suggests how this devaluation affected her experience of work, marriage, and motherhood:

> I married a fellow [in the mid-1960s] who did not want me to work. But I did. It was very important to me. I'd worked hard to get my RN and I worked for a year…then I had my first baby.

And I always worked but he did not want me to work. And in order to work I had to do everything first of all at home...after I had the baby I worked casual or permanent part-time and I did that on and off in between having my babies... but I had to get all the work done at home. I usually worked the afternoon shift so everything was done. The meal was ready for the evening. Anything the kids needed was organized...so it wasn't easy, but that's what I did and that kept him happy, as long as everything was done that needed to be done. He didn't like it, but we came to that—as long as I'd done things. It was hard, some of it was hard and I was tired. And I'd get home—I usually worked the afternoon shifts, so I'd get home at midnight...and I might have to be up with the kids at night time, right? And still be up in the morning, so there was never any, "boy, you did a good job" or "you must be tired." There was never any of that.[168]

Nursing offered young, white, working and middle-class women an opportunity for paid employment and social status that was unusual in the early postwar period. While it was expected that women would resign from nursing following marriage, increasingly, as was the trend in the broader society, more women were remaining in the paid labour force following marriage and even after bearing children. The demand for nurses under the expanding welfare state transformed nursing from an occupation suitable for single women to an opportunity for married women to forge a new identity as professional working wives and mothers.

At the same time that the three-year diploma offered an affordable option for young women from working-class families to obtain guaranteed employment, a university education afforded middle-class families the opportunity to educate daughters in a way that would maximize their social status as professionally educated women. Kelly, who graduated from the UBC School of Nursing in 1967, remembered:

When I graduated from university, people were banging on my door to work with them. There was a real shortage of nurses then. I could have worked anywhere. They hired me on the spot in a classroom at UBC; nobody was without a job. I found myself a head nurse on a psych ward within the fall of '69 two years after graduation. I had two years of public health nursing background, no experience of psych except for Riverview Mental Hospital. Then at the tender age of twenty-six or so, with very limited experience, I became the assistant director of nurses at a regional hospital.[169]

A university education, according to findings from the Royal Commission on the Status of Women, provided "more" equal access to social status, and opportunities for a career on par with male dominated professions.[170] The four- and five-year university degree programme offered at UBC provided the kind of access to advanced education and upward social mobility that liberal second-wave feminists might have envisioned. There were few professional programmes available to women in the 1960s at the university level; nursing was one such opportunity. Dora, a graduate of the UBC School of Nursing in 1972 expresses the growing status of a university education, and the opportunity that nursing provided for young women with families who could afford university tuition:

> I think that my friends and I, we probably considered ourselves a little bit above many of the other girls that we graduated with because we weren't, I mean, we had boyfriends and things like that...there were many girls who were very happy to stay in [small town on Vancouver Island] and get married and have children. That would have been the majority of our graduating class in high school. And so, the small little handful of us—we did see ourselves, I mean, at the time we didn't necessarily—well, maybe we did. I would have to say that we probably felt a little bit above them because we did well in school and we sort of, we would consider it of value to *not* be out looking for a husband....[171]

Nursing's essential position within the burgeoning health care system provided leverage for women as workers and professionals to place demands on employers for better wages and working conditions. For front-line staff nurses, this meant accommodation for the responsibilities of working motherhood. Wanda, a graduate of Vancouver General in 1969, remembers trying to work after the birth of her first child in 1970:

> Let me tell you how horrible it was being a breastfeeding mother going back to work in those days. Because it was so busy so I'd sit in the john on the toilet eating my sandwich and pumping my breasts. That was the only facility there was and, of course, nobody breastfed in those days. I was all alone and when I had to work late, overtime, the whole front of my scrub suit would be soggy with milk.[172]

In addition to demands for workplace accommodation for the responsibilities of working motherhood, Suzanne Gordon has argued that it was not always, or only, the so-called self-serving desire for better wages and fair working conditions that motivated nurses to join unions. Some leaders in the union movement saw the labour organizing as the most effective way to champion better working conditions that would, in turn, allow nurses to provide better patient care. Gordon comments that, "Conservative definitions of altruism posit an inevitable conflict between one's own need for decent wages and working conditions—making it impossible for nurses to assert that they, like other professionals, work for money and not love, and cannot deliver high-quality services if they are overworked and mistreated."[173] As Audrey, a graduate of the Holy Cross School of Nursing in 1964, remembered when I asked her about what difference the union made:

> A: I think it came in in the early eighties, I'm pretty sure. I think that the nurses just saw a need for better working conditions. We really were pushed around a lot in terms of our hours. We weren't being paid properly and I think there was a real need for it. And it did a good job for us. Now, there were times when, I mean, I'm not really a union person. And there were times I would get quite angry at what they were demanding.... On the whole I think that they [the union] improved our lot.

MS: Do you think they improved the quality of care?

A: Yes, in a roundabout way. If you were working a night shift and had to go back for evenings, you'd be pretty darn tired and your patients could suffer for it. Yeah, I think it improved the quality.[174]

Although nurses may have seen the necessity of striking for demands, concerns in the media about nurses striking were long-standing. The idea was that nursing is what comes naturally for women, but in a society that placed little value on paid or unpaid caregiving, there was little basis for increasing demands. While there were signs of change in the 1960s, the view that nurses should be caring for patients, not out on the street picketing still dominated the public's view of nursing. A *Vancouver Sun* reporter, covering the annual Canadian Nurses' Association (CNA) meeting at the University of Alberta in 1966, quoted from the address of Dr. Brian Williams on the topic of nursing and labour organizing. Williams is reported to have suggested that labour action and strikes were incompatible with the public's image of nursing. Williams warned the 1,500 attending nursing delegates at the national conference, that:

> Immediate adoption of collective bargaining by nurses might lead to a work stoppage and loss of the strong public support now held by the profession...in many cases employer negotiators are faced with fixed budgets and their sources of funds are largely restricted to city, provincial, and federal grants.... Why call a strike or a work stoppage [he argued] against a hospital that does not have the power to give you what you are demanding?[175]

As Janet Ross-Kerr explains, "The growing assertiveness of nurses and their willingness to challenge employers over wages and working conditions appeared to parallel increased activity in the women's movement in society generally."[176]

Indeed, it was not until 1966 that the *Registered Nurses Act* was amended "to allow for the process of collective bargaining."[177] In addition to the public's lack of familiarity with the image of striking women, striking nurses represented a contradiction to the image of nurses as selfless servants of society. The tensions between labour reform and liberal feminism continued to play out. Nursing's success in bringing attention to workplace conditions was a significant result of some nurses' ability to reframe their work as women's labour. But professional organizations at the provincial and federal levels discouraged collective bargaining and instead emphasized a professional identity based on "service, duty, and altruism."[178] As Suzanne Gordon has argued, "In hospital-organizing drives, management typically tries to exploit traditional gender stereotypes and women's socialization in passivity, while mobilizing conservative notions of altruism and service to perpetuate the subordinate status of nursing."[179] As Maria, a graduate of the Calgary General in 1962, recalls, traditions in nursing dictated that the relationship between money and nursing was complicated. Maria explains, "It was, it was really, and you know, the nurses…they just went on their way and didn't really worry about wages because you weren't really there for money, you were there to serve the people, you know, and take care of them."[180]

Melchior warned that, "as rank-and-file nurses became more vocal through unions, the division between them and nursing leaders who aspired to professional status for nurses became deeper."[181] As Mary, a graduate of St. Paul's School of Nursing in 1967 explains, class divisions developed between diploma (front-line unionizing nurses) and degree, a.k.a. "professional" nurses.

M: Here's my bias—I personally don't think that nurses who receive nursing education through a university get enough grounding in clinical skills. They learn a lot about critical thinking, but I don't think that it carries through all the time.

MS: To the skills part, you mean.

M: Right. And I know you went to UBC.

MS: Yes, that's right, I did.

M: And actually, once I was in—or out—of nursing school, I truly did not meet a UBC grad that I would ever take as a role model.[182]

For nurses such as Mary, the ascendency of academia created a division between herself and her nursing colleagues in which her own knowledge and sense of professionalism was challenged.This challenge has persisted since the 1960s because, as Wuest states, "In the health care field, patriarchal standards have reigned and the personal experience of professional caregiving has been devalued."[183] Expectations were that a commitment to nursing took priority over all other personal responsibilities: an expression of these standards embedded in the military and religious values of the profession. Shelley, a graduate of the Calgary General in 1966, remembers trying to balance professional standards and personal responsibility as she recovered from the birth of twins and returned to work after one month:

> My son was born in March of 1969. He was a preemie and he was in intensive care, so I had to quit work because I had him prematurely. I took a month off and they allowed me to do that but then they encouraged me to come back to work. I had only been off a month after losing a child—I had twins—and I just had my son who was a preemie of two pounds ten. So I went back to work in one month and I went to see him during my breaks and after work. When he was three weeks old I finally got to hold him and this continued until he was discharged in May. So he was in from March through to May and I was working full-time and seeing my baby son in between times. It was a time I got through and being only twenty-three years of age you had to develop the stamina.[184]

The rising power of academia and nursing's bid to expand its stake in academia privileged the status of a university nursing education to the detriment of acknowledging the value of the skills and knowledge base of the diploma-educated front-line nurse.[185] The result was that members of the nursing elite were working hard to strategically establish nursing as an academic discipline, rather than as a form of well-paid working-class women's labour. Thus, nursing, once seen as a respectable and suitable occupation for mainly working-class women, was more and more seen as a potential vehicle of upward social mobility for both working-class and middle-class young women.

While it was an accepted norm that working- and middle-class women worked hard in the 1960s, it was *not* the norm that these women worked in both the paid and unpaid labour market simultaneously. Nurses were unique in that their paid and unpaid roles both involved caregiving. In creating new ways of organizing their labour demands, while also claiming professional status, nurses played a significant role in highlighting issues of concern for many other working and middle-class women across Canada. Nurses did not passively accept workplace limitations or restrictions on claims to professionalism. Rather, nurses used both conformity to, and resistance against, gendered norms to re-shape their workplace and domestic realities. In reshaping workplace experiences, nurses drew on liberal feminist ideologies of equality in the workplace in order to make significant gains. In addition, labour feminist ideals of the right to fair labour practices were integrated into demands for changes in labour conditions. Thus, both labour and liberal feminisms contributed in distinct ways to changes for the better: progress in elevating both the status of nursing as well as the status of women.

BIBLIOGRAPHY

Baron, Ava. *Work Engendered: Toward a New History of American Labor*. Ithaca: Cornell University Press, 1991.

Baumgart, A. J. "The conflicting demands of professionalism and unionism." *International Nursing Review* 30(5) (1983): 150–55.

Boris, Eileen. "Roundtable on Dorothy Sue Cobble's *The Other Women's Movement: Workplace Justice and Social Rights in Modern America*." *Labor: Studies in Working-Class History of the Americas* 2(4) (2005): 43–62.

Boris, Eileen and S. J. Kleinberg. "Mothers and other workers: (Re)Conceiving labor, maternalism, and the state." *Journal of Women's History* 15(3) (2003): 90–117.

Cobble, Dorothy Sue. *The Other Women's Movement: Workplace Justice and Social Rights in Modern America: Politics and Society in Twentieth-Century America*. Oxford [UK]: Princeton University Press, 2004.

Gordon, Suzanne. "Institutional obstacles to RN unionization: How 'vote no' thinking is deeply embedded in the nursing profession." *Working USA* 12(2) (2009): 284.

Gordon, Tina. "Profits and prejudice: The undervalued work of nursing." *Dollars & Sense* 231 (2000): 26–38.

Luxton, Meg. "Feminism as a class act: Working-class feminism and the women's movement in Canada." *LABOUR-LE TRAVAIL* 48 (2001): 63–88.

McPherson, Kathryn. *Bedside Matters: The Transformation of Canadian Nursing 1900–1990*. Toronto: Oxford University Press, 1996.

Melchior, Florence. "Feminist approaches to nursing history." *Western Journal of Nursing Research* 26(3) (2004): 340–55.

Reverby, Susan. *Ordered to Care: The Dilemma of American Nursing, 1850–1945*. Cambridge History of Medicine. Cambridge and New York: Cambridge University Press, 1987.

Ross-Kerr, Janet C. "Milestones in Canadian nursing history." *Journal of Professional Nursing* 8(3) (1992): 139.

Roth, Mark. "The gendered workings of class in postindustrial, service sector capitalism: The emergence and evolution of the British Columbia Nurses Union, 1976–1992." Masters thesis. Simon Fraser University, 2008.

Strong-Boag, Veronica. "Canada's wage-earning wives and the construction of the middle class, 1945–60." *Journal of Canadian Studies* 29(3) (1994): 5–25.

Strong-Boag, V. "Making a difference: The history of Canada's nurses." *Canadian Bulletin of Medical History/Bulletin Canadien d'Histoire De La Médecine* 8(2) (1991): 231–48.

Timpson, Annis May. *Driven Apart: Women's Employment Equality and Child*

Care in Canadian Public Policy. Vancouver: University of British Columbia Press, 2001.

Wuest, J. "Professionalism and the evolution of nursing as a discipline: A feminist perspective." *Journal of Professional Nursing* 10(6) (1994): 357–67.

THE CANADIAN PUBLIC HEALTH ASSOCIATION AND ACCESS TO FAMILY PLANNING SERVICES IN THE 1960S AND 1970S

Kelsey Lucyk

I am a student, critical public health scholar, social historian, woman, and feminist. I first learned about second-wave feminism and the history of reproductive rights in Canada as an undergraduate student. Now, as a new PhD, I recognize the profound influence that my "Introduction to Women's Studies" course has had on my world view. Throughout my graduate training in community health sciences, I have questioned systems of power and privilege in Canadian society and have struggled to locate my own position within them. As a twenty-nine-year-old woman, I am indebted to the efforts of those who came before me and fought for the rights and freedoms that I have inherited and enjoy.

My dissertation was on the history of the social determinants of health in Canada, which is fundamentally about social justice. The unequal ways that power, money, and resources are distributed in Canada come to shape the conditions in which we live, grow, work, and age.[186] Historically, the public health community has recognized the influence of determinants such as gender, race, religion, and class on the health of Canadians. The efforts of the Canadian Public Health Association (CPHA) in bringing equitable access to family planning services during the 1960s and 1970s represents one instance where this influence was recognized.

The 1969 decriminalization of abortion and the sale and advertising of birth control legislated by amendments made to the *Criminal Code* mark a milestone in the history of family planning in Canada. Yet despite decriminalization, numerous social and economic restrictions remained for women who sought family planning services. In response, the public health community drew attention to the unequal access to family planning services that existed for Canadian women during the 1960s and 1970s, particularly those related to social, economic, and religious factors.

A study of the CPHA, a national non-profit organization, provides a historical window on the Canadian public health community as it existed during those two decades. The association has been an independent voice for public health in Canada since it was established in 1910 and throughout its history, the CPHA has also served as the professional association for the public health workforce that includes a broad range of individuals involved in protecting and promoting health and preventing disease. Accordingly, during the 1960s and 1970s, the CPHA gave a public health perspective on a number of topics and health issues, including those raised by the nurses, social workers, physicians, academics, and administrators who were involved in providing family planning services to Canadians. With respect to family planning, the CPHA provided the public health community with accurate information about population needs, birth control and abortion, and issues concerning access to family planning services. This role is clear in the institutional records of the CPHA and publications in the association's scientific journal, the *Canadian Journal of Public Health* (*CJPH*).

One key issue of concern for the public health community at the time was the accessibility of family planning services for women of different backgrounds. In the 1960s and 1970s, women of low socioeconomic status (SES) constituted one group that was experiencing limited access to family planning services compared to women of higher SES. Therapeutic abortion committees most frequently denied requests for induced abortions from women who faced social and economic disadvantage: poor, single mothers, immigrants, Indigenous people, and women of colour.[187] Women of low SES who were denied an abortion had no choice but to live with the committee's decision if they lacked the funds necessary to travel to another jurisdiction to have their case reviewed, or to pay for the procedure out-of-pocket at a private clinic outside of Canada.[188] The limited access to family planning services for women of low SES was an important issue for public health as they had the greatest number of children but were least able to afford their basic needs.[189] In the 1960s and 1970s, women of low SES were among those who needed and wanted these services the most.

Some members of the public health community questioned how discrimination among health workers contributed to unequal access to family planning services for women of low SES.

One professor of public health, Cope Schwenger, suggested that the public health workforce applied their profession's middle-class standards and Anglo-Saxon cultural stereotypes to women who sought family planning advice. He called to mind an unfortunate practice he witnessed among the "patronizing and smug health personnel" who dismissed women of low SES as too ignorant, apathetic, or hard to reach to benefit from family planning information. Schwenger suggested to his public health colleagues that they take a more open-minded approach when providing family planning services, as women of low SES "have simply not had the same access to birth control advice as the rest of the population."[190]

There were many articles published in the *CJPH* throughout the 1960s that addressed the unequal access to family planning services experienced by women of low SES. Some members of the public health community shared their ways of overcoming the financial costs associated with receiving family planning advice or birth control devices. For example, in 1967, members of the family planning clinic in Hamilton and Norfolk County, Ontario, reported that the local health unit covered the complete cost of running the clinic. This provided women of all SES backgrounds free access to oral contraceptives, intrauterine devices, as well as the physician fees related to family planning counselling and medical examinations.[191] Another article from 1967 reported on a clinic run by the Family Planning Association of British Columbia in Vancouver, British Columbia. Here, women paid for their birth control on a sliding scale from nothing to $15, depending on their financial circumstances.[192] Some clinics reported that they were able to offer family planning services free of charge in part due to the donations of contraceptives and informational pamphlets that they received from the companies manufacturing them.[193] Within the CPHA, the association adopted an internal position to further support the dissemination of family planning products and information. As recorded in the minutes of a 1967 meeting of the association's executive committee, members carried forward a motion suggesting that the *CJPH* seek advertising from companies that were actively involved in family planning at the time.[194]

In addition to focusing on women of low SES, the CPHA also drew attention to the unequal access to family planning services for Catholic women or for women with Catholic health care providers. In 1965, Vincent Matthews, a professor of social and preventive medicine at the University of Saskatchewan, identified family planning as "an essential part of maternal and child health programmes" that should be offered by all public health departments. He also suggested that the *Criminal Code* be amended to allow individuals "the right to make their own choice according to their moral code" on matters of family planning.[195]

The CPHA supported Matthews' position in 1969 by passing a resolution endorsing the position that family planning programmes be provided in accordance with the law "for all those who need them," drawing attention to the potential social, economic, and religious barriers that women faced in practicing family planning. Specifically, the resolution noted that "many Canadians practice family planning in a manner consistent with their personal religious, moral and ethical standards," and that "many families of the lower socioeconomic group...lack information or the means to obtain this information."[196] However, the above resolution fell short of challenging the newly amended *Criminal Code* or the legal barriers it introduced for women accessing family planning services. The *Criminal Code* would eventually be called into question two years later, in 1971, when the CPHA resolved that family planning services and education be provided "on request" and "in accordance with religious and ethical beliefs."[197] This position was much broader than the 1969 resolution, which had only recommended that services be provided "in accordance with the law."[198]

Throughout the 1970s, members of the public health community published articles in the *CJPH* on the fact that a woman's access to family planning services may be limited by conservative religious views, such as those held by Catholics. F. Michael Barrett, a former zoology professor at the University of Toronto, spearheaded the circulation of a series of opinion surveys on legalized abortion in 1968, 1971, 1974, and 1978 among students attending that institution. Barrett found that, compared to women of Protestant, Jewish, or no faith, Catholic women were most prohibitive regarding the conditions under which they would approve a legal abortion. The reasons that the surveys put forward included risks to the health of the mother, rape, child deformity, pregnancy out of wedlock, economic reasons, or that the child was unwanted.[199]

In 1973, another article published in the *CJPH* reported on the religious views of health care providers and how they might limit the access women had to family planning services. The authors surveyed gynecologists and obstetricians from the Ottawa area to determine how liberal they were in referring women for abortion procedures. Not surprisingly, the authors found that physician specialists who were Catholic were less liberal in referring women for an abortion procedure compared to specialists from other religious backgrounds. For instance, they reported that only 36 per cent of Catholic specialists considered economic circumstances as legitimate grounds for approving a woman's request for an abortion, compared to 85 per cent of Jewish specialists.[200]

For the public health community, the restrictive views of Catholics on birth control and abortion presented an unacceptable barrier for women needing access to family planning services. Some women may not have considered birth control or abortion as viable options when they (or their health care provider) opposed them. But despite assuming that holding Catholic views was a barrier to accessing family planning services, the *CJPH* reported findings that dispelled this. One article in the journal gave the results of a survey of a sample of women who had received abortions at a family planning clinic in Hamilton, Ontario in 1971–72. The authors found that 29 per cent of these women were Roman Catholic, illustrating that Catholic women did receive abortions, even though opinion surveys suggested otherwise. In fact, the authors of the study suggested that "the impact of religion was a less apparent factor" in a woman's decision to obtain an abortion compared to other factors, such as anxiety about being hospitalized for the procedure or family conflict arising from the unplanned pregnancy.[201] In 1973, another *CJPH* article reported on access to family planning among married women in Halifax, Nova Scotia. The authors found that among the women in their sample who took the birth control pill, just over 60 per cent were Catholic, in comparison to the nearly 44 per cent Protestants. As the authors described, Catholics in Halifax seemed to "find the pill acceptable, despite the continued opposition by the [Catholic] Church to chemical or mechanical contraception."[202] Both of these studies illustrate how the public health community played an important role in creating accurate information about the perceived barriers for women accessing family planning services, the different perspectives that existed, and evidence supporting the need for family planning services among diverse groups of women.

The *CJPH* also published articles about efforts to improve access to family planning for Catholic women who did not wish to pursue birth control options opposed by the Catholic Church. One example is the family planning clinic established in a Catholic-run hospital in an Ontario city, where health workers taught married couples methods of natural family planning, such as the sympto-thermal method. When this clinic surveyed couples who had attended their sessions on natural family planning, they found that 60 per cent of their clients were Catholic. Interestingly, however, only 17 per cent of couples responded that they had been motivated to learn about natural family planning because of moral or religious reasons. The authors noted that this finding was surprising and lower than expected, considering that the majority of the sample was Catholic. Instead, the primary reason that couples cited for pursuing natural family planning was concern about the safety of other contraceptive methods, such as the estrogen pill. Despite the reasons they reported for pursuing natural family planning, Catholic couples were among those most successful in continuing the practice, which the authors attributed to the status of the practice as "consistent with their religious beliefs."[203]

Health workers from another Ontario clinic, in Brantford County, reported on their attempts to improve access to family planning services. In 1967, Catholic women in Brantford were required to consult with their parish priest before accessing family planning services.[204] Health workers at the Brantford clinic sought to ensure that women could access services in ways that aligned with their religious beliefs.[8] The clinic maintained a room exclusively for use by Catholic women who wanted to learn about family planning and ensured a physician was on staff who understood natural family planning methods.[205] In this instance, the Roman Catholic fraternity had provided the Brantford clinic with information and ethical advice on family planning methods that were suitable to their faith.[206]

On the whole, the public health community played an important role in disseminating accurate information on family planning services in Canada to their community of programme planners, health practitioners, academics, and administrators. The CPHA used the *CJPH* to publish articles that enhanced the evidence base on birth control and abortion with regard to potential barriers, means of overcoming them, and how to meet the needs of different groups of women. Specifically, the public health community sought to improve access to family planning services and information for women of low SES and the Catholic faith due to the disadvantages they faced.

I have reflected on this history as an emerging critical public health researcher. I am grounded in the present and in the past. I recognize that the efforts of public health may seem modest when compared to the grassroots activists who fought and continue to fight for social justice, but they serve as a key complement to feminist activism. There is a long history of seeking social justice in the public health community which I am proud to share. While there remains work to be done in Canada to ensure the rights of *all* women are realized, public health scientists and professionals who were central to its history are also central to its future. I remain encouraged by my community's goal of health equity and will continue to pursue this end as a critical public health scholar, a woman, and a feminist.

HEALTHSHARING:
WRITING OUR WAY TO HEALTH

Connie Clement

I came of age—as a feminist and as a person—as a founding collective member of Women Healthsharing, best remembered as publishers of *Healthsharing,* the feminist quarterly published in Canada between 1979 and 1994. This is a personal reflection on my decade-long experience of being a part of Women Healthsharing and a bit about my sense of what Women Healthsharing contributed to the Canadian women's movement during the 1980s.

We coined the term "healthsharing" as a noun (the magazine) and, most of all, as a verb. By bridging health and sharing into a single word, we sought to convey an active, group process to generate conditions that support health. *Healthsharing* magazine was conceived to be a vehicle through which women would share knowledge, ideas, and experiences. Through writing, we hoped that contributors and collective members would challenge each other, our communities, and Canadian society to reimagine and recreate health.

From its inception until its doors closed, the magazine and the collective were at the heart of a pan-Canadian women's health movement within Canada's larger second-wave feminist movement. We didn't start as journalists or publishers; instead, we learned those crafts and used them to further the goals of an international movement.

From the beginning, *Healthsharing* chose to work in spaces of creative tension. Our audiences were lay women and health and medical professionals. We created space for stories and invited researched evidence and investigative articles. We questioned, yet also relied upon, science. We challenged the disease treatment system, sought to transform it and were open to non-allopathic treatments while not abandoning allopathy. All of these tensions were intentionally fostered by Women Healthsharing.

Our vision and *Healthsharing*'s focus was "health," very broadly defined using World Health Organization concepts that include social and environmental conditions and physical, mental, spiritual, and social well-being. This breadth allowed us to be a critic, a champion, and an explorer of new ideas.

Because the collective chose and maintained these tensions for at least a decade, the magazine was something of a hybrid, incorporating the style of a newsletter and of a magazine. In an early issue, the collective described "warmth" as an intentional attribute stating that, "We want the magazine to achieve journalist quality without taking refuge in the remoteness, the cool objectivity of most mainstream media and academic journals. We'd like to see *Healthsharing* become the kind of publication to which our readers feel personally connected. We'd like it to become, in a very real sense, yours as well as ours."[207]

Healthsharing's "My Story, Our Story" column and regular movement activity updates from regional reporters throughout Canada epitomized this balance for me. Publishing personal stories—forty-eight "My Story, Our Story" columns in all—"gave credence to women's stories. It provided a space for the voices of women who didn't often make it into mainstream press."[208] Some of the stories were about women's often frustrating and unsatisfying interactions with services and medical ill-treatment. Other stories were about the conditions of women's lives, family support or short-comings, friendship, choice, and the limitations of choice. Women wrote about depression, alcoholism, mastectomy, epilepsy, migraines, amniocentesis, and about choosing to parent, surviving incarceration, finding pride, being supported. These stories were, simultaneously, stories of resilience.

Healthsharing's writers were all volunteers. This applied equally to the stories, regional reports, and researched articles. Some authors were professional writers, yet most were women without extensive writing experience. Some authors were health, medical, or social service professionals, yet most were lay women without formal expertise in disease, sociology, or feminist critique.

Magazine topics ranged far beyond the narrow focus on reproduction that was at the time the typical approach to women's health, bringing a feminist analysis to the full range of influences on and experiences of health. "The collective tackled issues which got their public airing often for the first time in a national publication—like the debate over the use of Depo-Provera as a contraceptive, the harms caused by the drug DES, pesticides in breast milk, and the need for an expanded role for nurses—all before they appeared in the popular press."[209]

Writers were actively sought to bring experience of divergent cultural, racial, and ability differences into the magazine in order to create a composite sex and gender analysis in how health is understood and how the medical care system might be redesigned to respond to women. Yet Women Healthsharing began as a Toronto-based network of young, educated, white, Anglophone women, the majority of whom—not all—were middle class, heterosexual, and worked in or on the boundaries of the health system. Although some articles reflected lived experiences of and analysis by women of colour, lesbians, disabled women, Indigenous women, and Quebecoise, Women Healthsharing failed to "pioneer an analysis of diversity."[210] In this, the collective was a follower, not a groundbreaker. It was not until the last third of its existence that the collective critically assessed how it had contributed to suggesting universality based on a narrow range of experience and prioritized transforming itself to become a voice of and for women of colour, culturally diverse women, and working class women.

Although publishing *Healthsharing* was at the heart of Women Healthsharing's work, the collective was engaged in numerous women's health movement campaigns. The Healthsharing collective, from its inception, supported efforts to form a pan-Canadian movement. For example, Women Healthsharing co-founded the 1980 Committee for a Canadian Women's Health Network, was a partner in supporting the English and French-language tours of *Side Effects: A Play about Women and Pharmaceuticals,* and hosted grants to provide coordination for network development initiatives. In its last phase and as a precursor to the formalization of the Canadian Women's Health Network, Women Healthsharing produced six special regional issues of the magazine, highlighting women's health issues and activities across the country.

The boundary between what collective members did individually and what we did as a collective was flexible. Each member took on different roles and figured out different ways for our collective life to interact with our paid work and other volunteer and social activities. Collective members were involved in the abortion, midwifery, and wages for housework movements, in promoting the intersections of environment and women and health, in social service reform, and counteracting violence against women. Within the pages of the magazine, we published articles about research suggesting potential risks to women, especially young women, of medroxyprogesterone acetate (Depo-Provera) use and exposed the use of Depo by residential institutions to minimize menstruation by women with physical and mental disabilities. Outside the pages of the magazine, *Healthsharing* lent its voice to creating the eighty-five-member Canadian Coalition on Depo-Provera that advocated with the federal government to reject approval of Depo as a contraceptive. Similarly, a few years later, collective members were among the co-founders of Feminists against Reproductive Technology and the magazine published an interview with collective members who argued that establishing a federal commission about reproductive technologies would strategically carry risk for feminists.[211] Combined, these efforts led to a broadening of the eventual Royal Commission's mandate and greater space for lay and women's voices in the commission's processes.

We all learned about feminist theory and practice, and contributed and responded to feminism as the movement evolved. When I remember Women Healthsharing, what's most precious to me is how much I learned about friendship and being part of a group. With bumps and bruises, we learned about collectivity, moulded our own version of collective practice, experienced conflict, gained skills at debate and conflict resolution, and recovered from mistakes. We listened, asked, interrupted—loudly and softly—compromised, stretched our brains, strived to create trust, and sometimes did. We did this by writing, editing, and designing in pairs, in groups, and as the full collective. We also did this as friends. In this collective I attended my first labour, held a sobbing friend through a breakup, laughed with watering eyes, watched love bloom, and observed motherhood.

Women Healthsharing was founded amidst a proliferation of feminist and women's health organizations and projects in Canada and internationally. It was intoxicating as a young woman to be part of an international movement at the intersection of feminism, women, and health. It offered a stunning mix of being at the forefront and, even more importantly, learning from smart, committed women who were ahead of me and who challenged me in terms of analyzing, critiquing, and confronting sexism in conceptualizations of health, health and medical services, and in women's caregiving and paid labour.

Although we didn't start *Healthsharing* with a deep grasp of publishing, we ultimately became proficient writers and editors. I took copy-editing and proofreading courses, went to meetings of the Canadian Periodical Publishers Association, and negotiated magazine distribution. Because few of *Healthsharing*'s volunteer writers had writing experience, as collective member editors we partnered with authors to ready articles for publication. Often, we mentored, cajoled, coached, and reassured. I learned project planning and implementation, administration, budgeting, ledgers and spreadsheets, grant writing and rewriting to reflect funder objectives, and finding common interests with progressive bureaucrats. Before computer layout, each one of us learned to hold an Exacto blade steady while cutting along a straight edge, to lay a straight line with a sliver of tape, to cut and paste a tiny "i" into an already waxed-down block of type to correct a typo. We became used to fatigued eyes and aching shoulders.

And, oh, yes, I learned lots about health in its broadest senses. We each came to health as a means to feminist transformation for different reasons and by diverse paths. For me, I chose health as my life work because health touches everyone and everyone's everyone. Through health most people can be nudged towards recognizing societal biases and a few can be catalyzed to want and demand a sea change in how we structure society. Through my engagement in coalition and network development and advocacy, I gained vastly in terms of learning to negotiate common interests, conceive of and implement long-term change strategies, and manage short-term projects. I helped co-found Women Healthsharing when I was twenty-six years old and stayed for a decade. The movement and organizational skills I gained, I've subsequently applied throughout every step of my later professional career and volunteer experiences.

Even more than the movement skills, I hold dear the personal risk-taking inherent for women who published stories in *Healthsharing*. The women who wrote stories in *Healthsharing* worked hard to bridge the personal and the political, often disclosing very personal, previously private, stories. When I think of women being bold, I vividly recall leading vaginal self-examination groups—one of the many things I/we did, not formally as Women Healthsharing, but without ever quite leaving that identity behind. To help women equipped only with plastic speculum, mirrors, and flashlights to appreciate the varied shape and colour of female genitals and to see together what until then only MDs had seen, was both scary and exhilarating. Carol Downer of the US-based Feminist Women's Health Centres, called such groups revolutionary.

One of my life's greatest honours was being invited to lead a vaginal examination workshop with women whose mothers had been prescribed diethylstilbestrol (DES) during pregnancy to reduce risk of miscarriage. An effect of DES exposure in utero is an aggressive, and otherwise rare, cancer meaning that some of the DES daughters who took part in self-examinations in front of each other had had uterine and vaginal surgery. Tension filled the room as one after another woman said, "Me next. I'm ready." Together, we shared tears, laughter, and relief.

Women Healthsharing and its members, although at times demanding radical change and engaging in groundbreaking thinking, worked mostly for incremental change. We sought to transform how Canadians understood health, to change health-related services (allopathic and non-allopathic) to respond to the needs and wants of women, to encourage women to approach our own health with new knowledge, skills, and appreciation, and to use health as a lever for feminist societal change. It was life-changing for many of us in the collective and, I hope, for many of our contributors and readers.

Electronic versions of *Healthsharing* magazine are online at the website of the former Canadian Women's Health Network: http://www.cwhn.ca/en/node/46457.

VICTIMIZED OR VALIDATED? RESPONSES TO SUBSTANCE-USING PREGNANT WOMEN

Lorraine Greaves and Nancy Poole

Substance use among pregnant women is a major public health problem in Canada. Some studies estimate that approximately 20 to 30 per cent of pregnant women in Canada and the United States use tobacco,[212] with one study estimating tobacco use as low as 11 per cent.[213] Data suggest that the rate of smoking during pregnancy varies greatly with the age of the woman. In a 1998–1999 survey of mothers with children under two years of age, 53 per cent of mothers under twenty years of age had smoked during pregnancy, compared to 12 per cent of mothers aged thirty-five years or older.[214]

Approximately 10 per cent (9.6 per cent) of Canadian women who were pregnant at the time of the 2001 Canadian Community Health Survey indicated they drank alcohol *during the past week* (compared to 44.5 per cent of women who were not pregnant). Over 14 per cent of mothers indicated that they drank alcohol *during their last pregnancy*. These are likely underestimates, as surveys may miss accessing women facing serious health, economic, housing, and other social problems. In addition, the significant societal stigma regarding pregnant women's use of alcohol, drugs, and tobacco may also prevent some women from identifying use of any of these substances, even in the context of a survey.

Pregnant women who use substances come under considerable scrutiny in Canadian society. Analyses of public discourses regarding pregnant women as users of alcohol, drugs, and tobacco have revealed judgemental, blaming, and unsympathetic attitudes and practices.[215] The focus of legal, media, and public concern is usually on the health and welfare of the fetus and rarely on the health and welfare of the woman herself. This article examines the impact of perspectives that consider substance-using pregnant women primarily as "vessels" for producing children, and how such approaches fail to validate women's lives, health, and experiences, while ignoring structural circumstances that affect them. We argue that when a broader approach is taken, programmes and policies can be developed that reflect a concern about women, mothers, *and* children, and promote better health and well-being for all.

Seeing substance-using pregnant women primarily as "vessels" often leads to seeing them as entirely responsible for their situation and any potential damage to their fetus. In recent years this perspective has been evident across sectors: in legal cases, policies, media headlines, and treatment approaches. This perspective reflects a set of attitudes and practices that often puts substance-using pregnant women second, and sometimes casts their rights in conflict with those of the fetus or child. It also affects the way programmes have been developed to intervene with women and how policies have been used to respond to these issues.

In existing policy and law, the rights of mothers with substance use problems have been frequently set in competition with those of their fetuses/children. This is seen in child welfare policy, in drug policy, and in all-too-frequent media "cases" where mothers are publicly punished for using substances during pregnancy. For example, child welfare policy may refer to children's needs as "paramount" and use evidence of *any* alcohol or drug use to prevent mothers from retaining custody. In drug policy, Susan Boyd argues that "medical social and legal professionals consider persecuting mothers as 'saving' the fetus and the newborn from the risk of both the mother and the drugs they have consumed."[216] Unfortunately, and not surprisingly, this "competing rights" approach itself can become a barrier to women, resulting in substance-using pregnant women being afraid or reluctant to seek treatment partly out of fear of prejudicial treatment and eventual child apprehension.[217]

The tensions around this issue became very publicly evident in the key legal debate examined by the Supreme Court of Canada in the "Ms. G" case in 1997, which focused on the case of a woman from Winnipeg who was using solvents during pregnancy. In the Ms. G case, the pivotal point being tested was whether or not the state could apprehend Ms. G and impose mandatory treatment on her out of concern for her fetus. This case focused Canadian attention on the apparent conflict: In a case of potential harm due to substance use during pregnancy, whose rights should prevail?

The answer, as far as the media were concerned, was that "unborn children" needed protection from "abusive" mothers.[218] Such a view is a punitive approach akin to an American "war on drugs" policy because substance use by mothers was rarely explored or contextualized. In the media, substance use (whether of a legal substance like tobacco or alcohol, or an illegal drug) is often presented as an individual, deliberate choice that causes harm to fetuses and children.

In a study examining the content of Canadian news articles on substance-using pregnant women and mothers, we found headlines such as "Judge orders woman not to get pregnant for 10 years: Drugs affected child"[219] and "Save the Children."[220] This latter headline topped a review of a book that argues for understanding the context of the lives of women who use substances, and their capacities as mothers, but media articles rarely considered the social determinants of women's health.[221] Closely related was the lack of consideration for health and social interventions that might support women's improved health and, in turn, their capabilities as mothers.

Similar issues arise in policy application. When an agency committed to protecting child welfare assesses "risk" for the fetus or infant, measures are often used that reflect the interests of the fetus or child solely, and assess that risk in isolation from the welfare of the woman or mother, or from the perspective of the family system. For example, the *Risk Assessment Model for Child Protection*[222] in BC which complements the *Child, Family and Community Service Act*[223] has strongly worded risk criteria, suggesting that even occasional substance use (level two) can have serious negative effects on parents' behaviour such as "job absenteeism, constant arguments at home, dangerous driving," and "short-term stupor" impairing parental "childcare performance." These risk criteria can lead to dramatic results for parents including separation of a substance-using mother and child due to apprehension, fostering, or adoption. Sometimes life-long separation is the result, causing unmeasured impact on the long-term emotional health of both the child and woman.

The implications of a fetus-centred approach in all these arenas are significant and troubling to advocates of women's empowerment and equality. As Nancy D. Campbell argues, "beneath the legitimate and compelling concern for 'drug-addicted babies' lies a basic animosity to women's self-governance."[224] Many Canadians were affected by the Ms. G. case because it raised key questions about women's autonomy and bodily integrity, mandatory treatment and the comparative "rights" of mothers, women, and the fetus. However, key elements were missing from the public discourse in this case, such as a full discussion of the barriers to care for substance-using women, acknowledgment of the lack of visible, comprehensive, and welcoming treatment services, and exploration of the link between the substance use and the conditions and experiences in women's lives.

FASD AND TOBACCO USE

Although Ms. G's solvent use was a particularly dramatic case, in part because of the degree of her addiction and the public's judgement of solvent use as "scandalous," the judgements about her also resonate in discussions of tobacco and alcohol use by pregnant women, which are both more common practices. Alcohol and tobacco are the most commonly used drugs by women and have the most severe implications for fetal development. Through examining the dominant responses to two issues of substance use during pregnancy—Fetal Alcohol Spectrum Disorder (FASD) and smoking during pregnancy—we can identify and assess new approaches that could be more effective and validating of women.

FASD refers to a range of birth defects and developmental disabilities resulting from exposure to alcohol during pregnancy. While its diagnostic criteria continue to be refined and debated, it has gained acceptance in North America as a key condition resulting from heavy drinking while pregnant. FASD has primarily been regarded as an expensive health problem that is entirely preventable through individual behaviour change, with little attention and compassion paid to the difficult lives of women who have addiction and related trauma, mental health, poverty, or other issues. Janet Lynne Golden has documented how women who used substances during pregnancy were initially portrayed sympathetically in the American media as having health problems, but how this discourse changed under the leadership of government officials and legal professionals so that FASD came to be understood as a "*social*" deformity that expressed the moral failings of mothers and marked their children as politically marginal and potentially dangerous."[225]

In Canada, a dominant response to FASD has been the creation of public messages about the dangers of drinking during pregnancy, and a focus on diagnosis and intervention with those affected. Motivations for reducing the incidence of FASD are often framed in terms of preventing more births of affected children and reducing the economic burden of FASD. Less is said about improving women's health and launching successful prevention. Although much drinking can take place in the early stages of pregnancy when women do not know they are pregnant, there are still no wide-ranging health promotion initiatives that would serve to effectively help women of child-bearing years reduce their use of alcohol generally, as well as improve their overall health in pregnancy so that FASD would be reduced or prevented.

While prevention and treatment of FASD is clearly on the national agenda, it remains a struggle to keep support and treatment of women—mothers and pregnant women—as a focus. Women-specific and woman-centred alcohol and drug services have not been high priorities in addictions systems and are chronically underfunded. In Canada, Alberta is the only province that has a visible framework for women's alcohol and drug services.[226]

The impact of smoking on the health of women and their children receives much less attention in media and policy. This may reflect greater societal ambivalence about tobacco use in general because it is a legal substance but has no safe level of use. In addition, its overuse does not produce socially undesirable behaviours, nor does its consumption undermine women's socially prescribed roles, whereas overuse of alcohol and any use of illicit drugs are unlikely to facilitate women carrying out their roles. In addition, women smokers describe how smoking assists them in coping with difficult lives, stress, or poverty[227] and how tobacco use can assist in developing a socially endorsed image or identity.[228]

The one exception to this is smoking during pregnancy. A fetus-centric perspective in tobacco treatment mirrors legal and medical trends in maternal drug and alcohol use, as does the increase in fetal surgery, whereby the fetus is regarded increasingly as a "patient."[229] These trends have led to various suggestions for terms to describe the effects of tobacco use during pregnancy. For example, the terms "prenatal smoking" and "fetal tobacco syndrome," while not yet widely used, have been suggested to bring attention to the seriousness of smoking during pregnancy.[230] Laury Oaks reports that some advocacy groups suggest that newborns are addicted to nicotine when born.[231] In addition to increased medical attention, these trends contribute to an increase in litigation about tobacco use in pregnancy and around children, often centring on family law, custody, or abuse and neglect claims.[232] For example, the ASH[233] (Action on Smoking and Health) website exhorts separated and divorced parents to launch custody cases based on the issue of smoking around children.

The health interventions designed over the past twenty-five years to reduce smoking during pregnancy have not been resoundingly successful. While many women quit during pregnancy, both spontaneously and as a result of interventions, the relapse rate after birth is up to 90 per cent, according to some studies.[234] The approach to smoking cessation during pregnancy has been motivated mostly by a desire to lessen the deleterious effects on fetal health. Therefore most interventions are framed around fetal health outcomes and are confined largely to the period of pregnancy. As a result, pre-pregnancy and post-pregnancy tobacco cessation interventions, which would focus primarily on women's health, have garnered proportionately less attention and emphasis. As Bobbie Jacobson claimed in 1986, "in rich countries, *most* women are *not* pregnant *most* of the time," concluding that pregnancy tobacco cessation campaigns *ignore most women most of the time.*[235]

In short, there is little emphasis on women's health in campaigns for both FASD reduction and tobacco cessation during pregnancy. Similarly, there is also little emphasis on context—how poor nutrition and other factors interact with substance use to affect perinatal health. Overall, women's health advocates have found it difficult to establish pregnant women's substance use as a women's health issue of concern to funding agencies and policy-makers. As a result, all provinces lack services where women can access care with their children, women-specific detoxification services, or holistic, effective tobacco cessation programmes designed specifically for women, and health and social services that are welcoming and safe for pregnant women with substance-use issues.

VALIDATING SUBSTANCE-USING PREGNANT WOMEN

The issues involved in the Ms. G case were analyzed by Deborah Rutman et al. who concluded that there was a need for three key ideological "paradigm shifts": in the way substance use is treated and prevented (towards a harm-reduction/health promotion philosophy); in the mandate of child welfare (towards supporting families, not only protecting children); and in the way child apprehension is viewed (towards making social service systems accountable, not blaming mothers). They also reflect on how policy is disproportionately brought to bear on Aboriginal women who are pregnant, and how the conditions of Aboriginal women's lives make them more vulnerable to substance misuse.

Adopting a harm-reduction approach is a key suggestion for change that would validate women and their circumstances. Prevention of both alcohol and tobacco use during pregnancy would be improved by minimizing risk by encouraging reduction. There are several European examples that are models of harm reduction, where risk is calculated in a more fluid manner and decisions are made to support women as they minimize the risk to their fetus or child. A progressive example is the policy guideline published in 1997 by the Standing Conference on Drug Abuse (SCODA), associated with the local government associations in London, Scotland, and Wales, which looks at how harms associated with maternal substance use are being addressed and how children's needs are being met in the context of possibly continuing substance use.[236]

Essential insights on the effects of the policy and programme environment on substance-using pregnant women or mothers often come from the women themselves and those who work and live beside them. Their insights provide a unique, but often unelicited, perspective on how policy affects and responds to women who are often experiencing a range of pressures and disadvantages. In a study where sample scenarios were put to women who had substance-using issues during pregnancy and early mothering, women spoke of the importance of context, and a new approach to risk assessment and decision-making.[237]

In their view, the fetus or child at risk is seen within the context of the mother herself needing help and being at risk for harming herself (the participants never fully viewed mother and fetus/child as separate). For example, the child's health was seen as at risk due to the mother's smoking, but the mother was seen as struggling with addiction. Similarly, Ms. G was seen as at risk for giving birth to further affected children—but also as needing help for her own sake and in her own interest.

Using the women's perspective, a different assessment of risk was generated, which varies from the official assessment. Instead of examining only the facts surrounding maternal substance use, issues such as the patterns of drug use, and the viability and importance of the mother/child relationship, were taken into consideration by the women in a more "reality-based" assessment of risk. In contrast to a child welfare approach that focuses on child apprehension, the women suggested a different distribution of resources that would see some going to support the mother to bond with, keep, and support the child, instead of all resources going into apprehension, fostering, or adoption processes. They felt that ensuring the unification of mother and child might be more productive in both the short and long term. For women who were familiar with these issues on a first-hand basis, the intensity and inextricability of the mother/child bond and the damage done to it through child apprehension were serious long-term issues, often overlooked in policy and practice. As one woman articulated it:

> How is it good that the kid doesn't bond with the mother? How could it be that the child that you just gave birth to, this little person that is connected with you, like you just gave life to this child and then it's taken away from you, because you need to go through all the hoops that you were supposed to. Like, it's hard to quit drugs and they should be more empathetic to the mother and not just thinking whether it is safer for the child to go somewhere else…. Wouldn't it be better [than placing the baby into foster care] to have a group-type home with the mother and baby in the house together and to withdraw her that way?

Some treatment providers are beginning to examine their relationship to the dominant woman-blaming discourses in policy and media and are making efforts to provide welcoming, holistic, harm-reduction-oriented, woman-centred care that successfully engages pregnant women and ensures future health for *both* mother and child. For example, in the Fir Square Combined Care Unit at BC Women's Hospital and the Sheway Programme in the Downtown Eastside of Vancouver, providers have pioneered approaches that support pregnant women's self-determination of the services they need and enact an integrated and balanced approach to the needs of the mother and the child. Fir Square provides in-hospital antepartum and postpartum medical care to substance-using women, and at the time of birth involves mothers and a multidisciplinary team of health care providers together in the care of their newborns—it is an approach that supports the bonding and health of both mothers and infants. Most important, Fir Square is an "apprehension free" zone, preventing child apprehension by child welfare authorities in the period immediately following birth, while attachment and health stabilization are achieved and mothers' desires and needs can be assessed.

Sheway, a community programme located in the Downtown Eastside of Vancouver, provides help with the full spectrum of nutritional, social, and medical and related practical needs of pregnant women and new mothers, making all forms of care accessible and free of judgement for women in pregnancy and in the postpartum period. This programme has been evaluated, and significant benefits in both women's health and infant health outcomes, as well as reductions in child apprehension, were found. The women served by Sheway appreciated the welcoming, respectful approach that allowed them to determine the type and extent of change they wish to make.[238]

Some women's addiction recovery programmes, such as the Aurora Centre (women's day and residential treatment programme in Vancouver), are joining together with pregnancy-oriented services to smooth the transition to addiction treatment for pregnant women. This is accomplished by offering harm reduction and stabilization programmeming, such as short-term introductory group counselling where women can try to find balance and contemplate their readiness to change. Aurora is also successful at the development of internal motivation to quit that will outlast the pregnancy. These interventions do not assume that every pregnancy is a happy event, or that partners are either present or supportive. Indeed, these new approaches are more reality-based, dealing with issues of stress, violence, and stigma along with tobacco cessation.[239]

Unfortunately, these kinds of approaches are in the early stages of development and acceptance in Canada. While promising holistic programming for pregnant women such as pregnancy outreach programmes are being implemented in most provinces in Canada, there remains a long road ahead for these changes to be implemented on a system-wide basis supported by compassionate public policy, more progressive discourses, and new attitudes.

CONCLUSION

Pregnant women have often been regarded by health promotion advocates as presenting a "window of opportunity" for behavioural change. This notion has been applied to issues such as encouraging tobacco cessation and alcohol reduction during pregnancy, or improving nutrition and sleep habits. But this attitude can be seen as opportunistic, paternalistic, and inherently sexist for its exclusive (and temporary) focus that renders women's reproductive value superior to women's health for its own sake.

This view of women's health for the benefit of the fetus is consistent with a long "uterine tradition" of understanding women's bodies and health[240] where any compromising of the fetus as a result of women's behaviour is taken seriously by society, and women's ability to reproduce becomes the key reason to take notice of women's practices. Not only does this approach undermine women's health but it also produces guilt and self-blame in women who smoke and use alcohol and other drugs. This approach also allows stigma and punitive discourses about substance-using pregnant women to flourish. The alternative is to apply a critical analysis to practices such as women's substance use, where light would be shone on the material conditions and contexts affecting women's health in general.

As Oaks maintains, there is ample evidence that pregnant women are often reduced to being passive trustees of the fetus, not active makers of children.[241] Regarding women as vessels in this way has translated into treating women merely or primarily as vehicles or stewards who are working on behalf of society. Growing interest in the conduct of pregnant women is a significant issue in Canada and forms a crucial backdrop to the overall discourse surrounding substance use during pregnancy in contemporary Canada.

As part of this discourse on pregnancy, pregnant women themselves express a keen desire to do the right thing for their children, and want to create the healthiest conditions for their growth. They too see the advent of a pregnancy or the birth of a child as a significant life event where positive decisions can be made about someone else's welfare, so an opportunity exists for redirecting their goals and will. Indeed, substance-using women often remark that their children were the best motivation for change. These feelings are positive and hopeful and offer an important clue for transforming policy and protocol to take advantage of women's motivations and strong desires to protect and nurture their children.

Validating approaches to dealing with substance-using pregnant women are woman-centred and address the issues and experiences that lead women to use substances. But overall, they value and support the mother/child bond, by dealing with both the health of women as well as the health of the fetus, simultaneously and with equal respect.

ILL CONSIDERED: REFLECTIONS ON WOMEN, HIV, AND EXCLUSION

Jacqueline Gahagan

My interest in HIV in Canada started with thinking about men, especially gay men. As an undergraduate student in the 1980s, I was determined to focus my thesis on why there appeared to be such strong and negative reactions to HIV/AIDS in Canada, and toward gay men living with HIV or AIDS in particular. My passion for understanding the social diversity of the negative reactions to HIV/AIDS emerged from an incident at the local LGBT drop-in centre in downtown Ottawa where someone had spray-painted hate-filled slurs about gay men and AIDS on the brick wall just outside the front door. It was impossible to enter or leave that building without seeing these hateful words and, for me, without feeling a sense of outrage and frustration. This led to an increasing interest in how masculinity and gender-based social norms influence perceptions about HIV and AIDS.

I decided to do some research on these issues. My research consisted of sending out a fifty-question survey to five hundred undergraduate students in four different faculties—arts and social sciences, science, public affairs, and engineering—asking about their perceptions of HIV/AIDS and those living with HIV/AIDS. What I found was that when given the chance, individuals will freely share their visceral reactions when they can do so anonymously. While not a complete surprise to my thesis supervisor, there was a distinct pattern in the data based on age, sex (male/female), and by faculty. Younger, male students in engineering scored highest in terms of negative perceptions and attitudes towards people perceived to be living with HIV/AIDS. And, while not a requirement, many respondents took the time to write open-ended reactions to the issues of HIV and AIDS in Canada, including comments that were not unlike those spray-painted on the wall outside the LGBTQ drop-in centre. Again, there was a pattern in the comments that mirrored the analysis of the survey results—younger, male students in engineering expressed more discriminatory and angry sentiments about HIV and AIDS, who was at fault for the spread of HIV in Canada, and what should be done with those who are found to be living with HIV or AIDS.

Still wondering how masculinity and HIV fit together, I signed up for what I had hoped would be an enlightening "Men's Studies" course in which I posed a series of questions about why heterosexually-identified men felt such visceral anger at the thought of men having sex with other men; why there was such a strong need to blame gay men for the spread of HIV; why there was a sense of morality in relation to "non-normative" sexual orientations; and why anger was considered an appropriate way to respond to a health issue like HIV/AIDS. My hope in taking the course was aimed at achieving a better understanding of the ways in which both sex (biology and physiology) and gender (socially constructed and regulated expectations about how males and females should behave) individually and collectively contribute to our perceptions about HIV and AIDS, including our perceptions of who becomes infected with HIV and why.

As the only female in the class, I had hoped to hear outpourings about the challenges men faced in challenging homophobic social stereotypes, about their struggles with navigating masculinities, about ensuring that they model gender-appropriate heterosexual male social and sexual norms. Instead, I faced a room full of blank stares and complete silence. I left the course believing that perhaps these personal reflections between men and about men occur else-where—out of earshot of female classmates—in the gym? In the bar? In select conversations with certain other males? The issues of sex and gender in relation to our understanding of HIV and AIDS in Canada simply did not emerge.

Thankfully, other courses I took did lead to many heated conversations about how, for example, misogyny may impact the health of women, including the women whom men are intimately involved with, married to, have children with as well as men's role in HIV prevention strategies and infection rates among women in Canada. What emerged from these conversations and related media portrayals were two main themes. A silencing of ways in which masculinities, HIV, and AIDS were understood in the prevention/infection debate on the one hand, while on the other, a noticeable absence of the voices of women living with HIV or

AIDS. Even though media coverage in the mid-1990s began revealing some very concerning evidence of women becoming HIV positive through heterosexual sex with an infected male partner, for the most part media treatment perpetuated "othering" those perceived to be at risk. This meant focusing on injection drug users, sex workers, and gay men who were seen to be the "risk groups" for HIV. There was a strong media narrative about who is at risk despite the growing body of health research indicating that, as a blood-borne infection, HIV does not simply impact these select populations.

What was clearly and crucially absent from the media coverage was an in-depth discussion about heterosexual transmission of HIV based on the fact that, according to national data sources, most HIV positive women in Canada had contracted the virus this way. A great deal of media coverage of the World AIDS Conference in Vancouver in 1996 focused on the magic bullet of new medication that was paraded as the answer to this complex epidemic. But trading the "risk group" discourse for an HIV medication discourse was short-lived when the treatments were failing, particularly among populations with already complex lived experiences such as those who were unstably housed. But importantly, these new medications had not been tested on women due to women's exclusion from clinical drug trials, so it was not entirely surprising that women experienced significant challenges in embracing the magic bullet.

It was not until growing numbers of women became infected in Canada and mobilized for change that the discourse began to shift from gay men as the conduit for HIV infection to a more nuanced and inclusive understanding of the complex and intersecting determinants of HIV and AIDS. In fact, for heterosexual women, heterosexual transmission from unprotected sex with an HIV-infected male partner was one of the greatest risks for infection among women. However, even this fact failed to consider the many factors that place women at enhanced risk for infection, including women's economic, social, and cultural standing relative to men's. Epidemiological data continued to see high rates of new infections among men who have sex with men, and women continued to be largely absent from HIV prevention, treatment, and care infrastructure in Canada, including many AIDS service organizations.

Where was the prevention information for heterosexual women and for heterosexual men? Data collected at the time indicated that rates of transmission were increasing and yet about one quarter of those living with HIV remained unaware of their infection. Sadly, this still rings true today. Given the dearth of information on "heterosexual transmission" of HIV and the lack of women living with HIV included in HIV drug trials, I was not surprised to hear that women had more trouble adhering to HIV drug treatments based on drug trials with men. After reading a piece written in a local health magazine by an Ontario woman who described her HIV diagnosis and the lack of relevant prevention or treatment information for women, and the challenges in adhering to complex HIV drug treatment regimens, I became interested in understanding the unique challenges HIV-positive women experience in maintaining the level of adherence needed to maximally benefit from these new drug treatments.

In 1995 as I began a PhD, I considered this issue from a sex and gender-based perspective. Since women had been excluded from clinical trials for these new drug regimens, it was not surprising to find that women experienced both social and physiological issues with adherence. Unpredictable, and at times debilitating, side-effects emerged for women. Women had to hide their pills from those who were unaware of their HIV diagnosis for fear of HIV-related discrimination, of losing their children, their homes, or their family. These were just a few of the stories women shared with me over the years as they tried to maintain adherence.

As both improved medications and greater awareness of women's unique health and social care needs emerged, we saw a slow progression toward seeing HIV as a manageable, chronic disease. However, for many women who were diagnosed in the early days of the epidemic in Canada and who have survived, that is cold comfort. Issues of toxicity, heart-related health concerns, and social stigma, among others, remain important considerations today.

The issues of women and HIV remain intimately related to men, men's sexuality, masculinities, and fears. Years after completing my doctoral research, I was invited to attend a policy conference on HIV and gender in Dakar, Senegal. I recall sitting just inside a meeting room for a session focused on "Men who have sex with men" to get underway. Sheepishly, one person after another peered in and looked around as if searching for a friendly face before entering and then left the room. Those who came back, sat down as far away from the front of the room as possible. I remember leaning over to the South African Broadcasting Corporation (SABC) radio interviewer sitting next to me to ask if, as a woman, it was okay for me to be in the room. He reassured me that the situation was fine and that I should stay. Eventually the room filled, including with many imams and their colleagues.

The session began with four young men huddled around the microphone at the front of the room taking turns in various dialects to remind everyone in the room to look closely at their faces, to be able to notice if they went missing from the conference, to know that there are police nearby. They also pointed out that although they were men who have sex with other men, they were not looking to start a "gay pride" movement but rather they simply want to get on with their lives without fear of persecution for their same-sex sexual encounters. They also made it clear that they were brothers, husbands, and fathers and that many in the room knew of them as neighbours, as friends, as family members. Given the legal punishments sanctioned by government and religious leaders, these men were afraid for their lives. These efforts to recognize, if not normalize, same-sex encounters among men pointed out how fear of reprisal prevents many men from seeking health services, including sexual health and HIV testing services. And what is very clear is that these reprisals directly affect the women in their lives—wives, sisters, mothers, aunties. Access to accurate, timely and stigma-free HIV prevention information, care, and treatment is required for all regardless of how they may self-identify.

Although the absence of women in the early days of the epidemic in Canada cannot be forgotten, going forward, more attention must be given to the needs of cisgender and transgender women—both in terms of primary prevention as well as in terms of treatment options for those who become infected. So what, if anything, has changed? Medical treatments have advanced, but the social stigma surrounding the moral judgements about who is regarded as at-risk for HIV infection remains. With the Canadian government's recent reframing of HIV from a stand-alone illness to one that has become part of an integrated approach to sexually transmitted infections and blood-borne infections (STBBI), there is some hope for more widespread change to our national approach to STBBI prevention, care, treatment, and support.

While this shift may bring with it a lessening of the various forms of social stigma for women associated with HIV/AIDS, we need to ensure that we do not lose sight of the long history of the struggles women in Canada faced in HIV prevention and in relation to woman-specific care, treatment, and supports. To forget this history would serve to overlook the pioneers in the women and HIV work in Canada in terms of health and social care research, community mobilization, health equity, and activism. The future of women at risk or currently living with HIV will require a collective reframing of STBBIs to address both assumptions about HIV risk, as well as about "sex" and "gender," as key drivers in Canada. Still, women, remain largely a marginalized population in Canada when it comes to HIV prevention, treatment, and care, often coming second in the response to this ongoing epidemic.

DES CANCER AT AGE TWENTY: AN ACTIVIST IS BORN

Harriet Simand

I became a women's health activist at the age of twenty in 1981. And it happened not because of any ideological or political reasons, but because I was directly harmed by the pharmaceutical industry. I was a healthy young woman with no history of cancer anywhere in my family. Just before going off to university, I went for a check-up. The doctor examined me and said, "Did your mother ever take the drug DES [diethylstilbestrol] to prevent miscarriage when she was pregnant with you?" I had never heard of DES and had no clue what she was talking about. Within a week of that conversation, I had been diagnosed with vaginal clear-cell adenocarcinoma and whisked off to California for surgery. Later, I needed radiation back in Montreal when it was discovered the cancer had spread to my lymph nodes.

While I was recovering, my mother told me she had asked her doctor in 1971 if he had given her DES once the link to cancer had been established, and he said no, so I was never monitored. After my surgery, my mother went to her doctor to get her medical records because we learned that we might be able to get compensation from the drug companies. He held her records in his hands and refused to let her have them. She went to a lawyer who subpoenaed them, and that week they mysteriously "got lost."

This was my introduction to the women's health movement. Being naïve, I decided to write to the government to ask what had been done about DES because I was sure I was not the only Canadian affected by it. I was informed that DES was not a problem in Canada, only in the United States, but I knew this couldn't possibly be true since I was not adopted.

I began to do research, and was appalled to discover that early animal studies in the 1940s indicated DES caused cancer in rats, and that in a double-blind controlled study conducted in 1953, researchers found that DES was completely ineffective in preventing miscarriage, but it was still sold in Canada until 1971 when the link to vaginal cancer in daughters was made. After the thalidomide disaster in the early 1960s, the government had passed regulations requiring that drugs be shown to be effective to be able to come to market, but since DES was already being sold, it was not required to show it actually worked. It is now known that DES can cause a range of problems for daughters including ectopic pregnancy and T-shaped uteri, which can cause fertility issues. Mothers have a higher rate of breast cancer and sons can also have fertility issues.

My mother, Shirley, and I decided to channel our rage and sense of betrayal by starting DES Action Canada to try to alert other Canadian women. Our only support at the time came from DES Action USA, a volunteer group of mothers and daughters who had been affected in the United States. But there was nothing in Canada. The solidarity those women showed us enabled us to have the courage to do something in Canada. We created a pamphlet on the medical effects of DES on daughters, but we could not get the government or any organization to pay for the printing.

Undaunted, we reached out to the *Montreal Gazette* and local TV stations who covered our story. At the time, since we did not know how many people might have been affected, we gave out our home phone number. Suddenly, we were inundated with phone calls. My father was not particularly pleased that after the 11 p.m. news women were calling up asking him questions about vaginal cancer!

We were overwhelmed with the number of women contacting us. Fortunately I happened to attend a small conference on women and pharmaceuticals in 1982 and met Anne Rochon Ford and Barbara Mintzes, two veterans of the Canadian women's health movement, who agreed to help us by organizing groups in other parts of the country, arranging media conferences, and teaching us what it took to start a national organization.

As we branched out to Toronto, we were told that DES was only a problem in Quebec, not Ontario, but as soon as our story hit the papers, the phones started ringing. We were also told by members of the government and medical profession that we should not publicize the issue because informing women would "make them go hysterical." I stared at them, thinking, how I wish that someone had had the decency to tell me I needed medical care, and were more concerned about my health than about whether I might get angry. Maybe, just maybe, the appalling history of DES in Action Canada should cause women to be furious and organize instead of trying to sweep it under the carpet!

Over a period of twenty years we established groups across the country. One very important decision we made was that DES Canada would never ever accept money from pharmaceutical companies. Being effective and honest advocates for the DES-exposed meant that we had to be free to criticize the pharmaceutical industry.

By organizing local groups, we empowered DES mothers, daughters, and sons who had felt voiceless. We stood up for our rights and publicized the issue so that other DES-exposed people could receive the proper medical care. We learned that we could influence the government, pharmaceutical industry, and medical profession by speaking the truth and not backing down. And finally, we networked with other women's health groups who were facing similar issues of getting their message out when faced with a well-financed opposition.

We also felt that the DES story held important lessons for other women's health issues. We were concerned about the over-prescription of hormones for menopausal women. When we voiced our concerns, we were met with the argument that "there is no evidence the hormones are a risk." Years later, when studies were published showing that menopausal hormones were in fact a cancer danger to women, many specialists said that this was a complete surprise. Yet it was not a surprise at all for those of us working at DES Action. The message I have taken away from my experience is: Ask questions! Healthy women should not have to wait until a drug is proven to be dangerous; we need to know whether there is evidence the drug is safe! Stand up for what you believe in and refuse to be silenced.

CONCLUSION

Lorraine Greaves

Our health is central to our lives, our energies, and our well-being, and women and girls in Canada continue to enjoy the fruits of the amazing activism of the second-wave women's health movement. The tremendous rise of consciousness-raising (CR) activity in living rooms and halls across the continent in the 1960s and 1970s released a wellspring of ideas, emotions, frustrations, and plans, and laid bare scars, hurts, bonds, and passions. The second-wave women's movement emerged out of, and was fed by, those CR activities as women got together and shared information and experiences, often for the first time. It emerged in the context of progressive movements of the era such as the US-based civil rights and anti-war movements—and sometimes in response to ongoing sexism in the same progressive movements. It set the stage for immense changes for women.

Invariably consciousness-raising surfaced issues of the body as well as the mind and heart. The impetus for organizing around those issues was born of our frustration, anger, and need to govern our own bodies. We had a sense of some imposed collective ignorance and mystification about our bodies due to centuries of lost control over processes such as childbirth, contraception, abortion, and menstruation. As well, we developed a collective awareness that the information we did get about our bodies was filtered by a sexist, patriarchal medical system, with doctors as its agents and nurses as its handmaidens.

We also had a nagging feeling that we were not getting the facts from our point of view, and that we were not even considered reliable informants on our own health, health care, research, treatments, and diagnoses. Some conditions that were just part of living were deemed illnesses, and some illnesses were ignored. Hidden female experiences such as violence and sexual assault were not considered to be health issues, and overt experiences such as painful menses or traumatic childbirth were dismissed.

It was a lot to unravel. But it could not have been done alone, one woman by one woman. Once these fears and thoughts were found to be shared experiences, they gained mutual affirmation and were infused with credibility, and activism was born. Publications were written, self-help instructions were crafted, and handmade information sheets shared. Meetings were called. Lots of meetings. Collectives formed and actions began. This book describes some of those processes as well as the outcomes. It has helped us realize the immense job of filling the void of ignorance, self-blame, isolation, and the dereliction of the health care system when it came to women's health.

What difference did all of this organizing make? What are the links between the activism described in this collection and our current health concerns, care, policies, and research? The fruits of these activities were robust, detailed, often ingenious, and, in many cases, forced permanent changes in our society. For example, the notion that bodily autonomy was essential for women and that laws and regulations were directly impacting that autonomy was borne out by the long-term abortion rights movement. Relentless organizing and risk-taking were emblematic of the quest for abortions, illegal and legal. Decades of activism, legal challenges, criminal prosecutions, and quiet suffering ultimately won the day for women's right to choose.

The entire issue of reproductive freedom, including access to contraception, the right to choose not to have children, or to time pregnancy, or just to control fertility and take charge of our sexuality, independent of boyfriends, parents, husbands, priests, or other parties, was a key link to women's economic well-being. It gave women and girls freedom from early pregnancy, rushed marriages, unwanted children, lifelong childbearing, caregiving, restricted incomes, job loss, and poor health. The ramifications of controlling our fertility have been increased labour force engagement, more economic independence, smaller families, higher ages of motherhood, and fewer unwanted children.

We have gained something more intangible as well. Then, in the days before the beginnings of the second-wave women's health movement, there was the notion that men or patriarchal systems defined our health, including what was a diagnosis or an appropriate treatment, or what was ignored or dismissed about our bodies, or even what they should look like. Now, this has taken a backseat to women-defined body-positive movements, discussions about tax-free menstruation products, public breastfeeding, challenges to diagnostic and prescribing practices, and consumer-driven advocacy for better prevention and treatment of conditions such as breast cancer or heart disease.

Then, there was the notion that women's trauma, violence, substance use, and mental health issues were to be hidden and ignored, or worse, over-medicalized and suppressed with a surfeit of psychoactive drugs. Now, women's and girls' experiences of child sexual abuse, sexual assault, and domestic violence are recognized as public health issues, and health practitioners receive training in best practices on these matters. Not all is done, however. Women's substance use and addiction, especially when mixed with pregnancy or mothering, has had a much harder go of it, but is slowly pushing through a fog of stigma into a more sensitive and informed public discussion. Certainly, women's health issues are far from solved or remedied, but the second-wave activists had a lot to do with setting a new course.

It is no surprise that a good portion of the energy of the second-wave women's movement was focused on the relentless development of alternatives to what the health care system was offering—or not offering. As we have read, these "pop-up" services were sometimes fleeting, and sometimes not. They often operated on low overhead, volunteer work, collectives or flat organizations, and, of course, with not much money. They thrived on generating new information, providing education, a do-it-yourself approach, and taking risks.

Ultimately, demands for funding were made and sometimes met, and governments got involved. This often meant that these services evolved into a clash with pressures of professionalism and accountability, as they either entered the system and got credentials, or dissolved or went rogue. These were very debatable tensions that marked the service sector of the women's health movement. Some of these services split over these pressures to conform. Some anti-violence services resisted these pressures, and still do. Some midwives went rogue and offered services independently, and others, such as sexual assault services, were mainstreamed into hospitals or clinics. As we have read, feminist women who worked in "the system" as either doctors, bureaucrats, or politicians often became the midwives of many women's health projects and services as they made these difficult transitions.

But what of the larger issues? Not the issues pertaining to our-selves, our bodies, and our services, but the ones reflected in our systems? As the second-wave women's health movement matured and some of the initial wounds were staunched, collective efforts to look at the underpinnings of health and health care emerged. Then, there was no (broadly and positively defined) women's health research and no definitions of sex and gender to guide re-searchers, funders, and users of the evidence that was produced. Now, Canada has the only institute of gender and health research in the world, and the federal government requires a sex and gender-based analysis of all programmes and policies.

Then, the view of women's health focused on pregnancy and birth outcomes. Or on how to cure women's malaise from living in a patriarchy. Now, women's health is about the whole life course and the social context of health, including the direct ramifications of gender inequity. It is about seeking gaps in know-ledge and finding the rocks that need upturning, such as doctors who sexually assault patients. It is about the mistakes and faults in our system, and the gaps that reflect ongoing prejudice. Now, we are able to have discussions about over-prescription of pain medication, the exploitation of women by the tobacco, alcohol, and pharmaceutical industries, and how to support women with addictions in keeping their babies close by.

Then, there was a narrow medical view of health and illness; now there is a wide recognition that the social determinants of health (such as education, environments, culture, income, and gender) matter as much if not more to good health, and that equity is intertwined with health outcomes and access to appropri-ate care. There are consumer movements to pursue the causes of cancer, not just running after cures, and widespread worries about toxic environments and ill health. There is acute concern about Indigenous health and welfare in Canada, and the direct links be-tween poverty and health. Not all of these current movements are due to, or solely dependent upon, women's health activism, but their roots and concerns were seeded in the second-wave women's movement. It is fair to say the table was set by feminists for some of our key twenty-first-century concerns in health.

Most critical, however, is that our voices now count in defining our own health needs, our own care, and our own experiences of natural bodily processes. This recognition and placing of women's voices in women's health is the lasting legacy of the second-wave women's health movement. Women's health was, and remains, both political and personal. Even now.

CONTRIBUTORS

MARSHA ABLOWITZ has worked in community mental health. She was active in such feminist groups as the Western Canada Feminist Counselling Association and the Judaism, Feminism, and Psychology Association. Marsha ran Vancouver's first women's self defense groups, first lesbian support groups, and first incest survivors' groups before these issues became mainstream. She now writes as part of Quirk-e, the Queer Imaging & 'Riting Kollective for Elders, whose most recent book is *Basically Queer: An Intergenerational Introduction to LGBTQA2S+ Lives.*

GHISLAINE ALLEYNE has, since leaving the CWHN, continued her work as a communication and technology specialist with the University of Winnipeg and the University of Manitoba. She is a board member of *Herizons*—Canada's longest running feminist magazine—and uses her influence to ensure that women's diversity and strengths are recognized and represented in all aspects of her work.

CHERYL ANDERSON is a clinical associate professor at the School of Population and Public Health, Faculty of Medicine, University of British Columbia; panel physician for Immigration, Refugees and Citizenship Canada; and formerly a medical health officer in Vancouver, BC. A pioneer of midwifery services in British Columbia in the early 1970s, she practiced midwifery from 1972 until she became a physician in 1983. She also helped establish a midwifery education programme in BC in the 1980s, accredited by Washington state, whose graduates were amongst the first registered midwives in BC when midwifery was legalized there in 1998.

BETH ATCHESON specialized in the regulation of financial institutions and charities. Her volunteer work with the Ontario Committee on the Status of Women led to engagement in the women's constitutional lobby. Beth co-authored the study *Women and Legal Action,* leading to the formation of LEAF and the LEAF Foundation. She has served as member of the Canadian Human Rights Tribunal and of the National Advisory Council for the Canadian Human Rights Museum.

CONSTANCE BACKHOUSE has taught as a professor of law at the University of Western Ontario (1979–1999) and the University of Ottawa (2000 to the present). She has published a number of prize-winning books, including: *Petticoats and Prejudice: Women and Law in 19th-Century Canada; Challenging Times: The Women's Movement in Canada and the United States; Colour-Coded: A Legal History of Racism in Canada, 1900–1950; Carnal Crimes: Sexual Assault Law in Canada, 1900–1975;* and *Claire L'Heureux-Dubé: A Life.*

WENDY BARRETT was a well-known body therapist in Vancouver before her retirement. Her original training was as a physiotherapist in Britain and she used this training as she moved into body-centred psychotherapy through her involvement with Cold Mountain Institute (now Hollyhock) on Cortes Island, BC in the 1970s. She co-facilitated groups there and had a private practice in Vancouver for many years.

GWYNNE BASEN has, over her long lifespan, been a community organizer, a writer, a women's health activist, a documentary film-maker, an educator, and a farmer—her current (pre)occupation. The common thread in all these diverse endeavours has been her desire to make the world a better place.

SHARON BATT is an author and feminist activist based in Halifax. Following two decades of work as a magazine editor and writer, notably with the feminist magazine *Branching Out* and the consumer protection magazine *Protect Yourself,* a cancer diagnosis led her to activism in the breast cancer movement. She also began to explore health politics in her writing. Her books *Patient*

No More (1994) and *Health Advocacy Inc.* (2017) combine journalism, memoir, and scholarship.

SUSAN BAZILLI is the director of the International Women's Rights Project (IWRP). A feminist lawyer, educator, activist, trainer, advocate, and writer, Susan has worked for thirty years on women's equality rights, and, in particular, on issues of women, peace, and security. Her advocacy work has included legal director of the Metro Action Committee on Violence Against Women (METRAC); founder of the Ontario Women's Justice Network; executive director of the California Alliance Against Domestic Violence; manager of the Southern African Women's Legal Rights Initiative; and special adviser on violence against women to the American Bar Association in Moscow.

MADELINE BOSCOE has worked as executive director of a community health centre since leaving the CWHN in 2010, and is now managing community services for those living with mental illness in North Vancouver. She is a member of the Sex/Gender Methods Group within the Campbell and Cochrane Collaboration and continues to advocate for equity and healthy public policy that reflect the needs and perspectives of the most marginalized in society. Madeline is struck by how the challenges outlined in her article remain relevant but sadly, without the advocacy infrastructure and national presence the CWHN provided, still need to be addressed.

CARRIE BOURASSA is research chair in Indigenous & Northern Health, the scientific director of the Institute of Indigenous Peoples' Health at the Canadian Institutes of Health Research, and senior scientist at Health Sciences North Research Institute in Sudbury, Ontario. She served as a professor of Indigenous Health Studies at First Nations University of Canada for fifteen years, was a member of the Canadian Institute for Health Research Standing Committee on Ethics for six years, and is currently a member of the College of New Scholars, Artists and Scientists of the Royal Society of Canada, the Saskatchewan RESOLVE Steering Committee, International Indigenous Dementia Research Network, and a member of the Waakebiness-Bryce Institute for Indigenous Health at the University of Toronto. Dr. Bourassa is Métis, belonging to the Regina Riel Métis Council #34.

BARBARA BOURRIER-LACROIX has been working in public libraries since her time at CWHN, most recently as a collections librarian at Winnipeg Public Library where she advocates for a collection that is inclusive and represents the city's diverse population. She has served on the board of Réseau-action femmes (Manitoba) and the Mental Health Advisory Council of the Winnipeg Regional Health Authority.

KAREN BUHLER has been a family physician practising in Vancouver for more than thirty years, the past seven with a focused practice on maternity care, and a clinical assistant professor. Instrumental in helping midwifery become regulated in BC, Karen was head of the Department of Family Practice at BC Women's Hospital and founded the Sue Harris Family Practice Research Fund that provides grants for new researchers in Family Medicine women's health. She is currently a member of the Perinatal Addictions Service providing clinical care to pregnant and birthing women and their newborns. Promoting and facilitating group care for pregnancy (Connecting Pregnancy and Connecting Families) and bringing Mindfulness meditation practice into pregnancy care are two of her current passions.

CAMILLE BUSH followed her 1974 apprenticeship at the Vancouver Birth Centre with practising midwifery in the West Kootenays for eleven years. After becoming a licensed midwife in Washington State and fearing that midwifery might never become legal in BC, she earned a bachelor's degree in nursing. This enabled her to become part of the BC Women's Midwifery pilot programme and eventually catching the first BC registered midwife baby on January 1, 1998. Now, twenty years later, Camille has just retired from clinical practice but occasionally teaches aspiring midwives at UBC.

PAULA CAPLAN is a clinical and research psychologist, and was formerly head of the Centre for Women's Studies in Education, a full professor at the Ontario Institute for Studies in Education (OISE), and a lecturer in women's studies at the University of Toronto. She holds academic positions at Harvard University, the Washington College of Law, and Brown University. At Harvard, she is teaching Harvard's first course in the psychology of sex and gender. She is the author of ten books and editor of one. Paula has been awarded many honours for her work in the areas of women and psychology, women and body image, psychiatric diagnoses and their creations, sexual and child abuse, and women and science.

JAN CHRISTILAW is an obstetrician-gynecologist in Vancouver. She has held a number of leadership positions including president of the Society of Obstetrician-Gynecologists of Canada, and president of BC Women's Hospital from 2008–2017. She has been active in global women's health for many years and in 2017 was appointed to the Order of Canada for her leadership in women's health nationally and globally. Other awards include YWCA Woman of Distinction (2015) and the Queen's Diamond Jubilee Medal. Jan continues to work as a gynecologist in Vancouver, as a clinical professor of obstetrics-gynecology at the University of British Columbia. She also presently works with several community organizations in Vancouver.

CONNIE CLEMENT is the scientific director of the National Collaborating Centre for Determinants of Health at St Francis Xavier University, one of six Canadian public health knowledge centres. Connie was a Women Healthsharing collective member from 1978–1996, including serving as managing editor for two years. Connie has, among other positions, been a policy director at Toronto Public Health and executive director of Health Nexus. She divides her time between Toronto Island and Nova Scotia.

LEAH COHEN (1945–2007) was a prominent feminist, activist, and scholar in Toronto, Canada. She is the author of *Small Expectations: Society's Betrayal of Older Women* (1984), a provocative analysis of women's marginalization as they age that also contained a variety of creative and compelling societal responses to these experiences. She was a celebrated journalist on issues affecting women and is also co-author of *The Secret Oppression: Sexual Harassment of Working Women* (1979), the first substantial Canadian work on the sexual harassment of women in the workplace.

MELANIE CONN is a long-time feminist and community activist and one of the founders of the Vancouver Women's Health Collective. She has continued to work in the community economic development and co-op sectors as a consultant and practitioner with a focus on women's inclusion and economic security. Melanie is also a founding member of the Women's Economic Council and its current president.

LOUISE DESMARAIS has been employed by the Quebec government for many years, including eleven years at the Council on the Status of Women. For over thirty years, she was active in the Quebec feminist movement for the Right to Abortion. Her recent book, *La bataille de l'avortement, Chronique québécoise* (2016), tells the story of the abortion struggle between 1970 and 2010. Retired since 2007, she devotes her time as a consultant to women's and community groups.

MARY HAMPTON, academic research coordinator for RESOLVE Saskatchewan, is professor of psychology at Luther College, University of Regina, and research associate for the Saskatchewan Population Health and Evaluation Research Unit (SPHERU). She and her co-applicants currently hold a five-year, million-dollar CURA/SSHRC grant entitled "Rural and northern community response to intimate partner violence." Mary Hampton is a registered clinical psychologist in Saskatchewan.

REBECCA FOX, as a teenager, joined a women's consciousness raising group that met in the offices of Our Bodies Ourselves. She still has a thirty-cent copy of the original publication. She later joined the Vancouver Women's Heath Collective, where she was both a volunteer and a staff person for many years. The women's health movement has remained a part of her life as a health care worker, mother, and advocate for social change that includes support for science and our Canadian health care system.

SANDRA (SANDY) SUSAN FRIEDMAN is an educator and therapist in the area of girls' and women's development and issues, and in eating disorder and obesity treatment and prevention. She has extensive experience in facilitating professional training workshops and community education seminars across Canada and in the United States. Her group programme *Just for Girls* has become the prototype for a variety of programmes that address the health and social risks facing girls as they grow up. She is the author of *When Girls Feel Fat: Helping Girls Through Adolescence*; *Body Thieves: Help Girls Accept Their Natural Bodies and Become Physically Active*; *Just for Girls*; and *Nurturing Girlpower: Integrating Eating Disorder Prevention/Intervention Skills into Your Practice*.

JEANNETTE FROST graduated from UBC with a BSc in zoology. Post-graduation she worked as a lab technician and volunteered at the front desk of the Pine Free Clinic, where she became involved in the Vancouver pro-choice movement. This exposure to the women's movement and, in particular, to women's health care led to her involvement in the Vancouver Women's Health Collective's Diaphragm Fitters Group. She volunteered with the group for more than five years, until the group folded. She changed career directions and completed a technical programme in building mechanical services. She currently designs and project-manages institutional projects, with a specialty in health care facilities. In her spare time, she keeps busy travelling, cycling, and hiking.

JACQUELINE (JACQUIE) GAHAGAN is a medical sociologist and a full professor of health promotion in the Faculty of Health at Dalhousie University. Jacquie holds research associate positions with the European Union Centre of Excellence, the Health Law Institute, the Beatrice Hunter Cancer Research Institute, and the Healthy Populations Institute. Her programme of research focuses on addressing health inequities among populations at high risk for poor health outcomes through the development of effective policy and programming interventions. Before joining Dalhousie University, Jacquie worked in public health in the areas of harm reduction, HIV/HCV prevention, and tobacco use cessation.

LORRAINE GREAVES is a long-time activist and researcher in women's health, especially on issues of trauma, violence, addiction, and tobacco use. She is the author or editor of 11 books. She is senior investigator at the Centre of Excellence for Women's Health in British Columbia, and is its founding executive director. She is the founding director of the Centre for Research on Violence Against Women and Children. She led the health committee at the National Action Committee on the Status of Women, was the committee's vice president in the 1980s, and sat on the Interim Governing Council of the Canadian Institutes of Health Research.

CAROL HERBERT is professor emerita of family medicine at Western University and adjunct professor in the School of Population and Public Health, Faculty of Medicine at the University of British Columbia. She was a pioneer in developing services for sexually assaulted adults and children in BC and was co-founder and co-director of the Sexual Assault Service for Vancouver. A recognized leader in inter-professional education and collaborative practice, women's health and mentorship of academic women, she has chaired or served on multiple task forces on health policy and health professional education. She is currently a senior associate at In-Source, a Vancouver-based consulting company that applies a complex adaptive systems lens to health care issues.

ANDREA FOCHS KNIGHT began her work in women's health in Fredericton in 1975 as a member of the editorial board of *Equal Times: Fredericton's First Women's Newspaper*, coordinator of the women's centre, and co-founder of the city's first rape crisis centre. In Toronto, she became involved with the Ontario Coalition for Abortion Clinics and then worked as executive director of the Toronto Morgentaler Clinic from 1984 to 1989. She also served as a health policy advisor to two Ontario NDP ministers of health, where one of her areas of focus was women's health. Andrea works as a freelance editor in Toronto.

MICHELE LANDSBERG is a Toronto journalist and author. She wrote columns for the *Toronto Star* for twenty-five years and, for three years, was New York columnist for *The Globe and Mail*. She has written four books, been awarded six honourary degrees, has received the Person's Medal, and is an Officer of the Order of Canada. She is married to Stephen Lewis, CC; they have three children and four grandchildren.

KELSEY LUCYK is a PhD graduate from the Department of Community Health Sciences, University of Calgary, where she completed her dissertation on the history of the social determinants of health in Canada. She is a health policy researcher who is passionate about health equity and social justice. At present, Kelsey is completing a Mitacs Canadian Science Policy Fellowship with the Canadian government.

DIANA MAJURY was one of the founding members of Women Healthsharing who published *Healthsharing* magazine in the 1980s. She has been active on women's health issues in a variety of contexts before and since then, including the Toronto Women's Health Clinic Project, the National Network on Environments and Women's Health, the Regulated Health Professions Advisory Committee and the ECHO project. She has taught in the Law and Legal Studies Department at Carleton University since 1991, focusing on equality and human rights.

KIM MCKAY-MCNABB currently has a practice as an Indigenous therapist, researcher, and clinician. The research Dr. McKay-McNabb conducts is led by First Nation communities and is community-based with a focus on holistic health and guided by teachings from the Knowledge Keepers within Treaty 4 Territories and beyond. She is from George Gordon First Nation located in Treaty

4 Territory. Her most recent publication is "Miýo-pimātisiwin developing Indigenous cultural responsiveness theory (ICRT): Improving Indigenous health and well-being."

MARILOU MCPHEDRAN, a feminist human rights lawyer and professor, was appointed as an independent senator to the Parliament of Canada in 2016. She chaired Canada's first independent inquiry into the sexual abuse of patients that reported in 1991, a second such inquiry that reported in 2001, and a third that reported in 2016.

COLLEEN MACQUARRIE, professor in the Psychology Department, University of Prince Edward Island and active in feminist organizations for more than thirty years, is an academic activist and developmental health researcher. Her research integrates the perspectives of a feminist liberation psychology framework with an intersectional lifespan approach to examine how environments support individuals' and families' quality of life. Her collaborative approach informs critical participatory action research to initiate a range of social justice projects including reproductive justice and access to safe abortion services.

KAREN MESSING is an ergonomics researcher at the CINBIOSE research centre and professor emerita in the Department of Biological Sciences at the Université du Québec à Montréal (UQAM). She does most of her research in the context of formal partnerships between UQAM and various community groups, usually unions or women's groups. She is the author of *Pain and Prejudice: What Science Can Learn About Work from the People Who Do It* and *One-eyed Science: Occupational Health and Working Women*. She has received the Governor General of Canada's Persons Award for advancing the status of women (2009), as well as various academic awards.

RADHA NAYAR has been a consultant in the non-profit sector in Toronto for eleven years. She works to build the capacity of the women's sector and the settlement sector in their heroic efforts to address complex needs in the communities they serve. She is a fierce feminist, a *kundalini* yoga practitioner, and a singer. She is a loving friend and daughter. She is inspired by the new generation of young racialized women getting ready to take over the world.

FRANCINE ODETTE is a disabled feminist working on issues of violence against women with disabilities and access to services. Currently, she is working as a counsellor for women with disabilities.

INGRID PACEY is a psychiatrist who has worked her whole career from a feminist perspective, primarily with women, most often with childhood sexual abuse as well as the other issues that women face in a patriarchal society. She found support for her work from other women, particularly once the Feminist Counselling Association was formed. She had not found it in psychiatric training or psychiatric theory. Ingrid is still working part-time and continues to speak up about the need for the feminist perspective in therapy and in the role of women in society particularly now that she has a granddaughter (and a grandson who needs to learn too).

SARAH PAYNE trained as a midwife in the UK after training as a nurse in Canada. As well as a private practice, she worked in the Downtown Eastside of Vancouver in a community programme for pregnant women struggling with substance use. Sarah also pioneered a twelve-bed unit at BC Women's Hospital (BCW) for pregnant, substance-using women. She has been awarded the Governor General's Award of the Meritorious Service Decoration for her work at BCW.

N. JANE PEPINO is a Toronto lawyer. Actively involved in women's issues, she has been a member of the Ontario Human Rights Commission; the first woman appointed to the Toronto Police Commission; the founding chair of both METRAC (Action Committee on Violence against Women and Children) and the Ontario Women's Health Council. She has twice served full terms as a board member of Women's College Hospital (1995–2001; 2011–2017), and twice served as chair of the board.

NANCY POOLE is currently the director of the Centre of Excellence for Women's Health, a virtual non-profit research centre focused on sex and gendered approaches to health, with strong roots in policy, practice, academic and community networks. In this role, Nancy is still preoccupied forty years on, with women and substance use research and action, building on the early knowledge exchange work on the intersections among benzodiazepines, alcohol, and gender-based violence.

JERILYNN C. PRIOR is an endocrinology professor (University of British Columbia) working on women's health. She studies menstrual cycles, the effects of ovulation and its disturbances on women's later life osteoporotic fracture, heart attack, and breast cancer risks. She is the founder (2002) of the Centre for Menstrual Cycle and Ovulation Research (CeMCOR) whose website (www.cemcor.ca) makes informative, empowering information available worldwide garnering 3,500 to 7,000 page-views per day. She authored the award-winning *Estrogen's Storm Season: Stories of Perimenopause*.

ANNE ROCHON FORD is a long-time researcher, writer, and advocate in the field of women's health. She is the former executive director of the Canadian Women's Health Network and the National Network on Environments and Women's Health. In addition to multiple book chapters, she has published books on women and drug policy and the history of women's admission to the University of Toronto.

MARGARET SCAIA is a full-time teaching professor at the University of Victoria School of Nursing. Her area of research is women's labour history in post-war Western Canada, with an emphasis on nursing.

KAREN SEABROOKE has worked for international social justice organizations in the Netherlands, the UK, and Canada. She joined Inter Pares in 1982, managing programmes in Canada, the Caribbean, and in South and South-east Asia. She was a co-founder of Women's Health Interaction, coordinator of the Side Effects project, and has served on the boards of women's addiction centres and battered women's shelters in Ottawa, as well as on advisory committees of national and international agencies focused on women's health.

HARRIET SIMAND is a women's health activist who founded DES Action Canada with her mother, Shirley, after she was diagnosed with DES-related cancer at the age of twenty. She is currently an elementary school teacher in Toronto who teaches her students to use their voices to speak up when they see injustice. She was the recipient of the Prime Minister's Award for Teaching Excellence in 2012. Before beginning her career in teaching, she was a human rights lawyer for seven years.

RUTH SIMKIN is a retired physician, currently living in Victoria, BC. She has worked as a family physician and in hospice. She has a specialist degree in palliative care as well as family medicine. In 2010 she started writing books and has published memoirs, short stories, and a novel; she has also written countless medical papers and contributed to textbooks as well as doing many presentations.

BETH SYMES is a lawyer in private practice in Toronto. She was counsel for CARAL in the *Winnipeg v. G* case at the Supreme Court of Canada. Beth was counsel for the Medical Staff Association when the government was forcing Women's College Hospital to merge with Sunnybrook and she served on the first Board of WCH after the hospital achieved autonomy once again.

WILFREDA E. THURSTON is a professor emerita in the Department of Community Health Sciences, University of Calgary. Her specialization is population health with a focus on systemic determinants, particularly gender and racism as they affect women and Indigenous peoples. She was involved in the early women's health movement and maintained an action-policy-focused programme of research.

JANET TRAINOR received an MA from the University of Victoria in 2015. Her Canadian history thesis sought to discover whether lesbians were becoming extinct in a new age of identity politics. Her part of this book examines the elusive lesbian in the Canadian health care system.

SARI TUDIVER is a cultural anthropologist with a longstand-ing commitment to global social justice and improving women's health. Over four decades, she has engaged in teaching, research, gender-sensitive policy analysis and advocacy in academic and community health settings, with civil society organizations and with the federal government. In the early 1980s, Sari was a found-ing member of the Manitoba Side Effects Tour Committee and a decade later, of the Canadian Women's Health Network. She chairs the board of directors of Inter Pares, a Canadian feminist organization promoting global equality and social justice through international cooperation.

BILKIS VISSANDJÉE is a professor at the School of Nursing, University of Montreal. She is a Fellow of the Canadian Academy of Health Sciences and a researcher at the Institute of Public Health Research at the Université de Montréal. Her contributions to the scientific community along with national and international- ly based partners highlight the importance of accounting for sex, gender, migration, and ethnicity for providing quality and equity sensitive care within a diversified socio-cultural context. She was a board member of the Institute of Gender and Health, and the advisory body at the Ministry of Health in Quebec for access to health services.

ANN WHEATLEY has been active in the movement for repro- ductive justice in Prince Edward Island since 1988, the year of the Morgentaler decision. She is currently a co-chair of Abortion Access Now, the group that, with the support of LEAF and women from across Canada, challenged Prince Edward Island's discriminatory and unlawful abortion policy. As a result of the legal challenge, after more than thirty years, women finally have access to abortion services in Prince Edward Island.

SUSAN WHITE was assistant executive director of the Canadian Women's Health Network for thirteen years. Her main interests are the impact of racism on health and the health challenges of Indigenous and newcomer women and women of colour. After the CWHN office closed in 2013, Susan continued as the secretary-treasurer of the board. Her main goal is to preserve the rich information legacy of CWHN through its website (www. cwhn.ca) and the archiving of more than thirty years of records in the Canadian Women's Movement Archives.

ELIZABETH WHYNOT is a medical doctor who has been a family practitioner, public health officer, hospital administrator, and health consultant. She is the co-founder of the Vancouver Sexual Assault Service and was president of BC Women's Hospital from 2000 to 2008. Currently she is the vice-chair of the First Nations Health Authority board of directors and works as a part- time locum physician at the Vancouver Native Health Society and other community clinics.

WENDY WILLIAMS is a registered nurse whose feminism led her to work with the three levels of government as well as civil society agencies. She was the CEO of Planned Parenthood Newfoundland and of the NL Advisory Council on the Status of Women, a provincial think-tank; working as a nurse at an abortion clinic in Vancouver; and being elected to St John's city council. She was vice-president of the National Action Committee on the

Status of Women and a founding board member of the first transition house in Newfoundland. For two terms she also chaired Vancouver's first Women's Advisory Committee, work for which the City of Vancouver awarded her its Civic Award of Excellence.

ELLEN WOODSWORTH is an international speaker on urban issues using a gendered intersectional lens. In Vancouver, where she is a former city councillor, she founded and remains chair of Women Transforming Cities International Society (www.womentransformingcities.org), created the Hot Pink Paper Municipal Campaign, spoke at UN Habitat 3, and launched the Women-Friendly Cities Challenge (www.womenfriendlycitieschallenge.org) at World Urban Forum 9. Ellen also served on the national committee that created Advancing Equity and Inclusion: A Guide for Municipalities, a UN Habitat 3 Urban solution.

LINDE ZINGARO has spent forty years in direct service delivery, advocacy, and training with regard to the consequences of childhood trauma for adolescents and adults, and providing public education and professional development for programmes in Canada, the US, and Japan. In private clinical practice since 1985, she completed a PhD in educational studies at the University of British Columbia, and her adapted thesis has been published as *Speaking Out: Storytelling for Social Change*.

ENDNOTES

[1] Jane Austen, *Northanger Abbey* (Harmondsworth, UK: Penguin, 1972), 123–24.

[2] Barbara Freeman, *Beyond Bylines* (Wilfred Laurier Press, 2011).

[3] The first Canadian criminal law on abortion was passed in 1869. It incorporated pre-Confederation provincial statutes and provided for a penalty of life imprisonment for the person procuring the miscarriage of a pregnant female. Abortion would remain illegal until Parliament passed the *Criminal Law Amendment Act*, 1968–69, S.C. 1969–68, c. 38. This significant reform bill retained the overall prohibition on abortion, but created an exception, described in detail later in this article. The relevant section became section 251 of the *Criminal Code* when the statutes were consolidated in 1970, and that is how it was known during the work on the TWHC (RSC 1970, c. C-34). Homosexuality was also decriminalized in this legislation. The sale of contraceptives was decriminalized at the same time in a separate piece of legislation. See: Child Birth by Choice Trust, ed., *No Choice: Canadian Women Tell Their Stories of Illegal Abortion* (Toronto: Childbirth by Choice Trust, 1998).

[4] We sought, and received, professional advice from expert and generous people. Dr. M. Corinne Devlin, an obstetrician/gynaecologist from Hamilton, Ontario, acted as chief medical consultant. Dr. Sheila Cohen was also enormously helpful and supportive. Susan Lieberman, CA, advised us on accounting and cost projection. Geraldine Gonis, a student at the University of Toronto School of Architecture, created the architectural plans for the space at Lucliffe Place, a high-rise, multi-use building in downtown Toronto, close to all transportation. Dr. Richard Osborn, then "Chairman" of the Division of Preventative Medicine and Biostatistics at the University of Toronto, undertook to conduct an external examination of the operation of the TWHC and prepared a proposal explaining how that would be done. The TWHC logo was created by Ross Arnold.

[5] RSO 1990, c. P.40

[6] "There has been considerable debate over the limits of federal responsibility for, or jurisdiction over, abortion. Because abortion requires a medical procedure, it is a health issue. To the extent that it is desirable to prohibit abortions, or establish the conditions under which they cannot be performed, jurisdiction will lie with the federal government, because prohibition of an action for health or moral reasons is constitutionally associated with criminalization. To the extent that it is desirable to regulate abortions, or the conditions under which they can be performed, jurisdiction will lie with the government that has the right or duty to regulate health issues.... The establishment, maintenance and management of hospitals is specifically placed under provincial authority by section 92(7) of the *Constitution Act, 1867*." Mollie Dunsmuir, *Abortion: Constitutional and Legal Developments*

(Ottawa: Library of Parliament, 89-10 E, 1998), http://www.publications. gc.ca/Collection-R/LoPBdP/CIR/8910-e.htm, accessed on January 23, 2018.

[7] "The Toronto Women's Health Clinic: A Proposal, prepared in January 1978, for presentation to the Honourable Dennis R. Timbrell, Minister of Health for the Province of Ontario."

[8] The Royal Commission on the Status of Women reported in 1970 (http:// epe.lac-bac.gc.ca/100/200/301/pco-bcp/commissions-ef/bird1970-eng/ bird1970-eng.htm, accessed on January 23, 2018). It commented, with respect to section 251 of the *Criminal Code* and in particular on the requirement that abortions could only be accessed through a therapeutic abortion committee (TAC): "This formal procedure may make it even more difficult for some women to obtain a therapeutic abortion than it was in the past. The principal benefactor of this law is the medical profession which will know exactly under what conditions a therapeutic abortion can be performed and criminal responsibility avoided. It can even be argued, and illustrated by the experience of other countries, that a therapeutic abortion committee has the effect of reducing the number of abortions performed by a hospital" [footnote omitted], RCSW *Report*, 283–84. The majority recommended that the *Criminal Code* be amended to permit abortion by a qualified medical practitioner on the sole request of any woman pregnant for twelve weeks or less, and to permit abortion by a qualified practitioner at the request of a pregnant woman for more than twelve weeks if the doctor is convinced that the continuation of the pregnancy would endanger the physical or mental health of the woman, or if there is substantial risk that if a child were born it would be greatly handicapped either mentally or physically (RCSW *Report*, 286–87). Three commissioners issued "Separate Statements," a calibrated attempt to avoid taking away from the unanimity of their recommendations. Commissioner Doris Ogilvie opposed abortion on principle. Commissioner Elsie Gregory MacGill viewed abortion in all circumstances as a matter between a woman and her doctor. Commissioner Jacques Henripin supported section 251 of the *Criminal Code* with some modifications and additionally observed, "What is important now is that an honest effort be made, in hospitals and by doctors, to set up the machinery which the law provides for its application and which is still sadly lacking."

[9] Constance noted at our meeting that francophone women had been particularly effective in the course of events in Québec. Section 251 did not contain a requirement that any accredited or approved hospital in Canada have a therapeutic abortion committee. The federal government likely took shelter under constitutional law to avoid including such a requirement, as hospitals were so clearly under provincial jurisdiction. Such shelter also helped the federal government avoid some of the enormous political controversy of section 251 because it put any decision about day-to-day access to abortion in the hands of another level of government. In many parts of Canada, more so in Québec, many hospitals were Catholic hospitals and they refused to have TACs. Women in Québec, most of whom were francophone, could only look to public hospitals there, which were mostly anglophone. Allowing for abortions to be done in clinics relieved several

pressures in Québec. As charges under the *Criminal Code* are laid through the provincial justice system, it followed that Québec refused to lay any further charges against Dr. Morgentaler. He would be charged later in other provinces and eventually another one of his charges came before the Supreme Court of Canada after the coming into force of the Canadian Charter of Rights and Freedoms in 1982. Section 251 would be struck down as unconstitutional and Dr. Morgentaler vindicated in *R. v. Morgentaler* [1988]1 S.C.R. 30.

[10] *R. v. Morgentaler,* [1988] 1 S.C.R. 30.

[11] The Badgley report estimated that for every five women who obtained an abortion in Canada at least one left the country for this purpose: Between 1970 and 1975, 50,000 Canadian women underwent abortions in the *US Report of the Committee on the Operation of the Abortion Law* (Ottawa, 1977), 80–81.

[12] Under section 251, TACs could only be created in "accredited" or "approved" hospitals. Our research indicated that the TWHC could never meet the requirements of an "accredited" hospital, partly because it had to be a more full-service facility, and partly because it had to be in operation for at least a year before accreditation. Ontario was not creating any more "approved" private hospitals, but it was open to create an "approved" public hospital, that is, a hospital under the *Public Hospitals Act.* There were specialized clinics approved as public hospitals.

[13] In the course of our project research in 1977, we visited a Buffalo clinic. Beth A, Beth S, and Constance, together with Dr. Marion Powell (then a professor of medicine at the University of Toronto) squeezed ourselves into a small car loaned by some kind friend. We were warned by the Buffalo clinic to tell the truth at the international border, and, if asked, to declare that we were going to that clinic. At the border we were asked, and confirmed, where we were going. The guard, incredulous, looked at us and said, "All of you?" as though he was shocked to contemplate a car full of women seeking abortions. We have laughed about this ever since. Beth S and Constance also visited the Morgentaler clinic in Montreal, where on the spur of the moment they were invited to view an abortion procedure (Beth S observed at our April 2017 meeting that in 1977 privacy and consent considerations were less developed than today), which was challenging but instructive. In our meetings with young women doctors, we learned that abortions (like D & Cs) were often given to residents to conduct, that is, they were "beginner" surgeries, which explains why they were often performed more safely in clinics by specialists in the procedure. Constance noted that she learned from the young women doctors that when women patients were anesthetized they brought in residents to practice internal vaginal examinations without the knowledge, let alone consent, of patients. Constance and Leah Cohen wrote about this in *Upstream* magazine.

[14] See Atcheson, Beth, and Lorna Marsden, eds. *White Gloves Off: Work of the Ontario Committee on the Status of Women* (Toronto, ON: Second Story Press, 2018).

[15] We had been given a heads up by the deputy minister of health, Alan Backley, that being able to show cost savings to the health care system through clinic delivery of services might be persuasive. We took him at his word, although this may simply have been a way to divert our energies. We consulted with the Hospital Council of Metropolitan Toronto and were told that in a time of funding constraint no citizen's group would be able to negotiate bed closures with a hospital. In the next breath, after the minister made this request of us, in response to our push-back, he admitted that the information we would need to negotiate with hospitals would not be made available to us by the Ministry of Health. He offered to introduce us to hospitals.

[16] The *Indian Act* has had and continues to have implications for Aboriginal women in terms of identity. With the passage of Bill C-31, new divisions among Indian people were created. The bill limits the ability of women and their children to pass on their status beyond one generation. That is, grandchildren and great-grandchildren are generally not eligible to apply for status. In addition, while status can no longer be lost or gained through marriage, there are new restrictions on the ability to pass status on to children (Lawrence, "'Real' Indians and others." Unpublished PhD dissertation. Toronto: UMI Dissertation Services, 1999). For example, the bill divides Indian people into categories by using sub-sections of the act. A 6(1) Indian is defined as an Indian who had status in 1985. A 6(2) Indian is defined as a reinstated Indian under the act. If a 6(1) Indian marries a non-status Indian (including a Métis) then any resulting child from that union will be considered a 6(2) Indian. If that 6(2) Indian child grows up and has a relationship with a non-status Indian the resulting child is a non-status Indian. Thus, once again, status can be eliminated in two generations and grandchildren and great-grandchildren are excluded. It should be pointed out that if a 6(1) has a relationship with a 6(2), the resulting child is a 6(1) Indian. Furthermore, if a 6(2) has a relationship with a 6(2) the resulting child is a 6(1). The message is, if you don't marry back into your race, you risk losing status for your children or grandchildren. Although assimilation policy was supposedly abandoned in 1973 (announced by the minister of Indian affairs, Jean Chrétien), long-term effects of the *Indian Act* and Bill C-31 still promote assimilation. The federal government effectively controls the definition of "Indianness," but communities, families, and individuals live with the consequences and the confusion that arise from that control (Lawrence, "'Real' Indians and others."). McIvor points out that these violations of civic and political rights of Aboriginal women are violations of their "existing Aboriginal and treaty rights" (35). She argues that the Sparrow decision *(Sparrow v. The Queen 1990)* was a landmark Supreme Court ruling that upheld the notion of existing Aboriginal and treaty rights and that this forms part of the inherent right to self-government protected under s. 35 of the *Constitution Act,* 1982. She maintains that self-government is central to Aboriginal nationhood, culture, and existence and, if it is central to the existence of Aboriginal nations, then the ability to determine civil and political rights of members must also be central. This right to

self-government thus includes the right of women to define their roles in Aboriginal communities. She states:

> The right of women to establish and maintain their civic and political role has existed since time immemorial. These rights are part of customary laws of Aboriginal people and part of the right of self-government...they [rights] are those which women have exercised since the formation of their indigenous societies. In some cases, these rights were suppressed or regulated by non-Aboriginal law, such as the *Indian Act* (Lawrence, "'Real' Indians and others,"35).

[17] Haney, Catherine, "'Towards legitimate nursing work? Historical discursive constructions of abortion in *The Canadian Nurse*, 1950–1965," *Canadian Bulletin of Medical History/Bulletin canadien d'histoire de la médecine*, 31(2) (2014): 93–115.

[18] Chambers, Lori: *Misconceptions: Unmarried Motherhood and the* Ontario Children of Unmarried Parents Act, *1921–1969* (Toronto: Osgoode Society for Canadian Legal History, 2007).

[19] C. Sethna and S. Hewitt, "Clandestine operations: The Vancouver Women's Caucus, the Abortion Caravan, and the RCMP." *Canadian Historical Review* 90(3) (2009) 463–95. *Project MUSE*, doi:10.1353/can.0.0189.

In 1969, the reform of the Criminal Code legalized contraception, abortion, and homosexual acts between consenting adults. Yet the conditions under which legal abortion was now permissible were so restrictive that the new abortion law provoked widespread discontent. One women's liberation group, the fledging Vancouver Women's Caucus (VWC), outlined a plan to travel to Ottawa between February and May 1970 in an Abortion Caravan to protest the new law. The caravan's central feature was a van bearing a coffin filled with coat hangers to represent the deaths of women from botched abortions. Declassified RCMP files reveal that the Mounties were spying on the VWC and tracking the Abortion Caravan on its journey from Vancouver to Ottawa. An analysis of these files shows that the VWC, like other women's liberation groups, was targeted for surveillance because the RCMP was extremely concerned about women's liberation groups' real and putative connections to left-wing organizations. Indeed, the RCMP's approach to women's liberation groups was a crucial component of the climate of fear of subversion so prevalent during the Cold War. However, the files also reveal that RCMP surveillance of the VWC proved to be a major challenge because of the complex gendered nature of the force's surveillance of women's liberation groups. Ultimately, the files point to the importance of studying the ways in which state security interests intersect with variables such as gender, class, race, and sexual orientation.

[20] Slogan of the Front de libération des femmes du Québec. Founded in November 1969, it is the first francophone feminist group that, together with the Montreal Women's Liberation Movement, created in October 1969, marks the birth of a new feminism emerging in most western countries.

[21] Name given to family planning clinics set up in certain hospitals by Denis Lazure, then Quebec minister of health and social services. These clinics

received significant subsidies provided they offered abortion services, thereby forcing them to implement federal legislation. However, the boycott by pro-life doctors was instrumental in causing this project to fail.

22 CLSCs are public network facilities that provide front-line health services. Distributed throughout Quebec, they favour direct intervention within local communities by prioritizing a preventive approach and by encouraging citizens to take responsibility for their health. CLSCs reached a number of 160 in 1986. The existence of this network greatly promoted the setting up of abortion services in all Quebec regions.

23 This committee brings together on a regular basis people (doctors, nurses, and social workers) who provide abortion services in the public, community and private sectors.

24 According to the *Bottin des ressources en avortement au Québec 2014* (Directory of Abortion Resources in Quebec 2014), published by the FQPN.

25 Diane Siegel, personal communication, 2016.

26 Cheryl Hebert, personal communication, 2016.

27 *Planned Parenthood Newfoundland/Labrador v. Fedorik* [1982] 135 D.L.R (3d) 714 (Nfld. S.C.T.D).

28 *Planned Parenthood Newfoundland/Labrador v. Fedorik, supra.*

29 C. L. Hitchcock and J. C. Prior, "Oral micronized progesterone for vasomotor symptoms in healthy postmenopausal women: A placebo-controlled randomized trial." *Menopause,* 2012 19:886–93.

30 Walt Whitman, *Leaves of Grass.*

31 http://www.cemcor.ca/resources/qualitative-basal-temperature-qbt-method-ovulation-detection

32 http://www.cemcor.ca/resources/daily-menstrual-cycle-diary

33 C. Prior, Y. M. Vigna, M. T. Schechter, and A. E. Burgess, "Spinal bone loss and ovulatory disturbances," *New England Journal of Medicine* 323 (1990): 1221–27.

34 Prior et al., "Spinal bone loss and ovulatory disturbances."

35 Prior et al., "Spinal bone loss and ovulatory disturbances."

36 D. Li, C. L. Hitchcock, S. I. Barr, T. Yu, and J. C. Prior, "Negative spinal bone mineral density changes and subclinical ovulatory disturbances: Prospective data in healthy premenopausal women with regular menstrual cycles," *Epidemiologic Reviews* 36(137) (2014): 147.

37 K. J. Mather, E. G. Norman, J. C. Prior, and T. G. Elliott, "Preserved forearm endothelial responses with acute exposure to progesterone: A randomized cross-over trial of 17-b estradiol, progesterone, and 17-b estradiol with progesterone in healthy menopausal women," *Journal of Clinical Endocrinology & Metabolism* 85 (2000): 4644–49.

[38] J. C. Prior, S. Kirkland, L. Joseph, N. Kreiger, T.M. Murray, D. A. Hanley, et al., "Oral contraceptive agent use and bone mineral density in premenopausal women: Cross-sectional, population-based data from the Canadian Multicentre Osteoporosis Study," *Canadian Medical Association Journal* 165 (2001): 1023–29.

[39] J. C. Prior, "Perimenopause: The complex endocrinology of the menopausal transition," *Epidemiologic Reviews* 19 (1998): 397–428.

[40] J. C. Prior, "Adolescents' use of combined hormonal contraceptives for menstrual cycle-related problem treatment and contraception: Evidence of potential lifelong negative reproductive and bone effects, *Women's Reproductive Health* 3(2) (2016): 73–92.

[41] Boston Women's Health Collective, *Our Bodies, Ourselves: A Book by and for Women* (New York: Touchstone, 1976), 6.

[42] Eva Szekely, *Never Too Thin* (Toronto: The Women's Press, 1988).

[43] L. Laurence, and B. Weinhouse, *Outrageous Practices: The Alarming Truth about How Medicine Mistreats Women* (New York: Ballantine Books, 1994).

[44] J. Mason, "Midwifery in Canada," in S. Kitzinger, (ed.) *The Midwife Challenge* (London: Pandora Press, 1998).

[45] Mason, "Midwifery in Canada."

[46] H. Laforce, "The different stages of the elimination of midwives in Quebec" in K. Arnup, A. Levesque, and R. Roach Pierson, with the assistance of M. Brennan, *Delivering Motherhood. Maternal Ideologies and Practices in the 19th and 20th Centuries* (London and New York: Routledge, 1990).

[47] M. J. Relyea, "The rebirth of midwifery in Canada: An historical perspective," *Midwifery* 8(4) (1992): 159–69.

[48] K. Arnup, "Educating mothers: Government advice for women in the inter-war years" in *Delivering Motherhood.*

[49] See *Report on the Task Force on the Implementation of Midwifery in Ontario*, Task Force on the Implementation of Midwifery in Ontario, Toronto, 1987.

[50] C. L. Biggs, "The case of the missing midwives: A history of midwifery in Ontario from 1795–1900" in *Delivering Motherhood.*

[51] Star Delbert-Turner, "The golden speculum: A history of the Vancouver Women's Health Collective," unpublished thesis.

[52] This publication, available for the BC Ministry of Health, is still in use, having been revised in more than six editions to date.

[53] A year or so earlier, Dr. D. Hunt and Dr. H. Parkin, working in the emergency department at RCH hospital in New Westminster, had proposed wider use of "rape kits" to improve evidence collection by ER physicians.

[54] The flexibility in this contract was developed with the support of Leslie

Arnold, then MHR manager responsible for the Child Abuse Team and a significant driver of change within MHR.

55 The women physicians on the roster provided their medical services as volunteers in the early years of the programme until the provincial medical services plan added billing categories to cover their work. Police provided payment if a forensic report was filed, which happened about 50 per cent of the time.

56 The WAVAW Rape Crisis Centre was incorporated in 1982 as an alternative to the Vancouver Rape Relief collective, which had developed a radicalized strategy that proscribed collaboration with mainstream institutions such as the medical or legal systems. Both activist organizations continue today to provide effective support as well as political activism.

57 The "SAAS" (Sexual Assault Assessment Service) became the "SAS" (Sexual Assault Service) in about 1984 when BC Children's Hospital assumed responsibility for examination and support for children.

58 Delbert-Turner, "The Golden Speculum."

59 As of July 2016, these partners have facilitated development of eleven hospital-based services for sexual assault and domestic violence victims in Japan and there are a further twenty in development.

60 Holly Johnson, "Limits of a criminal justice response: Trends in police and court processing of sexual assault" in Elizabeth Sheehy, ed., *Sexual Assault in Canada: Law, Legal Practice, and Women's Activism* (Ottawa: University of Ottawa Press, 2012), 631. All data is from Statistics Canada.

61 Notwithstanding that the references and history herein are selective, I wish to acknowledge and thank Heather Gardiner, the archivist of Women's College Hospital, for providing extensive material documenting the efforts of Women's College Hospital to avoid being closed or disappearing as a result of actions of the Health Services Restructuring Commission.

62 Excerpts from the Affidavit of N. Jane Pepino, Q.C. dated April 8, 1997, filed in the Ontario Court of Justice (General Division) Divisional Court between Women's College Hospital as Applicant and the Health Services Restructuring Commission and the Minister of Health as Respondents.

63 *Final Report of the MTDHC Hospital Restructuring Committee: Directions for Change: Toward a Coordinated Hospital System for Metro Toronto.*

64 Affidavit of N. Jane Pepino, paragraph 58.

65 Duncan Sinclair, Mark Rochon, and Peggy Leatt, *"Riding the Third Rail": The story of Ontario's Health Services Restructuring Commission 1996–2000* (Montreal and Kingston: McGill-Queen's University Press, 2005).

66 Everyone knew the "party" under discussion was Sunnybrook.

67 The two academic health science centres, being Sunnybrook and Women's College, technically only "nominated" members to their boards; the University of Toronto then "appointed" directors.

[68] Women and Health Protection, *Remembering Ruth Cooperstock, Women and Pharmaceuticals Twenty Years Later*. Ruth Cooperstock Memorial Lectureship Committee, University of Toronto, and Women and Health Protection, Toronto, ON, 2006.

[69] Women and Health Protection, *Remembering Ruth Cooperstock, Women and Pharmaceuticals Twenty Years Later*, Ruth Cooperstock Memorial Lectureship Committee, University of Toronto, and Women and Health Protection, Toronto, ON, 2006.

[70] R. Cooperstock, "A review of women's psychotropic drug use," *Canadian Psychiatric Association Journal* 24(1) (1979): 29–34.

[71] R. Cooperstock and H. L. Lennard, "Some social meanings of tranquillizer use," *Sociology of Health & Illness* 1(3) (1979): 331–47.

[72] *All in the Same Boat*, videocassette, 1977, University of Toronto Libraries Catalogue.

[73] Natalie Zina Walschots, "This Isn't the witch hunt you're looking for—If witch hunts were historically about the privileged persecuting the vulnerable, why do people keep evoking the term to defend powerful men like Steven Galloway and Jian Ghomeshi?" posted on February 23, 2017, at 2:08 p.m. *BuzzFeed*. https://www.buzzfeed.com/nataliezinawalschots/this-isnt-the-witch-hunt-youre-looking-for?utm_term=.pswvvVdYr#.dfxpprNjZ

[74] Marilou McPhedran, "First, do no harm," *The Globe and Mail*, June 21, 2001. https://www.theglobeandmail.com/opinion/first-do-no-harm/article1338371/

[75] In 2015, the century-old libel law in Ontario was replaced by the *Protection of Public Participation Act* making such SLAPP suits (selective litigation against public persons) more difficult to use to silence critics and public debate.

[76] McPhedran, Marilou and Wendy Sutton, *Preventing Sexual Abuse of Patients: A Legal Guide for Health Care Professionals* (Markham, ON: LexisNexis Butterworths, 2004).

[77] Judith Herman, *Trauma and Recovery: The Aftermath of Violence—from Domestic Abuse to Political Terror*, (New York: Basic Books, 1997). Reprinted in *"What About Accountability to the Patient?" Final Report of the Special Task Force on Sexual Abuse of Patients*, November 10, 2000, released to the public in 2001.

[78] On my recommendation, in 1991 the CPSO also appointed Dr. Harvey Armstrong (psychiatrist), Dr. Rachel Edney (general practitioner), Patricia Marshall, and Roz Roach (psychiatric specialist and nurse) as task force members, as well as Briar Long (who went on to become a psychiatrist) as the executive coordinator. In consultation with the task force, the CPSO also established an advisory council for the task force.

[79] *Health Professions Procedural Code*, being Schedule 2 of the *Regulated Health Professions Act*, S.O. 1991, c. 18.

[80] McPhedran et al., *What About accountability to the patient? Final Report of the Special Task Force on Sexual Abuse of Patients,* available online [MMc Senate facebook].

[81] Clementine Ford, *Fight Like a Girl* (Crow's Nest: Allen & Unwin, 2016), 273.

[82] Constance Backhouse, Donald Mcrae, and Nitya Iyer, *Report of the Task Force on Misogyny, Sexism, and Homophobia in Dalhousie University Faculty of Dentistry,* June 26, 2015, 12.

[83] Dr. Mark D'Souza, Chair of Ontario Medical Association District 11, presentation to the Standing Committee of the Ontario Legislative Assembly regarding *Bill 87—Protecting Patients Act,* April 3, 2017 in Toronto, Ontario.

[84] Acadia University, "Women's and Gender Studies at Acadia University," http://womenstudies.acadiau.ca/Home.html, accessed on November 21, 2016.

[85] Vanessa Milne, Christopher Doig, and Irfan Dhalla, "Less science, more diversity: How Canadian medical school admissions are changing," http://healthydebate.ca/2015/12/topic/canadian-medical-schools-admissions, accessed on November 21, 2016.

[86] *The Canadian Encyclopedia,* "Women's movements in Canada: 1960–85," http://www.thecanadianencyclopedia.ca/en/article/womens-movements-in-canada-196085, accessed on November 2, 2016.

[87] Ontario Coalition of Rape Crisis Services, *OCRCS Herstory,* http://www.sexualassaultsupport.ca/page-418416, accessed on November 2, 2016.

[88] John R. Barner and Michelle Mohr Carney, "Interventions for intimate partner violence: A historical review," *Journal of Family Violence,* 26(2011): 235–44.

[89] Leslie Tutty, "Shelters for abused women in Canada: A celebration of the past, challenges for the future," Family Violence Prevention Health Issues Division Health Canada: Project #H5227-7-K002, https://www.academia.edu/1590855/Shelters_for_abused_women_in_Canada_A_celebration_of_the_past_challenges_for_the_future?auto=download, accessed on November 2, 2016.

[90] Marcel Roy, Minutes of proceedings and evidence of the Standing Committee on Health, Welfare and Social Affairs respecting: Inquiry into violence in the family including: The third report to the House (wife battering), House of Commons, Issue No. 34, Thursday, May 6, 1982.

[91] Marcel, 26.

[92] White, Nancy (2008). "MPs laughed when she spoke on battered women," *Toronto Star* https://www.thestar.com/life/2008/06/13/mps_laughed_when_she_spoke_on_battered_women.html, accessed November 21, 2016.

[93] Kathleen J. Tierney, "Social movement organization, resource mobilization, and the creation of a social problem: A case study of a movement for battered women." Doctoral dissertation, Ohio State University, 1979: 194.

[94] John M. Johnson, "Programme enterprise and official cooptation in the battered women's shelter movement," *American Behavioral Scientist* 24(6) (1981): 827–42; Kathleen J. Tierney, "The battered women's movement."

[95] R. Tobias, "*Continuing education and professionalization:* Travelling without a compass," *International Journal of Lifelong Education,* 22(5): 445–56.

[96] White Ribbon. "Who are we?" http://www.whiteribbon.ca/who-we-are, accessed on November 21, 2016.

[97] Barner and Carney, 237

[98] S. Paterson, "What's the problem with gender-based analysis? Gender mainstreaming policy and practice in Canada," *Canadian Public Administration* 53(3) (2010), 395–416.

[99] Kendra Nixon, Colin Bonnycastle, and Stephanie Ens, "Challenging the notion of failure to protect: Exploring the protective strategies of abused mothers living in urban and remote communities and implications for practice," *Child Abuse Review* (2015) DOI: 10.1002/car.2417; Karen Swift, *Manufacturing "Bad Mothers": A Critical Perspective on Child Neglect* (Toronto: University of Toronto Press, 1995).

[100] Paterson, 165.

[101] Roy, "Minutes of proceedings."

[102] Government of Canada, "National Inquiry into Missing and Murdered Indigenous Women and Girls," https://www.aadnc-aandc.gc.ca/eng/1448633 299414/1448633350146, accessed on November 23, 2016.

[103] *Side Effects* group interview participant, October 2015. We are very grateful to our "*Side Effects* sisters" Jean Christie, past executive director of Inter Pares; Rose Mary Murphy, retired nurse educator and stalwart member of Women's Health Interaction; and Mary Ann Mulvihill, former Inter Pares staff person and *Side Effects* tour coordinator, who participated with us in a group interview about *Side Effects* in October, 2015. The process of reconstructing and sharing our varied experiences with the *Side Effects* project laid the groundwork for this article. The group interview was hosted by Inter Pares and facilitated by two Carleton University student interns, Kenneth Boddy and Ethan Lamirande, based at Inter Pares who organized the considerable *Side Effects* archives. Special thanks to Inter Pares co-manager Jack Hui Litster and all the staff for ensuring the *Side Effects* story is told.

[104] P. Freire, *Pedagogy of the Oppressed* (Harmondsworth: Penguin, 1972).

[105] Inter Pares, "Does it work? Feminist analysis and practice at Inter Pares," *Inter Pares Occasional Paper Series* (8) (March, 2011): 33.

[106] Inter Pares, "Women and pharmaceuticals workshop," Aylmer, Quebec, Educational Kit Working Papers (June, 1983, unpublished).

[107] Inter Pares (2011), 33.

[108] *Side Effects* group interview, October 2015.

[109] "Side Effects: The National Tour" programme handout, 1.

[110] I. Boucher, M. A. Mulvihill, Y. Mennie, and K. Seabrooke, for Women's Health Interaction, "Side Effects: A dramatic presentation," *Healthsharing* (Fall, 1996): 13–17.

[111] Boucher et al., 15.

[112] *Side Effects* group interview participant, October 28, 2015.

[113] The archives contain English and French scripts; published and unpublished articles and reports; "tool kits"; original evaluation forms and data summaries; correspondence with individuals and groups across the country; project art work; and many other documents.

[114] See https://www.copasah.net/naripokkho.html.

[115] See http://nijerakori.org; https://interpares.ca/news/nijera-kori-through-eyes-canadian-interns.

[116] Some examples of this work include A. R. Ford and D. Saibil (eds.), *The Push to Prescribe: Women and Canadian Drug Policy* (Toronto: Women's Press, 2009); B. Mintzes, J. Lexchin, and A.S. Quintano, "Clinical trial transparency: Many gains but access to evidence for new medicines remains imperfect," *British Medical Bulletin* 116 (2015): 43–53; J. Lexchin, *Private Profits versus Public Policy: The Pharmaceutical Industry and the Canadian State* (Toronto: University of Toronto Press, 2016).

[117] Canadian Women's Committee on Reproduction, Population and Development, "Canadian policies and practices in the areas of reproduction, population and development," *Canadian Woman Studies* 15 (2 & 3) (1995): 159–165.

[118] Inter Pares (2011), 35–37.

[119] Government of Canada, news release, "Canada announces support for sexual and reproductive health and rights," March 8, 2017.

[120] Winnipeg Consultation Coordinating Committee, "The strength of links: Building the Canadian Women's Health Network," (1994), http://www.cwhn.ca/en/node/21670, accessed on May 22, 2017.

[121] See https://interpares.ca/womens-equality.

[122] *Side Effects* group interview, October 28, 2015.

[123] B. Hartmann, *Reproductive Rights and Wrongs: The Global Politics of Population Control* (Chicago: Haymarket Books, 2016).

[124] Association of Workers' Compensation Boards of Canada, *2015 Injury Statistics Across Canada* (Toronto: Association of Workers' Compensation Boards of Canada), http://awcbc.org/?page_id=14.

[125] I. Niedhammer, M. J. Saurel-Cubizolles, M. Piciotti, and S. Bonenfant, "How is sex considered in recent epidemiological publications on occupational risks?" *Occupational and Environmental Medicine* 57(8) (2000): 521–27.

[126] Danièle Kergoat, *Les ouvrières* (Paris: Sycomore, 1983); Pat and Hugh Armstrong, *Double Ghetto: Canadian Women and their Segregated Work* (Toronto: McClelland and Stewart, 1978).

[127] Maria De Koninck, *Elements pour une problematique de la santé des femmes au travail* (Direction de la santé communautaire Ministère des Affaires sociales du Quebec, 1983).

[128] Jeanne M. Stellman, *Women's Work, Women's Health* (New York: Pantheon Books, 1985).

[129] K. Messing, B. Neis, and L. Dumais, (eds.), *Invisible: Issues in Women's Occupational Health and Safety/Invisible: La santé des travailleuses* (Charlottetown, PEI: Gynergy books, 1995).

[130] Donna Mergler, "Worker participation in occupational health research: Theory and practice," *International Journal of Health Services* 17 (1987): 151–67.

[131] Anne-Renée Gravel, Jessica Riel, and Karen Messing, "Protecting pregnant workers while fighting sexism: Work-pregnancy balance and resistance of pregnant nurses in Quebec hospitals," *New Solutions: A Journal of Occupational and Environmental Health Policy* 27(3)(2017): 424–37.

[132] K. Hohenadel, P. Raj, Paul A. Demers, Shelia Hoar Zahm, and Aaron Blair, "The inclusion of women in studies of occupational cancer: A review of the epidemiologic literature from 1991–2009," *American Journal of Industrial Medicine* 58(3) (2015): 276–81.

[133] Karen Messing and Piroska Östlin, Gender Equality, Work and Health: A Review of the Evidence (World Health Organization: Geneva, 2006), http://www.who.int/gender/documents/Genderworkhealth.pdf.

[134] Katherine Lippel, *Addressing Occupational Violence: An Overview of Conceptual and Policy Considerations Viewed Through a Gender Lens* (Geneva: International Labour Oorganization, 2016).

[135] Karen Messing, *One-Eyed Science: Occupational Health and Working Women* (Philadelphia: Temple University Press, 1998).

[136] Jean-Anne Bouchard, *Les effets des conditions de travail sur la santé des travailleuses: actes du Colloque international sur les effets des conditions de travail sur la santé des travailleuses* (Montréal: Confédération des syndicats nationaux, 1983).

[137] Patrice Duguay, François Hébert, and P. Massicotte, « Les indicateurs de lésions indemnisées en santé et en sécurité du travail au Quebec : des différences selon le sexe. *Comptes rendus du congrès de la Société d'ergonomie de langue française* » vol. 6 (Montreal, 2001): 65–69.

[138] Karen Messing, *Pain and Prejudice: What Science Can Learn about Work from the People Who Do It* (Toronto: BTL Books, 2014).

[139] Julie Côté, "A critical review on physical factors and functional characteristics that may explain a sex/gender difference in work-related neck/shoulder disorders," *Ergonomics* 55(2) (2012): 173–82.

[140] B. Gushulak, K. Pottie, J. Hatcher Roberts, and S. Torres, "Migration and health in Canada: Health in the global village. Canadian guidelines for immigrant health," *Canadian Medical Association Journal* (2011) 183:12, DOI:10.1503/cmaj.090287; Z. Vang, J. Sigouin, A. Flenon, and A. Gagnon, "Are immigrants healthier than native-born Canadians? A systematic review of the healthy immigrant effect in Canada. *Ethnicity and Health* (2016), http://dx.doi.org/10.1080/13557858.2016.1246518; B. Vissandjée and A. Battaglini, Santé des femmes : A la croisée des questions de genre, ethnicité et migration," in A. Battaglini, ed., *Santé et services sociaux de première ligne en milieu pluriethnique* (Éditions Rémi Saint Martin, Québec, 2010), 277–92; B. Vissandjée, M. DesMeules, Z. Cao, S. Abdool, and A. Kazanjian, "Integrating ethnicity and migration as determinants of Canadian women's health," *BMC Women's Health* 4 (Suppl. 1) (2004): S31, www.biomedcentral.com.

[141] W.E. Short and B. Vissandjée, "Women Living with HIV in India: Looking up from a place of stigma, identifying nexus sites for change," *Diversity and Equality in Health and Care* 14(3) (2017): 159–66.

[142] http://www.historyworld.net/wrldhis/PlainTextHistories.asp?historyid=ad26.

[143] http://www.historyworld.net/wrldhis/PlainTextHistories.asp?historyid=ad26.

[144] Donna Dickenson, *Margaret Fuller: Writing a Woman's Life* (New York: St. Martin's Press, 1993), 45–46.

[145] Paul Gordon Lauren, *The Evolution of International Human Rights* (Philadelphia: University of Pennsylvania Press, 2003), 18–20.

[146] https://en.unesco.org/node/265103.

[147] https://Declaration_of_the_Rights_of_Woman_and_of_the_Female_Citizen.

[148] http://constitution.org/fr/fr_drm.htm.

[149] K. B. Jones, *Compassionate Authority: Democracy and the Representation of Women* (New York: Routledge, 1993).

[150] Jones, *Compassionate Authority*.

[151] https://plato.stanford.edu/entries/beauvoir/.

[152] https://plato.stanford.edu/entries/beauvoir/.

[153] L. Hengehold and N. Bauer, eds, *A Companion to Simone de Beauvoir* (Hoboken, NJ: Wiley Blackwell, 2017).

[154] https://www.reuters.com/article/us-g20-women/canada-best-g20-country-to-be-a-woman-india-worst-poll-idUSBRE85C00420120613.

[155] http://www.trust.org/trustlaw/.

[156] https://www.gardeningknowhow.com/ornamental/trees/baobab/baobab-tree-flowers.htm.

[157] https://www.gardeningknowhow.com/ornamental/trees/baobab/baobab-tree-flowers.htm.

[158] Constance Backhouse and David H. Flaherty, *Challenging Times: The Women's Movement in Canada and the United States* (Montreal: McGill-Queen's University Press, 1992); Madeline Boscoe, Gwynne Basen, Ghislaine Alleyne, Barbara Bourrier-Lacroix, and Susan White of the Canadian Women's Health Network, "The women's health movement in Canada: Looking back and moving forward," *Canadian Woman Studies* 24(1) (2004): 7.

[159] Dorothy Sue Cobble, *The Other Women's Movement: Workplace Justice and Social Rights in Modern America* (Princeton: Princeton University Press, 2004).

[160] Boscoe et al., "The women's health movement in Canada," 7.

[161] Linda Duxbury and Christopher Higgins, *Work-Life Issues in Canada: The 2012 National Study on Balancing Work and Caregiving in Canada* (Ottawa: Carleton University Press, 2012).

[162] Annis May Timpson, *Driven Apart: Women's Employment Equality and Child Care in Canadian Public Policy* (Vancouver: University of British Columbia Press, 2001), 3.

[163] Momin Rahman and Anne Witz, "What really matters? The elusive quality of the material in feminist thought," *Feminist Theory* 4(3) (2003): 243–61.

[164] Cobble, *The Other Women's Movement*.

[165] Cobble, *The Other Women's Movement*.

[166] Timpson, *Driven Apart*.

[167] Eileen Boris, "Roundtable on Dorothy Sue Cobble's *The Other Women's Movement: Workplace Justice and Social Rights in Modern America*," *Labor: Studies in Working-Class History of the Americas* 2(4) (2005): 62.

[168] "Rona," interview with the author, January 25, 2011.

[169] "Kelly," interview with the author, January 28, 2011.

[170] Royal Commission on the Status of Women in Canada and Florence Bird, *Report of the Royal Commission on the Status of Women in Canada* (Ottawa: Information Canada, 1970).

[171] "Dora," interview with the author, January 19, 2011.

[172] "Wanda," interview with the author, January 8, 2011.

[173] Suzanne Gordon, "Profits and prejudice: The undervalued work of nursing," *Dollars & Sense* 231 (2000).

[174] "Audrey," interview with the author, February 8, 2011.

[175] *Vancouver Sun*, July 10, 1968.

[176] Janet C. Ross-Kerr, *Prepared to Care: Nurses and Nursing in Alberta, 1859 to 1996* (Edmonton: University of Alberta Press, 1998), 270.

[177] Ross-Kerr, *Prepared to Care*, 270–271.

[178] Mark Roth, "The gendered workings of class in postindustrial, service sector capitalism: The emergence and evolution of the British Columbia Nurses Union, 1976–1992," masters thesis, Simon Fraser University, 2008, 25.

[179] Suzanne Gordon, "Institutional obstacles to RN unionization: How 'vote no' thinking is deeply embedded in the nursing profession," *Working USA* 12(2) (2009): 280.

[180] "Maria," interview with the author, January 7, 2011.

[181] Florence Melchior, "Feminist approaches to nursing history," *Western Journal of Nursing Research* 26(3) (2004): 344–45.

[182] "Mary," interview with the author, January 12, 2011.

[183] Judith Wuest, "Professionalism and the evolution of nursing as a discipline: A feminist perspective," *Journal of Professional Nursing* 10(6) (1994): 364.

[184] "Shelley," interview with the author, January 10, 2011.

[185] Mark W. Risjord, *Nursing Knowledge: Science, Practice, and Philosophy* (Ames, IA: Wiley-Blackwell, 2010): 66–75.

[186] Commission on Social Determinants of Health, *Closing the Gap in a Generation: Health Equity through Action on the Social Determinants of Health. Final Report of the Commission on Social Determinants of Health* (Geneva: World Health Organization, 2008).

[187] Sandra Rodgers, "Abortion denied: Bearing the limits of the law," in *Just Medicare: What's In, What's Out, How We Decide*, Colleen Flood (ed.) (Toronto: University of Toronto Press, 2006).

[188] Christiabelle Sethna, Beth Palmer, Katrina Ackerman, and Nancy Janovicek, "Choice, interrupted: Travel and inequality of access to abortion services since the 1960s," *Labour/Le Travail* 71 (Spring 2013): 29–48.

[189] C. J. G. Mackenzie, G. P. Evans, and J. G. Peck, "The Vancouver Family Planning Clinic: A case study," *Canadian Journal of Public Health* 58, 2 (1967): 53–60.

[190] Cope W. Schwenger, "The way ahead," unpublished article from CPHA, ca. 1967, submitted in correspondence with *Canadian Journal of Public Health*, 7.

[191] H. H. Washburn, "The administration and operation of the Norfolk County Family Planning Clinic," *Canadian Journal of Public Health* 58, 6 (1967) 277–79; Ian Bain, "The development of family planning in Canada," *Canadian Journal of Public Health* 55, 6 (1964): 334–40.

[192] C. J. G. Mackenzie, et al., "The Vancouver Family Planning Clinic: A case study."

[193] Mackenzie, et al., "The Vancouver Family Planning Clinic: A case study"; Henry Fitzgibbon, "The forming of a family planning clinic," *Canadian Journal of Public Health* 58, 4 (1967): 182–25.

[194] Canadian Public Health Association, Minutes of the Executive Committee, September 16, 1967.

[195] Vincent Leon Matthews, "The public health implications of population trends," *Canadian Journal of Public Health* 57, 2 (1966): 62.

[196] Canadian Public Health Association, Minutes of the Annual General Meeting, May 23, 1969, 8.

[197] Canadian Public Health Association, Minutes of the Annual General Meeting. April 22, 1971, 4.

[198] Canadian Public Health Association, Minutes of the Annual General Meeting. April 22, 1971, 6.

[199] F. Michael Barrett and Malcolm Fitz-Earle, "Student opinion on legalized abortion at the University of Toronto," *Canadian Journal of Public Health* 64, 3 (1973): 294–49; F. Michael Barrett, "Changes in attitudes toward abortion in a large population of canadian university students between 1968 and 1978," *Canadian Journal of Public Health* 71, 3 (1980): 195–200.

[200] Murray C. Diner, "Survey of Ottawa area general practitioners and obstetrician-gynecologists on abortion," *Canadian Journal of Public Health* 65, 5 (1974): 351–58.

[201] Joan M. Rogers and David W. Adams, "Therapeutic Abortion: A multidisciplined approach to patient care from a social work perspective," *Canadian Journal of Public Health* 64, 3 (1973): 254–59.

[202] Virginia K. Elahi, "A family planning survey in Halifax, Nova Scotia," *Canadian Journal of Public Health* 64, 6 (1973): 515–20.

[203] Kerry J. Daly and Edward S. Herold, "Who uses natural family planning?" *Canadian Journal of Public Health* 76, 3 (1985): 207-8.

[204] E. Aenid Dunton, "A family planning cinic in a county health unit," *Canadian Journal of Public Health* 58, 4 (1967): 181–82.

[205] Henry Fitzgibbon, "The forming of a family planning clinic"; E. Aenid Dunton, "A family planning cinic in a county health unit."

[206] Fitzgibbon, "The Forming of a Family Planning Clinic."

[207] M. Boscoe, et al., "Collective notes," *Healthsharing*, Vol 2, No 1(1980).

[208] Anne Rochon Ford, "The Healthsharing connection," http://www.cwhn.ca/en/node/46098 (retrieved October 10, 2016).

[209] Rochon Ford, "The Healthsharing Connection."

[210] E. Dua, et al., "Introduction" in E. Dua, et al, *On Women Healthsharing* (Toronto: Women's Press, 1994) 14.

[211] C. Clement and D. Majury, "Visions for women's reproductive care," *Healthsharing* Vol 9, No 2 (1988): 18–22.

[212] G. J. Coleman and T. Joyce, "Trends in smoking before, during, and after pregnancy in ten states," *American Journal of Preventive Medicine* 24(1) (2003): 29–35; Connor, S. K., and L. McIntyre. "The sociodemographic predictors of smoking cessation among pregnant women in Canada." *Canadian Journal of Public Health* 90 (1999): 352–355.

[213] Health Canada, *Tobacco Control Programme: Canadian Tobacco Use Monitoring Survey* (Ottawa: Health Canada, 2002), www.hc-sc.gc.ca/ hec-sesc/tobacco/research/ctums/.

[214] Health Canada, *Canadian Perinatal Health Report 2003* (Ottawa: Minister of Public Works and Government Services Canada, 2003).

[215] L. Greaves, C. Varcoe, N. Poole, M. Morrow, J. Johnson, A. Pederson, et al, *A Motherhood Issue: Discourses on Mothering Under Duress* (Ottawa: Status of Women Canada, 2002); D. Rutman, M. Callahan, A. Lundquist, S. Jackson, and B. Field, *Substance Use and Pregnancy: Conceiving Women in the Policy Process* (Ottawa: Status of Women Canada, 2000).

[216] S. C. Boyd, *From Witches to Crack Moms: Women, Drug Law, and Policy* (Durham, NC: Carolina Academic Press, 2004), 93.

[217] N. Poole and B. Isaac, *Apprehensions: Barriers to Treatment for Substance Using Mothers* (Vancouver: BC Centre of Excellence for Women's Health, 2001).

[218] Rutman et al., 51.

[219] "Judge orders woman not to get pregnant for 10 years: Drugs affected child," *National Post*, February 18, 2000.

[220] P. Pearson, "Save the Children," *National Post*, May 8, 1999.

[221] Greaves et al. (2002).

[222] BC Ministry for Children and Families Child Protection Consultation Services, *The Risk Assessment Model for Child Protection in British Columbia* (Victoria, BC: Queen's Printer, 1996).

[223] Province of British Columbia, *Child, Family and Community Service Act* (1996, amended 2002).

[224] N. D. Campbell, "Regulating 'maternal instinct': Governing mentalities of late twentieth century U.S. illicit drug policy," *Signs: Journal of Women in Culture and Society* 24(4) (1999): 918.

[225] J. Golden, "'A tempest in a cocktail glass': Mothers, alcohol, and television, 1977–96," *Journal of Health, Politics, Policy and Law* 25(3) (2000): 2.

[226] Alberta Alcohol and Drug Abuse Commission, *A Framework for Addictions Services for Women* (Edmonton, 2003).

[227] H. Graham, *When Life's a Drag: Women, Smoking and Disadvantage* (London: HMSO, 1993).

228 L. Greaves, *Smoke Screen: Women Smoking and Social Control* (Halifax, NS: Fernwood Publishing, 1996).

229 M. J. Casper, *The Making of the Unborn Patient: A Social Anatomy of Fetal Surgery* (New Brunswick, NJ: Rutgers University Press, 1998).

230 L. Oaks, *Smoking and Pregnancy* (New Brunswick, NJ: Rutgers University Press, 2001), 79–82.

231 Oaks, 83.

232 Greaves, *Smoke Screen*; Oaks, *Smoking and Pregnancy*.

233 Action on Smoking and Health (ASH), http://www.ash.org/ custody-and-smoking.html, accessed on March 3, 2005.

234 L. M. Klesges, K. C. Johnson, K. D. Ward, and M. Barnard, "Smoking cessation in pregnant women," *Gynecological Clinics of North America* 28(2) (2001): 269–82.

235 B. Jacobson, *Beating the Ladykillers* (London: Pluto Press, 1986).

236 Standing Conference on Drug Abuse, *Drug Using Parents: Policy Guidelines for Inter-Agency Work* (London: Local Government Association Publications, 1997).

237 Greaves et al. (2002).

238 N. Poole, *Evaluation Report of the Sheway Project for High Risk Pregnant and Parenting Women* (Vancouver: British Columbia Centre of Excellence for Women's Health, 2000).

239 L. Greaves, R. Cormier, K. Devries, J. Bottorff, J. Johnson, S. Kirkland et al., *Expecting to Quit: A Best Practices Review of Smoking Cessation Interventions for Pregnant and Postpartum Girls and Women* (Ottawa: Health Canada, 2003).

240 J. Matthews, "Building the body beautiful: The femininity of modernity," *Australian Feminist Studies* 5 (1987): 17.

241 Oaks, 21.

INDEX

AAA (Association pour l'accès à l'avortement), 132
Aberman, Arnold, 262
Ablowitz, Marsha, 302–4
Aboriginal women. See Indigenous women
abortion, access to: inequity of, 109, 138, 146, 147, 381–82; need to travel for, 62–63, 119–20, 146, 147, 149, 158–59; for NL teachers, 158–59; outside system, 106–8, 109; PEI loss of services, 140–41, 142–43, 146–47; quotas and delays, 61–62; and TACs, 38–39, 41, 138–41, 381, 432n8, 433n12
abortion, fight for: at clinics, 37, 39, 41, 130, 435–36nn21-22; demonstrations, 113, 115–16, 129, 149; in NL, 94–95; in PEI, 139–43, 144–46, 148–53; in Quebec, 128–33; at VGH, 122–27
abortion, legal/political aspects: Badgley Report, 41, 42–43, 61, 62, 433n11; federally, 38–39, 41, 61, 112, 152, 431n3; levels of jurisdiction, 431–32n6, 432–33n9; in Ontario, 44–47; in PEI, 138, 143–46, 151, 154–56; provincially, 33; in Quebec, 41, 129–30; Supreme Court ruling on, 38, 116, 131. See also section 251 of Criminal Code
abortion, safety of, 42–43, 62, 105–6, 121, 433n13

abortion, social aspects: arguments against, 109–10; attacks on providers, 121, 134–36, 268; and Catholicism, 382–84; PEI abortion survey, 145; pro-life movement, 131, 132, 137–38, 140–44, 162–64; stigma of, 108–9. See also women's bodies
Abortion Caravan, 71, 111, 112–16, 435n19
Abortion Information Line (PEI), 148
abuse. See rape; sexual abuse headings; violence
AC+T (drug combination), 176
Ackerman, Katrina, 140
ACSW (NL Advisory Council on the Status of Women), 96, 99
ACSW (PEI Advisory Council on the Status of Women), 140, 142, 145, 146
Act Respecting Assisted Human Reproduction and Related Research, An, 27
Action on Smoking and Health (ASH), 397
addiction, 51, 269–70, 306, 394–401. See also smoking; substance use
advertising aimed at women, 27–28, 49, 193, 323, 324
Advisory Council on the Status of Women (NL), 96, 99
Advisory Council on the Status of Women (PEI), 140, 142, 145, 146

Ages, Alice, 304
Agnew, Bonnie, 305
AIDS and HIV, 268, 403–8
alcohol use, 393, 396–97. See also
substance use
All In The Same Boat (film), 288
Allemang, W.H., 45, 50, 55, 58, 64
Alliance for Breast Cancer Survivors,
180
Alliance for Life, 162
amenorrhea, 184, 186–87. See also
ovulation
anaesthesia, 59–60
analgesics, 59
Anderson, Cheryl, 210–11, 215, 219,
223
Anderson, Doris, 239
anti-abortion forces. See pro-life
movement
Archer, Robyn, 149
ASH (Action on Smoking and
Health), 397
Ashford, Margaret, 140
"Ask Jerilynn", 183–84
Association of Ontario Midwives,
204
Association pour l'accès à l'avorte-
ment, 132
Atcheson, Beth, 37–38, 46
Atkinson, Marian, 95
Aurora Centre, 401
Austen, Jane, 33
Austin, Donald F., 58
Aylmer workshop, 335, 340, 341

Baby-Friendly Hospital Initiative, 270
Backhouse, Constance, 37–38, 39,
46, 298
Backley, Alan, 434n15
"Backyard Abortion Waltz, The"
(Archer), 149
Badgley Report, 41, 42–43, 61, 62,
433n11
Ballem, Penny, 268, 269, 270, 327
Bangladeshi activists, 334–36
Barker-Benfeld, G.J., 52
Barnett, Robin, 329
Barr, Susan I., 183
Barrett, F. Michael, 383

Barrett, Wendy, 300, 311
Batt, Sharon, 170–71, 172, 182
Bay Centre for Birth Control, 237
Bazilli, Susan, 118–21
Bazowski, Peter, 127
BC Women's Hospital and Health
Centre: as beacon, 275; FIR Square,
269–70, 400; funding, 271–72;
services at, 268–71, 273–74. See also
Grace Hospital (BC)
BC Women's Milk Bank, 270
BCA (Breast Cancer Action) (US),
178
BCCEWH (British Columbia Centre
of Excellence for Women's Health),
269, 327
Beauvoir, Simone de, 365
Beckwoman, Bonnie, 113–14
Bell, Ilene, 63, 64, 65
Bennett, Carolyn, 239, 243–44, 245
Benoit, Cecilia, 93
Benston, Margaret, 304
benzodiazepines, 27, 286, 327
Beral, Valerie, 183
BFHI (Baby-Friendly Hospital
Initiative), 270
Bill 51 (ON), 243
Bill C-31, 86, 87–88, 434n16
Bill C-43, 152
Bill C-484, 132
biomedical model of health care,
26–27, 173–74, 201, 287
birth: changes in practices around,
222–23; experience for unwed
mothers, 105; in hospitals, 206,
273–74; mortality, 215, 275; natural v.
medical, 59–60, 201–3, 209–10, 211.
See also midwifery; pregnancy
birth control pills. See under
contraception
Birth Options for Nanaimo District
(BOND), 219
Bitonti-Brown, Victoria (née Morris),
213, 223
Blackwood, Joan, 36
bodies. See women's bodies
body image, 192–95, 310
Body Politic (periodical), 34
BOND (Birth Options for Nanaimo
District), 219

CEQ (Centrale des enseignants du Quebec), 360
cervical caps, study on, 159
cervical dysplasia, 330
cervical self-exams, 75, 391–92
cervical/uterine cancer, 54, 58, 392. See also pap tests
Chapman, Carol, 149
Cheverie, Wayne, 142
child sexual abuse. See sexual abuse of children
childbirth. See birth
children, 282, 394, 395, 397, 399–401. See also fetuses
Christilaw, Jan, 266, 272
chronic illness in Indigenous women, 80
Chronic Pelvic Pain clinic, 270
cigarette advertising, 323, 324
CIHR Act, 351–52
CIHR (Canadian Institutes for Health Research), 25, 349, 351
CJPH (Canadian Journal of Public Health), 381–82, 383–85
Clark, Christy, 235
Clement, Connie, 387, 390–91
climate change, 364
clinics: family planning, 382; fighting for abortions at, 37, 39, 41, 130, 435–36nn21-22; refusal to privatize, 132; secret, 163; specialized, 132. See also hospitals; specific clinics, e.g. Morgentaler
Clinton, Hillary, 117
clitorectomies in 19th c., 52
clitorises, 348
CLSCs (centres locaux de services communautaires), 130, 436n22
CMHA (Canadian Mental Health Association), 282
CMPA (Canadian Medical Protective Association), 297
CNALG (Coordination nationale pour l'avortement libre et gratuit), 129–30
Coalition québécoise pour le droit à l'avortement libre et gratuit, 130, 131–32
Coats, Daniela, 305

Cobble, Dorothy Sue, 368, 369–70
Coffin, Kathy, 95
Cohen, Leah, 37–38, 46, 67
Cohen, Marcy, 114
Cohen, Sheila, 58, 61, 64, 65
College of Midwives of BC, 219
College of Midwives of Ontario, 204
College of Physicians and Surgeons of Ontario, 293–95, 297
colonialism, 80–89, 434–35n16. See also discrimination; Indian Act
Comité de lutte pour la Contraception et l'avortement libres et gratuits, 128–29
Comité de vigilance, 130, 436n23. See also Coordination nationale pour l'avortement libre et gratuit
Common Ground (PEI periodical), 151
Comprehensive Abortion and Reproductive Education (CARE), 268
Confédération des syndicats nationaux (CSN), 359, 360
Conn, Melanie, 77–79
Conservative government (ON), 240, 252
contraception: access to, 118–19, 157–58, 382–83; birth control pills, 155, 190; and Catholicism, 384; Diaphragm Fitters Collective, 74–76; dispensaries for, 237; hysterectomies as, 55; legality of, 104, 380; in NL, 157–58, 163; reluctance to use, 168; stigma of, 109, 154–56. See also population control; specific types, e.g. diaphragms
Cooperstock, Ruth, 50–52, 279, 286–87
Coordination nationale pour l'avortement libre et gratuit, 129–30
Corbiere decision, 86–87
Corea, Gena, 50, 55, 56, 57, 59–60
councils on status of women: federal, 94, 98, 323–24, 372, 432n8; in NL, 93; NL, 93–99; in NL, 94–95; PEI, 140, 142, 145, 146
Cowan, Carol, 244
CPHA (Canadian Public Health

Early Pregnancy Assessment Clinic (BC), 270–71
Eberts, Mary, 257
École Polytechnique Massacre, 131
elective labour induction, 59
Eli Lily, 284
Emmott, Kirsten, 304
endocrinology. See menstruation; ovulation
endometriosis clinics, 270
Enovid, 155
environmental contaminants, health effects of, 26–27, 181–82
episiotomies, 59
Epp, Jake, 324
ERT. See hormone replacement therapy
estradiol, 188
estrogen, 189. See also progesterone
estrogen replacement therapy. See hormone replacement therapy
ethnicity v. race, 81
European Trade Union Institute, 360
European Trades Union Congress (ETUC), 358
Everything You Always Wanted to Know About Sex (Reuben), 57
examinations. See internal pelvic examinations; rape examinations

Family Crisis Service (NL), 94
family planning, 380–85. See also abortion headings; contraception
Family Planning Association (NL). See Planned Parenthood Newfoundland and Labrador
Farm Midwifery Center, 202
FASD (Fetal Alcohol Spectrum Disorder), 396–97
Fat Is a Feminist Issue (Orbach), 309–10
FCA. See Western Canadian Feminist Counselling Association
FDA (US), approving Prozac for PMDD, 284
Fédération des femmes du Québec (FFQ), 132
Fédération des travailleurs et travailleuses du Quebec, 360

Fédération du Québec pour le planning des naissances (FQPN), 132
Fedorik, Vera, 160, 162–64
Feminine Forever (Wilson), 57
feminism: birth and, 202; lesbianism and, 34, 72; liberal feminism, 369–70, 377; publications, 22–23, 33–34, 66, 203; of younger generation, 116–17. See also health movement
Feminist Approach to Pap Tests, A (Barnett/Fox), 329
Feminist Counselling Association. See Western Canadian Feminist Counselling Association
"Feminist Therapy Now" (conference), 301
Feminists against Reproductive Technology, 390
Fetal Alcohol Spectrum Disorder, 396–97
fetal monitoring, link to Caesarean section, 60
fetuses, 144, 393–97, 401–2. See also children
FFQ (Fédération des femmes du Québec), 132
Fidell, Linda, 49
FIR Square Combined Care (BC), 269–70, 400
Fisher, Bernard, 172–73
Flynn, Laurie, 123
Focus Theatre (NL), 159–60
Food and Drug Administration (US), approving Prozac for PMDD, 284
Forbes, Jack, 268
forced sterilization, 112, 114, 336
forceps delivery, 59
Ford, Anne Rochon, 178, 410
Ford, Clementine, 297
Forsyth, Dan, 215
Fox, Morgan, 72
Fox, Rebecca, 328
FQPN (Fédération du Québec pour le planning des naissances), 132
Free Childbirth Education Centre. See Vancouver Birth Centre
"Free Delivery" (booklet), 212
French Revolution, sexism of, 365
Friedan, Betty, 36

misogyny. See sexism
Mitchell, Margaret, 211, 304, 317
MLF (Mouvement de Libération des
Femmes), 365
Money, Deborah, 268
Montreal Gazette, 360
Montreal Women's Health Centre,
130, 132
Montreal Women's Liberation
Movement, 435n20
mood-altering drugs, overprescribing
of, 27, 48–52, 50–52, 59–60, 286–88
Moore, Teresa, 226
Morgentaler, Henry: 1976 court case,
38, 41, 432–33n9; 1988 court case,
131, 137–38, 142–43, 432–33n9; 1994
PEI court case, 151; lobbying for free
abortion, 131; PEI gift to, 149
Morgentaler clinics: in Atlantic
Canada, 146, 149–50; attacks on, 121,
134–36; illegality of, 39
Morgentaler v. The Queen (1976), 38,
41, 432–33n9
Morrison, Pat, 211, 224
mothers, valued less than fetuses, 144,
393–97, 401–2
"Mothers' Little Helper" (Jagger
song), 287
Mouvement de Libération des
Femmes, 365
Moyer, Cheryl, 325
MRC (Medical Research Council),
351, 353
Ms. G case, 394–96, 398, 399
MTF (Midwifery Task Force BC),
203
MTFO (Midwifery Task Force
Ontario), 203–4, 205
Mulroney, Brian, 98, 152
MUN (Memorial University of
Newfoundland), 93, 98, 100, 158
Murphy, Cathy, 93, 94
MWHC (Montreal Women's Health
Centre), 130, 132

NAC (National Action Committee
on the Status of Women), 98, 323–24
Nain Women's Group (NL), 99
Naripokkho (Pro Women), 340

National Action Committee on the
Status of Women, 98, 323–24
National Breast Cancer Coalition
(NBCC) (US), 172
National Cancer Institute (NCI)
(US), 56, 176
National Inquiry into Missing and
Murdered Indigenous Women and
Girls, 322
natural childbirth, 59, 60. See also
birth; midwifery
Naylor, David, 264
NBCC (National Breast Cancer
Coalition), 172
NCI (National Cancer Institute),
56, 176
"necessity defence" (of abortion), 38
New Brunswick: lack of midwifery
in, 207; Morgentaler clinic in, 146
New Democratic Party government
(ON), 240
New England Journal of Medicine, 58
Newfoundland and Labrador:
abortion in, 94–95, 158; contraception
in, 157–58, 160; women's health
movement in, 93–100
Newfoundland and Labrador Sexual
Assault Crisis & Prevention Centre,
95
Newfoundland and Labrador
Women's Institutes, 97
Newfoundland Medical Association,
158
Newfoundland Status of Women
Council, 93–99
Nijera Kori, 340
NLWI (Newfoundland and Labrador
Women's Institutes), 97
Non-Smokers Health Act, 324
Nous aurons les enfants que nous
voulons (manifesto), 129
NSWC (Newfoundland Status of
Women Council), 93–99
nurses: diploma v. degree, 375–77;
interviews with, 370–74, 376; in
labour movement, 368–69, 370,
373–75; as mostly women, 369;
opposing midwives, 201, 204, 205;
as supposedly selfless, 370–71, 373,

374–75. See also caregivers
nursing as opportunity, 371–72, 377
"nymphomania", 19th c. "cures" for,
52

O&A (Orthopaedic and Arthritic
Hospital), 256, 259, 261, 264
Oaks, Laury, 397
"Oakville Orange, The", 119
occupational health, 355–61;
conferences on, 358, 359; low priority
sectors, 355–56; progress made,
360–61; research on, 358–59, 360; risks
specific to women, 355–58; and trade
unions, 357, 358, 359, 360–61. See also
labour feminism
O'Connell, Patricia, 246
Ogilvie, Doris, 432n8
OHIP (Ontario Health Insurance
Plan), 43, 46
"Oil in the Family" (radio drama), 163
OMA (Ontario Medical Association),
290–91, 296, 297
OMA v. McPhedran, 290–91
"On to Ottawa Trek" as inspiring
Abortion Caravan, 112
Ontario Coalition for Abortion
Clinics, 134
Ontario Coalition of Rape Crisis
Centres, 316
Ontario Health Disciplines Act,
amendments to, 204
Ontario Health Insurance Plan, 43,
46
Ontario Medical Association, 290–91,
296, 297
Ontario politics in 1977 regarding
abortion, 44–47
Orbach, Susie, 309
Orthopaedic and Arthritic Hospital,
256, 259, 261, 264
osteoporosis. See bone health
Our Bodies, Ourselves (Boston
Women's Health Collective), 10, 68,
77, 103, 330
ovariotomies, 52, 55
over-prescribing: of hormones, 57–58,
180–81; of mood-altering drugs, 27,
48–52, 50–52, 59–60, 286–88

ovulation: as a vital sign, 191; disturbances in, 184, 186–87; protective
effects of, 189–90; research on,
183–84, 186–91. See also menstruation

Pacey, Ingrid, 300–304, 308, 311–12
pain killers. See anaesthesia;
analgesics
pain response, gender differences, 361
painful periods, 154–55
Palm, Jocelyn (Joc), 239, 246
Palmer, Hazelle, 246
Paltiel, Freda, 356
Pandora (periodical), 33–34
pap tests, 329–30. See also uterine/
cervical cancer
Parti Québécois, position on
abortion, 41, 129–30
Patient No More (Batt), 172
patriarchy. See sexism
Payne, Sarah, 201, 205
Peckford, Brian, 161
Pedestal, The (periodical), 71, 72
PEI Advisory Council on the Status
of Women, 140, 142, 145, 146
PEI government, on abortion,
142–43
PEI Hospital and Health Services
Commission, 138
PEI Standing Committee on Health
and Social Services, 144–45
pelvic examinations, 48, 69, 75,
391–92
pelvic pain, clinics, 270
Penfold, Sue, 305, 308
People's Health Centre (Bangladesh),
333
Pepino, Jane, 250–55, 257–60, 293,
294, 296
periods, painful, 154–55
pharmaceutical industry: advertising
by, 27–28; harm caused by, 409;
influence on DSM, 284; sponsoring
breast cancer groups, 178; as
subverting public health care, 175–77,
334–35. See also drugs; Side Effects
(play)
PHSA (Provincial Health Services
Authority BC), 271, 274

race v. ethnicity, 81
racism, 81, 82–84, 282. See also discrimination
radical mastectomies. See mastectomies
Rae, Bob, 240
Ransom, Joanne, 305
rape: conferences on, 64; rape crisis centres, 65, 95, 237, 316; responding to, 65, 226–27, 235, 437n53; services, 225, 229–31, 233–34, 237; statistics on, 234; writing on, 35. See also sexual abuse headings; violence
Rape Crisis Centre of Toronto, 65. See also Bell, Ilene
rape examinations, 63–65
RCMP spying on Abortion Caravan, 114, 435n19
REACH Centre (BC), 228
REAL women (PEI), 146
Regan, Gail, 239, 245
Registered Nurses Act, 375
Regulated Health Professions Act, 1991 (ON), 295–96
Report of the Committee on the Operation of the Abortion Law, 41–43, 61, 62, 433n11
reproductive freedom/rights. See abortion headings; contraception; sterilization
research. See medical research; women's health research
Resolution 17 (PEI), 143–44
Reuben, David, 57
RHPA, 1991 (ON), 295–96
Richardson, Bev, 239, 243–44, 245, 246, 248, 263
Richardson, Luba Lyons, 219
Ridgley, Sharon, 62
Right to Life Association (NL), 160, 162–64
Right to Life Association (PEI), 138, 141
Risk Assessment Model for Child Protection (BC), 395
Roach, Roz, 295
Robinson, Gail, 293
Rochon, Mark, 258–59
Rock, Allan, 349, 353

Rolling Stones, 287
Romalis, Gary, 268
Roome, Becky, 164
Ross, Becki, 36
Ross-Kerr, Janet, 374
Royal Commission on Health Care, 25
Royal Commission on the Status of Women, 94, 372, 432n8
RTLA (NL Right to Life Association), 160, 162–64
RTLA (PEI Right to Life Association), 138, 141
RU-486 abortion pill, 131
Rutman, Deborah, 398

SAAS. See Vancouver Sexual Assault Assessment Service
Sabia, Laura, 39
Salson, Sharon, 257
Salvation Army: and Grace Hospitals, 267, 268; Home for Wayward Girls, 105; transition house of, 96
Sanders, Bernie, 175
Sandinista! (Milner play), 333–34
SANE (Sexual Assault Nurse Examiner program), 233
Sarafem, 284–85
SAS. See Vancouver Sexual Assault Assessment Service
Saskatchewan, rates of hysterectomy in, 53–54
Saxell, Lee, 205
School of Midwifery (BC), 203
Schooley, Jill, 93, 95
Schwartz, Pepper, 304
Schwenger, Cope, 382
science, politics of, 350
SCODA (Standing Conference on Drug Abuse, UK), 399
Scott, Robert, 136
Scott, Ted, 44
SDG 5 (Sustainable Development Goals), 364
Second Sex, The (Beauvoir), 365
Secret Oppression (Backhouse and Cohen), 46
section 251 of Criminal Code: creation, 38, 431n3; criticism, 129,

founding of, 209–12; impact of, 223; post-grant, 218–20; staff, 219–22
Vancouver Cool-Aid Clinic medical bus, 210–11, 217
Vancouver General Hospital, 122–27, 267–68
Vancouver Rape Relief, 226, 227
Vancouver Sexual Assault Assessment Service: background, 232–33; beginnings of, 225, 229–30; name change, 231, 438n57; politics and, 233–34; protocols at, 231, 233
Vancouver Women's Caucus, 111, 112, 435n19
Vancouver Women's Health Collective: activities of, 70–72, 77; beginnings of, 70–71; commitment of, 77–78; Diaphragm Fitters Collective, 74–76; experiences at, 68–69, 225–26; feminism of, 232; funding, 70, 71; struggles of, 78–79; studying at, 213
VAW (violence against women). See rape; sexual abuse headings; violence
Vayda, Elaine, 57
Vayda, Eugene, 51, 53–54, 60
VBAC (Vaginal Birth After Caesarean), 215
VGH (Vancouver General Hospital), 122–27, 267–68
Victoria General Hospital (NS), abortion services at, 146, 149
violence: against Indigenous women, 80–81, 315; categories of, 315; demographics of, 320; extent of, 93, 304; research centres, 321; resulting in death, 131, 305; shelter from, 94, 95, 96, 313–14, 316–22, 317; statistics on, 80–81, 304, 364; writing on, 35. See also rape; sexual abuse headings
Vissandjée, Bilkis, 363, 366–67
Voyageur, Cora, 87
VRR (Vancouver Rape Relief), 226, 227
VWC (Vancouver Women's Caucus), 111, 112, 435n19

Walter, Helen, 307
WAVAW (Women Against Violence Against Women), 231, 232, 438n56
WCFCA. See Western Canadian

Feminist Counselling Association
WCH. See Women's College Hospital (ON)
We will have the children we want (manifesto), 129
Wedge, Catherine, 304
Wellesley Hospital, 240, 255
Wells, Andy, 163
Wendall, Sue, 304
Western Canadian Feminist Counselling Association, 300–312; conferences, 301–4, 305–6, 307, 310, 311; donations from, 307, 311; social action, 308–9; start of, 300–301; support groups, 307, 310
What Women Should Know About Breast Cancer (Crile), 56
WHDI (Women's Health Development Initiative), 270
Wheatley, Ann, 148–49
WHI. See Women's Health Initiative (US study); Women's Health Interaction (committee)
White Ribbon campaign, 319
WHO (World Health Organization), 358, 388
WHP (Women and Health Protection), 170
Whynot, Elizabeth, 69, 104, 225–26, 227
Wiebe, Ellen, 229
Williams, Brian, 374
Williams, Wendy, 93–98, 157–58, 161, 163
Wilson, Bertha, 137
Wilson, Elinor, 325
Wilson, Robert A., 57
Wine, Jeri, 282
Witmer, Elizabeth, 295
woman-centred health care, 22, 271–72, 272–73
Women's Place, The (NL), 93–94
women's shelters. See shelters
"Women—Visions of the Future" (conference), 302–4
Women, Work and Health (conferences), 358
Women Against Violence Against Women, 231, 232, 438n56

Women and Health Protection, 170
"Women and Pharmaceuticals"
(Aylmer) workshop, 335, 340, 341
Women Healthsharing (collective),
387–92
Women Recovering from Abuse, 237
women's bodies: control over, 11–12,
201–3, 395–96; as unwilling models
for doctors, 48, 194–95, 206. See also
abortion headings
Women's Centre (NL), 93, 94
Women's College Hospital (ON),
236–49, 250–65; board memberships,
238, 239–40, 243, 249; early history,
236–37, 250–51; friends of, 238,
239–41, 242, 243–45, 246–47, 248;
legal challenge to HSRC, 257–59;
merger with Sunnybrook, 243, 251,
251–54, 256–57; negotiations on
merger, 245–46, 248, 255–56, 259–65;
principles, 252; Star column on,
241–42; taking back, 244–47; under
threat, 237–38, 240, 252
Women's Committee, 340–41
women's health. See health; health
care
Women's Health Bureaus, 21
Women's Health Contribution
Program, 269, 349
Women's Health Development
Initiative, 270
Women's Health Initiative (US
study), 180–81
Women's Health Interaction
(committee), 335, 340–42
women's health movement. See
health movement
Women's Health Network (NL), 100
women's health research, 347–54
Women's Health Research (Friends
of WCH), 242
Women's Health Strategy, 271
Women's Legal Education and Action
Fund, 46
"Women's Mental Health and Sexual
Orientation" (conference), 301–2
Women's Network (PEI), 144–45, 151
women's organizations, 140
Women's Place, A (BC), 71

Wood, Betsy, 114
Woodsworth, Ellen, 111, 115
Working Group on Women's Health
(NL), 99
working women, 370–71. See also
labour feminism; occupational health
workplace health. See occupational
health
World AIDS Conference (1996), 405
World Conference on Tobacco or
Health, 326
World Health Organization, 358, 388
WRAP (Women Recovering from
Abuse), 237
Wright, Judith, 286
Wuest, Judith, 376
Wynne, Kathleen, 235

YWCA (NL), 94

THE FEMINIST HISTORY SOCIETY SERIES

The Feminist History Society is committed to creating a lasting record of the women's movement in Canada and Québec for the fifty years between 1960 and the year of the Society's founding, 2010. Feminism has a history that predates the 1960s and continues long after 2010.

The energy that women brought to their quest for equality in these decades is beyond dispute, and it is that energy that we capture in this series. Our movement is not over and new campaigns are upon us. But the FHS series presents an opportunity to take stock of the wide-ranging campaigns for equality that occurred in Canada between 1960 and 2010. There was much transformative social, economic, civil, political, and cultural change.

We maintain an open call for submissions (https://secondstorypress.ca/submissions/) across a full range of approaches to the period, including autobiographies, biographies, edited collections, pictorial histories, plays and novels. There will be many different authors as all individuals and organizations that were participants in the movement are encouraged to contribute. We make every effort to be inclusive of gender, race, class, geography, culture, dis/ability, language, sexual identity, and age.

Beth Atcheson, Constance Backhouse, Lorraine Greaves, Diana Majury, and Beth Symes form the working collective of the Feminist History Society. Margie Wolfe, Publisher, Second Story Feminist Press Inc. and her talented team of women, are presenting the Series.

https://secondstorypress.ca/feminist-history-society-series/